D0871429

THE PEDESTRIAN IN THE CITY

The Pedestrian in the City

Edited by David Lewis

D. VAN NOSTRAND COMPANY, INC.
PRINCETON, N.J.

©Paul Elek 1965

Published by
D. Van Nostrand Company, Inc.
Princeton, N.J. 08540
        1966

Printed by
The Garden City Press Limited
Letchworth Hertfordshire
England

Printed in Great Britain

CONTENTS

NOTES ON CONTRIBUTORS

DAVID LEWIS – author of monographs on Constantin Brancusi and Piet Mondrian and also (with Hansmartin Bruckmann) 'New Housing in Great Britain' is Andrew Mellon Professor of Architecture and Urban Design at the Carnegie Institute of Technology, Pittsburgh U S A

ELEANOR SMITH MORRIS – an American planner, at one time a planner with the Philadelphia Planning Commission, is currently Senior Lecturer in Civic Design at the University of Edinburgh and is author of the special issue on Philadelphia published by Architectural Design in 1962

JANE JACOBS – is the author of 'The Death and Life of Great American Cities' 1961 and lives in New York

VICTOR GRUEN – American architect, famous for his Fort Worth plans and Northland Shopping Centre outside Detroit, author of a recent book, 'The Heart of our Cities'

JOHN ALEXANDEROWICZ – a U S photographer whose documentations of American industrial cities have a wide reputation, an exhibitor at New York's Museum of Modern Art

ROGER MAYNE – an English photographer internationally known for photography that is a sharp social summation of city life

ANTHONY HILL – works and teaches in London. He has exhibited internationally, and has a large relief in the Tate Gallery

STEPHEN GILBERT – works in Paris, has received a Gulbenkian Award and has a sculpture in the Tate

PETER CARTER – is an English architect who has been working with Mies van der Rohe in Chicago for some years. He was premiated in the National Theatre Competition for London

BEN NICHOLSON – an internationally famous abstract painter whose works are included in every important public collection of modern art throughout the world, currently concentrating on large scale reliefs to act as walls, preferably free-standing, in architectural and urban settings

GUNTER NITSCHKE – is a German architect-planner who collaborated with Alison and Peter Smithson on their Berlin Haupstadt plan and now lives and works in Tokyo

GEORGES CANDILIS, Alexis Josic and Shadrach Woods – are an international team of architects in Paris; members of TEAM X and perhaps the best-known young firm of architects in France, they have recently begun work on a new city beside Lake Chad, where they are using an extension of the principles used at Toulouse

GEORGE R COLLINS – is Professor of the History of Architecture at Columbia University, New York. Among his books is a monograph on Antonio Gaudi. He is completing a book on the history of linear planning

CHRISTIANE COLLINS – with husband George R Collins she is the translator of 'City Planning According to Artistic Principles' by Camillo Sitte, and together they have written 'Camillo Sitte and the Birth of Modern City Planning', both books recently published in New York

KENNETH CAMPBELL – is Principal Housing Architect in the Department of Architecture and Civic Design, Greater London Council

GEOFFREY COPCUTT – was the principal designer of Cumbernauld's central areas. He has been special adviser to the United Nations at the National Research Institute in Dublin, and is currently Visiting Andrew Mellon Professor at the Carnegie Institute of Technology in Pittsburgh, U S A

LAWRENCE FRICKER – teaches landscape architecture at the University of Edinburgh

VICTOR PASMORE – this internationally known English painter gained first prize at the Pittsburgh Carnegie International 1964/65

COLIN HUNT – is a Director of the Taylor Woodrow Property Company, London

JACK LYNN – was the principal designer responsible for the Park Hill and Hyde Park developments, Sheffield, and is now in private practice

JOHN ALLAMAND and ANTHONY MEATS – work for the Liverpool City Centre Planning Group

EDUARDO PAOLOZZI – a British sculptor of Italian parentage who has been a leader of the European post-Dada avant-garde since 1950

THEO CROSBY – for some years was Technical Editor of Architectural Design (London) and until recently architect in charge of the design team for Euston Station and the Fulham Study, author (with Monica Pidgeon) of 'Houses', 1961, he won the Gran Premio at the Milan Triennale 1964 for his design of the British Pavilion. He is now in private practice, and his most recent book, 'Architecture: City Sense', has just appeared

H R WEDGWOOD – is doing graduate research at the University of Edinburgh and worked with Doxiadis in Athens

E MAXWELL FRY – received the Gold Medal at the Royal Institute of British Architects, 1964. Other recent recipients have been Le Corbusier, Mies van der Rohe, Sven Markelius, Sir William Holford. In the 1930s he was in partnership with Walter Gropius; and in the 1940s and 50s he pioneered modern architecture in hot climates, particularly in West Africa, the Middle East and India. He was in partnership with Le Corbusier in the design of Chandigarh, new capital of the Punjab; and is now in practice in London with Jane Drew

JANE DREW – with husband Maxwell Fry she has designed Universities in West Africa, collaborated with Le Corbusier at Chandigarh, and is now in practice with Maxwell Fry in London. With Maxwell Fry she is author of 'Architecture for Tropical Countries'

KENT BLOOMER – is a well-known U S sculptor; he is also Assistant Professor and teaches basic design in the Department of Architecture, Carnegie Institute of Technology, Pittsburgh

BHANU MATHUR – is Senior Architect for the Punjab University at Chandigarh

MARGARET GRENFELL – is a British architect who worked for some time in Lima, Peru, with the Peruvian architect Diego Robles Rivas, in the barriadas

WILLIAM TURNBULL – the work of this British sculptor in recent years has been closely concerned with the problem of interrelating sculptural and architectural form

HERMAN HAAN – is a Dutch architect in practice in Rotterdam who is also an explorer of the remote regions of North Africa

DEREK COUTTS, RICHARD DOUST, and LAWRENCE CAREY – are at the Royal College of Art, London

JOE TILSON – this young British artist was responsible for the ceiling of the British Pavilion designed by Theo Crosby which won the Gran Premio at the Milan Triennale 1964

WARREN CHALK, PETER COOK, BEN FETHER, RON HERRON, PETER TAYLOR and MICHAEL WEBB – were members of the Euston team led by Theo Crosby, collaborated on the Fulham Study, and made The Living City exhibition at the Institute of Contemporary Arts, London, in 1963

ACKNOWLEDGEMENTS

2

THE PEDESTRIAN IN THE CITY marks a new direction for the Architects Year Book series. Each new volume in this second decade of year books will have a subject (thus the title) around which contributions are grouped, and so will tend to become a separate book in its own right besides being a volume-in-series

The delay between the publication in journals of some of the projects and their appearance in book form is unavoidable. I hope that in presenting an inter-relationship – and occasionally a conflict – of projects and essays, the usefulness of ideas will be more important than news value. With only one exception, all the writings in this volume are published here for the first time

The editor wishes to thank particularly Maxwell Fry, Jane Drew, and Theo Crosby for the help they gave in the early stages of putting the book together; he wishes also to thank Donal Pierrucci, Donn Allen Carter, and Surendra Ahuja, Andrew Mellon Fellows at the Carnegie Institute of Technology, Pittsburgh, USA; he wishes to acknowledge the assistance he received from the editors of Architectural Design (London), Architectural Forum (New York), Richard Saul Wurman and Eugene Feldman of The Falcon Press (Philadelphia), Le Carré Bleu (Paris); he wishes to acknowledge the courtesy of the Trustees of the Tate Gallery, London, and of the Carnegie Museum, Pittsburgh, and also the courtesy of the Marlborough-Gerson Gallery (New York), the Marlborough Gallery (London), and Professor Bode of Documenta II; he wishes to acknowledge the courtesy of the Cities of Sheffield, Liverpool, and Philadelphia, the Development Corporation of Cumbernauld, and the London County Council; and to acknowledge the following photographers in connection with New Urban Design Concepts – Laurence S Williams, Philadelphia Skyphotos, Claire Kofsky, Tom McCaffrey, and the Philadelphia City Planning Commission; in connection with Mies' Urban Spaces – Hedrich-Blessing (Chicago), Erza Stoller Associates (New York), Russ Fraser and George Fletcher (Des Moines, Iowa) and Baltazar Korab (Birmingham, Michigan); in connection with Do Not Segregate Automobiles and Pedestrians – John Alexanderowicz and Roger Mayne; in connection with the reliefs of Anthony Hill and the sculptures of Stephen Gilbert – Henk Snoek (London), Tommaso d'Elia (London), Bertrand Weill (Paris); in connection with Cumbernauld New Town – Douglas Scott (Glasgow), Bryan and Shear Ltd (Glasgow), The Glasgow Herald, and Donn Allen Carter (Pittsburgh); in connection with Sheffield – Roger Mayne; in connection with Liverpool – John Mills (Liverpool); in connection with Ben Nicholson – Documenta II (Germany), Studio St Ives (Cornwall), and Felicitas Vogler (Switzerland); in connection with Chandigarh – Rondal Partridge (Berkeley, California), and R J. Chinwalla of the Camera Press (India); in connection with Squatters in Peru – John Turner (Lima, Peru); in connection with the sculptures of William Turnbull – Kim Lim; and Thad C Grabowski; of Jaybee Studios, Pittsburgh; the editor also wishes to thank Messrs Hutchinson, publishers, for permission to use illustrations from 'Architecture in Transition' by Constantinos A Doxiadis; likewise the editor of Uppercase and the Whitefriars Press (London); the illustrations for The Linear City were derived from the following sources – H González del Castillo, 'Ciudades jardines y ciudades lineales', Madrid 1913; Arturo Seria y Hernandez, 'The Problem of Land in Spain', Madrid, 1926; Compañi a Madrilena de Urbanización, 'Ciudad Lineal', Madrid 1930; the Journal of the American Institute of Architects; J. Raymond, 'Guide practique de l'urbanisme', Paris 1933; Edgar Chambless, 'Road-town', New York 1910; E McCoy, 'Richard Neutra', Braziller (New York) 1960; S Freese, 'The Ten Year Plan, a dream of 1940', London 1932; Reginald Malcolmson; Landscape Architecture (USA) T Adams, 'Design of Residential Areas', Harvard University 1934; The Architects' Journal (London); Tom Hancock; Le Corbusier, 'Oeuvres Completes', Girsberger 1938; 'The Nation's Capital', Washington D C, 1961; L Hilberseimer, 'The New City', Theobald (Chicago) 1944; Sert in Zucker, 'New Architecture and City Planning', New York, 1944; The MARS Group, London, 1938; Bernard Reichow, 'Organische Stadbaukunst,' Braunschweig, 1948; Alcan Industries Ltd; plans and line drawings for Theo Crosby's essay on Greece are derived from Roland Martin, 'L'Urbanisme dans la Grèce Antique', Editions A & J Picard & Cie, Paris, 1956; the chapter on The Living City is derived from the exhibition of that name at the Institute of Contemporary Arts, London, 1963. The editor wishes also to thank Simon Nicholson for his help in the early stages of establishing a new typography for the series; also Mrs Valerie Groenewald for her invaluable secretarial assistance – D L

INTRODUCTION

DAVID LEWIS

This is both an optimistic and a pessimistic book

It is optimistic because it publishes large projects from cities in a number of countries. And these reflect the growing concern of architects all over the world for urban – as distinct from more narrowly architectural – problems in the second half of our century. In many cases their thinking is built up from first principles, ending in the achievement of new urban forms on massive scales, radical, and without doubt far-reaching in their future influence

The book is pessimistic, however, because in comparison with the vast crisis in cities and the urgent need for action, the projects published here are but fragments in a general sea of indifference. How are we going to awaken in time those in every country, and city, who are in control of the necessary powers? Awaken them, not only to the crisis itself, but to the fact that no solution is possible without deeply committed and intelligently programmed inter-relationships of power, political and economic, on scales far larger than anything we have seen so far

At present rates of growth the world's population will almost treble during the next fifty years. Many demographers agree that the present total world population of 3.2 billion will reach 7 billion by the year 2000.[1] One of the most important points about this acceleration in the growth of world population is that it will not echo present patterns of distribution. Agriculture-oriented populations will, if anything, diminish in size. The vast majority of these new people will cluster in nodal cities

In a recent book[2] Charles Abrams points out that 'the impact will be felt most in the cities of the less developed world' – that is to say, those cities least able to cope. He quotes some alarming figures. In Africa, the present urban population of 58 million people will grow to 294 millions by the year 2000. In Latin America, the present urban population of 144 millions will grow to 650 millions; and in Asia the present urban population of 559 millions will grow to 3,444 millions, over the same period of thirty-five years[3]

Whether or not one wants to dispute these figures, there can hardly be any doubt that the world faces gigantic problems of urbanisation. For many cities the crisis has already arrived. Peru has a squatter history of only twenty-five to thirty years, yet the number of people living in the squatter settlements – or 'barriadas' – on the fringes of the major cities already amounts to some forty per cent of the country's total urban population

To be more specific, outside Lima the Caraballa group of barriadas was first settled in 1957 and today has a squatter population of over 100 thousand.[4] Squatter slums, composed of hundreds upon hundreds of appallingly impoverished shacks, put together with rubbish-dump materials, rolled out rusty kerosene tins, rags, and straw matting on crude frameworks of poles, without piped water, drainage or electricity, are to be found on the edges of almost every city in the underdeveloped countries of the world. Brazil has an annual population growth index of 3.2 per cent (compared with India's 2.5); in the 'favellas' or squatter slums, or the hillsides above Rio, there is already a population of 800 thousand people. In Caracas, 65 per cent of the city's population are squatters. In Calcutta, 600 thousand people sleep in the streets without shelter. Charles Abrams' forlorn cry should not surprise us. The world's engineers could make a greater contribution to society by inventing a chemical or other simple means for disposing of human excrement on earth than by making contact with the moon'[5]

But the crisis is not restricted to the underdeveloped countries. To what degree are cities, even in the highly industrialized countries, able to deal with the new pressures? In Britain the drift of population to the south-east is reaching critical proportions. London already occupies over 600 square miles.[6] One way of stemming the tide of migrants is to accelerate the massive reconstruction of northern cities such as Liverpool, Sheffield, and the enormous industrial conurbation of the Clyde, not simply as cities, but on an interrelated regional basis, as a means of creating counter-magnets to London.[7] In the United States the situation has become sufficiently serious – and its importance still sufficiently under-estimated – to merit on March 1 1965 the first-ever presidential Message to Congress on the subject of cities[8]

On the basis of current growth, President Johnson forecast that 'during the next fifteen years 30 million people will be added to our cities – equivalent to the combined populations of New York, Chicago, Los Angeles, Philadelphia, Detroit and Baltimore'

I think that this statement is probably conservative. As in the underdeveloped countries, the whole balance of population in the United States is rapidly shifting. By the turn of the century the population of the USA will not only have almost doubled (from 180 to some 330 million), but 90 per cent of all these people will live in urban areas. That percentage has already been reached in Britain. But the difference is that Britain is implicitly urban. The US, in addition to her industrial size, is one of the world's major agricultural countries, on whose shipments of agricultural surpluses many underdeveloped countries at present depend

And as in the underdeveloped countries, the gravitational pull is not just to cities; but to a few major cities. The effects of this process in the US are already visible. Countless small rural towns and cities are losing population and beginning to decay, with little chance of attracting new investment; a process which starts in the central areas, the fulcrum of the community's life – many of which, with their broad treelined streets and simple colonial architecture, have considerable eighteenth century charm, precision and proximity of scale. And the crucially important population they are losing is the talented young, their future community leaders, who leave the rural cities for college education, and do not return

Meanwhile the principal cities are growing rapidly, gaining new population at a rate of considerably more than 100,000 people a week – with four great population concentrations accumulating, on the eastern seaboard; the Milwaukee–Chicago and Detroit–Toledo areas of the Great Lakes; California; and to a lesser extent in the cluster of cities on the Gulf of Mexico. Already 38 million people live in the eastern seaboard strip, from New Hampshire in the north to northern Virginia in the south. This represents 21 per cent of the total US population concentrated into 1.8 per cent of its area. In thirty-five years the population of this same area is expected to reach some 120 million[9]

President Johnson is clearly not referring therefore so much to the small towns and cities of the US when he says that, in scarcely more than a generation, 'we will have to build in our cities as much as all that we have built since the first colonist arrived on these shores. It is as if we had forty years to rebuild the entire urban Unites States.' He is referring to the major cities, especially those whose growth will form the megalopoli of the future

Many architects and planners consider a city of ten million people too large to be comprehensible, and that optimum (static) sizes for cities should be established. Such arguments overlook the fact that modern systems of mobility and communications have smashed the sound-barriers of past urban forms. I do not believe that it is sensible, or possible, in an age of unprecedented dynamism, to seek answers based on formal and static conceptions – or that the growth of cities would take much notice if one attempted to. As we have said, the US eastern seaboard is developing into a single conurbation, stretching across several states, not of 10 million people, but 120 – in which the presently separate cities of Boston, New York, Newark, Philadelphia, Baltimore, and Washington, will be separate cities no longer, but a series of interrelated centres, or cores, in a continuous urban belt

The problem is fundamentally a question of urban structure itself, and its capacity to evolve new and creative urban forms, in response to these fantastic population pressures and new patterns of physical growth. In previous epochs, systems of defence were the powerful elements in imposing on cities their basic skeletal structure, in other periods theories of mathematics predominated

Today the most powerful elements of urban structure are systems of circulation, and the insatiable urge for mobility. This applies no less to Europe and Japan than it does to the US. And is there any reason to suppose that, as standards of living rise, the vast urban populations of the future Asia, Africa and South America will be satisfied with being less mobile than, say, contemporary Britain?

So far, it is true, we have been subjected more to the dangers of mobility than we have been awakened to its creative possibilities. The sheer magnitude of the highway engineer's decimation of the traditional concept of the city – as major highways cut through the hearts of cities, and as the commuter city extends its formless low-density periphery along highway routes into the countryside – reveals the incontrovertible power of this single factor

And the fact remains that a megalopolis of the kind which is developing on the U S eastern seaboard is of course absolutely dependent on fluent circulation systems. The major cities – New York, Philadelphia etc – already act as concentrators, and generators, of extremely dense intercity activity. Between them runs a traffic system which carries 27/35,000 vehicles a day on each of the major highways, and these volumes are increasing dramatically. Within the cities themselves, however, the crosstown throughways handle volumes far in excess of these intercity highways. Traffic comes into the central areas of the city from all directions, without differentiation between types, destinations, or speeds of the vehicles. London has a rush-hour of between one and one and a half million people a day; but most of these people travel on public mass transit systems. The US is an automobile oriented society. In New York, the US city with the largest rail transit commuter network, nearly fifty per cent of the city's commuters travel by private car. In Los Angeles, the percentage is ninety-two[10]

Top: Lloyd Center, Portland, Oregon. Architects: John Graham and Company. Photo: Delano

Centre: Antonio Sant' Elia. Stazioni Aeroplani, 1912, a drawing from the Citta Nuova series, showing tall buildings, linked by pedestrian decks and bridges, rising above several traffic levels, with an airport in the background

Bottom: Le Corbusier. Ville Radieuse, 1924/5. This drawing shows tall blocks rising from parkland and pedestrian squares and bridges which – by using air rights over the fast traffic ways – continue unbroken the texture of the city. The pedestrian squares and bridges have restaurants, entertainments, and shopping precincts, and are landscaped

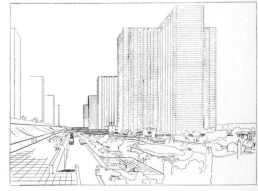

Certain clear results emerge from this. One of them is that the old closed-form city is a thing of the past. In spite of its green belt, the population pressures on London have forced thousands of families to live beyond the belt, and commute greater and greater distances daily. Within the widening commuter radius, previously autonomous rural towns and cities are now expanding, with untidy and unbalanced rapidity, as they become metropolitan satellites

In the United States, despite mounting population pressures, many of the major cities continue to lose population to their surrounding counties, as the demand for suburban split-levels – on one acre lots, within easy reach of a super highway on which to swing into the city – remains undiminished. For these two-automobile families it is not the city's centre which is their immediate centre, but the suburban shopping drive-in, of which Victor Gruen's Northlands, outside Detroit, was a pioneering example. Because wide acres outside dense cities are still available, the economics of the drive-in are such that a huge sea of parking tarmac surrounds the shopping island in the middle. But already land prices, responding to density, and traffic congestion, are beginning to change this. The first compact and integrated, multi-level park-and-shop structures are beginning to appear in the US

Nevertheless the theory remains unchanged. And it is perhaps important to realize the irony of how close to the classic, early modern movement theories of Sant' Elia and Le Corbusier the idea essentially is. The shopping drive-in is pedestrian/traffic segregated. Whether you have had to walk across quarter of a mile of tarmac – or simply had to ascend by escalator from parking decks contained within the structure beneath – once you are in the centre, you are implicitly in an air-conditioned, pedestrian-dominated city, to which you have travelled along your six-lane throughway

The qualitative poverty of the suburban shopping drive-in, whatever its form, as an urban centre in microcosm, is demonstrated by the new multi-level centres, such as Cumbernauld, which are developing in Britain and Europe. However carefully and sympathetically the suburban drive-in is designed, an air-conditioned market place with flowering trees, and tropical shrubs, and aviaries, and 'outside' cafés umbrella'ed in internal plazas, and children's

Right: J. B. Bakema. Sketch of the 'core wall', 1958

5

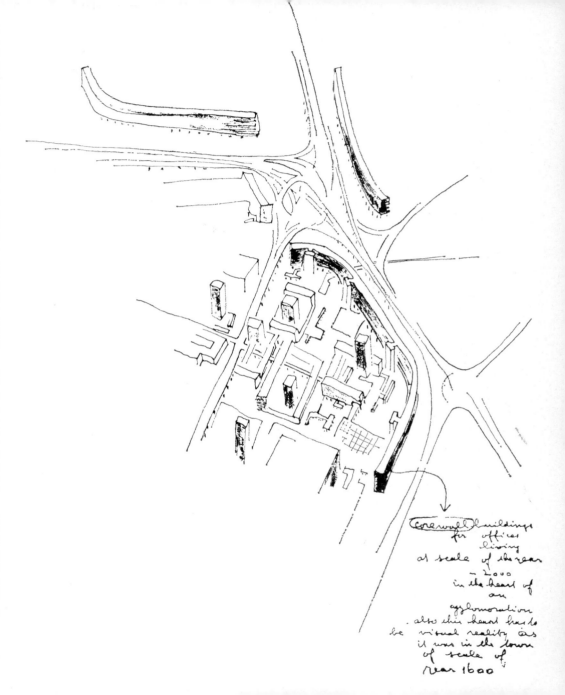

Corewall buildings for offices living at scale of the year – 2000 in the heart of an agglomeration. also this heart has to be visual reality as it was in the town of scale of year 1600

play areas on the mezzanines, it is still conceived only as a shopping centre, closing at nine Mondays through Saturdays

The design for Cumbernauld, on the other hand, includes in its multi-deck structure many of the multiplicity of functions which an urban core is all about – civic administraion buildings, law courts, company and professional offices, hotels, markets, and a central library, auditoria and cinemas, and housing, in addition to shopping, in a complex interplay of spaces

The distinction here is crucial, as it emphasizes the difference between a true urban centre – the intricate and vibrant and dense place of human exchange – and the suburban drive-in, designed as it is at the moment for only one activity. At the same time the distinction also shows how, step by step, a new urban structure may rationally and even inevitably evolve, based on high mobility

The facts of the new urban structure were foreseen by the pioneers of the modern movement in its heroic years. Today a humanist insistence begins to breathe a complex life into the basic theory. Sant' Elia's series of drawings for his Citta Nuova, before the first world war and parallel with cubism in painting, appears to have originated in reconstruction proposals for Milan Central Station, and to have developed into an incredibly prophetic document of fundamental urban thinking

He spoke in 1914, in the foreword of the exhibition of the Citta Nuova series, of the modern city 'like an immense and tumultuous shipyard, active, mobile, and everywhere dynamic.'[11] His drawings show the core of the Citta Nuova conceived as a single building, massive but differentiated, a series of skyscraper blocks rising from decks which are given over to various uses, an airport, and pedestrian decks and

Below: Peter and Alison Smithson, plan for Hauptstadt, Berlin, 1960/61. Friedrichstrasse, looking towards the Museum of Technology

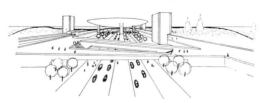

causeways, below which there are elevated railroads, and automobile highways

One of the most prophetic of Sant' Elia's ideas was his conception of the Citta Nuova as a whole series of such multi-level cores, occurring periodically through the urban fabric and linked by these immense traffic routes – surely an outrageous exaggeration of the power of mobility in terms of 1912, and yet not in the least implausible in today's reality of superhighways cutting through the fabric of new and existing cities

Behind this conception of Sant' Elia's lies another of equal importance. For the speed of travel so contracts the time/space dimensions of geographic distance, that it undermines and ultimately destroys the closed and formalist boundaries of urban comprehensibility. In its place he substitutes the open-endedness of successive fields of urban experience

The influence of Sant' Elia on Le Corbusier's Ville Radieuse is well known. Although in the twenties Le Corbusier was working in a strictly axial classicism, he clarified and humanized many of Sant' Elia's ideas without destroying their power. In the Ville Radieuse traffic flows freely and swiftly along divided highways beneath pedestrian bridges and plazas at various levels which, although they use air rights over trafficways, are really the urban squares of the old city, with restaurants and cafés, shops and theatres; and the towers rise on piloti from these plazas and from parkland

A drawing by Bakema, the Dutch architect, as part of a sheet of notes done in May 1958 on this dilemma of urban scales, shows a fragment of an imaginary but existing city. A superhighway cuts through it. He shows a vast curving slab-block, put like a shielding arm between the tender and intimate scale of the traditional city, and the irrefutable power of the highway with its huge insensitive scale – a shielding arm which he calls a 'core wall'. And the drawing then shows other core walls, the inference being that each protects the intimate scale of its own community, as highways cut the city into a succession of quadrants

The drawing is just, because it challenges both the creative and the destructive aspects of such giant systems of circulation. One might say that in stressing the immense importance of protecting the human-pedestrian scale of whole areas at once – whole sectors, large enough to harbour the incredible

Above: Square in Society Hill, Philadelphia

multiplicity of the city, yet compact enough to be geographically comprehensible – Bakema is revealing how highways may be creatively definitive, endowing the city with an organic, cellular infrastructure of communities

On the other hand, it is the obverse of Sant' Elia's Citta Nuova and Le Corbusier's Ville Radieuse, putting very bluntly the conflict of scales between large-scale mobility and the intimate social scale of pedestrians, which, if not resolved, shatters any city to fragments. In that case the concept of the core wall is wrong, since each community turns its back on its neighbour, and looks only inwards. What Le Corbusier demonstrates, in essense, in his Ville Radieuse, is the value of exploiting at first the highway, and then the air rights over them, as the means of at once dividing the city into sectors, with a comprehensible urban structure – and then of continuing the texture of the city unbroken across the platformed links

Of course in the Ville Radieuse, Le Corbusier was theorizing mainly about the new city, built specifically for twentieth century conditions. Nevertheless, in terms of an existing city, the idea is substantially the same. Highway and rapid transit networks should not be planned simply as high-density corridors. They should be designed with the

Above: One of the residential towers rising above car parking spirals in Bertand Goldberg's Marina City, Chicago, 1964

Right: This project for four sixty-storey towers by Urban Design Associates (David Lewis, Donn Carter, Raymond Gindroz) in the Golden Triangle, Pittsburgh, uses air rights over the cross town highway network and rapid transit concourses for pedestrian decks with offices, shops, restaurants, townhouses, and a conference centre – thus continuing unbroken the texture of the city across the large-scale throughways. The first phase of the project area, the US Steel tower on the right, will be in construction in 1966

conscious and sensitive intention that they will perform, in the social sense, as the new, large scale, geographically definitive urban structure[12]

For what we are talking about, then, is the emergence of cellular cities on enormous scales, organic, rapidly changing – in which systems of mobility act as the hard structure, the urban skeleton; and each city is an additive cluster of quadrants – some being the older areas of the city, and some the new; with each quadrant at once differentiated, defined geographically by this huge weblike infrastructure of transitways, and each by the same means indissolubly linked

In the huge industrial cities of Europe and the US, it

is absolutely pointless to attempt to banish automobiles because of their effect on the accepted or traditional shape of cities.[13] Modern systems of communication have blasted open the old closed urban forms. The notion of a city 'core', a single central area, with its seats of administration and investment houses – a commuter core round which the (now vast) urban agglomerate is grouped – every day becomes less meaningful. The City of London has long been an anachronism, along with the bowler hat; Manhattan is rapidly becoming so

It is important to realize that urban development of the kind which is now remorselessly threading together the previously independent giant cities of the US seaboard into a single super-giant megalopolis, which will cross several states, and will have several interdependent centres or sub-cores – of which Manhattan will be one – is a macrocosm testifying to the sheer power of circulation systems as the basic element in the new theme of urban structure. And when one looks at all that peripheral sprawl, which is these cities' means of growth, one sees, in the drive-in shopping centres, even the meanest of them, a microcosm of exactly the same form – a series of interconnected highway-oriented commuter centres

In the formative years of this new structure, the automobile and the highway, with other transit and communication systems, including aircraft and television, fragmented the city with the reality and the dream of free mobility, and incredibly extendible – and contractible – horizons in time and place. The same factors which fragmented the city are now the means for achieving its unity in a new way

We are approaching the time, during the coming decade, of fast and automated mass transit for passengers and freight, of closed circuit television in general industrial and administrative uses, of computer processing, and of far shorter lives for certain kinds of building. As a result, the need for enormous centralized clusters of offices and industries begins to decline – and so do the disadvantages of decentralization

Highways and rapid rail transit are the key; large-scale in speed and volume, they maintain the infinitely open-ended city, linking nucleus to nucleus in a continuous chain of compact, decentralized centres. By designing these cores on the basis of traffic-pedestrian segregation, you can come up on ramps, escalators or elevators, from transit concourses or parking decks beneath, to the pedestrian

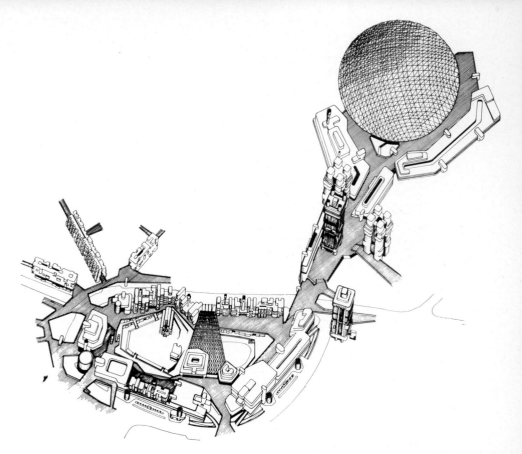

plazas above – and these continue unbroken the texture of the human-scale city on each side, uninterrupted by massive transit-scales. And into each centre would be concentrated all the plurality and vibrancy of any true urban core, the traditional core recreated in terms of today's special needs, not simply shopping, but, like Cumbernauld, the Barbican in London, or Sheffield, containing office blocks, entertainments, restaurants and hotels, cultural facilities, education, high density housing, and even industry

In an excellent and recent short book, Architecture: city sense, Theo Crosby speaks about those considerable areas in our cities which, without necessarily containing marvellous individual works of architecture, add up to splendid human scale

Above: This multi-deck central area for the Fulham district of London, based on principles of traffic/pedestrian segregation, was designed by Taylor Woodrow Group (Theo Crosby, Ron Herron, Frank Linden, Peter Cook, George Gaits, and Robin Middleton). The project has parking and service access at basement level, and shops, a department store, and a market square at the main pedestrian level, 6ft 6in above the existing ground. Above this, the main pedestrian deck which connects the commercial centre with Stamford Bridge Stadium, upper right, is punctuated by cinemas, penthouses, shops, office and apartment towers, swimming baths and bowling alleys

environments. He mentions Chelsea, and the squares of Bloomsbury, in London, Georgian Edinburgh and Bath. To these one could add Georgetown in Washington DC, Society Hill in Philadelphia, or Pittsburgh's Manchester area – or areas from your own city: all of them sectors with streets and tree shaded squares of eighteenth or nineteenth century townhouses. 'Areas such as these could and should be protected, by a simple blanket decision.' And the definition of the city by quadrants would enable the architect-planner, the developer, and the citizens themselves, to work together towards rehabilitation within specific and comprehensive boundaries. For the urban infrastructure of fast mobility would siphon all through-traffic off street systems which were never designed for today's loads, releasing them for manageable local traffic. And this, in turn, will allow communities to function, in a highly mobile society, with all the traditional plurality of the urban street at human scale[14]

The point about this is that Crosby is not talking about preservation in the historic sense, so much as protecting the quality of environment, pedestrian scale, and the social coherence of community. He is talking, as Jane Jacobs does, about cities which simply can't exist as fine but empty shells, aggregates of architecture and engineering, nor as endless low-density suburbia; and can only exist as vital and enjoyable environments for people – people in continuous, multiple, differentiated contact

These are qualities which do not properly belong to any one period or place. They are timeless qualities, the mainsprings of urban life, and have to be created in each period in its own way. 'Like individuals, cities should have character and flavour; like individuals, this flavour is made up of numerous characteristics or identifiable elements.' In some societies, the ability to reflect in physical environment the multiplicity of human contact, as well as its habitual patterns, exists traditionally – outside time, as it were – in, for example, the traditional Greek village, which has remained virtually unchanged for two thousand years, or the urban clusters of the Dogon. But what we have to understand is that even for the people in these environments, these qualities are not traditional in the dead sense; but very much alive, and dependent on each generation for their recreation

In what one might call the first generation of the new city, the new systems of mobility undermined these traditional and timeless qualities of community. The middle income populations rushed to low-density suburbs, leaving enormous areas in the inner rings of our cities to decay and become slum

But more than urban fabric decayed. What decayed was urban quality itself, that intensive plurality and intricate wonder of private and public life infinitely in dialogue, out of which our western civilization has grown. In one sense the mobility of this first generation is symbolic of the many incredible extensions of experience which have occurred right across the board of our mental and physical lives – into space with mathematicians, and from Cape Kennedy; into remote past cultures with archaeologists, in every provincial museum; into fantastic possibilities for the creation and control of life (and death) with biologists, and into frightening probabilities of universal destructors; all of which is reflected in much of the finest art of our period, in the concern with the dynamics of space and time, and with the open forms of line and surface as opposed to the closed forms of mass, of the constructive sculptures of Gabo, Pevsner, and Stephen Gilbert, and in the painting of Mondrian, Malevich, Pollock, and Nicholson

But just because of all these extensions and specializations – rather like the inner, taut disciplines which govern the dynamics of these art forms – man needs more, not fewer, opportunities for exchange and understanding with his fellow man. He needs contemporary environments reflecting his capacity for choice and synthesis. And it is ironic that in our realization of this need for creative urban dialogue, studies by sociologists of urban slums have provided the most recent generation of planners and architects with important stimulus – for in the slums the urban fabric has decayed, but the intensive plurality of urban exchange has not

Thus the need for new nuclei, new high density focal centres, for all quadrants of the city becomes an inescapable corollary of the new urban infrastructure itself – in exchange for the outdated forms of our present cities, with their overworked commuter cores which die at night, jammed rush hour transit routes, and suburban sprawls of thin depressing sameness. Already in some cities, prototypes such as Bertrand Goldberg's Marina City in Chicago are beginning to appear, with origins in Sant' Elia and in Le Corbusier's Ville Radieuse but wholly translated into the vision and needs of the nineteen sixties, with its lower levels of shopping concourse, restaurants and plazas, its middle levels of parking spirals, and its residential and office towers rising into the city skies above. And, backed up by recent legislation concerning comprehensive acquisition of land and air rights, the economics of investment and development in both Britain and the US are now moving very rapidly in this direction

The effect of the new high density nucleus, linked on the one hand to every part of the city by its web of large-scale high speed mobility systems, and on the other to its immediate community, will be that of a stimulating catalyst, for only through identifying themselves as a community can people feel a working loyalty and pride for the place in which they live. In the traditional parts of the city, Bloomsbury or Society Hill, there is an implicit pluralism of urban experience to be rescued and built upon, an image of identity in squares and courts, townhouses and shopping precincts, of historic continuity and place, out of which such nuclei can rise. To the people in the vast thin areas of suburbia, the situation is much more difficult, as these images of identity and pluralism have still to be made; and the suburban drive-in, minimal though it may be, is the thing to work with, for, socially speaking, it is the one potentially dense and multiple thing, the one comprehensible and communal nucleus, they have on which to build. The whole theory is, in fact, one of cities made up of decentralized cells, each with its high density multi-purpose nucleus, at once autonomous as an urban totality, and yet linked by mobility systems to every other part of the urban complex. In macrocosm, one sees whole cities linked in regional and national interdependence. As cities expand, the new opportunities for the dynamic enclosure, release and interrelation of urban spaces offer a fantastic design challenge, from the seclusion of the in-city pedestrian-scale court, to the interrelation of giant urban aggregates, across the breadth of a continent, along 1,000 m.p.h. transit corridors

Thus the city's cellular form which is now emerging reflects the structure of mobility systems. It also represents its pattern of growth. And fundamentally the pattern of cellular growth for, say, the US eastern seaboard megalopolis is similar in striking respects to the gigantic barriada slums on the outskirts of cities such as Lima in Peru – for these barriadas also expand by the addition of cells of community of 50 to 100 thousand people. Here, too, it is the large-scale elements which need to be inserted by government intervention – utilities, schools, and industries – as catalysts to the vast resources of self-help energy and community incentive which are based on human dignity and pride

FOOTNOTES

[1] It took from the dawn of evolution to about the time of the 'Mayflower' for the gross human population of this planet to reach its first half billion people. By 1830, the gross population of the world stood at one billion. By 1930, just one century later, the second billion mark was reached. By the early 1960s, just one generation later, we reached our third billion. If present rates of growth continue, it is expected that the four billion mark will be reached by 1975; by 1985, ten years later, there will be five billion people; and there will be seven billion by the year 2000. 'World Population Growth', by Harold F. Dorn, in The Population Dilemma, edited by Philip M. Hauser, Prentice-Hall, New York 1963, pp. 7–29; papers from the Twenty Third American Assembly, 1963

[2] 'Man's Struggle for Shelter in an Urbanizing World', by Charles Abrams, MIT Press, Boston 1964

[3] Estimates, quoted by Charles Abrams, by Homer Hoyt, Study of International Housing, United States Senate, Eighty-eighth Congress, First Session, March 1963, p. 17

[4] 'Dwelling Resources in South America', by John C. Turner, William Mangin, Patrick Crooke and Catherine S. Turner, Architectural Design (Special Number), London August 1963. One of the most interesting aspects of the barriada situation which this special issue emphasizes is that, in spite of government incapacity or refusal to intervene at anything like a large enough scale, the people of the barriadas have organized themselves into democratic co-operatives, initiating self-help house construction programmes, and even building schools, virtually unaided. Today the older barriadas contain thousands of primitive but acceptable structures, built painfully slowly by neighbours in mutual aid, and assisted by the co-operatives in the larger elements. However slow and painful progress may be these barriadas represent socially a significant and purposeful moment in modern urbanization

[5] Charles Abrams, op. cit., p. 294

[6] 'Architecture: city sense', by Theo Crosby, Studio Vista, London, and Reinhold, New York, 1965, p. 13

[7] The South East Study, critical statement by the British Town Planning Institute, submitted to the Ministry of Housing and Local Government, 'The Architects' Journal', London, 8 July 1964, pp. 71, 72

[8] President Lyndon B. Johnson, Message on Cities to the US Senate and Congress, 'Congressional Record', vol. 111, No. 39, p. 2312–16, 2 March 1965

[9] A description of the factors encouraging the coalescence of the US eastern seaboard cities into a continuous conurbation is given in 'Megalopolis, The Urbanized Northeastern Seaboard of the United States', by Jean Gottmann, MIT Press, Boston 1961

[10] In other major US cities the percentage of commuters who travel by private automobile is Detroit 86 per cent, St Louis 83 per cent, San Francisco 82 per cent, Pittsburgh 80 per cent, Washington 76 per cent, Boston 75 per cent, Philadelphia 73 per cent, Chicago 68 per cent. Statistics compiled in 1960, from Developing Metropolitan Transportation Policy, Committee for Economic Development, New York

[11] The full text of Sant' Elia's Messagio, and a discussion of his Citta Nuova, occur in Reyner Banham, 'Theory and Design in the First Machine Age', Architectural Press, London 1960, pp. 127–37

[12] 'Mobility is the key both socially and organizationally to town planning, for mobility is not only concerned with roads, but with the whole concept of a mobile, fragmented, community. The roads (together with the main power lines and drains) form the essential physical infrastructure of the community. The most important thing about roads is that they are big, and have the same power as any big topographical feature, such as a hill or a river; to create geographical, and in consequence social, divisions. To lay down a road, therefore, especially through a built-up area, is a very serious matter, for one is fundamentally changing the structure of the community

'Traditionally some unchanging large-scale thing – the Acropolis, the River, the Canal, or some unique configuration of the ground – was the thing that made the whole community structure comprehensible and assured the identity of the parts within the whole

'Today our most obvious failure is the lack of comprehensibility and identity in big cities, and the answer is surely in a clear, large-scale road system – the URBAN MOTORWAY lifted from an ameliorative function to a unifying function. In order to perform this unifying function all roads must be integrated into a system, but the backbone of this system must be the motorways in the built-up areas themselves, where their very size in relationship to other development makes them capable of doing the visual and symbolic unifying job at the same time as they actually make the whole thing work.' Peter & Alison Smithson, Uppercase 3, Whitefriars Press, London, 1961

[13] In the decade 1951–61, the number of motor vehicles in the London region rose from 1,137,000 to 2,679,000; and at present rates of increase the total number of vehicles in the nation in 1970 will be 17 million, and 25 million by 1980, compared with 9 million in 1960

[14] Theo Crosby, op. cit.

PETER CARTER

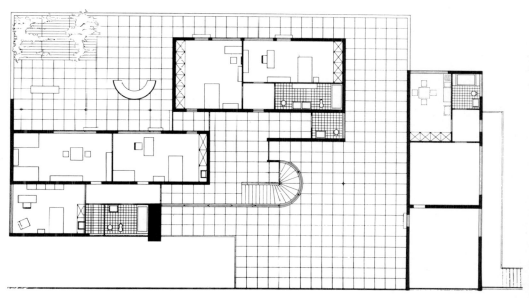

11

The late 'fifties and early 'sixties have seen a great expansion in metropolitan populations and a growing affluence in many sections of society. In the cities, these factors have engendered a sudden acceleration in the pace of rebuilding at a time when co-ordinated urban planning is virtually unknown. Circumstances, therefore, have dictated piecemeal development and the failure of this approach to rejuvenate the urban fabric as a whole is obvious from the parade of unrelated events which characterizes the city today

In democratic societies the protection of individual liberties – which in economic terms, means competitive free enterprise – and the creation and maintenance of the highest social good, are paramount aims. Yet, the desired balance between individual gratification and social well-being is rarely achieved. This failure is particularly apparent in the field of

Right above: Brick Country House, project, 1923 Plan

Right below: Tugendhat House, Brno, Czechoslovakia, 1930. Plan of upper floor. Photo: Hedrich-Blessing

urban rebuilding, where the most flagrant statements of social irresponsibility pass without censure

To educate public opinion and thereby create a sense of involvement in urban matters should not be by-passed on account of the apparent insuperability of the task. For until such an educated public exists and responsible leadership is established, political opportunism will continue to maintain its control of the planners and the onus and liability for the urban environment will be left largely in the hands of private owners and developers – men who have usually remained innocent of the prodigious responsibilities involved

The most effective method of educating public opinion is through good examples of urban planning and building. When such exceptions to the prevailing pattern occur, the degree to which these contribute to the urban environment is directly proportional to the social conscience displayed by the developer, as well as to his architect's ability to comprehend the wider implications of the project

The seven schemes by Mies van der Rohe which are discussed in this article, while subject to the limitations of the prevailing situation, show, most forcefully, what independent projects can accomplish in stabilizing the present transitory and anarchical urban matrix

The structural and spatial concepts which have determined the character of Mies van der Rohe's work have a particular bearing on his urban projects. These concepts may be summarized as follows:

(1) the interpenetration of the spaces between buildings and building elements resulting from their open as opposed to closed placement;

(2) the establishment and scale breakdown of a building's magnitude through a clear expression of the structural system and the components of its construction;

(3) the open ground floor, which adds clarification to the structural system, sets a transitional scale between exterior and interior, and visually and physically opens one street to another;

(4) the introduction of single storey structures into the larger plaza spaces establishes an intermediate scale gradation between the pedestrian and the big space;

(5) the achievement of a scale range within which the buildings and the outside spaces may be harmoniously related to the human being – a cardinal architectural

12

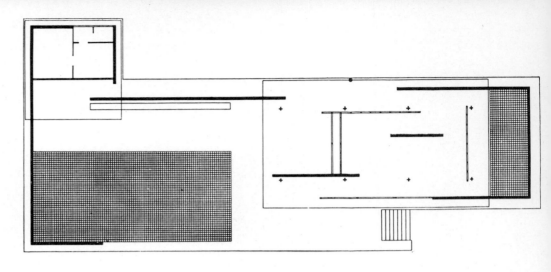

Above and Below: Barcelona Pavilion, 1929. Plan and view from court

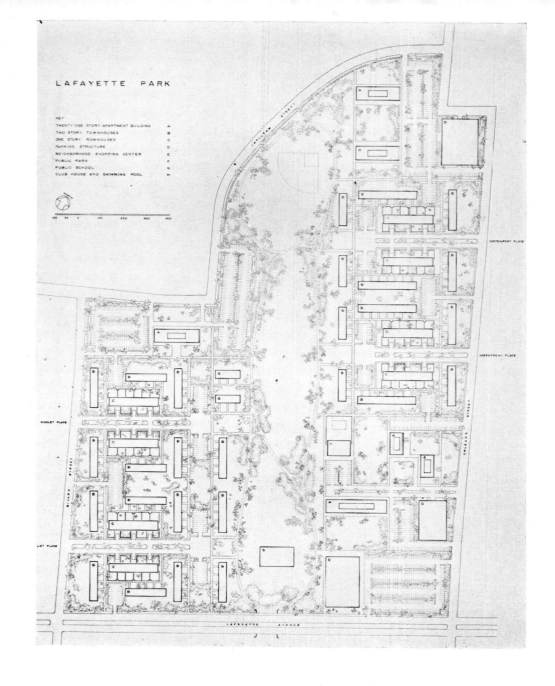

LAFAYETTE PARK

KEY

TWENTY ONE STORY APARTMENT BUILDING   A
TWO STORY TOWNHOUSES   B
ONE STORY ROWHOUSES   C
PARKING STRUCTURE   D
NEIGHBORHOOD SHOPPING CENTER   E
PUBLIC PARK   F
PUBLIC SCHOOL   G
CLUB HOUSE AND SWIMMING POOL   H

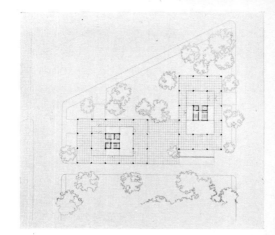

Above: 860/880 Lake Shore Drive, Chicago, 1951.
Site plan
Photo: Hedrich-Blessing

Left: Lafayette Park, Detroit. Master plan, 1956
Photo: Hedrich-Blessing

consideration for a democratic society (cf the neo-fascistic style of Lincoln Center in New York);

(6) the use of landscaping to supplement and comple-ment the interpenetration of space at pedestrian level and, when necessary, to provide privacy and screening;

(7) the consideration of the immediate visual and tactile experiences of the pedestrian by the choice of fine materials and their careful juxtaposition, even on limited budgets

These seven factors are central to Mies' urban work, they determine the character of an environment which is, at one and the same time, in scale with the city, its traffic, and the pedestrian

The projects selected for examination here cover both single and multi-building complexes and a wide variety of metropolitan site conditions. The multi-building complexes – by their nature indicative of a wider city concept – are of particular interest for the development they show of the spatial decellulariza-tion which was characteristic of Mies' earlier work

The decellularization of space in this context first appeared in a primitive form at Frank Lloyd Wright's Oak Park residence of 1889, and although Wright continued to develop this idea in his subsequent work, by the time he had built the Martin House in

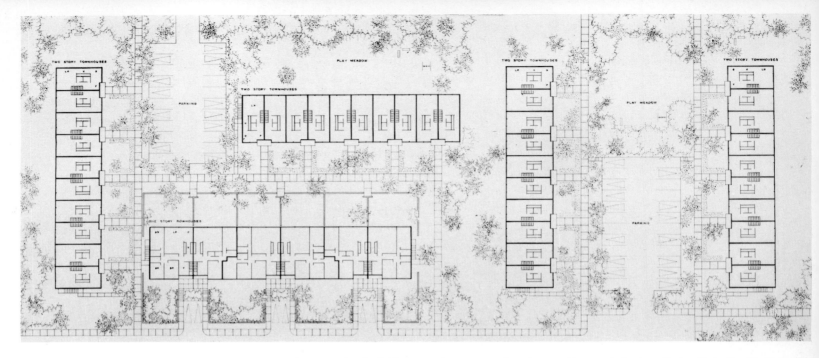

1904 he appears to have advanced its possibilities as far as he felt it necessary. The further development of this seminal concept was to await the introduction of the free-standing wall in Mies' 1923 project for a Brick Country House. Here the walls were treated as clearly defined individual entities placed in a semi-overlapping manner such that any one area of the house was not rigidly enclosed, but rather subtly defined, in its relation with others. By this arrangement space flowed as a continuum throughout the house, and since walls were often pulled out into the landscape the defining line between interior and exterior was minimized. This liberation of interior space was developed further in the Barcelona Pavilion of 1929 where the horizontal planes were also brought into the system. Spatially, no section of the plan was closed but became a natural part of adjacent areas. The character of this space possessed a fluid contiguity where, unlike the compartmentalized plan, a greater whole might be sensed at any one moment, although not actually seen

A year later, at the Tugendhat House, Mies gave this spatial concept a further development. On the upper level of this house the master suite, the children's rooms, and the garage were accommodated in three separate rectangular enclosures placed in a somewhat similar manner to the walls of the Brick Country House and the Barcelona Pavilion. Although the resulting spatial character had already been hinted at in the site layout of Mies' initial project for the Weissenhofsiedlung exhibition at Stuttgart in 1927, it was not until he undertook his first major American work – the campus of the Illinois Institute of Technology – that the potential of this idea in terms of exterior space became more fully realized

A CAMPUS IN THE CITY

The Illinois Institute of Technology occupies 110 acres of flat land a short distance from Chicago's central business district. When Mies became director of I.I.T.'s school of architecture in 1938 he was asked to prepare the master plan for a new campus. The exterior spaces in Mies' plan are individually articulated but never closed; they open freely into adjacent areas, achieving a sense of the larger whole without loss to local intimacy. The plan is remarkable for this integration of separate and individually

Above: Lafayette Park, Detroit. Master plan, two-storey town houses and one-storey row houses

identifiable spaces into a total unity. The fact that the buildings never oppress or impinge, although the physical distances are not always great, is particularly apparent while one is walking around the complex. These spatial qualities have resulted from the open placement of the buildings; the clear expression of a generously proportioned skeletal construction (which establishes the module and gives both order and unity to the buildings and spaces); and from the natural counterpoint provided by Alfred Caldwell's free flowing landscaping

While the spatial characteristics of earlier works certainly influenced the form of the campus plan, the project set entirely new problems, not the least of which was to achieve a workable unity for a large group of buildings accommodating diversified functions whose construction period would extend over ten or more years

Mies' solution to this problem was to plan the campus on the basis of a 24 ft square 12 ft high module. This

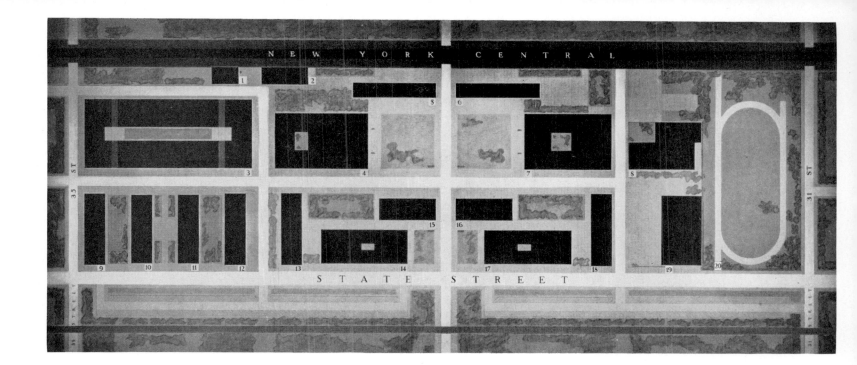

1 Power House
2 Metals Research
3 Engineering Research
4 Auditorium and Student Union
5 Electrical Engineering
6 Civil Engineering
7 Library and Administration

8 Gymnasium and Natatorium
9 Institute of Gas Technology
10 Lithographic Technical Foundation
11 Research Laboratory
12 Armour Research Foundation
13 Humanities
14 Mechanical Engineering

15 Architecture and Applied Arts
16 Chemistry
17 Metallurgy and Chemical Engineering
18 Military Tactics
19 Field House
20 Athletic Field

ILLINOIS INSTITUTE OF TECHNOLOGY   I.I.T. Campus Master Plan, Chicago, 1940

module was derived from the requirements of a typical classroom; its multiplication provided laboratories, drafting rooms and workshops. The Student Union and the Library and Administration buildings planned by Mies, retained reference to this module although the specialized functions of these buildings required different structural dimensions. Nevertheless, although greater in scale than the typical campus buildings, they were designed from a similar structural viewpoint and utilized the same steel, glass and brick vocabulary which he felt would ensure consistency of character for the campus over the prolonged period of its construction

860 LAKE SHORE DRIVE

At the 860/880 Lake Shore Drive Apartments the spatial ideas of I.I.T. were extended into the field of high-rise structures, a development which was later to be continued in the larger scale urban projects at Lafayette Park in Detroit and the Federal Center in Chicago

In contrast to the impenetrable wall of apartment blocks which line Chicago's Lake Michigan shore, the non-formal placement of the two 860/880 towers permitted areas further inland to enjoy contact with the lake

A clear expression of the structural skeleton of these buildings establishes the initial scale breakdown from their total volumes. The structural bay is openly stated at each building's base where the columns stand free of enclosing elements. A further scale reduction is made on the apartment floors by the subdivision of each structural bay into four parts

Although the 860/880 site is small, a sense of almost unlimited spatial extension pervades the area, setting its particular character. The following factors contribute towards this situation:

(1) the creation of open as opposed to closed spaces due to the non-formal placement of the two towers;

(2) the sense of physical and visual penetrability at pedestrian level due to the ground floor glass enclosures being set well back from the peripheral columns;

(3) the sense of easy access resulting from this penetrability is emphasized by the contiguity of the ground plane throughout interior and exterior spaces;

(4) the physical link established between the two buildings by a paved concourse and a protecting canopy

On the limited site of 860/880 a new urban pattern has been suggested, a pattern which is in scale with the pedestrian as well as with the fast moving traffic of a major thoroughfare

LAFAYETTE PARK

At Lafayette Park, a 78 acre urban renewal scheme in Detroit, the spatial characteristics of I.I.T. (low-rise) and 860/880 (high-rise) are brought together for the first time in a large-scale project. However, at Lafayette Park, the exterior spaces assume new functional importance as private courts, public gardens, children's play areas, and community park land

Access is gained to the various building groups via cul-de-sacs from the city roads which enclose the site. All traffic is therefore local and none crosses the central park area

Below left: One Charles Center, Baltimore, 1962. Site plan

Below: Seagram Building, New York, 1958. Site plan   Photos: Hedrich-Blessing

16

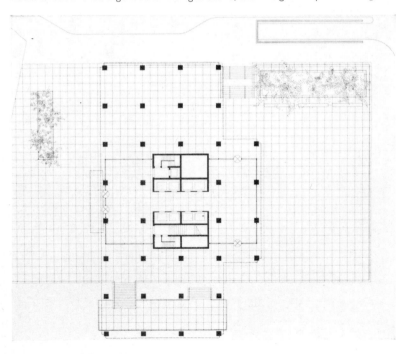

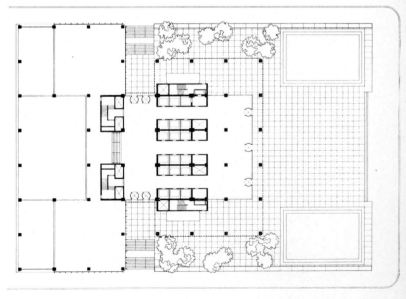

Top: I.I.T. Campus, Chicago. View

Below: I.I.T. Campus, Chicago. View

Right: 860/880 Lake Shore Drive, Chicago. View of the towers at night

Photo: Hedrich-Blessing

In the low-rise groups, which consist of one-storey row houses with court gardens and two-storey town houses planned around cul-de-sacs, a considerable degree of privacy has been achieved due to the scale of the buildings, the careful landscaping, the cul-de-sac road system, and the suppression of car parking areas. The high-rise groups consist of twenty-one storey apartment buildings (accommodating 84 per cent of the project's dwelling units) planned with underground and partly underground parking facilities. Throughout the site landscaping complements the architecture and furthers the interpenetration of both small- and large-scale outdoor spaces[1]

The plan of Lafayette Park was the outcome of collaboration between Mies and the city planner Ludwig Hilberseimer. Professor Hilberseimer's concern with the problems of traffic hazard, air pollution, and proximity of living areas to schools and places of work, have become salient aspects of his city planning theory. His copious proposals for the rehabilitation of cities are discussed in practical and non-utopian terms in 'The Nature of Cities' (Paul Theobald and Company, Chicago 1955). In Mies' hands at Lafayette Park the architectural potential of these ideas was forcefully demonstrated

By 1956 the first portion of Lafayette was complete, but the sudden death of Herbert Greenwald (the project's developer) and the subsequent introduction of work by other architects in addition to Mies' was to seriously affect the architectural unity of the project. Nevertheless, the initial concept was strong enough to absorb the non-Mies buildings to the degree that Lafayette Park is probably one of the most spatially successful and socially significant statements in large-scale urban renewal[2]

FOUR DOWNTOWN PROJECTS

Populous buildings demand adequate physical space at ground level for efficient admission and emission; the number and positioning of doors and the general openness of the space will either ease or hinder these operations. Under stringent site conditions the widening of a sidewalk under the building itself may be the least that can be achieved to ease access, while at the same time, extending a gesture towards the pedestrian

The Seagram Building (Mies van der Rohe and Philip Johnson, architects) stands on a site which is essentially a three-sided pocket off a major thoroughfare. During the planning stage Mies took into consideration the possibility of a typical New York envelope being erected on the then free site to Seagram's north. His reasons for introducing the plaza may be summarized as:

(1) a half-acre pocket of space establishing a point of reference amongst New York's ubiquitous canyons;

(2) a space for the building to stand in, in concordance with its magnitude;

(3) a small, although workable, public plaza; such reasons are particularly convincing now that the site to the north is occupied. In addition, the Seagram plaza allows McKim, Mead & White's Renaissance style Racquet Club to be seen to great advantage, probably for the first time in its life

The New York zoning code does not limit the height of a tower provided that it occupies no more than 25 per cent of the site area: the Seagram tower is exactly this proportion of the 200 ft by 300 ft site. The building contains 530,000 sq ft of office space with 90 ft on the Park Avenue frontage left open as plaza space

[1] Landscape architect: Alfred Caldwell (who was also the landscape architect for the I.I.T. campus.)

[2] The Lafayette Park project was initiated in an interesting way. In 1953 the first portion of a 78 acre plot of condemned property located half a mile from the centre of Detroit was cleared in preparation for the initial stage of an extensive urban renewal programme. After two years' study, the Citizens' Redevelopment Committee, a body of civic-conscious citizens collectively financing urban renewal in Detroit on a non-profit basis, who were to act as co-developers on the project, presented a scheme for the site's redevelopment which had been prepared by a group of well-known architects. This proposal failed to attract developers and it was not until Herbert Greenwald and Samuel Katzin of Chicago took up the options a year later on the basis of a design prepared by Mies and Ludwig Hilberseimer that the future of this important site was determined. The area was divided into a number of 'parcels' on each of which Greenwald and Katzin took out an option. This arrangement allowed the developer to purchase the individual parcels as the project's construction advanced, while at the same time, it gave a commitment to the Detroit urban renewal authorities for the completion of the whole scheme

Federal Center, Chicago (under construction).
Site plan. The architects of the Chicago Federal Center are: Schmidt, Garden & Erikson; Ludwig Mies van der Rohe; C. F. Murphy Associates; and A. Epstein & Sons, Inc.

18

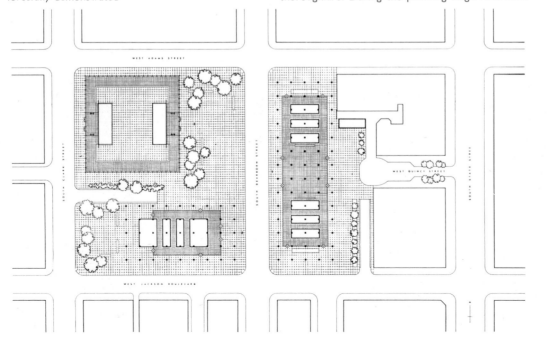

Left and below: 860/880 Lake Shore Drive. Garage
entrance and ground floor concourse

Above and next page: Lafayette Park. Detroit. Views
and model

Photos: Hedrich-Blessing

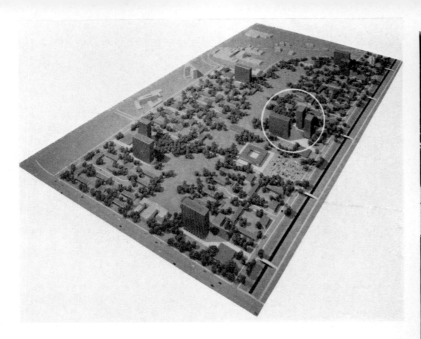

20

Previous page, extreme left: Seagram Building, New York
Photo: Ezra Stoller Associates

Previous page, right, above and below: One Charles Center, Baltimore
Photos: Hedrich-Blessing

This page, left: Seagram Building, New York
Photo: Ezra Stoller Associates

This page, right, above and below: Home Federal Savings and Loan Association of Des Moines, Iowa: view, and model
Photos: Hedrich-Blessing

23

The plaza is paved with granite and raised a few steps above the Park Avenue sidewalk; its north and south boundaries are defined by wide marble benches which also act as parapet walls. Effective foreground elements are provided by two groups of fountains; these help to set the scale of the space which extends from the street back to the building and also give a moment of relief for pedestrians walking the 200 ft from street to street. By locating the trees so that they partially screen the buildings on adjacent sites, the plaza environment is contained more effectively. At night a peripheral band of light illuminates each floor of the building, making both structure and plaza alive for the general public after office hours

The great popularity of this free space with the pedestrian is certainly a tangible acknowledgment of the Seagram Company's social act. One hopes that this gesture will often be emulated, for New York is a city singularly lacking in small, convenient public spaces[3]

[3] At a time when the City of New York is moving towards a zoning law which would encourage a finer quality of building and provide more open space, the city's tax commission has introduced a drastically increased tax assessment policy for what are termed 'prestige' buildings: i.e. buildings which do not sacrifice every inch of land for the maximum rental area at the minimum permissible budget. The owners of the Seagram Building fought their case in the courts and unfortunately lost, which means that all future building development in New York City will be designed with this penalty for the civic act in mind

The American Institute of Architects issued the following statement with regard to the Seagram case:

'The recent New York State Court decision upholding the additional taxation of more than a third of a million dollars per year against the owners of the 375 Park Avenue Building, based on the "prestige value" of the building, sets a dangerous precedent which, if followed by other municipalities, could seriously threaten the quality of future city development

'In effect, the new tax ruling penalizes the owners of the Seagram Building for making a great contribution to the urban environment of New York City. The owners of the building displayed a remarkable degree of civic pride and concern for the citizens of New York when they decided that the building was to occupy only a small percentage of its site and that the remaining area was to be developed as an open

Federal Center, Chicago (under construction).
Model of project   Photo: Hedrich-Blessing

The recently completed One Charles Center office building in Baltimore is located on a site which has two important points of approach, at opposite sides of the lot and at greatly differing levels. Through pedestrian traffic is therefore invited and the immediate response of the public to the plaza areas provided confirms the desperate need for such pedestrian cells in our cities

The building for Home Federal Savings and Loan Association of Des Moines was completed in 1962. It is a three-storey structure on a relatively small downtown site. The opening up of a limited area under and around the building as an extension of the sidewalk has demonstrated that even a small concession to the pedestrian may contribute to the city environment to a degree out of all proportion to its actual physical dimension

In 1959 Schmidt, Garden & Erikson; Ludwig Mies van der Rohe; C. F. Murphy Associates; and A. Epstein & Sons, Inc. formed Chicago Federal Center Architects in order to undertake the design of the new federal government offices and courts in Chicago. The Chicago Federal Center is the most extensive of the downtown projects under discussion here – covering a block and a half of the 'Loop' business district. Past experience had convinced the architects of the need for adequate public space in such congested environments and they felt this to be of particular importance in a project of this magnitude

The placement of the three buildings which comprise the Center creates two interlinked plaza areas, the smaller is approximately the size of the Seagram Building plaza. The ground floors of the two tall

---

space to be enjoyed by all citizens. Now, it appears, these owners are to be taxed for their goodwill. They are to pay a price for their public-spirited actions

'The American Institute of Architects strongly opposes this tax ruling and the concepts therein. This nation is engaged in an era of unprecedented city development, and it is vital to the welfare of our urban population that private developers be encouraged to construct buildings which contribute to, rather than detract from, the quality of urban living

'Continuation of the New York tax policy, and its possible adoption by other cities, would render this goal impossible. It would discourage the nation's best hope for revitalizing our great cities'

Federal Center, Chicago. View of plaza
Photo: Hedrich-Blessing

---

office and court buildings are given over entirely to lobby space, with access from every side. The enclosing glass walls of the lobbies are set well back from the peripheral columns, thereby increasing the physical width of the sidewalks and providing protection from rain. The general openness at pedestrian level visually and physically connects one street with another, and greatly increases the apparent size of the plaza areas. By maintaining illumination in all ground floor areas after normal business hours the plaza spaces will be kept alive and inviting

THE PEDESTRIAN CONSIDERED

The foregoing examples illustrate the degree to which architect and client may contribute towards a humane environment for the urban pedestrian. The large-scale projects of I.I.T., Lafayette Park, and the Chicago Federal Center make significant city planning statements within the context of existing conditions, and without special concessions from local planning codes

The interpenetration of space which characterizes these projects gives identification to individual areas while allowing a larger whole to be sensed. Interpenetration, through extension and contiguity, brings spaces of various sizes towards a common equilibrium, and results in a spatially varied, yet conceptually unified, environment

Parallel to Mies' concept of space is his establishment of a harmonious scale range spanning from the clear statement of a building's magnitude (through structural system and construction components) down to the building elements which confront the pedestrian. The latter, whether benches, steps, landscaping, fountains, or pools, enrich the major spaces at pedestrian level with fine materials and careful detailing

These are the characteristic qualities of Mies' urban work, they enable the buildings and the spaces between the buildings to contribute on equal terms towards the creation of a unified environment. His is an environment which is restrained and humane, and, at one and the same time, in scale with the city, its traffic, and the pedestrian

24

Above: Federal Center, Chicago. View of plaza
Photo: Hedrich-Blessing

Right: Model of Mies' site plan for the Weissenhofsiedlung, Stuttgart, 1927

26

Skyphotos, Philadelphia

NEW URBAN DESIGN CONCEPTS
GREENWAYS AND MOVEMENT STRUCTURES
THE PHILADELPHIA PLAN

ELEANOR SMITH MORRIS

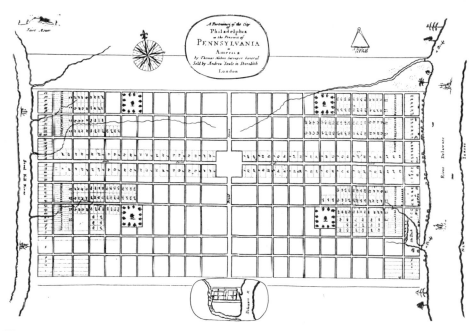

Urban designers are striving to understand the implications and problems of twentieth century living. For the most part urban design is still conceived in terms of the medieval precinct, the renaissance piazza, the baroque esplanade and the beaux arts City Beautiful avenue. It is with difficulty that these traditional design concepts are translated directly into the present-day city. Rather these same design concepts must be re-interpreted in physical forms which can cope with overpopulation and the automobile, to mention but two of the complex facets of twentieth-century life

Philadelphia, U.S.A. is making as brave an attempt as any city to find new urban design forms and the new city structure. So far their explorations have resulted in two concepts; that of the greenway system based upon domestic human needs, and that of the multi-level centre based upon movement needs. Slowly over the past twenty years, Philadelphia designers have evolved both systems to complement each other. Eventually the greenway system will filter through the residential areas and the continuous multi-level buildings will command the civic centre

THE GREENWAY SYSTEM

One of the lasting principles of urban designers has

Above: William Penn's grid plan, 1682, for a greene countrie towne' of about 1,200 acres situated at the narrowest point between the Schuylkill River and the Delaware River. Notice the four green squares

Right: Independence Hall where the Declaration of Independence was written and proclaimed is one of the best of the eighteenth-century buildings on Society Hill

been that individual buildings must be related to each other and to their environment by a clear space organization system. In the medieval period, the very small size of most towns and the few buildings of obvious authority meant that a single space organization system happened unconsciously, or with a minimum of planning. In the Renaissance and Baroque periods, with society growing in population and complexity, a planned space organization of squares, piazzas, parade grounds, etc, evolved. But these were mostly static concepts, generally not related to each other. Hausmann's Paris and the City Beautiful Movement related these static spaces out mainly for the use of the monarchical or governmental authorities

Now we come to the twentieth century, when mobility of the population is paramount, and hence a new

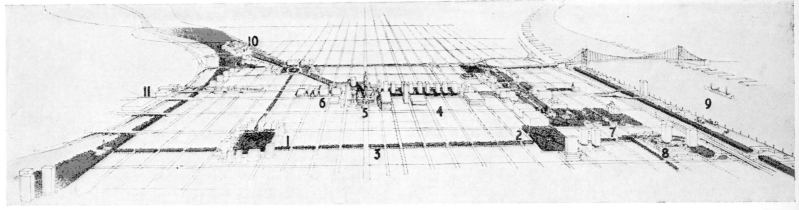

space organization system must reflect this changing need. The greenway system attempts to do this. On the domestic scale, the greenway system acts as public open space for the democratic use of every citizen and exists as landscaped pedestrian ways which lead to and from important local institutions and landmarks which act as focal points in the system. The greenway deliberately follows the wayward path of the pedestrian, catching hidden vistas of church spires and reflecting human needs in human scale spaces

More importantly the greenway system becomes the order which determines the location and general form of the principal buildings in the urban area. This kind of structuring of the city is strong enough to be a unifying device for all new buildings, and yet allows continuing freedom in the individual building design. The architect's freedom of expression is maintained, while at the same time the individual building is re-emphasizing a total city greenway network

Edmund Bacon, Planning Director of the Philadelphia Planning Commission, began experimenting with the greenway concept after World War II, and encouraged consultant architects to emphasize a greenway network

One of the early expressions of the greenway principle is shown in the proposed scheme of consultants Louis Kahn and Christopher Tunnard for the redevelopment area of South-West Temple Philadelphia. In this scheme, on the main central street, an ample set-back was proposed to allow for a shady promenade lushly planted with green shade trees. From this main promenade, minor greenways penetrating back into the housing areas linked with established community institutions such as the local Armenian

church. At a pivotal point of the promenade, a thirteen-storey point block with its own piazza was proposed as a new landmark

The Society Hill Washington Square Redevelopment Plan afforded the first chance of putting the greenway concept into effect. Covering approximately 286 acres of the eastern portion of William Penn's original city, the Society Hill area houses about 15,000 people. Part of this area has been redeveloped to provide 1,476 new dwellings, but most of the area has been rehabilitated. The design problem lay in co-ordinating the many historic eighteenth-century dwellings with the new housing, institutional landmarks and the expansion of the two major hospitals in the area

An early design attempt in Society Hill created three vast malls in front of Independence Hall, causing disharmony between the automobile scale of the malls and the human scale of the eighteenth-century State House. A further mall on the east-west axis repeated the mistaken interpretation of scale leaving a small eighteenth-century Guild Hall and Bank as islands in a green sea. Having learnt their lesson, Philadelphia's designers created the greenway system with its landscaped walks which restored the compact and tight scale that a sense of urbanity requires

In the proposed Society Hill Plan, the central design concept is based on a major east-west axis from Washington Square turning along Locust Street and running to Rittenhouse Square. This major east-west axis links two of William Penn's four eight-acre open spaces of his 'greene countrie town'. To this day these open spaces are important breathing spaces for centre-city residents. Subsidiary greenways 'dog leg' northwards to the Customs House and to Indepen-

Above: The Philadelphia City Planning Commission's redevelopment of the central areas of the city
1 Rittenhouse Square. 2 Washington Square. 3 Locust. 4 Chestnut. 5 City Hall. 6 Penn Center. 7 Society Hill. 8 I. M. Pei project area. 9 Delaware River. 10 Art Museum. 11 Main Line Railway Terminal on the Schuylkill River

Below: The 'B-Mall' greenway opening on to the pedestrian square and leading to the Old Customs House is settling into the urban landscape. Photo: Claire Kofsky

28

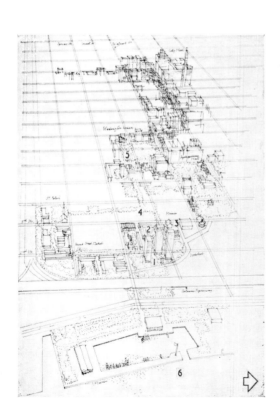

Above left: One of the original streets laid out by William Penn in the Society Hill area and now part of the greenway system. The houses have been rehabilitated recently by private individuals. Photo: Lawrence S. Williams, Inc.

Above: The greenway from Third Street leads through a rehabilitated area of old houses, and new town houses, to the apartment towers designed by I. M. Pei. Pei's town houses are on the right and the towers are now occupied

Left: The greenway system provides the framework for I. M. Pei's project for Society Hill as shown in this sketch by I. M. Pei, architect
1 Apartment Towers. 2 New town houses. 3 Rehabilitated houses. 4 Greenways. 5 Washington Square. 6 Delaware River waterfront and marina

Next page: The eighteenth-century guildhall known as the 'Head House' sits at the pivot point of the greenways leading from the rehabilitated houses to the new Society Hill towers

dence Hall, and southwards to old St Peter's Church via 'Old St Peter's Way'. A further greenway turns around the new development, leads the pedestrian to St Paul's Church Hall and alongside it to enter into the new development. The Customs House greenway includes a toddlers' playground as does the greenway at 3rd and Delancey Streets. The materials used so far are indigenous to the area, red brick paving, flowering trees, white painted clapboard fencing, low concrete benches and wooden litter bins

The success of the greenway system in structuring the new development is shown in the architect I. M. Pei's scheme for the redevelopment portion of Society Hill. Unlike the other competitors, I. M. Pei purposely kept his tower blocks to the extremities of the area, where either Washington Square or the open expanse of the Delaware River afforded breathing space to the towers. In between, the new town houses fit in with the rehabilitated houses, maintaining the same scale as the existing three-storey row houses. The town houses reinforce the direction of the greenways, while each of the three Dock Street towers are carefully placed in relation to the greenway system. One tower 'closes' the greenway view along St Paul's Mission while another tower B turns the pedestrians towards the Head house greenway

Left: The before photograph of a greenway concept. St Peter's Way is shown as the slum it was; St Peter's Church spire can be seen in the distance. Photo: Claire Kofsky

Centre: The after photograph of the greenway concept. St Peter's Way is shown as the greenway it is now, with a children's playground and rehabilitated eighteenth-century houses. St Peter's Church spire can be seen in the distance. Photo: Lawrence S. Williams, Inc.

Below left: Greenway plaza with the Pennsylvania State Office Building in the background. The greenway was designed by Ian McHarg; the fountain was designed by James Morris. Photo: Tom McCaffrey

The irregular pattern of the greenway system leads the pedestrian in a complete round trip. The pedestrian starts from the B Mall of the Customs House, goes along Willings Alley to the greenway alongside St Paul's Mission, through the park of towers by I. M. Pe, south along the tree-shaded greenway to the historic Head house and eighteenth-century Market Place. At the Head house, the Stampler Street greenway links with Old St Peter's Church, which also acts as the terminus for the north-south greenway from Willings Alley. The pedestrian has made a complete circuit. Subsidiary greenways lead off to other rehabilitated alleys of town houses, while a major greenway on Spruce will link under the Delaware Expressway with the Waterfront Marina

Other greenways are proposed for the University area of the city, Broad Street and for the smaller community development projects in residential areas. A unique variation on the greenway scheme is that proposed for Chestnut Street. In the new plan, along one of the best shopping streets in Philadelphia, Chestnut Street will lose its vehicular traffic and keep only a two-way electric tram which will go the full breadth of the city from the western parking garage on the Schulkill Expressway to the eastern parking garage on the Delaware Expressway. The existing pavement will be widened to use the former vehicular space of the sixty-foot wide street, thus creating a shopping promenade which eventually reaches the historic Independence Hall. Chestnut Street would become the only 'greenway Promenade' in Jane Jacobs' terms, whereas all the other greenways are meandering pedestrian ways

The greenway concept hearkens back to Patrick Geddes' idea of Conservative Surgery, which Geddes discussed in a report on Balrampur, India, a long time ago

'Some of the principles of conservative surgery can be illustrated in a quarter south of the palace of Balrampur. Here are two plans. The first, a tracing from the Municipal Survey, shows the existing labyrinth which is crowded and dilapidated, dirty and depressed. The second shows a plan that has resulted from an intensive study of the area, house by house as well as lane by lane. It will be seen that the lanes have now become reasonably spacious and orderly, though not formally so, and that open and easy communications exist in every direction

'Here, as so often, the right starting points have been provided by the existing open spaces, each with its well and temple

'These spaces have been slightly extended by clearing the sites of all fallen buildings and planting trees to protect the enlarged spaces against future encroachment. The open spaces can then be linked by further small clearances, mainly at the expense of ruined and dilapidated buildings

'As this study of the locality proceeds, one is encouraged by the results, alike for sanitation and for beauty. As these depressed and dilapidated old quarters re-open to one another it can be seen that the old village life with its admirable combination of private simplicity and sacred magnificence is only awaiting renewal

'Even in the beautiful old cities of the west we have rarely such a wealth either of open spaces or of antique shrines. In fine old European towns, as of Belgium or Italy, the churches are larger and more magnificent, but the great number of these small shrines, with their domes and spires always pleasing and often admirably proportioned and wrought, makes an effect which, though less magnificent, is in a way even more delightful . . .'[1]

'The conservative method, however, has its difficulties. It requires long and patient study. The work cannot be done in the office with ruler and parallels, for the plan must be sketched out on the spot, after wearying hours of perambulation'[2]

These snatches from Geddes' reports illustrate a method of individual improvement over wholesale clearance, a more subtle and painstaking approach than razing an entire area and relocating the inhabitants elsewhere. The greenway system helps to

[1] 'Patrick Geddes in India', edited by Jacqueline Tyrwhitt, Lund Humphries, London 1947, p. 48. Taken from the report, 'Town Planning in Balrampur': a report to the Honourable the Maharajah Bahadur, 1917, p. 41

[2] Patrick Geddes. Taken from a report on 'The Towns in the Madras Presidency,' 1915, Tanjore, p. 17

31

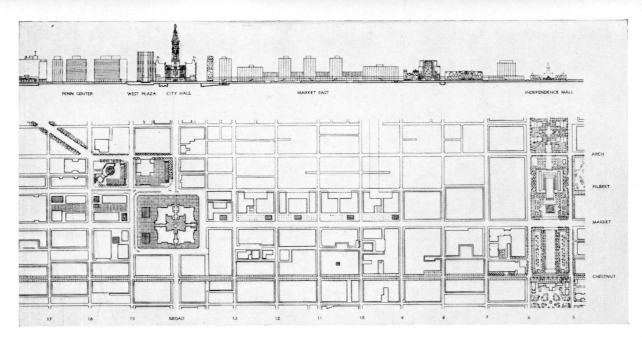

PENN CENTER   WEST PLAZA   CITY HALL   MARKET EAST   INDEPENDENCE MALL

ARCH

FILBERT

MARKET

CHESTNUT

17   16   15   BROAD   13   12   11   10   9   8   7   6   5

structure such an approach. It is an urban design device whose potential has not yet been disclosed
As Geddes reminds us, the greenway system depends on an intimate knowledge of the individual characteristics of an area. For instance, the civic design possibilities of each dwelling and every public institution must be studied. A complete landscape survey of existing trees, existing floorscape, and existing street furniture must be made. Finally each citizen needs to fulfil his own individual act of expression in the city's townscape
The greenway system in Society Hill has been successful at the level of the consideration of relationships of buildings to each other. It has not yet been entirely successful on the townscape details of floorscape, landscape and integration of street furniture. Telephone wires still criss-cross between old and new development, 'stop' signs, 'no parking' signs and all the sign paraphernalia of street life still clutter the corners. However, Philadelphia's designers are aware of this and in time will encourage 'non-wirescapes' and street furniture worthy of the area
Citizens have helped a lot to improve individual houses, develop individual patio gardens and window boxes, and upkeep in this particular area. Citizens have also been encouraged by the Redevelopment

Authority to plant street trees. The Redevelopment Authority sells the trees at one-third the cost, since the other two-thirds is paid from Federal Funds
The greenway system is excellent for reflecting the individual characteristics of an urban area. As a space organization system it must fulfil the desired lines of pedestrian paths going to specific places in the particular urban area. As a landscape concept, the greenway must grow trees and the flowering shrubs indigenous to the soil and climate of the urban area. And as a civic design concept the greenway system organizes the relationship of particular buildings to each other and to the particular topographic situation of the city. Hence no greenway system can ever be exactly repeated in the way that previous urban design concepts have been totally copied. Paris' Place Vendome can turn up in Philadelphia's Logan Square, but Philadelphia's greenways cannot be faithfully reproduced on the Paris Right Bank. Greenways in Paris will be thoroughly Parisian. In an age of mass production, the individuality of the greenway concept offers a healthy release
The greenway system also reflects a relative space-time relationship which previous urban design concepts have not been able to do. The greenway system is continuous in space: it never begins, it

never ends, and there is no middle. The organization of greenway spaces continues as long as there is a need. Portions of the system can disappear and new portions can be structured into the system. This flexibility means that the greenway system is also continuous in time and variations of the original space system can be everlasting. Thus Philadelphia's greenway concept is the beginning of new space-time urban design concepts

MULTI-LEVEL CENTRES

The problem of movement—arrival and dispersal—from centre city is one of the most involved problems confronting planners today. Movement cannot be isolated, or zoned into neat categories; rather the urbanist is confronted with many different kinds of movement occurring simultaneously. It is the simultaneous demands of movement systems demanding co-ordination with the normal everyday facts of city life of working, shopping, eating and playing which have forced the creation of the multi-level building complex
All types of movement systems: the underground railway, the surface transit systems of bus and tram, the pedestrian, the commuter railway system, and the automobile on both the expressway and arterial

streets; all these systems must enter centre city at the same spot and the same time. Vertical segregation, as well as horizontal segregation of all movement systems is imperative, and when civic activities are co-ordinated in the same building envelope, one avoids creating monuments of movement and instead builds citadels of civic activity

Philadelphia has been experimenting with multi-level centres and is slowly evolving a new urban form of importance

THE MOVEMENT PLAN OF LOUIS KAHN

One of the earliest proposals for new multi-level centres occurred in Louis Kahn's proposed movement plan for Philadelphia. First published in 1953, Kahn's movement plan was not radical, but a pragmatic theoretical interpretation of contemporary movement systems overlaid on William Penn's original scheme

Louis Kahn devised a symbology – his own inimitable expression to explain his Movement Plan:

Expressways are like RIVERS
    These RIVERS frame the area to be served
        RIVERS have HARBOURS
            HARBOURS are the municipal parking towers
From the HARBOURS branch a system of CANALS that serve the interim
The CANALS are the Go Streets
    From the CANALS branch cul-de-sac DOCKS
        The DOCKS serve as entrance halls to the buildings

The Expressway 'River' system contains the centre city, much as the River Ouse contained medieval

Above: One of Louis Kahn's many drawings for his 1956 study for Center City, Philadelphia. Cylindrical parking towers (harbours) ring the downtown area. The existing City Hall is on the extreme left with high rise structures to house municipal offices. The truncated pyramid on the right is a department store

Below: Kahn's movement plan. Pedestrian ways are primarily shopping streets unharassed by motor vehicles. The 'go' streets afford free motor access to Center City while 'stop' streets provide for parked vehicles, buses, etc

▦	pedestrian ways
▤	squares, parks and malls
▬▬	expressways
>>>>>>	'go' streets – through motor traffic; no parking; no trolley cars or local buses
⌐	'stop' streets – parking and service; trolleys and buses; no through traffic
■	municipal parking buildings
●	commercial parking garages

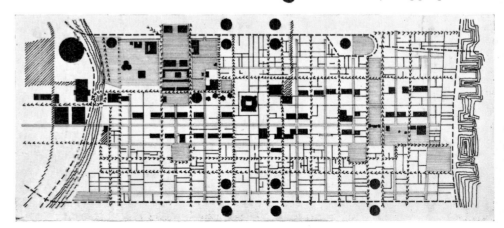

33

York. Most of the planners and engineers were also thinking of the loop expressway – which is now three-quarters built. It is noticeable that the containment of the expressway is not visual. The expressway is depressed below the normal street level, and thus does not create a psychological or physical barrier to urban development

Philadelphia's gridiron pattern is already a system of alternating one-way streets, but Louis Kahn segregated his 'Go' Streets still further to create larger superblocks alternating with greenways. His 'Go' Streets permit through automobile traffic, but do not allow for curb parking, the staccato movement of trams, cars or local buses. The stopping and starting of public transit facilities and of short-term parkers produces a staccato movement alien to the non-stopping 'Go' movement of vehicular movement. For the staccato movement, Louis Kahn set aside the cross streets, also alternating with greenways. These staccato 'Stop' streets allow for parking and servicing of buildings and for trams and the local buses

Kahn's plan does not reflect the small-scale greenways that Bacon is creating. In Kahn's plan the alternating east-west greenways are primarily shopping promenades, as the Chestnut Street green tramway, which Kahn shows leading from the commercial garage in the Schuylkill across the city to Independence Hall. These shopping promenades would be alive with people milling in and out of trees, gardens, exhibits and escalator entrances. Unlike many purist planners, Kahn accepts all the most human honky-tonk activities of our black leather jacket age and wants to place pin-ball machines, shooting galleries and juke boxes on these greenway shopping promenades

The important 'stop' streets terminate in Kahn's docks, or municipal parking garages. Off important exits from the expressway loop, Kahn suggested the new movement symbol of the spiralling street in the air forming commercial parking garages. These

circular movement towers are constructed as part of the expressway system. In Kahn's further proposal for Center City, these circular parking garages are placed round the inner core of the multi-level Center City. Shopping units hang like the Gardens of Babylon from these shopping and parking multicolumnar towers, with parking in the interior

Kahn's building plan for Philadelphia shows other multi-level centres, for culture at Logan Square and for sports at 9th and Market Streets

MARKET EAST MULTI-LEVEL CENTER PROPOSALS OF LOUIS KAHN

Recently Kahn has been given a further chance to present his ideas in the Graham Foundation Study sketches of Market East. His earlier proposals suggested a form, but now the Market East sketches show forms developed into a systematized Order. This order Louis Kahn calls 'Viaduct Architecture', and in strength and its circular form, Viaduct Architecture is very similar to the medieval urban components of the wall and the circular castle form

Kahn has been searching for an urban form which will dominate and control the automobile and which will elevate civic activities to their proper importance. Kahn's wall of 'Viaduct Architecture' surrounds Center City very much as medieval Carcasonne was protected by a wall. In this respect Kahn has said:

'Carcasonne was designed from an order of defence. A modern city will renew itself from its order concept of movement which is a defence against its destruction by the automobile

Center City is a place to go to – not to go through'

In the Viaduct, cars are raised on long expressways, beneath which are tucked levels of buses, trains and warehousing. His Viaduct architecture is another form of the multi-level centre where the viaduct becomes part of a great sports centre structure of circular shopping areas and an elliptical stadium whose cars are parked under the podium

Civic activities of shopping, and recreating in a great sports centre, become important through the strength of the new Form. Within the continuous multi-level centre there is a glimmer of an architectural concept of 'served' and 'service' spaces evolving into new urban spaces. It is here that Kahn

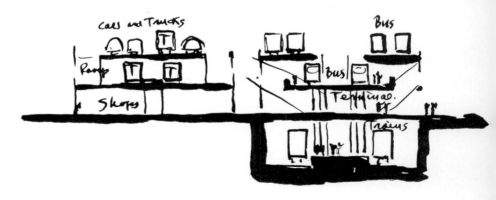

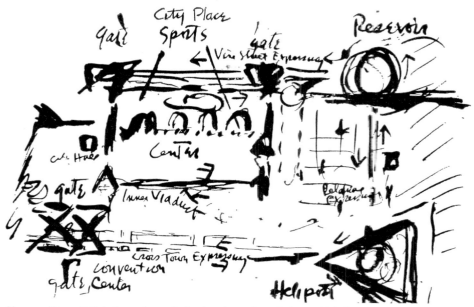

Above: One of Kahn's early analysis sketches of Market East in Center City for the Graham Foundation Study 1961-62, showing an early stage in the evolution of his viaduct architecture

Below: Kahn's model of his 1961-62 Graham Foundation Study for Center City showing how new structural orders emerge from a clear statement of traffic hierarchies

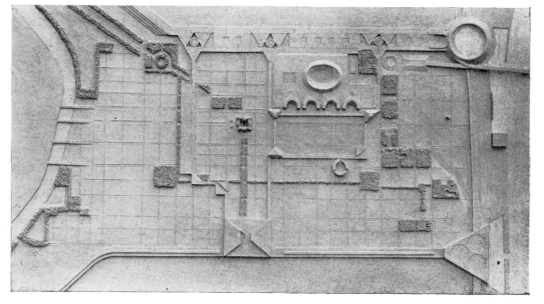

believes the medieval Scottish castle points to new directions for urban components

The interpretation of the solidity and scale of the Scottish castle and the medieval town walls appears in Kahn's viaduct architecture. In these Market East sketches, the suggestions of new form and new strength are there, but the attitude is still too Roman, too authoritarian. The human being and his freedom of choice has still to be expressed in Kahn's great centre. This will be in the next design stage, when Kahn's ideas about his centre are detailed

THE PRINCIPLES OF BACON'S CENTER CITY PLAN

The most exciting reward for Edmund Bacon and his Philadelphia planners is to see the many different ideas for Center City finally develop into one coherent plan. Organizing the problems of movement has been at the heart of the many different concepts pursued

Center City, Philadelphia, has complex movement problems because it is the regional capital of an eight county metropolitan area, whose present population of 4 million people will increase to 6 million by 1980. Center City, Philadelphia includes 25 per cent of the region's employment, all its banking, insurance, advertising and governmental facilities, serves as the dominant retail centre and is the home of some of the nation's outstanding cultural and entertainment facilities

As a result, Bacon's Center City site plan is based on the following principles:[3]

1. An efficiently concentrated core to house a thriving centre of private commerce and public services for a region of 6 million people

2. A modern, balanced transportation system (auto, bus and rail) penetrating close to the heart, with easy and pleasant transfer from vehicle to foot; and the exclusion of traffic not destined for the core

3. Major parking facilities and bus terminals directly connected with the expressway system to reduce congestion of local streets

4. Pedestrian movements in the core separated from automobile traffic in so far as practicable by upper and lower level concourses, and the removal of automobiles from the city's primary retail street

5. Parks and open space to provide an appropriate and dignified setting for public buildings and historic shrines, squares for public gatherings

[3] 'Center City, Philadelphia', Philadelphia City Planning Commission, 1960

and celebrations, quiet spaces for relaxation and places for enjoying the bustle and excitement of the crowd

TRAFFIC PLAN

The Traffic plan for Center City proposes the efficient and safe interlocking of three different types of movement; automobiles via an expressway system linked to parking terminals; commuters and passengers via the underground, the railway system and the bus system, and pedestrians via separated below level or upper deck walkways

The Expressway Loop around Center City provides a by-pass for all traffic not intended for Center City, and provides controlled access to Center City via key exit points which are purposely related to major parking garages

The underground system (known as Rapid Transit) is to be improved both by lengthening strategic sections and by rebuilding existing elevated portions underground

The suburban commuter railway system, consisting of two different railway lines, the Pennsylvania and the Reading, will be connected underground at Filbert Street, bringing passengers to stations at Penn Center and Market East. Existing stations will be either relocated or extended to conform to the proposed plan. The resulting system of combined underground and commuter passenger stations and adjoining parking garages is purposely related to the office, commercial and retail centres of Center City

Eight major parking terminals providing a total of approximately 17,000 parking spaces are also to be connected to the expressway by special access ramps and to the major passenger stations

The largest parking garage is that proposed underground at Broad and South Streets and is for 6,000 cars. A second 2,000-car parking garage will be located on the western side of the Schuylkill River at the end of Chestnut Street tram line. At the opposite end of Chestnut Street on the eastern side of the city connecting to the Delaware Expressway is another 3,000-car garage

Above: The Philadelphia Planning Commission plan for Center City 1952-62
Key: 1 art museum, 2 railroad station, 3, 4 Penn Center, 5 municipal service building, 6 City Hall, 7 Logan Square, 8 Rittenhouse Square, 9 Market East, 10 Washington Square, 11 Independence Square, 12 Independence Mall, 13 Franklin Square, 14 Federal Hall, 15 Society Hill, 16 Delaware River

Right: N-S section looking east through the plaza project now being developed immediately west of the City Hall and the Municipal Services Building

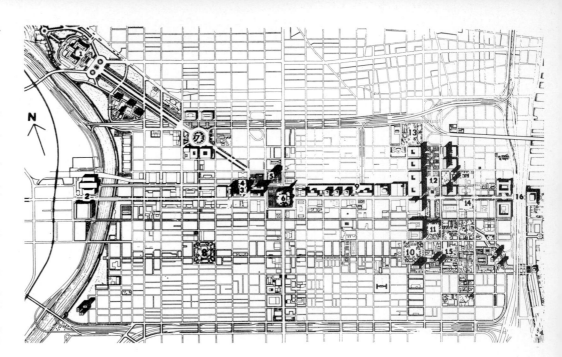

36

Scattered parking garage complexes, related to the Vine Street Expressway, will be built to house a total of 6,000 automobiles

The pedestrians will be able to walk from one side of the city to the other via the Chestnut Street pedestrian mall. All automobile traffic is to be removed from this mall, leaving only the two-way tram system. The tram system will terminate at both the eastern and western end in the proposed parking garages

The pedestrians are also able to reach either passenger stations or business complex under cover in the existing or to be expanded underground concourses

CENTER CITY: THE SITE PLAN AND CO-ORDINATION OF MULTI-LEVEL CENTERS

The site plan shows the gingerbread Victorian City Hall in the centre of the plan. Two main axes run north-south, Broad Street, and east-west, Market Street. The skyscraper office core concentrates on Broad Street south of City Hall. The department store complex concentrates along East Market Street at 8th Street. The west Chestnut Street area contains the better retail shops

Penn Center is completed just west of City Hall along Pennsylvania Boulevard which ultimately terminates at the grandiose neo-classic Pennsylvania Railroad Station on the west side of the Schuylkill River

East of City Hall the Market Street East scheme is proposed to link the Penn Center complex with the existing department store group at 8th Street

Further east are suggestions for parking terminals. There, the partially completed Independence Mall focuses on Independence Hall doglegging to the east with the Independence Hall National Historical Park. South and east is the Society Hill area redevelopment scheme from Washington Square to the Marina on the Delaware River

MARKET EAST: CENTER CITY

The Market East proposal presents the most complete concept of the continuous multi-level centre yet to appear in an American city. Its objectives are:[4]

[4] 'Center City, Philadelphia', Philadelphia City Planning Commission 1963

Above left: Penn Center lower level restaurant looks over the sunken plaza towards the Transportation Building. Photo: Claire Kofsky

Below left: In winter the sunken plaza becomes a gay ice skating rink. Penn Center office buildings frame the City Hall and William Penn in the background. Photo: Claire Kofsky.

1. Distribution of all pedestrians arriving at Market East Center on a series of separate levels from Penn Center to Independence Mall
2. Rebuilding and rehabilitation of the Market Street underground stations
3. The interconnection of the suburban railway commuter lines of the Pennsylvania and Reading railways
4. A new bus terminal which will remove all New Jersey commuter buses from Market Street
5. A parking garage for 3,000 cars with direct access to the Vine Street Expressway

The architectural form integrates the communications centre with the vast shopping possibilities in four major department stores and future office development. Covering over 70 acres, this one multi-level complex weaves its way across the city, around City Hall and out into the completed Penn Center

1964 MARKET EAST STUDY

The Market East multi-level centre has been under continuous study, and appears to be closer to a solution with the 1964 scheme. This 1964 study shows an entirely new structural form with functions more clearly defined and thus the centre becomes easier to implement. A single great esplanade extends the length of the complex, separating public and private sectors. This great esplanade is considered a public pedestrian street and thus is serviced by the police, firemen, etc. as any normal street. On its street side are the shops which can be built as independent units, under overall design control, and which feed into the lower department stores. These can be reached either from the street level or from the lower level pedestrian concourse, or esplanade level. In contrast to earlier schemes, the shops cannot be reached on the upper level. Access on three levels left too many confusing choices to the shopper, so now in this design there is a clear and definite decision that the lower level esplanade is the principal level. On the non-street side of the esplanade rises the upper level bus deck, four levels of parking for 2,000 cars and then office space above. In this scheme the release of air rights for office space can now be controlled

MARKET STREET LEVEL

Because of existing shops, the street level will remain a typical street with shops off a deep set back. The design of the street level follows the gridiron street pattern uninterrupted for eight blocks along Market Street from City Hall to Independence Hall. A unique feature of this design is the proposal to encase the cross streets within a glass frame such that the cars will seem to float above the esplanade

Above right: Separated model of Penn Centre, showing the first portion of the multi-level complex to be completed. The model base shows the lower level concourse, underground tracks, underground bus terminal, and sunken plaza. Photo: Lawrence S. Williams, Inc.

Below right: One of the first views taken from an underground subway train looking into a sunken, lower-level pedestrian plaza. Penn Center rises above with the Municipal Services Building in the background

LOWER LEVEL: THE PEDESTRIAN ESPLANADE

The backbone of the Market East Center is the interconnecting link between the two commuter railways and the new railway stations to be placed on the lower level pedestrian esplanade. In this 1964 study, this Lower Level concourse has become the principal concourse, designed as a vast esplanade with celestial glazing. The pedestrians arrive by trains or by underground into a light, airy atmosphere and not into the normal dingy tunnel. This pedestrian esplanade continues the length of the complex, and is punctuated by hothouse landscaping, interior shops and, of course, the commuter railway stations
This later Market East study is a vast improvement over the first concept. Several major difficulties seem to have been resolved. The first Market East scheme was not as free of the rigid grid system as this later scheme. Functions are now more clearly separated, and uses and directions are more obvious. Separating out the great esplanade gives tremendous freedom to the entire concept and allows complementary uses to join on to it where desired
A second major conflict over the number and use of pedestrian levels has been resolved. In the previous scheme the poor pedestrians were bewildered by three levels, all of equal importance, equal length, with equal shopping facilities. In this scheme there is definitely one major pedestrian level, that of the esplanade. The esplanade is the grand concourse with every mode of transportation entering or leaving its airy space. The esplanade, like an Italian galleria, will contain the main entrances to the shops, and will be dominated by the commuter railway stations. The Market street level is definitely now subsidiary to this main esplanade level
One of the best features of the previous scheme has been retained in this present scheme – that of the segregated but interlocked transportation systems at each level, such that each level is an arrival platform
Commuter buses and long distance buses from the region arrive at the upper level via access ramps which lead straight off the Expressway system into

38

the integral complex, thus ensuring that no city traffic interferes with the picking up and depositing of passengers. The pedestrian reaches the street level and esplanade level by escalators. The esplanade level is serviced by both the commuter trains and the underground railway

DOWNTOWN PHILADELPHIA

When seen as a whole, the Market East Center will unite with the existing Penn Center and West Plaza multi-level complexes to create a continuous urban form. It is not only the continuity and variety of these proposals that stimulate new ideas for new urban design, but also the scale of the proposal. At last in Philadelphia the designers are trying to think of the whole of Center City in one concept, as one continuous interlocking three dimensional space, volume, time concept

Above left: Interior view of the pedestrian esplanade of Market East Project. Note the underground train arriving far left and the automobile traffic crossing the concourse in the background

Below left: Section through the Market East project, Philadelphia, showing within the building complex: parking garages, bus terminal, service vehicles' access and loading bays; passengers' bus concourse and terminal, commuter railroad concourse, esplanade; Market Street subway and commuter railroad station

Next page: Aerial view of downtown Philadelphia showing the City Hall and partly completed multi-level Penn Center in the middle of the photograph. Market East multi-level complex will continue in the right-hand corner. Photo: Skyphotos, Philadelphia

List of references

Edmund N. Bacon: 'The Space Between Buildings', a speech delivered to Harvard University, April 14, 1962

Edmund N. Bacon: 'Basic Design Structure', a speech presented to the Harvard Conference on Urban Design, Cambridge, Massachusetts, April 12, 1957

Edmund N. Bacon: 'Civic Design': a speech presented to an Invitation Conference on Urban Design, Harvard University, Cambridge, Massachusetts, April 9-10, 1956

Eleanor S. Morris: 'Philadelphia Plan', Architectural Design', August, 1962

Wurman and Feldman, 'The Notebooks and Drawings of Louis I. Kahn' (The Falcon Press, Philadelphia, 1962)

Philadelphia City Planning Commission, 'Center City, Philadelphia', 1960

Philadelphia City Planning Commission, 'Center City, Philadelphia', 1963

SKYBORNE
STRATFORD NEW

CONSTRUCTED ART

ANTHONY HILL

Here are some considerations to be resolved by artists who like myself have left the traditional domains of painting and sculpture to move into an unprecedented field – the constructed art work

These considerations focus on some signal differences that too often get lost or overlooked and although not independent of the theoretical standpoint can be treated as such

The problem starts when such art works leave the studio to confront a public in the various settings in which they are to be encountered

Clearly such works no longer fit comfortably in either of the categories 'painting' or 'sculpture' and this alone has triggered off numerous problems for all concerned

Perhaps one of the first questions concerns the idea of a work of art being original, that is to say unique. This is best explained, I think, with reference to actual practice rather than to some ideal concept or principle

Right: Relief construction, 1960. 36 × 42½ × 1⅞ in. Aluminium and vinyl. Collection: the Tate Gallery, London. Photo: Tommaso D'Elia

In my own case I have made project versions, sometimes models, sometimes scale projects, always using the destined materials; thus there is no question of a mock-up and ultimately such works may become small works in their own right, but more often they are just a stage in the realization of a work of more fulsome dimensions

This must not be confused with the issue that a particular theme may give rise to a number of distinct versions, each being a unique work rather than a transcription. (A parallel might be the use of a tone row in serial music rather than the transcription of a work – say an orchestration of a piano piece or vice versa)

Thus 'unique' has two distinct meanings, a unique work is certainly going to give rise to a number of more or less identical 'performances', serial production in the sense of a limited series of replications

Although the means of replication could be put on a 'production belt' process, in practice it is as unlikely to really amount to this any more than it involves the notion of replication that has always existed in cast sculpture or printing

It is up to the artist to decide how limited an 'edition' any one work will have

Such works are principally 'designed works' and the work methods will involve prefabricated components and the completion of an individual work happens when the components are assembled and fixed into position; arising out of this is the factor of renovation, the work allows for 'self-renovation' or more strictly perpetuation through replacement of any damaged parts

For the artist who uses uniform surfaces it becomes increasingly possible to maintain a 'standard of performance'. In the past, and equally with most forms of modern art this is seldom a requirement, only in architecture have we become accustomed to this idea within the realm of fine art

Thus even when adverse conditions interfere with the artist's intentions these can be written into the constitution of the work and less and less will they be merely suggested in token

As a consequence of this all the components of the work can be codified and interference at the level of decay, etc (noise) can be clearly distinguished from the original 'message'

All these topics are emergent, continual and we hope becoming more controllable so that fuller discussion and the linking of these with other factors becomes more fertile all the time

So much for some thoughts on the bodily constitution of this kind of work. It will probably be agreed that all this is as nothing compared to the question of how and where such works are to be utilized. Discussion of this does well to bear in mind some of the topics raised here

Photographing this kind of work, at least two courses are open, neither really satisfactory. In a single view of a work one must hope to have chosen the best from many trials, including the best lighted; if a selection of views is chosen – front, side from the top and so on, one will hope to present a complete account taking in colour, scale and the overall spatial context

In the illustrations shown the 1963 work was photographed front on in strong artificial lighting, extracting nearly all shadows and reflections, flattening the work by excluding all perspective. It could be argued that a plan, elevation and projection – engineer's drawing – would best convey the structure and a mental picture could then be formed that would convey clearly the whole of one aspect of a work

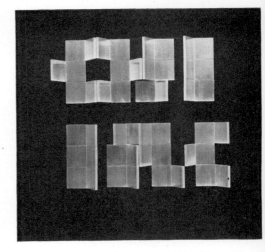

Above: Relief construction, 1963. 24 × 27 in. Aluminium and vinyl. Photo: Tommaso D'Elia

Below: Project model for I.U.A. screen, 1961. 7 × 48 in. Aluminium, Perspex, formica, etc. Photo: Henk Snoek

42

43

Constructional screen, 7 x 48 ft., by Anthony Hill in the International Union of Architects' conference headquarters, South Bank, London, 1961. This building by Theo Crosby demonstrated the most successful artist-architect collaboration of the past decade. Among the artists who collaborated were William Turnbull, whose mural-wall can be seen in the background, Kenneth Martin, Mary Martin, John Errest and Edward Wright. Photo: Henk Snoek

PLANNING IN LIVERPOOL TODAY

ANTHONY MEATS
JOHN ALLAMAND

44

INTRODUCTION

In common with many cities in Britain, Liverpool is faced with a serious and urgent urban renewal programme, aggravated by a persistently high rate of unemployment and high natural increase in population within the Merseyside Region. In order to deal with this situation Liverpool has established a highly organized and competent city planning machine and this machine is unique in current British town planning practice

In February 1962 the City Council realized the enormous scale of the problem which faced them and recognized their inability to deal with it within the existing planning framework. They took the bold and far-reaching decision of appointing a private planning consultant to advise them in relation to the central areas. The man chosen for the task, Graeme Shankland, was formerly the Senior Architect Planner on the London County Council new town project for Hook and he set up a highly qualified inter-professional team to deal with the problem of the 1,400 acres which form the inner area of the city

The essence of his terms of reference were 'to advise the city on the three-dimensional redevelopment of the inner area including road proposals'. That is, to provide a three-dimensional blue-print for the future aimed at securing the continuance and strengthening of this area as the main economic, commercial, shopping and entertainment focus for the Merseyside Region. The City Council realized that should the central area cease to maintain its status the problem of solving the rest of the city's difficulties would become increasingly more difficult

In December 1962 Walter Bor, formerly Deputy Planning Officer in the London County Council, came to Liverpool as the first City Planning Officer, and established a department of 120 people to produce, with as much speed as possible, a new plan for the redevelopment of the city. In one year, therefore, Liverpool appointed a Planning Consultant with central area responsibilities and also established a new and large City Planning Office. The planning of the city centre has now reached a point where a combined office is being formed, which will be jointly led by Walter Bor and Graeme Shankland, to resolve the final Central Area Plan as the key element to be integrated, in its policies of employment, relocation and primary road network into the new plan for the whole city. A comprehensive transport and land use survey is being conducted at present towards this end

Membership of this new team will be provided from both the City Planning Office and the Planning Consultant's Office and the venture will be known as the Liverpool City Centre Planning Group. Thus the final inner area plan, the broad framework of which has already been established by Graeme Shankland in ten reports submitted to and approved by the City Council, will be completed by a group of men and women from both the public and private sectors of the Town Planning profession

With regard to the new plan for the city as a whole, Walter Bor's planning department has produced the first part of a City Planning Policy Report which is an amalgamation of fifteen previous reports dealing with planning standards, problems of the city within its regional context, with employment and unemployment, population and housing, shopping, education, open spaces, social and community facilities and transportation. Special reports are being prepared of three-dimensional planning aspects such as high buildings and comprehensive landscape policy and detailed design projects such as the development of the precinct of the Anglican Cathedral

THE PROBLEM: THE GROWTH OF LIVERPOOL

The rapid industrialization of Eastern Lancashire at the end of the eighteenth century and the need to find an outlet for the world-wide distribution of its products laid the foundations of the modern city of Liverpool. The following two centuries saw the expansion of dock and port facilities and the establishment of the great shipping, banking and insurance houses that are at the commercial heart of the city today and which give it a distinct and well defined architectural expression centred on the Town Hall, and a sense of city scale unusual in British cities

The commercial nucleus of the city attracted industries which were based on the manufacture of imported 'colonial' raw materials, and a main shopping centre was established to serve the needs of a growing community. Added to this were entertainment and administrative functions so that today, in the centre of the city, there exists a highly concentrated and very sophisticated pattern of land uses

The growth of Georgian and Victorian cities was typified by very powerful 'forces of aggregation' and these had their full effect in Liverpool. Commerce and industry sought positions close to the centre of activity and sources of raw material. People crowded in and lived close together within walking distance of their work. This applied as equally to the prosperous as to the working-classes. Admittedly, the former lived in larger houses but these were built in compact streets and squares on a ridge overlooking the central areas of the city. Development took place on every available piece of land. Conditions were appalling

The net was loosened a little by two factors. Firstly, the reform movement and the institution of building bye-laws gave people minimal standards of living which were at least better than anything produced hitherto. Liverpool played a leading part in the pioneer work of these improvements. Secondly, the romantic vogue for the spacious villa set in parkland and the 'Gothic' revival drew the more wealthy out of the very heart of the city

As soon as communication systems allowed, the middle classes emulated them but in a smaller way. This situation existed from the middle of the nineteenth century until the First World War. It is in these Victorian areas that one has today the bulk of the slum clearance problem (in 1955 some 40 per cent of the housing in the city was unfit for habitation) and those areas which are not yet slums form a very large twilight zone which present enormous problems of relocation and rehabitation

Meanwhile in the 'twenties and 'thirties 'forces of dispersal' gathered pace and resulted in a massive suburban sprawl which continues today unchecked

Above: Liverpool today, looking towards Pier Head from the River Mersey

LIVERPOOL AS A REGIONAL CAPITAL

Liverpool is a city of 750,000 people at the heart of a total region of 2.5 million. Those living within the area from which people make their journey to work into the city number about 2 million people

Liverpool however finds itself as a part of the 'Other Nation'—that of the 'have nots'. Its rate of net population growth in the 1950s was 2 per cent per annum compared with the national figure of 5 per cent. If this pattern was to continue until 1981, the 'Journey to Work' region would hold something less than 2.4 million people rather than the potential 2.5 million derived from natural growth. One of the prime purposes of a plan for Liverpool will be an attempt to hold those citizens who might otherwise leave (inevitably the younger and more ambitious) by providing them with a better physical and social environment and sufficient employment

Because of the nature of the city's economic development there is a marked imbalance of employment opportunities—60 per cent of employment is in the service categories. By 1981 20,000 jobs are expected to be lost in the transport section alone. In addition, the high natural increase of population means that in total some 200,000 new jobs will be required over the next twenty years. About half of this need will be met by local firms. The other half will have to be brought in from outside the area. The possibilities of this occurring will be greatly increased if the physical environment generally can be made much more attractive and if the efficiency of the communications system can be improved

THE CENTRAL AREA

Nowhere is this more true than in the central area. Indeed, redevelopment here is seen as the spearhead of an attack on the slum environment and unemployment situation of the whole city. This area provides 25 per cent of the city's rateable values. Investment on this scale must be maintained if the projects elsewhere are to be economically possible. Similarly the regional shopping centre must be made more attractive and efficient and be able to cope with the increases in regional population and spending power expected by 1981. The central area too, is the most important single employment concentration of the region, providing one job in every five within a ten-mile radius from the centre. Its efficiency, however, is being strangled by its traffic congestion. Equal to all this is the fact that the heart of the city in its role as the hub of the community must be made more spacious and attractive if it is to become a resort of pleasure rather than of duty

A SOLUTION
THE ESTABLISHMENT OF A BROAD PLANNING FRAMEWORK

The design approach is to establish a clear, broad framework which must be a flexible one in order to absorb any future change. Therefore, it will be administered flexibly. A finite and rigid plan is seen as being unworkable. This broad framework will aim at total design and it will be concerned with both the functional and visual aspects of the city. The plan must be capable of reflecting future changes in society, of increasing mobility, and of increasing social mobility which will lead to a more fluid society; and the urban forms suggested by the plan should be expressive of the cultural, economic and social structure of society in the latter half of the twentieth century. It is acknowledged that an urban

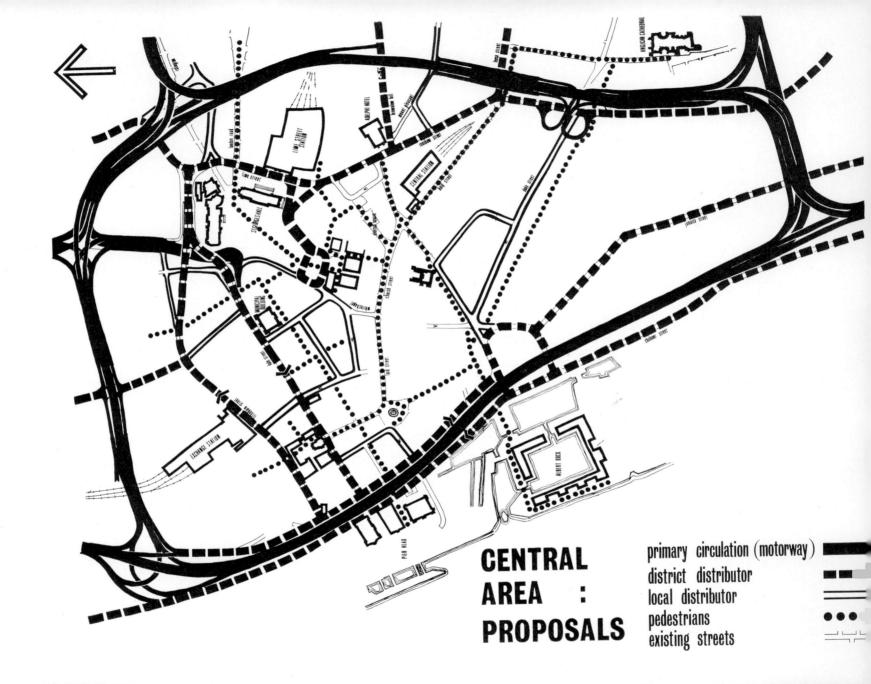

46

CENTRAL
AREA :
PROPOSALS

primary circulation (motorway)
district distributor
local distributor
pedestrians
existing streets

region serving the varied needs of 2.5 million people is a complex organism and Jane Jacobs is right when she talks of 'planning for organized complexity'

The broad planning framework must hinge on the correct analysis of the major land use components to ascertain their correct quantity and disposition related to supply and demand. Having the proper balance of land uses in relation to needs is seen simply as having 'the right things in the right places'. To this end a city policy and structure map is being prepared showing the overall framework and designating certain areas as 'action' areas to be designed in detail

IMPLEMENTATION OF THE PLAN

The implementation of the plan will involve physical alteration to the fabric of the city over a long period of time and will consist of three basic processes: Rehabilitation, Conservation and Redevelopment

With redevelopment, the collecting together of small units of land at present under multiple owner-ship is a crucial part, especially in the central area. The purpose of gathering small units of land into the freehold of the City Council is so that larger units of land may be leased out for development; in many cases modern development introduces larger scale buildings and building complexes due to tech-nological advances in building and civil engineering and sophisticated patterns of interrelationship in urban usage; and the traditional patterns of streets and individual freeholds is totally unsuited to accept this. In some cases the city may have to resort to using its powers of compulsory purchase, for without these powers the community may be held to ransom by recalcitrant owners hoping to capitalize on inflated land prices. In the future the city will be able to share in the increasing prosperity, which its own planning effort and expenditure will have helped secure, by owning the freeholds and collecting the betterment. However, the fact that all redevelop-ment must be economically viable cannot be for-gotten. It is encouraging that as a result of an aware-ness that 'something is happening in Liverpool', private capital would seem prepared to invest in redevelopment on a large scale in the central area, and is now doing so. In some cases redevelopment will be the joint enterprise of the City Council and private enterprise but it is essential that the projects are executed by a single city planning and design agency within the framework of the overall officially agreed plan

THE NEW CITY STRUCTURE

The city's transportation pattern is a key factor in the new city structure. This pattern of movement is made up of road system hierarchy, in terms of urban motorway, ground level distributor street, local access to buildings and service street, and patterns of pedestrian movement related to major land uses; points of pedestrian generation, such as bus and railway stations, and to the major green open spaces in the city

This latter pattern is a system of pedestrian streets, based on pedestrian flow, linked to the city's major parks, both new and existing, which will act as environmental spaces related to groups of develop-ment. The new space system will be grafted on to the existing city space pattern. Thus the new urban structure will be built and integrated from these systems, and the new three-dimensional content of the city will be designed to reflect the basic sense of order and structure, along with those parts of the city which have such visual significance that they can be regarded as fixed design points

VISUAL AIMS

The ultimate visual aim will be to achieve a clarity of city form by the correct plastic distribution of new parts, with the siting of tall buildings and the city's tall buildings policy playing a vital role in attaining this aim. But, the achievement of 'Identity, Structure and Meaning', to quote Kevin Lynch, as the overall urban design aim, cannot be got by a single architect-ural idea, as obviously development will take place over a long time with many architects making con-tributions, and a degree of architectural diversity will exist. It is felt, however, that certain urban design rules can be laid down in terms of the assessment of visual quality in the city today, and a respect for this insisted upon, once an indication of height, general massing, and relationship to the city structure of new development has been established

FORM OF THE PLAN

The form of the plan is as follows: the central area of Liverpool is planned to remain as the dominant economic, commercial and entertainment focus for the Merseyside Region, as mentioned earlier, and surrounding the central area at distances up to six miles will be a series of district centres, some new, some existing. These district centres are conceived as being major shopping and social centres related to a wide catchment area, which in some cases may

exceed a population of over 100,000 people. The centres will be planned to have a compact and visually controlled urban environment, and visual emphasis will be introduced by the siting of large scale building forms, which will give greater ex-pression to these nodal points in an essentially flat landscape. A major design objective is to accept the motor car; and separate vehicle and pedestrian circulation systems will be designed. Car parking space will be provided for 2,500 cars on average, at each commercial-social centre. There will also be an allocation for industrial development making a valuable social contribution to the areas

It is the policy of the city to plan for three categories of shopping:

1 Central Area shopping containing the major department stores and 'specialist' shops
2 District Centre Shopping, for daily and weekly needs
3 The 'local' shop

It will be seen from this that the traditional neigh-bourhood concept has been abandoned in favour of the district centres serving a much wider area

Linking the district centres to each other and to the central area will be the Urban Motorway pattern. Thus fast communications will exist between the district centres and the main focus. The urban motorway structure will be a grid superimposed over the city. The section which will serve the central area is known as the inner loop, and is really one sector of this grid, adjacent to the River Mersey

THE CENTRAL AREA

The inner loop will be a six lane (three in each direction) part elevated, part sunk highway and its purpose is to facilitate the ease with which vehicles can get to the centre and also to provide a very important connection with the Mersey Tunnel—which is right in the heart of the central area. In the future traffic emerging from the Tunnel Mouth will be able to gain direct access on to the motorway pattern and

Opposite. Bird's-eye view of major central area proposals. The pedestrian network is shown in a dark grey stipple. The large pedestrian area in the upper part of the plan is the Civic Centre site. The site in the lower part of the plan where the five tower blocks are located is the Strand Street/Paradise Street site

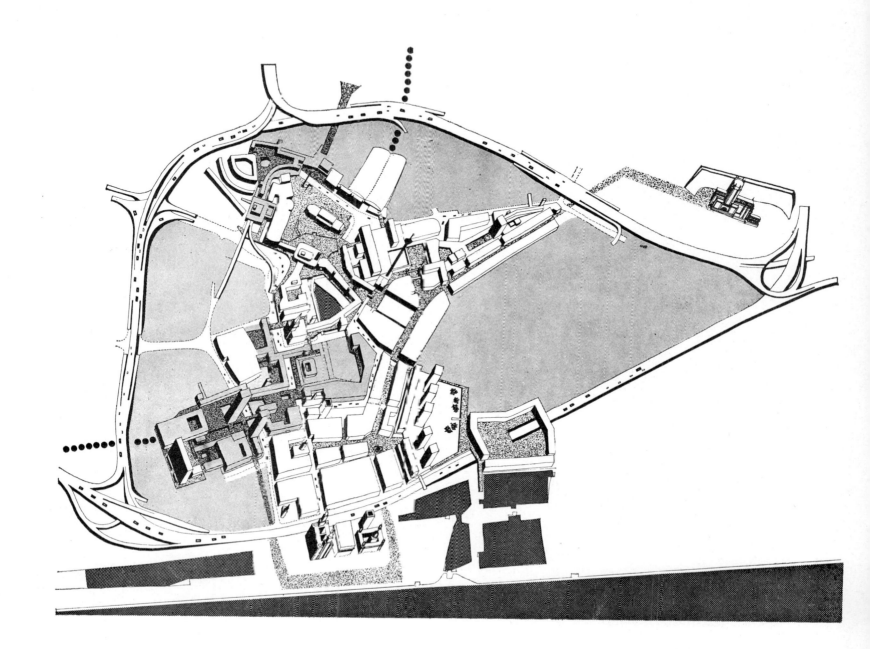

49

50

have rapid exit from the central area instead of causing congestion on the central area streets as happens at present

The inner loop will also take cross-city traffic which generates from the large dock estates on the north and south sides of the centre. It will be three and three-quarter miles in circumference, embracing an area of approximately two square miles and will give direct access to large car parking zones which will permit shopping and business motorists to penetrate close to the shopping and business zones

The structure will be superimposed over the main street network; and the main street system will take the public transport routes as it does at present. This will allow public transport to enter into the core of the city centre, and serve the office and shopping zones. The public transport routes will terminate in a new bus station. This bus station will be part of a development known as the Strand/Paradise Street Scheme which is situated on a twenty acre site overlooking the River Mersey. Above the bus station will be an arcaded extension to Lord Street and Church Street, which are the city's principal shopping streets and which will then become precincts. Rising again above the shopping arcade will be a car park for 2,500 cars. Five tower blocks of apartments and a low block of maisonettes will rise from the roof of the complex overlooking a six and a half acre park. The five towers will visually locate this multi-use development in its immediate context, and within the overall

51

Opposite: This view of the model of the Civic Centre proposals shows St. George's Hall and the large pedestrian plaza in the lower part of the photograph; the five towers rise above the Strand Street/Paradise Street site, and beyond them lies the River Mersey

Above: This view from the pedestrian plaza alongside St. George's Hall is towards the north; the high towers mark the new office zone and the northern edge of the central area

Right: This view shows the Inner Loop from the south. Pier Head buildings are on the skyline and in the middle distance are the Strand Street/Paradise Street towers. For much of its distance the Inner Loop is an elevated highway, and car parking warehousing and light industries, reached from ground level, are integrated in its structure

high-building policy for the central area will mark the southern edge of the city core by their grouping in echelon

The centre of Liverpool falls into three well defined zones to which the plan will give added significance. These zones are offices, shopping, civic and cultural. At the heart of these zones, wholesale redevelopment is unlikely due to the existence of many buildings having either an architectural or historic merit, or a still useful life. Therefore, the existing ground level street access must be maintained, and this means the introduction of horizontal pedestrian and vehicular segregation. In the plan the main shopping streets as mentioned, and Castle Street, the main business street, are to be precincted. However, on the periphery of the zones there is the prospect of large scale redevelopment and the introduction of vertical segregation of pedestrian and vehicles. This will mean a system of pedestrian movement at two levels operating throughout the city centre and they will be related at key nodal points, such as existing squares and new piazzas, by escalators and ramps. The pedestrian network will also relate to bus stops on the main streets. The main street network will demarcate a number of environmental areas, but each area will have a different environmental standard. One question, for instance, is the amount of traffic noise a shopping street can absorb compared with that of an office precinct

CAR PARKING

An upper limit of 35,000 car parking spaces—to serve the central area—has been set and this is determined in relation to the capacity of the approach roads. A six lane highway was decided on as being the optimum width for an urban motorway, after consideration of land acquisition costs, construction costs and environmental intrusion and finally the capacity of the central area itself to accept large scale parking. However, it is physically impossible to provide enough car parking space in the city centre for all future commuters, and if car ownership in the Liverpool region reached the saturation level predicted by the Road Research Laboratory, space would be required for over 100,000 vehicles. The aim is to get a balanced car-parking system which will give certain types of car user a priority due to the inability to adapt the city to full motorization. Special emphasis is laid on the need to provide short-term car-parking space relating to the shopping centre with a continued dependence on mass public transport during the morning and evening peak hours. The car parking policy is recognized as relating to an overall public transport policy for the region

CONCLUSION

This total planning effort will mean that Liverpool will become an attractive shopping and employment centre for all its inhabitants. It will be pleasurable to live in, to work in and just to walk around in. As a modern city it should regain its lost social and economic vigour and prestige, which years of unemployment and hardship have sapped away: and the future will be faced with confidence

Above left: A view of Bold Street and integration of ground and high level pedestrian systems

Above right: Williamson Square, with its theatre and traffic on the right, are retained, but related to the south-west end of the high level pedestrian platform of the Civic Centre

JACK LYNN

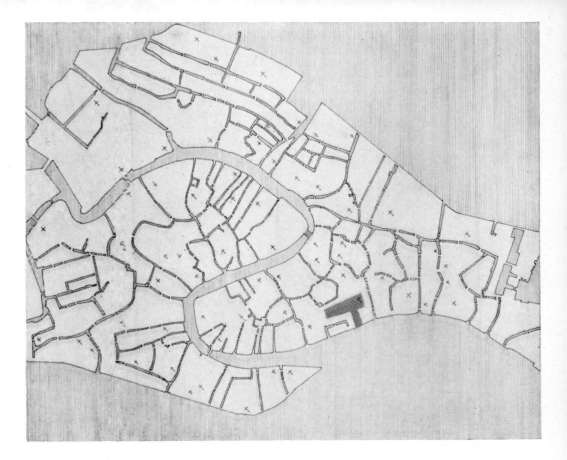

53

The form of the city has always been governed by the manner in which man considers he will move about in it. This is, in many places, conditioned by site peculiarities but is determined largely by the most common form of transport available to him at the time. Venice is characterized by the conjunction of its pedestrian and canal networks, Los Angeles by the predominance of the motor vehicle as the accepted means of getting about, and each gives rise to its own peculiar environment. In Britain there are few towns and no cities which have been conceived in the motor age. Here lies the urban dilemma of our time for there is a universal urge to full motorization and a chronic incapacity in our towns and cities to cope with this condition. There arises a conflict between man and his neighbour's motor in which man is imaged as a pedestrian

This image can be a misleading one. Pedestrian is merely a state of motion on foot – and man spends part of every day in the city in other states of motion which might be called motorized, whether they are in individual vehicles or in units of mass transport. Throughout the day the same person will pass from one state of motion to another

It has been the motor car's attraction that the process of translation from pedestrian to motorized move-

ment has been possible informally because the motor vehicle has been free to use any route and to stop and start, to be left and rejoined anywhere within the street network of the city. This state of affairs is rapidly being overtaken in towns and cities by the increasing number of vehicles on the roads. The overcrowding of the road system at certain times has necessitated restrictive measures being taken to control the areas or the direction in which cars may move and the places where they may stop. Within the city the scope of the motor vehicle is rapidly being reduced to movement characteristics similar to those of all other forms of unit transport – a highly canalized route and a rigorously controlled terminal and interchange point

Plan of Venice, and on the next page, a small section of Los Angeles to the same scale

At the birth of a new town or city the issues are clear and a solution can be postulated in terms of a new concept of in-town movement. A system capable of growth can be generated by a plan. The initiative is held by the designer. Resources can be programmed and used to full effect. In a city ages old, the dilemma remains and its resolution is a matter more subtle and often elusive. For a city is an organism capable of responding to any significant mark made upon it. A building or a stretch of motorway correctly sited in space and time can start a chain reaction of further developments which will eventually affect the whole city. Equally, the organism can be blighted by lack of watchfulness, for initiative is dispersed throughout the city, resources are scattered, and at the present time no machinery exists for effective programming of their use

Sheffield is such a city, typical, in its dilemma, of the provincial cities of this country. One-third motorized. Enigmatic. For so long the filthy home of Britain's steel industry, notorious for its polluted air and its decayed housing, it has shown in the past few years an astonishing vigour in rebuilding its major industrial plant, cleaning its air, clearing its slums, so that today it is one of the few cities capable of exciting the eye and making the heart leap

Rarely in a city of half a million inhabitants is it possible to perceive the basic structure of the place. Suddenly, this is becoming so in Sheffield. The building developments are clarifying the land form of the whole locality and fresh vistas are opening up as the topography is revealed from new vantage points in the buildings themselves

Sheffield has grown up on one of the loveliest sites in the whole of England, a fact appreciated by few of those who know it only through its industrial products. It lies in the foothills of the Pennine range where the river Don is joined 145 ft above sea level by the Sheaf from which the town derives its name. Both these rivers with their tributaries drain the moorlands which rise to 1,350 ft within the City boundary to the west and which end dramatically on a rock face of millstone grit overlooking the Hope Valley. The 'edge' is popular with climbers, and the softer landscape of the limestone country – the Derbyshire Peak District – is a haunt of hikers from miles around

The coal measures underlying the region from the westerly escarpment some 3,000 square miles to the east, are the richest in Britain with reserves estimated at 3,000 million tons of high grade coal. It was probably this availability of fuel for steam power combined with the steady home demand from the cutlery trade which led to Sheffield becoming a town of steel. Iron production in the area dates back to pre-Roman times. The manufacture of edge tools was established very early in the Sheffield region where the fast streams provided the source of power and the local gritstone the wheels for grinding.

54

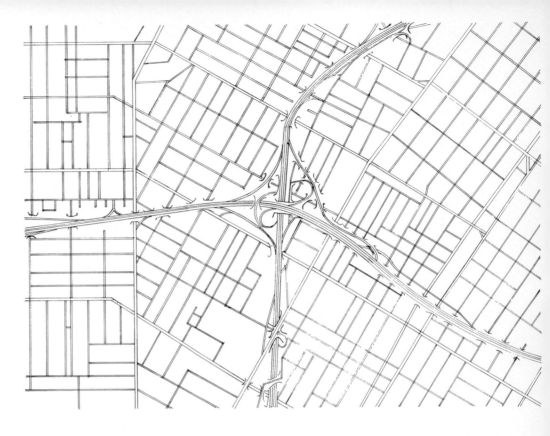

Whirlow Brook Park, Sheffield. One of the many parks within the city boundary

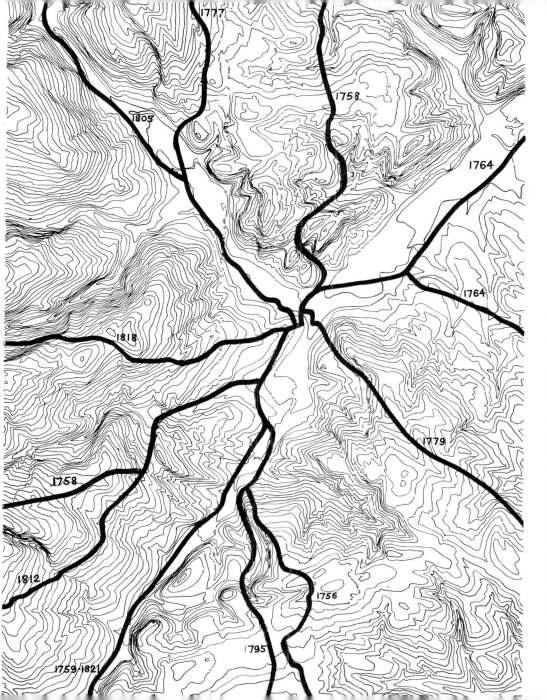

Whilst grinding developed into a specialized business, the production of cutlery was carried on in home workshops all over the expanding town. Because the town was so isolated from main communication networks trading was established by 'chapmen' who visited Sheffield regularly. The first manufacturer to travel to London himself on business did so only in 1723, even though a stage wagon to London had been operated from 1710, and the first direct trade link with the Continent was made in 1740. The hilly country made what roads there were difficult to travel until a series of twenty-two Turnpike Acts between 1739 and 1818 improved Sheffield's links with the rest of the country. The development in Sheffield of crucible steel hard enough for the new machines of the industrial revolution and the boosting of steel production for Army ordnance at the end of the eighteenth century made the town the centre of a new industry which was to be relied on more and more as Britain's economy changed from an agricultural to an industrial one. By the time Bessemer opened his factory in 1858, the Railway Age was in and the demand for steel increased still more, so that the second half of the century saw the establishment, from parent companies in Sheffield, of most of the major shipbuilding and armament combines. The transport of heavy goods had always been difficult, the easiest way being by road to Bawtry and thence by river to Hull and by sea to London. But the lower Don Valley was prone to flooding and it was to relieve this condition that the river was diverted in 1626 into the Ouse and so made navigable. Although plans were laid in 1696 to extend the system of water transport within easy reach of Sheffield, the steelworks were developing along the river banks, making river improvement difficult, and it wasn't until 1819 that the canal was cut through to the town centre. It was not long before the railways were competing for freight traffic

The North Midland line, passing on easier terrain five miles to the east of Sheffield, had a branch brought through to the Wicker Station in 1838 against the opposition of the canal company and the Duke of Norfolk who had enjoyed a local monopoly in coal hitherto. A railway connection with Manchester was made with great difficulty through three miles of tunnel at Woodhead and a station terminus built on arches at Bridgehouses, the high level system being extended later to Victoria Station and beyond. Sheffield was still off the main

Turnpike roads out of Sheffield

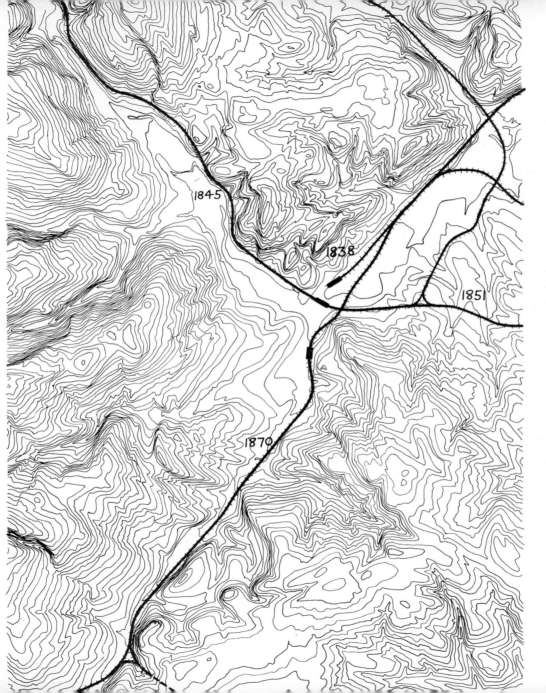

1845

1838

1851

1870

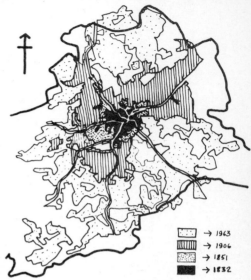

→ 1963
→ 1906
→ 1851
→ 1832

line system until 1870 when the tunnel was cut through to Chesterfield, the Midland line extended up the Sheaf Valley and a new station built there

All these developments in industry and communications were accompanied by a rapid expansion of the town's population. From a township of 2,000 when Mary Queen of Scots was imprisoned in the castle, Sheffield grew by 1801 to have a population of 35,000; by 1851, 120,000; by 1901, 381,000; and today about 500,000. The rate of growth was highest between 1821 and 1831 when there was a cutlery boom following the lifting of the wartime blockade of trade with North America. The severe overcrowding made worse the ravages of a cholera outbreak in 1832

Progressively after that time, housing in the central area was replaced by larger scale commercial buildings. The new steel industry tended to attract workers in large numbers from the surrounding countryside and these were accommodated in a belt of artisan housing around the old town. Most of this housing is on the north-facing slopes of the hills, the southerly aspect being usually developed previously by the factory owners for their own spacious homes. The pattern of development outside the central area is thus an alternating one, corresponding

Left: Railway development

Above: Growth of the built-up area

closely with the undulating ground, of beautiful well-wooded suburbs and tightly packed rows of brick terrace houses, blackened by the smoke from hundreds of furnaces and steam engines scattered among them

This, too, has been the pattern of the redevelopment problem as the older properties wear out. Most of the major housing reconstructions are on north-facing slopes. The three most central lie on the three hills surrounding the valley intersection

One of them, Park Hill, can be taken as typical of the way in which successive developments have taken place. The hillside is in two steps, the lower of which has a shoulder on the south-west. The rest of the hill slopes generally at 1 in 10 to the north, with narrow sections falling away more steeply to the west. The earliest development was at the north end nearest to the town. The Mansfield Road turnpike drove out up the hill to the south through Sheffield Park. The rapid growth of population in the early nineteenth century spread a new kind of housing development up the hill in the form of back-to-back houses, the outer one facing on to a street and the one at the rear into a courtyard surrounded by others like it. Each house consisted of one down-stairs room 12 ft square with one or more of similar size above. Privies serving the whole block, together with the inadequate water supply, were located in the courtyard and access to it was by narrow tunnel entrance between the houses. Frequently a small workshop formed part of the courtyard structure and often provided employment for the families attracted there from the surrounding countryside. These were moving in large numbers from the land which was being 'improved' by the Enclosure Acts. Often workshop and courtyard would be built as one industrial/residential expansionist enterprise

This form of development enforced a community life from which there could be little escape. The over-crowding which ensued eventually resulted in a cholera outbreak becoming a serious epidemic killing off some 400 people including the Lord Mayor. Yet, even with this stimulus to action, it was another thirty years before the age of reform could bring about legislation designed to guard against the worst evils of this sort of housing

The great Victorian 'housing drive' of a hundred years ago was carried on in a spirit of fervour and civic pride that has scarcely been equalled since. If the

Distribution of high and low density

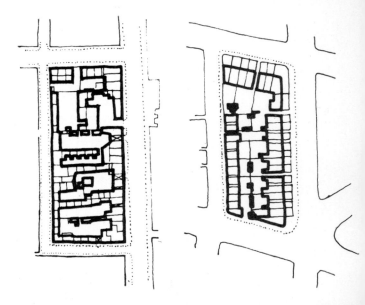

Above: Back to back courtyard housing, Sheffield

Right: Managerial housing; Back to back housing; Bye-law housing; all at Park Hill and all drawn to the same scale

architectural result appears bleak and depressing to twentieth-century eyes it should be remembered that the forms of housing which this century has bequeathed to later generations are for the most part scarcely less dismal in appearance

If we compare the degree of social advance made in the housing of the last fifty years with that of the preceding fifty, there can be little doubt that the Victorians made much greater progress than we have done, for the improvements they made were basic ones concerning arrangements of space and access. The simplified street form represented a return to the great urban residential developments of the eighteenth century and away from its debased and exploited form of back-to-back

It was an expression, if you like, of the new urban democracy. Yet it was something more than symbolic for it conferred upon the artisan the very solid social advantages of the street pattern and gave his family a new dignity. This was real and derived first of all from the separateness of his house within the row; it was no longer necessary to pass through someone else's place nor any shared space other than the public street to reach his own front door. Then, there was always more than one way home as a rule; it was possible for him to approach

his house from a variety of directions, meeting or avoiding neighbours as he chose. Further, the side by side arrangement did not thrust him or his wife into any special relationships with any other household so that acquaintances were not forced upon them. Lastly, the open street pattern had an element of continuity which allowed all the other ingredients of a happy neighbourhood, the 'local' pub, the corner shops, workshops and agencies to develop naturally, being accommodated in the same cellular structure as the houses themselves. In a word the street form had the supremely appropriate virtue of neutrality, allowing maximum freedom of movement and association

Today when we are prone to consider that housing standards are raised by improvements in equipment or by the provision, simply, of more houses, it is easy to 'turn a blind eye' on some of the socially retrogressive steps taken in the last few years. One of them is the adoption in England of forms of collective houses imported from other European countries. 'Tower' or 'Point' blocks of flats or apartments interpose between the individual front doors and the open air an indoor no-man's-land through which inhabitants must pass. It is an ambiguous space, being neither public nor private and, as such, it can

make a positive contribution neither to the life of the individual family nor to the social life of the community. Worse than that, it has an inhibiting effect on both. This form of housing has none of the social advantages of the house in the street, yet many are built

Another form of housing development which is commonly used as a means of increasing housing density and reducing costs with too little consideration for the social consequences is the superimposed flat or maisonette, apartment or duplex, form with either staircase or narrow gallery approach. As in the point block, the element of access is inherently anti-social in the context of general housing. At best these forms are economical solutions of a storage problem

The bye-law street development, despite its sanitary shortcomings, fostered a community life essentially healthy in that it was free from those unreasonable pressures which can be brought about by the physical structure of an environment

However, not all the back-to-back and courtyard dwellings were cleared away and many existed on Park Hill until 1955. Indeed in other parts of the city

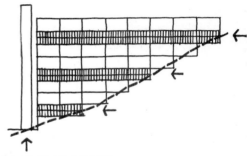

Schematic arrangement

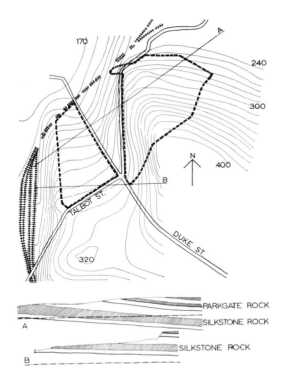

Site plan. Site sections

they exist still. During the 1920's and 30's they were the breeding grounds of terrorism and vicious gang warfare which was broken up only by a vigorous combination of Police action and slum clearance programmes. The worst areas, which lay on the steepest part of the site with courtyards built against the side of the hill, were cleared first and redeveloped between 1936 and the outbreak of the war. This is why, today, Park Hill is separated from Hyde Park by a triangle of brick-built walk-up flats. This kind of development stopped during the war and the sites which had been cleared and not built upon were used for American types of prefabricated house. It was as if a social wound had been cauterized

In 1953 there was a hint that the Government would resume the slum clearance programmes interrupted by the war and the Park Hill area was the worst of those needing redevelopment in Sheffield. It was possible to see then the pattern of the community structure and how this related to the environment—ragged and incomplete as this was. The essential

gregariousness of the people and the way this depended on the open air spaces around the front doors was made even more clear during the Coronation celebrations of that year when the unit of collective participation was everywhere in the street. Decorations, bunting, food, drink, and entertainment were organized spontaneously on a street by street basis. Flags, crowns and loyal slogans were painted on walls and only removed when those walls were brought down

It was obvious that despite the evils arising out of a lack of proper water supply, sanitation and ventilation, here was a structure of friendliness and mutual aid which had somehow to be salvaged from the demolition. At this stage the brief was simply 'to investigate and make recommendations'

A rapid survey revealed that there were natural limits to the area formed by the Midland Railway Station in the valley bottom to the west and the lines approaching it from the north in a cutting. To the south, the classified route along Talbot Street was the clearest line dividing the unfit from the not so unfit houses. On the east side the ground rose steeply to the hilltop where the development stopped at the edge of a quarry and a greyhound stadium. The prevailing wind was noted to be from the south-west while the heavy concentration of industry lay to the north and north-east. The site lay on coal measures with the Silkstone seam worked out well below the ground and the Silkstone rock, a fairly massive sandstone, outcropping over the area of the lower part of the site (now Park Hill) and forming a shelf sloping to the north at about 1 in 10. The upper site (now Hyde Park) was much more varied in its structure and its slope, the crown of the spur being formed by the outcropping Parkgate rock and the steep land to the west consisting of layers of rock, coal, shale and fireclay in thin seams all with a dip to the north-east

On this ground were nearly 800 houses, including sixty-three prefabs and a small number of properties which were not then classified as unfit. One hundred and eighty of the houses were on the land sloping steeply down from South Street to the Midland Station which had been scheduled in the City Development Plan as proposed open space. Being so close to the Wholesale and Retail Markets in Sheaf Valley and to the canal, the railway, the steel and engineering works, there were strong links with the city

What was called at the time a 'visual analysis of the site' made note of the strongly contrasted character of the two parts of the site; the upper one craggy, precipitous in places, with slopes and views out in all directions; the lower site enclosed by the hillside on the east but opening to a valley to the west. The problem arose of their developed relationship, for the two parts together were prominent from the city centre and the hill to the north. Certain vantage points on the site were noted, some of them at that time, of course, having no outlook at all because of the standing property, places which could nevertheless be imagined to command exciting views over the city. The whole complex site had a vast potential in the topography for the creation of an entirely different kind of place

PARK HILL

Previous studies in house design and grouping for other sites, reinforced by observations of the community life engendered by the old environment had led to a programmatic approach to this particular problem. It seemed to the designers that certain basic concepts were valid and particularly potent in this situation. These were:

(a) That the primary grouping of houses should be a linear one

(b) That the exciting prospects outward from the site should be exploited to the full by the superimposition of one street above another in the form of decks

(c) The slope of the site could be utilized to give walk-on access to most of these decks somewhere on the site, thereby allowing the provision of elevators to be as economical as could be wished and the lift disposition to be determined by ground level development

(d) That the street system at all levels should be as continuous as possible

(e) That along any street or deck level there should be maximum variety in the size and type of house or flat

(f) That this should somehow be achieved within a repetitive framework of structure and services

The first complete layout for the site, produced in July 1953, planned for 2,000 new dwellings to be built, giving a surplus of 1,200 over what existed on the site and providing a useful reservoir of dwellings in hand for further redevelopment areas. It had the lower area developed with a continuous building making right-angled changes of direction to follow the existing road pattern as it was still considered then that, for reasons of economy, the existing roads and services should be used. (It was subsequently discovered that all the services were so old, in such a poor state of repair and in many cases so inadequate for the increased demands which would be placed upon them that it became possible to think in terms of a completely new ground and services layout)

The road pattern on the upper site had always been much less regular, corresponding with the irregularity of the slopes of the ground and it gave rise to Y-shaped connections of blocks much shorter in length and made less continuous as a safeguard against uneven settlement due to the widely different kinds of sub-strata existing under the area. During these early stages a variety of cross-wall dwelling types were being explored, including central corridor arrangements. These had small flats for old people at the deck level and family flats above and below reaching the full width of the block. Some of these were incorporated into the first layout for the upper site in short lengths between changes of direction so that daylight could be seen at each end. Under these conditions it was felt that the central corridor was acceptable and might in fact offer an interesting change in the kind of space experienced in a walk along a deck

This initial scheme was carefully programmed for the simultaneous development of both parts so that the least number of people would need to be moved out of the area to enable a start to be made and the great majority of the local residents could be rehoused without leaving the district at all. This, it was felt, would be an important factor in preserving the community life which existed in the area. In the four months which elapsed between the preparation of the scheme and its presentation to the council, the investigation into services and possible contract arrangements had led to the conclusion that each

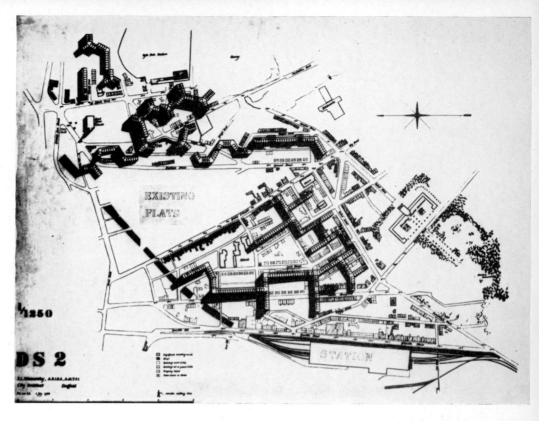

First layout plan of Park Hill and Hyde Park, 1953

site should be developed as a separate building contract, entailing the clearance of most of the property before rebuilding commenced. There were some misgivings among us that the community structure would be irrevocably upset, as indeed it was, but the rapidity with which a new one was formed somewhat alleviated these fears and revealed certain things about the nature of a community in the process

It was now possible to recast the programme in the light of the particular problems of the site and the times. The latest housing requirements gave percentages of different house sizes including, for the first time, large numbers of one and two person units—many of the people being displaced under the slum clearance schemes were old couples and pensioners living alone. Certain items of a technical nature which had strong design implications were settled at this stage, such as the adoption of some form of central heating and a water-borne system of refuse disposal. The aim was now to be:

(a) To design a repetitive structure with a standardized service unit or units which would allow different sizes of apartments to be provided according to the Housing Manager's requirements, by means of varying the position of non-structural party walls. The structure and service arrangement to be capable of adaptation to the requirements of shops, pubs, laundries and other ancillary uses

(b) To achieve full continuity of access, avoiding pedestrian cul-de-sacs by placing vertical circulation at the ends of the block

(c) To use all the frontage, including corners, for

60

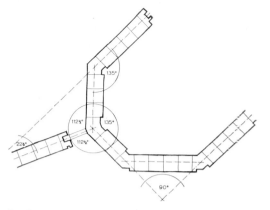

Setting out

dwellings by the development of a structure which, with as little modification as possible, could negotiate corners, with junctions of five types:

1 Access deck moving around internal angle

2 Access deck moving around external angle

3 Access deck crossing from internal to external face

4 A three-way junction combining 1, 2 and 3

5 A three-way junction spaced out to incorporate a bridge connection

The next twelve months were devoted to finding a solution of these problems. We were fortunate in having the advice of Ronald Jenkins of Ove Arup & Partners from the beginning of the investigations. Of immense value was his patience in giving detailed reasons why the various stages we reached were inadequate structurally and in always insisting that the plan must come first. Economy would follow when 'plan and structure fit like a hand in a glove'. These were exciting days when we felt we were on the threshold of what would now be called a 'break-

through'. The cross wall plans had given insufficient variety in the size of flat and had proved intractable at the corners, creating conditions of serious over-looking between apartments on the internal angle and leading to excessive unlit floor space. Moving around right-angled corners in two stages opened up the frontage on both sides of the block and allowed the block to change direction at 135°. The Y-unit and the bridge connection were made from the 135° bend with the outside angle bisected by the third arm. This set up, in an extended layout, a rogue angle and a second setting out grid at 22½° to the first giving greater vitality to the block relationships than were developed out of a 60° angle. It was in this way, out of the study of the house form as a microcosm of the total environment, that the environment itself arose After many months chasing hares – some of which might still be worth catching – the necessary economy was found in a three-bay plan unit with a double-sided duct serving internal bathrooms. The centre bay provided the interlocking and back-to-back staircases within an H-shaped wall layout and the flexible bays of floor space which could be allocated

61

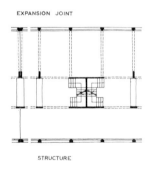

STRUCTURE

BELOW

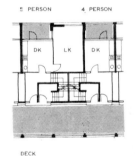

DECK

ABOVE

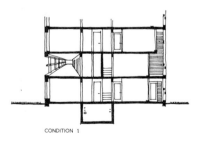

CONDITION 1

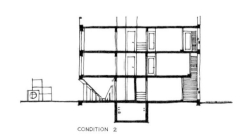

CONDITION 2

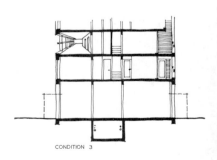

CONDITION 3

2 PERSON   2 PERSON

4 PERSON   5 PERSON

4 PERSON   5 PERSON

STRUCTURE

BELOW

DECK

ABOVE

62

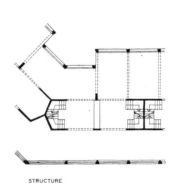

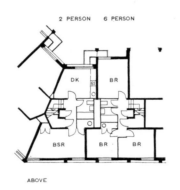

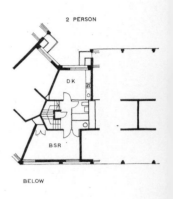

2 PERSON   6 PERSON

6 PERSON

2 PERSON

STRUCTURE

ABOVE

DECK

BELOW

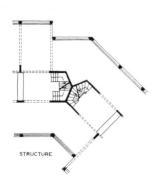

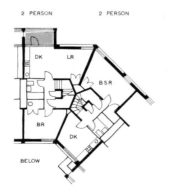

2 PERSON   2 PERSON

6 PERSON

6 PERSON   2 PERSON

STRUCTURE

BELOW

DECK

ABOVE

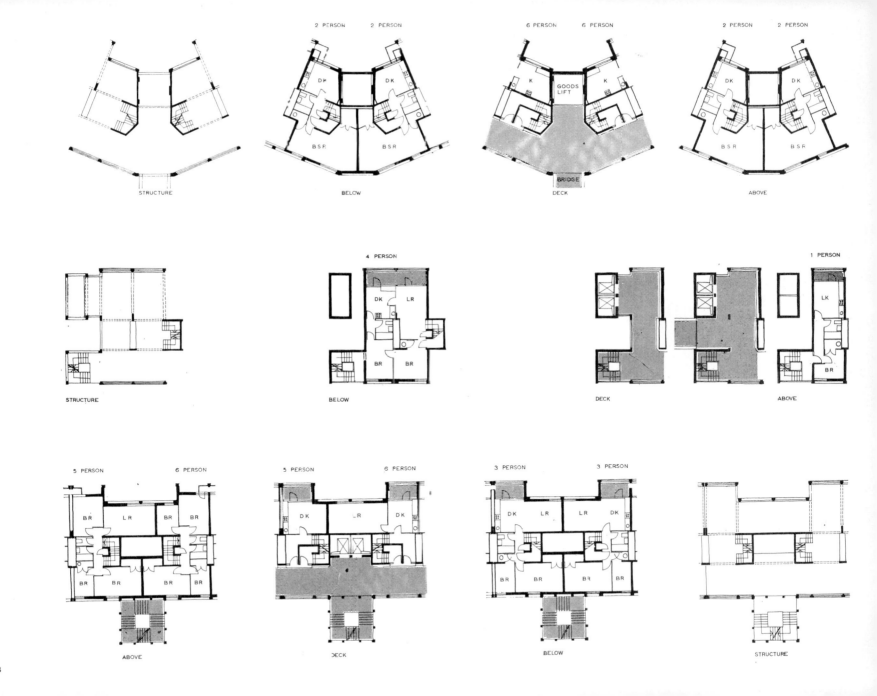

63

5*—AYB

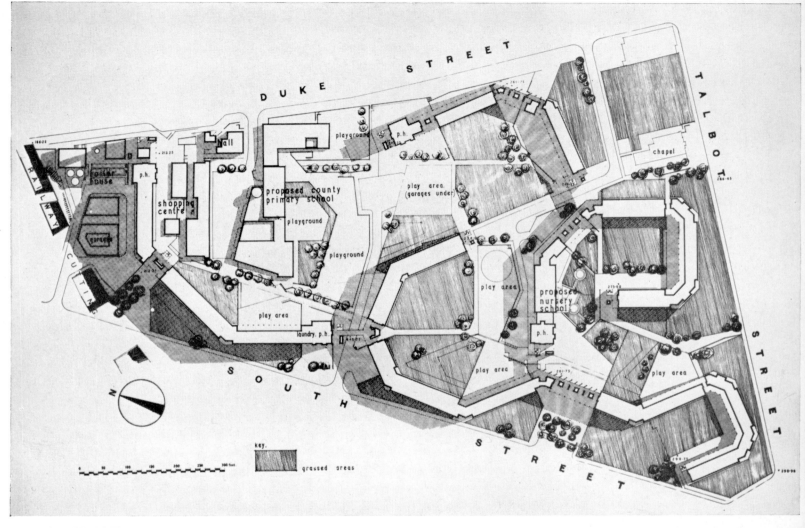

Layout plan of Park Hill

to either side in a variety of ways. This could provide all sizes of dwelling from one-person to five-person in roughly the right proportions. It also worked well on the corners as the service duct could remain standard, the angle being negotiated by altering only the outer wall of the staircase enclosure. Further variations of house types were possible in the corner

units, including some for six persons. Structurally the scheme was satisfactory; all the wind loads were taken on the very rigid H-walls enclosing the stair-cases. Beams transferred much of the floor loads also to these wall members and all the floor spans were of the same order, about 10ft. This gave the minimum room sizes of the current Housing Manual, which was the conditional basis of the Ministry's financial aid

At all stages in the development of this family of house plans, they had been tested for layout potential, so that layout principles evolved at the same time. The simple idea of having a constant roof line and a direct walk in to all deck levels posed the problem of space between parts of the building, because it increased in height as the ground fell away to the north. A 30° light angle was made a constant between any two parts and on this an irregular grid was

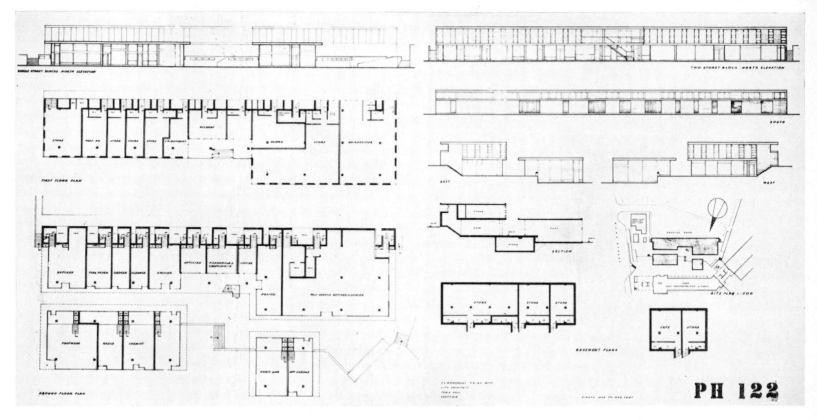

PH 122

Park Hill shopping centre

developed over the whole site map which showed how big a space would need to be to give every room at ground level anywhere on the site 60° of sky. This became the regulator for many sketch layouts which were assessed in terms of the number of plan units provided, the number of 'specials' in the form of ends, corners and bridges, as well as their space characteristics. The three-floor unit of section used in conjunction with sloping ground gave three different conditions of ground connection, each with its own implications for ground finish and location of extra mural activity

Condition I Below deck level, for a flat on the ground with private balcony and living room on one side and bedrooms on the other, it was essential to have grass on each side for outlook and privacy, pedestrians at

ground level being kept away from the facades at this condition

Condition 2 Deck level, on the ground. Pedestrian entry via the colonnade on the deck side; also a point of release where deck ran to ground, an obvious spot for small children's play. On the opposite side the living rooms of the maisonette where it was essential to have grass for privacy and outlook

Condition 3 As it was desired to have all dwellings opening off the decks, this condition became an open colonnade available, in places where openness would not be required for ancillary uses such as shops, public houses, laundries, nursery school, lavatories, etc

The imposition of a cellular structure of this scale on an irregular site created a wealth of incident at ground level. It can be imagined how every sketch

layout set up its own pattern of ground development and even the alteration of the single datum level up or down moved the groundwork events about correspondingly. Practice led to the acquisition of a high degree of control over site potentialities

The layout of Park Hill and Hyde Park was determined primarily by the assumption that people would move about the area on foot and the whole environment is conditioned by this. Vehicles are allowed to penetrate the site but not allowed to pass through, so that the character of pedestrian movement is continuous and that of the vehicles interrupted or terminal

In this way the dominance of the pedestrian is asserted and immediately the environment is freed from the conflict in pace of the two kinds of movement. The layout of pathways, ways under and through the building forms are designed to exploit

66

the pedestrian's capacity for abrupt changes of direction and level with all the excitement of rapid contrast in space and light experience which this can bring. Gradual changes of level are used too, so that there is always a choice, in moving about the site, between steps and a ramp, the fast and the slow way, to suit varying mood or differing ages. There is also a choice between moving around under cover within the horizontal street deck system and moving in the open air between the building forms, so that changes in weather cause changes in the routing of journeys through the site

At Park Hill there is some 78 ft difference in level between the shopping pavement and the ground at the most remote corner of the site and it is the negotiation of this change of level which gives the area its major interest. The shops are located at the bottom of the hill on the south side of the tallest part of the building. Some of the shops are underneath twelve floors of the housing block, the shopfronts set back behind the columns to give weather protection to the shoppers. One- and two-storey blocks are built close up to these frontages to make a compact centre of thirty-two shop units arranged so that everywhere there is shop frontage on both sides of the pedestrian pavement. The site slope makes for two distinct levels of shopping pavement 4 ft apart and connected by ramps and steps. Trees are planted where the pavement is wide enough. Pairs of elevators up to the four deck levels serving the houses are sited at both ends and the whole shopping area is sheltered from wind by the tall building. Main street traffic can be seen passing at one end but all vehicles are kept to a service reserve at the rear

Away from the shops a wide spine footway ramps up the hill and into the court system. It is a straight, direct route connecting major areas of activity together. Because changes of level at the building face are accomplished abruptly in storey heights with retaining walls cutting away at right angles, the ascending path attains a sequence of terraces of varying kinds of surface finish, most often of grass in

Top left: Spine footpath

Top right: A street in the air
Photo: Roger Mayne

Left: Play area

Preceding page: Park Hill was completed in 1961. Note the streets-in-the-air, and the shops in the ground floor of the structure
Photos: Roger Mayne

Above: Stepping of ground
Right: View of city from deck of Park Hill
Right below: View of city from Hyde Park

large areas, alternating with paved play areas for children where a deck runs out to ground level, or forecourts to a laundry, public house or lift entry point. At the same time the path system moves alongside a wall retaining these terraces which rises and falls constantly, broken occasionally by entry points or a flight of steps giving rapid access to an upper terrace level. And always beyond this close range wall and path relationship, the building itself moves towards or away from the route

Major ground level space incidents occur when the route penetrates the building form into another court entirely, emerging in two stages; through the building first of all, but in a cutting, so that by the time it attains the court level there is a junction with other routes occurring at a point of tension within the space. All the walls, radiating from the building, appear to hold the path inevitably in this position and indeed they do locate it in this way, canalizing all movement to the pathway system and protecting the lawns from casual use. In this way, in a development with a housing density of 200 people to the acre including a high percentage of children, the grass is preserved without any resort to tiresome notices

While the children use the whole site area as their playground, the ramps being particularly attractive for roller skating and go-karting, and the multitude of spaces lending themselves to all the fantasy of a child's imagination, certain places are laid out specially for particular age groups. Climbing frames

and sandpits are located where decks meet the ground and these tend to hold the smaller children from straying too far from their own street level. They are lively places where the ground footpath system is joined by the street deck and it is here that people are likely to meet and stop to chat. The play equipment has been given the same scale as the building forms to preserve its congruity when not in use

A walk along the horizontal deck system is a completely different experience. Here the route moves within the building along the edge of spaces varying in two ways simultaneously. The courts themselves are of differing shapes and sizes, differently lit because of the angles of the blocks to one another and with changing ground patterns but, surprisingly, the ground itself moves further and further away and gives the impression of one having become very securely airborne. This feeling is strengthened when, rounding a corner, the deck leads through the width of the building and suddenly there below is the rest of the city across the valley and beyond, a broad sweep of open view with a horizon of farm and moorland. Walking in the city has acquired some of the quality previously found only on the fells or on cliff tops by the sea

Left: Hyde Park, the small block connected to the others by a bridge across the road at the upper level

Above: Hyde Park, under construction

Next page: Views of the model of Hyde Park; and a view of the first completed section – the long low apartment terraces seen on the left of the upper photograph – with vehicle turning point

HYDE PARK

At Hyde Park the ground level of the central square is 14 ft higher than the roof of Park Hill and the view from it substantially broader. The highest rooftop flat is 250 ft above the lowest point of the site 450 ft away. This distance can be traversed completely under cover using the street deck system and the elevators. Because the site falls away in all directions, the elevators are utilized in journeys across the site so that their significance in the movement pattern is of a different kind from those in Park Hill. Indeed the largest pair of elevators is installed in a tiny block containing only twenty-eight dwellings but it is through this block that most journeys to and from the city will be made by people living in all other parts of Hyde Park – even those who live in the larger maisonettes entered off a ground level street serving the long terraces. For this reason the elevators have been given large windows and a slot has been left in the elevator shaft so that the vertical movement can become a positive visual experience. The towers containing elevators are expressed as sheer shafts of black brick. At night the moving lift will be seen from great distances across the city

On its completion and occupation, Hyde Park will become a twin neighbourhood to Park Hill, made of the same parts, derived from the same social premises, but utterly different in the character of its environment. At the same time the two are complementary and together they will have a profound effect on the areas of the city immediately adjacent

Before considering the seminal effect of the Park Hill redevelopment on that part of the city centre, it is necessary to see the way in which the city reconstruction has been proceeding

SHEFFIELD CENTRE

The commercial centre of Sheffield developed in a linear form about a mile in length away from the River Don in a south-westerly direction. Both the Wholesale and the Retail Markets had been long established near the confluence of the two rivers and a shopping centre grew up on the west side of them expanding further up the hill encompassing Waingate, Haymarket, Angel Street, High Street and Fargate. On the flatter land away from the steep valley slopes, the character of the shopping gradually changed and the larger establishments of local catering firms and department stores flourished. Beyond the Town Hall, over the ridge and down the gentle south slope, the long straight street called The Moor was popular both as a city shopping street and a local centre serving a concentration of small terrace houses along the west side and at the southerly tip

In December 1940 two bombing raids brought about serious destruction and damage to Sheffield's commercial area, most severely at the north and south ends. Unlike some other cities, however, the destruction was nowhere complete and many properties were able to be patched up and carried on trading. This created difficulties in redevelopment

69

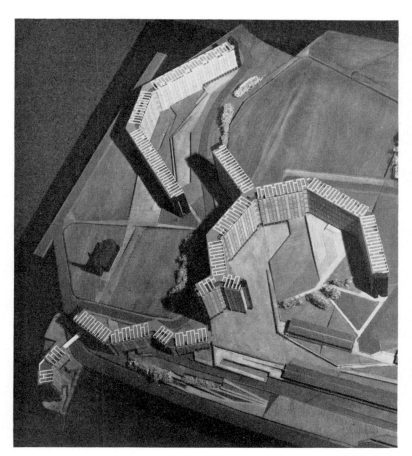

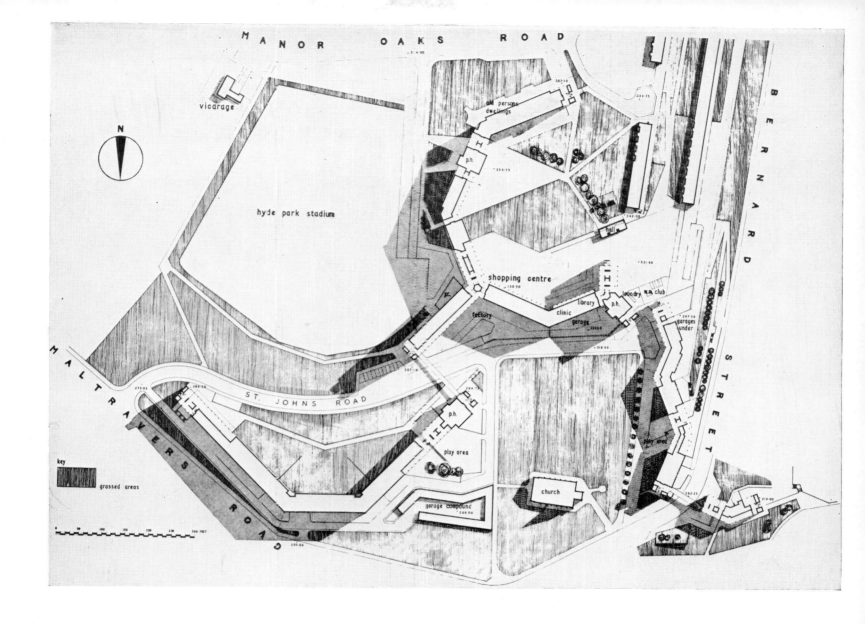

Layout plan of Hyde Park

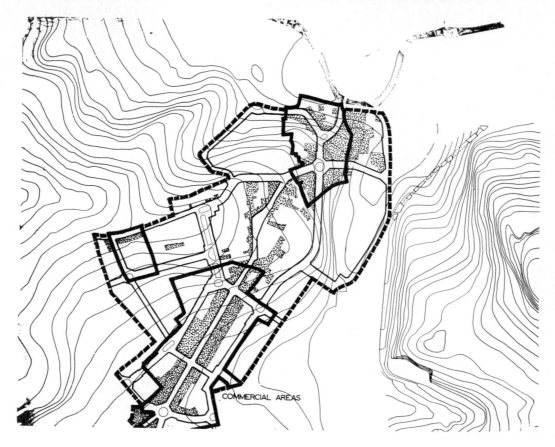

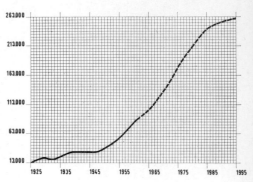

COMMERCIAL AREAS

as the damage was on a sufficient scale in some places to warrant extensive reconstruction, yet, close by, the existence of substantial undamaged properties made it financially impracticable to take full advantage of the opportunities apparently presented by the bombing

The City Council made an order for treating 198 acres of the central city as a war-damaged area and subject to compulsory purchase. This order was eventually confirmed but with the acreage reduced to 92½. With a strong desire to conserve capital funds the Compulsory Purchase Orders were not proceeded with immediately and as much as possible of the property required for redevelopment was acquired by the Corporation through agreement with the owners. In this way war damage compensa-

tion payments were preserved to help finance the rebuilding

The City Engineer is the Town Planning Officer and the reconstruction conformed with road plans prepared before and during the war, modified in places in the light of the extent of the bomb damage, and published in 1945 in a book called 'Sheffield Replanned'

These provided for an inner ring road area roughly a mile in diameter with another ring road within that, to be called the Civic Circle, encompassing some fifty acres of land in the very heart of the city. A series of radial roads joined the inner circle and some penetrated through to the Civic Circle. The Moor was one of these, being conceived in the immediate post-war plans as a dual purpose street, for shopping and

Left: Post-war comprehensive redevelopment areas in relation to road proposals and the commercial zone. The firm line shows those areas confirmed by the Minister. Contours at ten feet intervals

Above: Graph of vehicle licences issued in Sheffield since 1925. Future projection shown dotted

Alker Tripp's road classification for urban areas

traffic. At the same time traffic relief roads were planned on each side of The Moor running parallel with it. The Moor itself was to be widened and new frontages were set back accordingly. With the intention of achieving a measure of architectural uniformity, a height of three storeys on the main

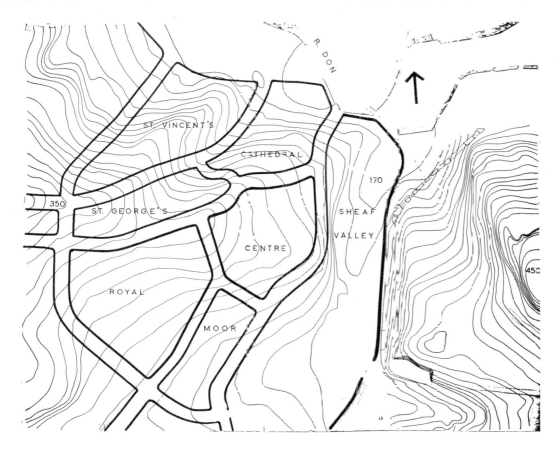

Precinct structure in Sheffield as it would be defined by the City Engineer's current road proposals

street frontage was insisted upon and the facing material was required to be Portland Stone

Within the Civic Circle, a precinct was envisaged in which were sited the major civic buildings placed around a civic square which was to be opened up between the City Hall and the Town Hall. The principal shopping streets within this precinct were to be developed as the 'first class' shopping area

To the north the Haymarket/Waingate area was seen as the site for 'second class' shopping and it was intended to remove the Wholesale Market from the valley bottom to free traffic movement in that

vicinity. The Angel Street/High Street junction was planned as a traffic roundabout with elaborate provision made at basement level in the surrounding properties for pedestrian subways under the traffic roads at this intersection

Much of the property destroyed in the war has been replaced in the commercial centre and the reconstruction is now entering a new phase. Two major factors have emerged in the intervening years which have altered the tenor and orientation of city planning

One is the phenomenal growth of the market in land and property accompanied by a continual state of inflation in the national economy. The other is the rapid increase in vehicular traffic in towns. The 1945 twenty-year road plan had anticipated twice the pre-war level of car registrations, which stood

at 30,000 vehicles in 1939. The figure reached 60,000 by 1956, stood at 90,000 in 1963, and could become 270,000 before saturation point is reached. Whilst the pre-war figure has trebled with very little of the proposed road network carried out to cope with the increased traffic, it is obvious that the city environment could never absorb anything like full motorization if everyone tried to use their cars for everyday journeys to work and for city shopping trips. Already during the 'rush' hours traffic flow is impeded by the inadequacy of the road system, a system which so far manages well enough at other times of the day. City parking is still on derelict or war-damaged lots and in the streets, where it further holds up traffic flow and endangers pedestrian and motorist alike

H. Alker Tripp, writing in 1942, put forward principles for resolving these problems of road traffic in existing towns but his writings seem to have been largely ignored. He advocated a classification of the existing road network into a strict hierarchy of roads which he called (1) arterial—dedicated to fast moving vehicular traffic only, no parking, no pedestrians, connecting only with (2) sub-arterial roads whose function was to distribute traffic from the arterial system into (3) local roads which would connect only with each other and with the sub-arterial roads with T-junctions. Frontage development would not, he proposed, be allowed on the arterial roads, the entire building development within the road system being designed in precincts served by the local road system only. In this way, he claimed, traffic would be speeded up and civilized life made possible again within the precinct structure

One of the main forces resisting such a clear, economical and sensible reorganization was, of course, the pressure of real estate interests which claimed that business would suffer if shopping were separated from the traffic street. Now, under the greater pressure of acute traffic congestion with its concomitant evils of increasing atmospheric pollution, noise and sudden death, Tripp's ideas are finding new champions. Notable among them is Professor Colin Buchanan whose paper 'Towns and Traffic', read at the Coventry Conference of the RIBA 1962, consolidated them into a general theory, and whose book 'Traffic in Towns' appeared at the end of 1963 and is beginning to exert considerable influence. By clarifying the connection that exists between vehicles and buildings he accounted for environmental factors as measurable items and related them to problems of accessibility, the control of the generative capacity of the built-up area within the major

THE MOOR

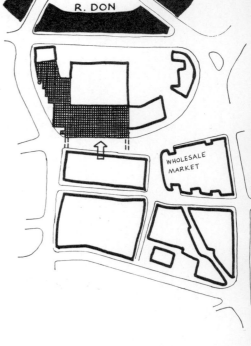

The Moor. Frontage redevelopment of an existing traffic street which could be made a pedestrian precinct. All new buildings are provided with rear loading arrangements

Top: Plan showing old and proposed road patterns with the possibility of making the Moor itself a pedestrian shopping precinct

Programme of Markets area reconstruction

road network and the discharge capacity of the network itself

The City Engineer's road plan for the central area divides up the city into a number of precincts, three of which together make up the present commercial zone. They are Moor, Sheaf Valley and Centre and, because their problems are different, they can be used to illustrate various ways in which precinct development can take place producing different kinds of environment

The Moor has been reconstructed as a dual purpose shopping and traffic street. Being simply a straight mall, there need be no complication about revising this idea when the alternative vehicular relief roads are ready. All the new premises have been arranged with rear loading so that when alternative routes are available, traffic can be diverted from The Moor itself and the full width of the street used exclusively

by pedestrians. As a pedestrian street, The Moor would be excessively long. This could be overcome by the provision of a two-way travellator moving along most of the length. The street could be given added interest by planting trees and the development of kiosks and places to sit within the central space. Traffic segregation in this environment would be by place separation

In the Sheaf Valley, on the other hand, the possibilities are for separation by grade or level. Here the Corporation has embarked upon a complete reconstruction of the Markets area. Owning most of the land in the vicinity, it has been possible to programme in stages:

1 The building of a new Retail Market for dry goods on a war-damaged site adjacent to the Meat and Fish Markets, all under one roof

2 The demolition of the old Market Hall and leasing of the site to a developer for the erection of a multiple store

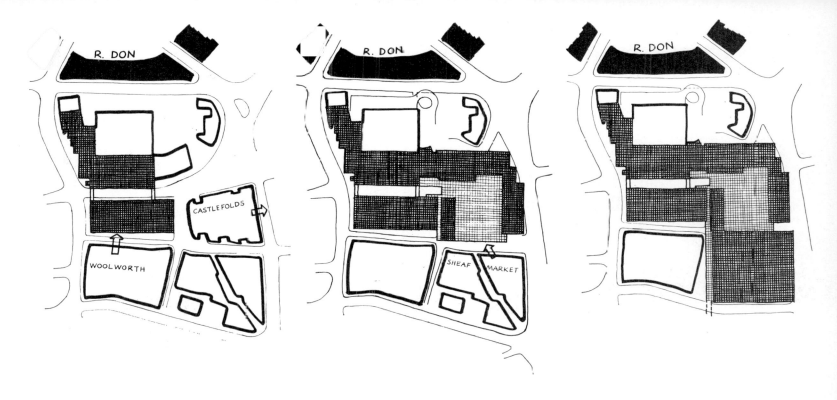

3   The demolition of the Wholesale Market adjacent to the old Market Hall after building a new Wholesale Market out of the central area

4   The development of the old Wholesale Market site (Castlefolds) as a new Market Square to rehouse the existing Sheaf open Market

5   The clearance of the old Sheaf open Market site and leasing of the site for further commercial development

The case for redeveloping the Sheaf Valley rests ultimately on its central location in the topography of the city. Because of the hill formation, almost all the routes across the city intersect in the valley bottom. This means that its nodal situation would make it especially attractive to commerce. That this has not happened hitherto is also due to history and the same topographical formation. The earliest trading centre was undoubtedly in Sheaf Valley at the northerly end. With the growth of Sheffield, expansion had to take place up the hill, due to the

presence of the ponds which flooded the valley immediately to the south, and the many industrial enterprises which were grouped around the waterways. The commercial centre of gravity has moved and the industrial use of the valley has largely waned, leaving a dereliction of old warehousing, some industry and open ground now used as a bus station, bus stacking space and surface car parking. Attention was drawn away from the Sheaf Valley in the immediate post-war years by the desire to rebuild the city centre where it had been damaged. But inevitably the basic underlying factors determining land use are being recognized and the full commercial potential of the Sheaf Valley is beginning to emerge. Reconstruction has been proceeding on the entire perimeter of the slopes surrounding the valley. The building of Park Hill and the clearance and planting of the area between it and the railway have given the valley a new prospect to the east, one on a truly city scale and including, for the first time in 150 years, extensive areas of grass and trees.

Progressively, too, the westerly slopes are being rebuilt with the new Technical College, workshops and a large multi-level car park, making a continuous development connecting with a cinema at Fitzalan Square. To the south a new office block for the British Transport Commission is under construction outside the Midland Railway Station and, at the north end, the Markets development is generating a progressive reconstruction of the valley proper

The latest road plan of the City Engineer proposes an urban motorway connection with the M1 entering the city from the east and the traffic load being taken on a north-west to south motorway running along the upper Don and Sheaf Valleys, with a multi-level intersection on redundant railway land

Visually, the land form can allow this major element to intrude into the urban scene without their mutual destruction. The railway exists already as a fence along the eastern boundary, preventing cross valley movement except at the north end where it becomes

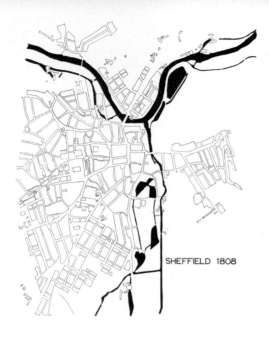

SHEFFIELD 1808

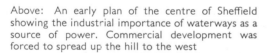

Above: An early plan of the centre of Sheffield showing the industrial importance of waterways as a source of power. Commercial development was forced to spread up the hill to the west

Right: New developments around Sheaf Valley. Recent buildings shown in solid black. Current proposed schemes shown with heavy line

Opposite: Sheaf Valley, looking north-west from Park Hill. Castle Market and Woolworth's are in the centre. Castlefolds in use as a car park until building operations commence on the new Sheaf Market Square

a tunnel and cutting construction. The motorway is sited parallel with the railway and on a shelf of the hillside above it so that, whilst becoming another barrier to be passed by any cross valley pedestrian link, it poses no essentially new problem. What the urban motorway does mean, however, is a reinforcement of the eastern boundary of city centre commercial development clearly defined previously by the railway sidings and canal terminus

The Sheaf Valley development area, therefore, is an unusually well-defined one having a clear generating zone in the busy shopping streets, Waingate, Haymarket and Fitzalan Square, and an equally finite eastern limit of extension at Sheaf Street. Its northern boundary is the River Don and to the south the limit need only be fixed by the dimension of time

The form of the development becomes equally straightforward – an extension of the city shopping levels out over the valley to the line of Sheaf Street as commercial floorspace, with vehicular access, loading bays, warehousing and car parking in the lower levels of the structure. By this means a clear and logical separation of traffic by level is proposed

The phasing of such a scheme is of great importance

Sheaf Valley, looking west from Park Hill. In the foreground some of the last remaining industries in the valley.
Beyond is the clock tower of the Town Hall and the
spire of St Marie's Church with the moors beyond

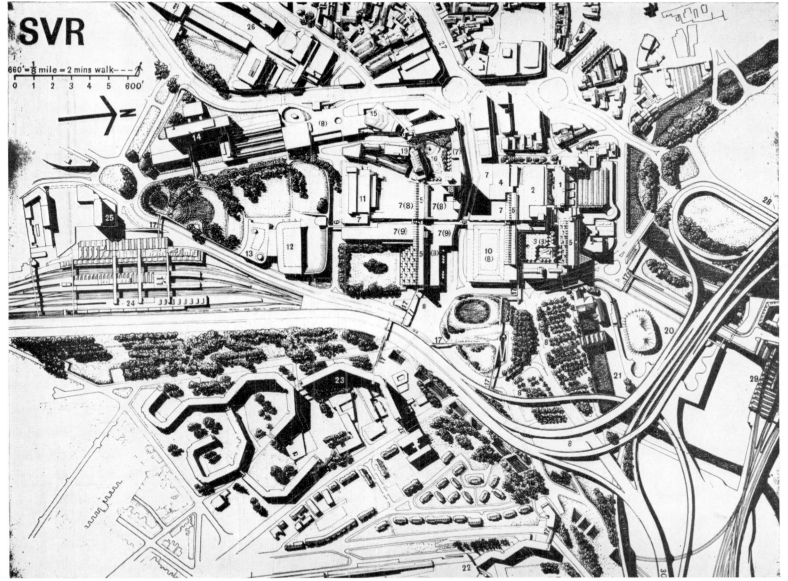

SVR

660' = 1/8 mile = 2 mins walk - - - - -

0 1 2 3 4 5 600'

N

Sheaf Valley Redevelopment Proposals

1 Castle Market (Retail), 2 Woolworth's, 3 Sheaf Market Square, 4 British Home Stores, 5 Housing, 6 North-South spine pedestrian route, 7 Shopping,

8(8) Car park (under), 9) Bus Station (under), 10 Ice Rink and Bowling Alley, 11 G.P.O. Sorting Office, 12 Indoor Sports, 13 Swimming, 14 Technical College, 15 Cinema, 16 Fitzalan Square, 17 Overhead pedestrian route, 18 Barclays Bank, 19 Head Post

Office, 20 Fair-ground, 21 Canal wharf, 22 Hyde Park, 23 Park Hill, 24 Midland Railway Station, 25 British Railways Offices, 26 Civic Centre, 27 High Street, 28 Wicker, 29 Victoria Station, 30 Link to Motorway

since at all times the area must continue to function within the city structure. Fortunately the City Corporation owns a large proportion of the land in the valley and by this means can retain the initiative throughout the programme. At the same time, however, certain substantial sections will have to proceed under the detailed control of others. It is vital, therefore, that some stimulating theme of redevelopment should unify the pattern of reconstruction. Providing the location is right, commercial development is most easily stimulated by an increase of accessibility. The theme in Sheaf Valley being vehicular access from the road network at valley bottom level and pedestrian access at one or more upper levels, with the creation of a considerable amount of new frontage on a pattern relatively free from the old street layout below, the commercial development should be a lively one

At the shopping levels the unifying element is a pedestrian spine route running north/south and linking all phases of the development in a continuous new frontage. This is at levels which can extend southward across Commercial Street in the form of a bridge. Blocks of multi-level development can extend in depth away from this spine on either side with feeder routes through them making further connections with the city centre shopping streets and squares to the west and, via bridges, with the residential areas of Park Hill and Hyde Park to the east. Again, largely because of the topography, the commercial viability of this development will tend to fade south of the Fitzalan Square feeder route, this being the last connection from the spine which is possible at ground level and because of the presence further to the south of a new G.P.O. Sorting Office creating a barren zone. The spine route is proposed to continue south beyond this point as a pedestrian connection with the temporary bus station and the site for a central swimming pool and park on the valley floor outside the Midland Station

THE MULTI-LEVEL RETAIL MARKET

The germ of this whole development is the Retail Market building erected in 1959. In this, the levels of the site are used to give pedestrian access to an extensive retail area on several levels, the vehicular access being kept separate. Servicing is via trolleys

Castle Retail Market building showing offices over the gallery access system, perimeter shops and bridge to adjacent development

moving along a perimeter subway at the lowest level which connects with the loading dock at one end. The Retail Market is on two levels placed in a mezzanine arrangement with the existing Meat and Fish Market. Every effort has been made in the planning to equalize the accessibility of all the stalls. The upper Market level has large voids left in the floor to provide a visual contact between it and the lower level and stairway correction plays an important part in the design of the interior. Most of the stalls have a small stockroom immediately above and this subsidiary level is used in areas adjacent to the stairways for cafés, showrooms, display and stock

The Market is a completely interior organization. The perimeter is surrounded by shop units at the street level and at a gallery level which connects by bridges with a similar gallery around the Woolworth building across the street. Inside Woolworths there are escalators to this upper shopping level and a staircase on the Market side connects it with street level

The next stage, the provision of a new Sheaf Market, which is the open-air trading centre for Sheffield, is conceived as a traditional Market Square surrounded by new buildings on the north, south and east, the west side being the Woolworth east front. In form it is like the Retail Market turned inside out. The floor of the square is the site for the six-day Market traders under a lightweight translucent roof. Other stallholders operating on two or three days a week are accommodated at another lower level, so that on their non-market days their absence will not depress the scene. Exchange Street, which will be closed to vehicles, slopes down to the east from its connection with Waingate and will lead directly into the lower Market level. Ramps up on either side of the street and down from the gallery will lead to the upper Market level. A large rectangular void pierced through the upper level will light the lower one and draw shoppers through to where a further ramped connection will be made within the void. Further stalls are located at Market Square level under the building on the east side which is an office block for

Above: Cross section of Castle Retail Market showing relationship with the existing Meat and Fish Market and with the Woolworth building

Below: Castle Retail Market. Service to perimeter shops and market stalls is by a subway connecting a loading dock and hoists to upper levels

81

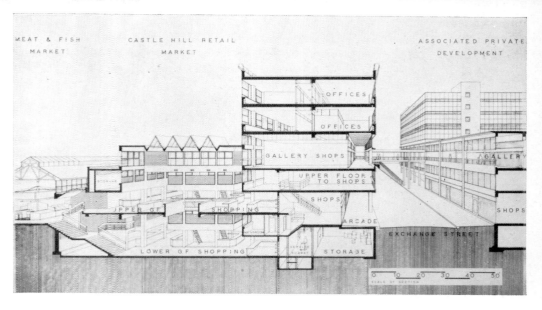

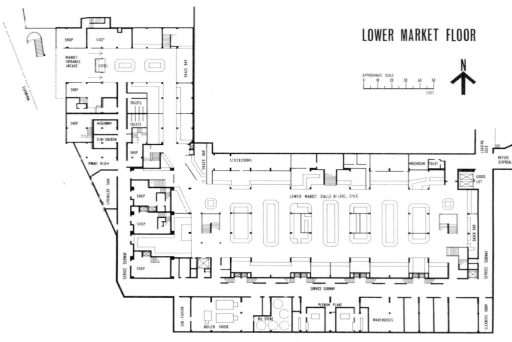

LOWER MARKET FLOOR

the Transport Department. The north block has a supermarket and shops facing both on to the square and into a short arcade leading from the upper floor of the Retail Market building. Above these shops the gallery level is extended with further shops and a staircase connection down to the square. The Transport Club premises with kitchen and restaurant for employees use the rest of this upper level. Above this further, are housing units facing south over the square and set back in grandstand pattern for privacy

The south block has shopping at Market Square and gallery level with a similar housing terrace above. At the west side a small block of shop units carries the gallery level out from the Woolworth building and forms the start of the spine valley route with ramped connections down to Market Square level. Below the lower Market deck are two floors of car parking, loading docks and warehousing with its own vehicle service entry under the Transport building and a motor showroom on the Sheaf Street frontage

Within the square the fullest advantage is taken of the linking of levels possible in an exclusively pedestrian environment. Here the square can be moved into and through not only from all quarters but from below and from above as well. Interest and movement in such an area is stimulated by the extent of the variety of the immediate environment in terms of surfaces, planes, textures, light and shade. In an environment freed from the oppression of the moving vehicle which imposes its own scale deriving from its mode of movement, man's potential enjoyment of architecture and of human society can be realized to the full

THE CIVIC CENTRE

Reconstruction in the centre of the city, that is the area to be within the proposed Civic Circle road, has a potentiality for traffic–pedestrian separation, by place and by level. It is here that positive planning initiative is most urgently required, if great opportunities are not to be lost. These opportunities are being created by two main factors. One is the imminence of the construction of the Civic Circle

Above: Both upper and lower retail floors connect on a mezzanine with the existing meat and fish market

Below: The long block has two floors of offices and the short block five

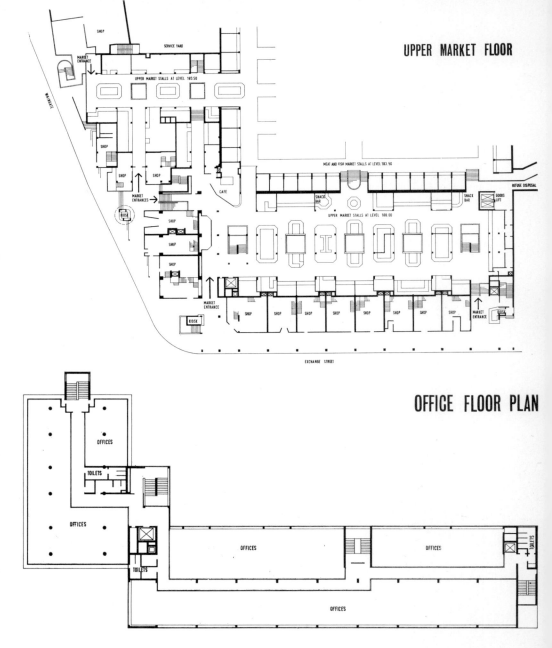

UPPER MARKET FLOOR

OFFICE FLOOR PLAN

82

Top: Lower market interior

Upper market level

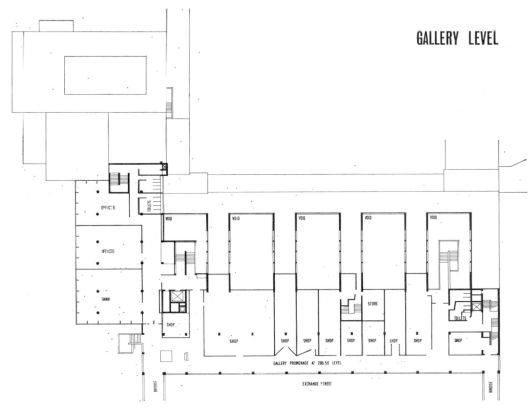

The gallery level connects via bridges over Exchange Street with the Woolworth building which has shops at gallery level. The gallery system will be extended by further market developments to the east

Next pages: Exchange Street looking east towards Hyde Park. This street will be closed by the next stage of the Market development—the building of Sheaf Market Square
Upper and lower market levels from the mezzanine meat and fish market

road, which raises the question of the immediate future of the road network within the 49 acres enclosed by it. The other is the desirability, which has emerged since 1945, of linking together the main shopping areas to the north and to the south by a revision of the land use proposals. This revision has moved the site for Civic buildings to the easterly edge of the area, previously occupied by industry and away from the central position where it interrupted the continuity of the commercial development

The building of the Civic Centre here will enhance the total city structure in three important ways. It will fulfil an urgent need in the city for new accommodation for the expanding administrative, social and legal services in the best possible location relative to transport facilities and other city functions. It will round off the substantial area of comprehensive rebuilding which the Corporation has undertaken, centred on the Sheaf Valley and including the Park Hill and Hyde Park housing redevelopments, the Retail Markets, the Technical College and car parks,

84

87

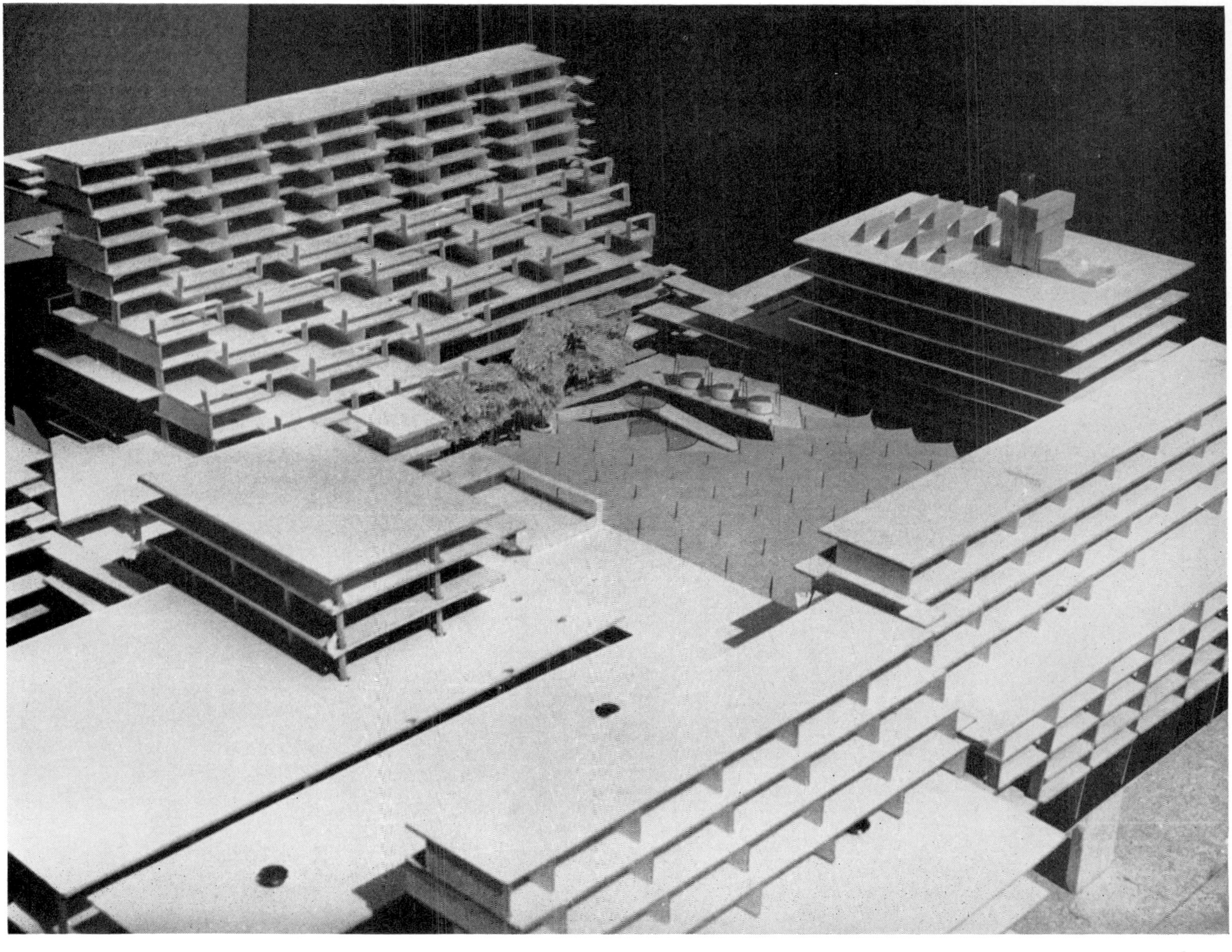

enclosing the entire valley with new works. Furthermore, by withdrawing into the Civic Centre site many departments at present occupying premises elsewhere, it will stimulate the commercial reconstruction effort in the very heart of the city, permitting it to develop in a continuous and concentrated form

The new site for the Civic Centre is an elevated one on the edge of the plateau on which the city centre is located. Beyond the Civic Circle road which skirts it to the east and south-east, the ground falls sharply away giving excellent prospects outwards from the site towards Norfolk Park and the Sheaf Valley. Conversely, its situation ensures that from many parts of the city the location of these civic buildings will be easily recognized

The programme called for three main groups of buildings; Law Courts and Police Headquarters, extensions to the Town Hall, and an Arts Centre. The design is proceeding on the lines of a closely knit development in which each element will play its part in the total environment. Wherever possible, existing buildings of architectural significance on and around the sites have been respected and incorporated in the sequence of spaces engendered by the new work. The general height of the new buildings is to be kept below that of the existing ones so that the Town Hall will continue as the dominant feature in the city centre. The Law Courts will together form the largest single mass, but the placing of this building will be such that the greater height and the slim outline of the Town Hall tower will always predominate. The buildings themselves will be disposed to create a sequence of spaces exclusively pedestrian in their use and providing some three acres of additional traffic-free open space in the city centre as an extension to the St Paul's Garden

The new squares will be partly grassed and partly paved and are intended to provide sheltered areas of quiet space contrasting in prospect and proportion. All the present streets within the site will be closed and the whole site will be accessible to motor vehicles from only one new road, which will run from Charles Street at the south end to Norfolk

88

Preceding pages: Sheaf Market Square. View of model from north east

Sheaf Market Square. View of model from south west showing the grand-stand housing above the north block

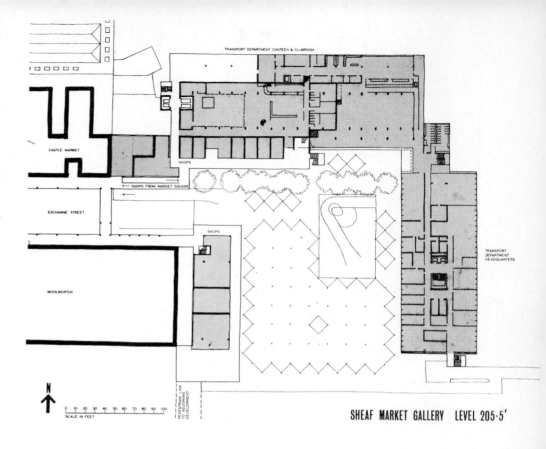

SHEAF MARKET GALLERY LEVEL 205·5'

Street at the north and serving all the buildings and car parking on the site. This will run at low level and be roofed over so that the whole of the upper levels of the site will be available for pedestrian use

To break up direct noise paths from the traffic street to the office buildings within the precinct, a high earth bank will line the Civic Circle road, faced with stone on the outside and planted with grass and trees on the inner face. A walkway for pedestrians will be provided along the top of the bank with access down to road level at bus stops. Three pedestrian subways under the eastern section of the Civic Circle road develop into four pedestrian routes across the Civic Centre site and into the Central Area. Substantial parts of these routes are in the

form of covered ways along the perimeter of the open spaces or through the buildings themselves. The Arts Centre, in particular, is designed to exploit the route from the existing bus station into the city centre, as a means of bringing the arts and the public into easy contact

The Civic Centre, including the existing Town Hall and the public garden, accounts for $14\frac{1}{2}$ of the 49 acres within the perimeter road. Within the area as a whole, about one-third is at present roads and footpaths, of which $9\frac{3}{4}$ acres is surfaced for vehicles Large numbers of vehicles at present using those roads are simply traversing the area and will be catered for in the future by the circular road. The internal road network can be redesigned, therefore to serve the existing buildings and to prevent short-

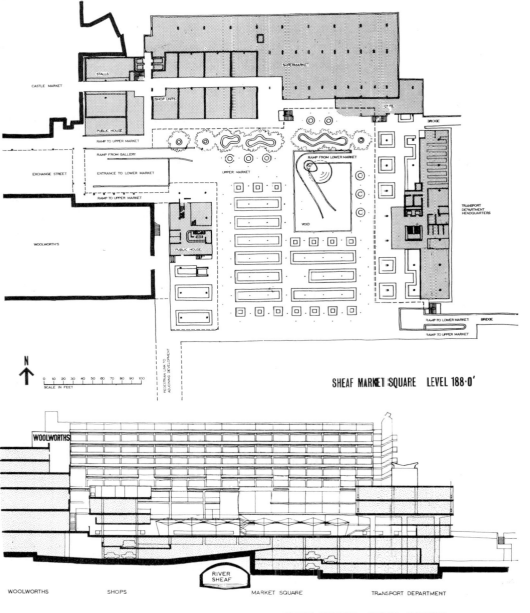

STALLS

CASTLE MARKET

SHOP UNITS

SUPERMARKET

PUBLIC HOUSE

RAMP TO UPPER MARKET

RAMP FROM GALLERY

EXCHANGE STREET

ENTRANCE TO LOWER MARKET

UPPER MARKET

RAMP FROM LOWER MARKET

RAMP TO UPPER MARKET

WOOLWORTH'S

PUBLIC HOUSE

VOID

TRANSPORT DEPARTMENT HEADQUARTERS

BRIDGE

RAMP TO LOWER MARKET   BRIDGE

RAMP TO UPPER MARKET

PEDESTRIAN LINK TO ADJOINING DEVELOPMENT

N

0 10 20 30 40 50 60 70 80 90 100
SCALE IN FEET

SHEAF MARKET SQUARE   LEVEL 188·0'

WOOLWORTHS

RIVER SHEAF

WOOLWORTHS   SHOPS   MARKET SQUARE   TRANSPORT DEPARTMENT

0 10 20 30 40 50 60 70 80 90 100
SCALE IN FEET

SHEAF MARKET CROSS SECTION

CITY HALL

TOWN HALL

LIBRARY

N

Civic Centre as planned in 1945 showing new law courts and other public buildings grouped with the City Hall and the Town Hall and making a complete break in the shopping conformity

circuiting the perimeter system by stopping off all through routes across the centre. One way in which this can be done, in an area as small as this, is by restricting traffic movement to a number of one-way loop roads penetrating the area but never crossing it. In this way continuity of pedestrian movement over most of the area can be achieved. If, within the central precinct, the pedestrian is given the right of way across the loop roads then full continuity can be assured. This would be a workable arrangement providing car parking within the area is located near the perimeter road. Such a system of limited penetration loop roads requires only 3¾ acres for vehicle movement, thus releasing 6 acres of valuable city centre land for building

With a radically different vehicle movement pattern the environment could be reshaped to become pedestrian dominated. The pedestrian movement pattern could cease being a system of ribbon-like routes hugging the building faces. Greater freedom

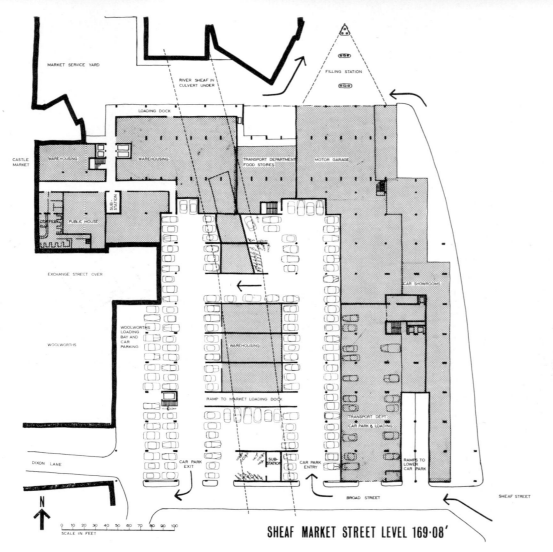

SHEAF MARKET STREET LEVEL 169·08'

Labels within the plan:

MARKET SERVICE YARD

RIVER SHEAF IN CULVERT UNDER

FILLING STATION

LOADING DOCK

CASTLE MARKET

WAREHOUSING

WAREHOUSING

TRANSPORT DEPARTMENT FOOD STORES

MOTOR GARAGE

SUB STATION

PUBLIC HOUSE

EXCHANGE STREET OVER

CAR SHOWROOMS

WOOLWORTHS LOADING BAY AND CAR PARKING

WOOLWORTHS

WAREHOUSING

RAMP TO MARKET LOADING DOCK

TRANSPORT DEPT. CAR PARK & LOADING

DIXON LANE

CAR PARK EXIT

SUB STATION

CAR PARK ENTRY

RAMPS TO LOWER CAR PARK

BROAD STREET

SHEAF STREET

N

0 10 20 30 40 50 60 70 80 90 100
SCALE IN FEET

90

regular crowds of worshippers who go there, by opening up the church building to the newly created square and, at the same time, would add a new urbanity to Fargate itself. The Town Hall tower is another building which could be more eloquent within the city if it could be seen up the length of Fargate. The old building which blocks the view is an awkward shape in plan and faces north and north-west. The demolition of this building and its replacement across the street, over the present highway, would open up an excellent view of the tower and provide a new building with faces to the east, south and north which, by its siting, would improve the shape of Fargate and of the square outside the Town Hall as well. The Town Hall square is capable of great improvement by these means. The corners, at present gashed open by roads, could be closed up to contain the space, making it more attractive for people to use, less windy and with more activities made possible around the perimeter

The difficulties in the way of such a reconstruction largely derive from questions of land ownership. The situation is bristling with contradictions. The most attractive shops internally have the noisiest, the smelliest, the most dangerous shopping conditions outside their doors caused by motor traffic. At the present time these cars are allowed to penetrate the centre of the city but are not allowed to stop. In this area of the highest land values in the city, one-fifth of it is dedicated to moving vehicles. Because of the self-consuming market in land, there is the strange paradox of plots being redeveloped twice, within sight of others which still have Georgian cottage properties converted to other uses. In this situation the currently accepted techniques and procedures for comprehensive redevelopment are inadequate. The bringing of all this expensive land into one ownership, whether by negotiation or by compulsory purchase, would be so time-consuming and costly that rentals in the new development would be prohibitive. Voluntary land pooling would seem to be the only practicable way of achieving a

of movement could also allow greater freedom in the siting of new buildings

With the release of new building land converted from highway use, some judicious demolition could be afforded which would open up new prospects for those few buildings in the city centre deserving a better setting than they have at present and, at the same time, provide the sort of public spaces required for city functions. St Marie's Catholic Church is such a case, where a fine tower and spire are so built-in that they cannot be seen and the church is without the space outside its door which it requires. The clearance of the old buildings between its walled-in west front and Fargate would provide a space for the

Right: Model of Civic Centre looking north towards the Arts Centre. To the left is the old town with St Marie's Church above. To the right is the existing library building. All vehicular traffic serving the 14 acre site is channelled into a new underground road. The roof of the two-storey car parking and storage served from the new road becomes a civic square giving pedestrian access to all the buildings

92

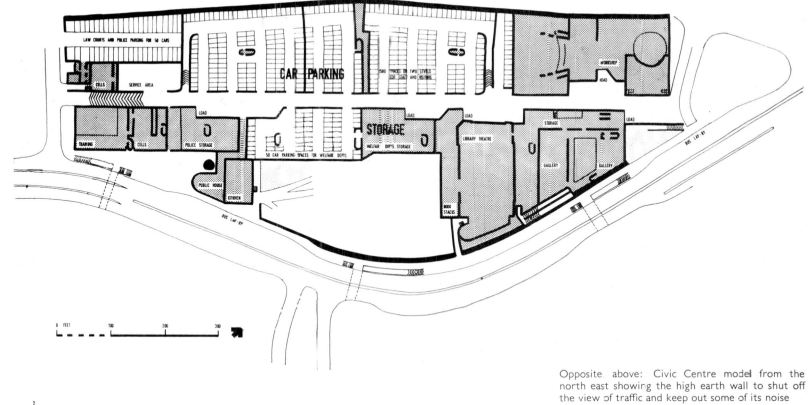

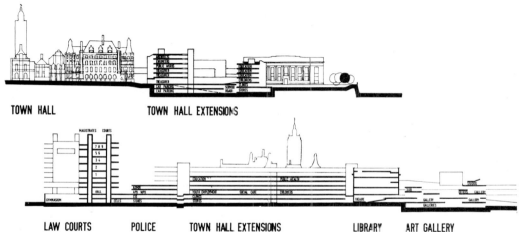

TOWN HALL   TOWN HALL EXTENSIONS

LAW COURTS   POLICE   TOWN HALL EXTENSIONS   LIBRARY   ART GALLERY

Opposite above: Civic Centre model from the north east showing the high earth wall to shut off the view of traffic and keep out some of its noise

Opposite, below: Civic Centre model from east. The tall Court building has been kept away from the old tower and the office accommodation kept relatively low. The level of the pedestrian square in the centre is projected past the library to improve its entrance and returns as a walk way along the top of the earth wall with a restaurant at the south end and the entrance foyers to theatres and galleries at the north end. Extensive views open out from this level

Above: Civic Centre. Plan at vehicle level. A new one way road, giving access to car parking on two levels and loading bays for all buildings above, is made across the site from south to north. Access from the car parking is up into the Civic Square around which are grouped the entrances to particular departments

Left: Civic Centre. Sections across the site

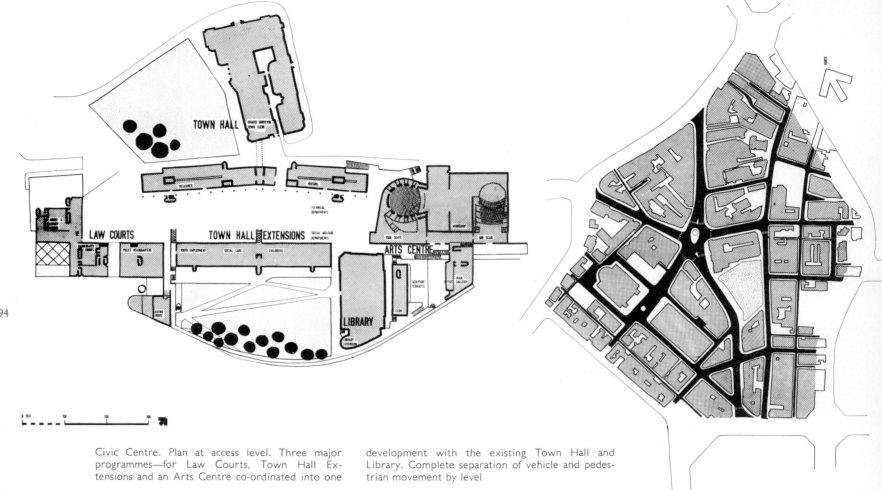

Civic Centre. Plan at access level. Three major programmes—for Law Courts, Town Hall Extensions and an Arts Centre co-ordinated into one development with the existing Town Hall and Library. Complete separation of vehicle and pedestrian movement by level

redevelopment on this scale. Previously the major objection to land pooling schemes has been that the benefits of the redevelopment brought about by the pooling scheme cannot be confined to its own boundaries. In an area such as the centre of Sheffield within the Civic Circle such an objection could be said to be less strong since the perimeter road around the area forms an effective break. The size of the area, too, would be a reasonable one within which to operate such a scheme. The Corporation

is already committed to redeveloping about one-third of it in its Civic Centre proposals and owns certain other sites which will become progressively released for redevelopment as the Civic Centre is built and traffic movement amended. In this way, and by producing an overall plan for the centre, the Corporation could initiate the reconstruction of the entire city centre

If the principle of land pooling were adopted, land

ownership could be one of the bases of the shareholding of a development company formed for the purpose of the redevelopment and in this way land costs need not enter into the financial programming of the scheme. The subsequent developments would need to cover only building costs before showing a profit, so that there would be every likelihood of the scheme proving very attractive to all concerned, not least the Local Authority, who would obtain extra benefits from the rateable values

94

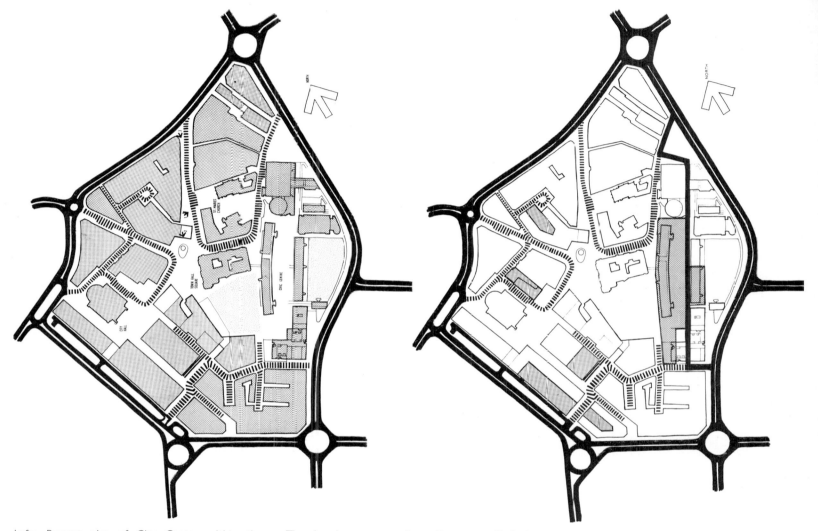

Left: Present plan of City Centre within the proposed Civic Circle road. Total area 49 acres of which $9\frac{3}{4}$ acres are roads. Pedestrian movement confined to the white areas

The plan shows new works on those areas likely to be reconstructed first

Right: Proposed plan of City Centre. Showing limited penetration system of one way loop roads for vehicles. The reconstruction will be gradual and many older properties will continue to require service to the street frontage for a number of years.

Above, right: St Marie's Church from Fargate

Above: St Marie's Church after proposed demolition to make a small square at the west end

Right: Town Hall from Fargate. The black building screening the tower is lit only from the north and north west and is an awkward shape in plan

Below: Fargate after removal of black building and its replacement across the street with north, east and south light

Right: Town Hall Square. At present a traffic roundabout exposed to the wind

Below, right: Town Hall Square with traffic passing only at the corners. The space reshaped by demolition and rebuilding across existing roads

VICTOR PASMORE

Projective Relief in black, white, maroon and cedar
Painted wood and plastic 1963 48 × 48 in (122 ×
122 cm)

CHRISTIANE AND GEORGE COLLINS

99

The most eloquent critic of mechanical planning and of city planning in terms of traffic was probably Camillo Sitte, whose book 'Der Städtebau' appeared in 1889 in Vienna. Sitte spoke for the man of taste against the paper-planners who seemed to be out to annihilate him – psychologically at least – with their enormous Babylons. The most modern scientific methods are to be applied to alleviate over-crowding, to restore circulation, and to improve sanitation, but true city planning (city-building as Sitte called it) should operate on a totally different level from that of such practical technicalities. Sitte applied himself to the matter of 'public life' in the city and explored the problem of whether in a modern metropolis the setting for it could still be scaled to the individual citizen

To many his search for rules that underlie the essential beauty of towns and cities of the past seemed to be nothing more than a sentimental romanticism, without application to modern times. And, indeed, the social, utopian, and engineering aspects of city planning seem to have largely diverted progressive planners away from his artistic orientation for several decades now

However, Sitte's 'principles' quickly permeated both the literature and the educational system of architecture and planning in Germany over the turn of our century when that country was the exemplar to modernists everywhere. By World War I the type of planning that grew out of Sitte could be detected throughout Western Europe and America. How subtly this came about is demonstrated by the fact that the leaders of the British planning profession were expressing themselves in his terms by 1910, although his book was not to appear in English for them to read until thirty-five years later. Thanks in part to Raymond Unwin, garden cities (and garden suburbs) the world over exhibit some of the most picturesque traits of the Sittesque style

As today we have become more and more disenchanted with the ruthless, chaotic commercialism and the doctrinaire municipal uniformity that mark our 'new' cities, we find that creative architects and planners are beginning to express themselves much

Above: One of Sitte's favourite plazas, that of St Peter's in Rome, formed solely by colonnades

Right: Old street in the Moorish Section of Palma de Mallorca

as Sitte did when they describe to us their new building groups, their civic centres and city extensions, or even their latest tours of Europe

Sitte's message for his day and ours was a relatively simple and quite unforgettable one: namely, that, regardless of the scale and general monotony of the modern metropolis, there must be certain open spaces in it where a person on foot can find himself in scale with his surroundings. Such a scale does not depend on size alone (and, in fact, Sitte gives no absolute rules for the size relationships), but also involves the element of 'closure' of the space. Closure means, simply, that from a given point in an urban space the pedestrian can see few if any breaks in the 'wall' of the space around him. Such breaks would normally be streets, of course, and Sitte found upon examination of old cities that most streets angled away or bent away so as to close themselves off to the viewer; in more formal planning, arches or colonnades covering the point where the street joins a square can give a sense of closure to the space (illus. p99). Sitte's equal enthusiasm for such different styles of urban space and closure led to contradictory estimates of his position; he was ultimately credited with giving rise to both a medieval and a Baroque revival in civic design!

He himself seems to have considered matters of architectural style less important than other principles in the building of cities. He limited his purpose, moreover, to that which is immediately and practically achievable:

'Artistically contrived streets and plazas might be wrested even from the gridiron system if the traffic expert would just let the artist peer over his shoulder occasionally or would set aside his compass and drawing board now and then. If only the desire were to exist, one could establish a basis for peaceful coexistence between these two. After all, the artist needs for his purpose only a few main streets and plazas; all the rest he is glad to turn over to traffic and to daily material needs. The broad mass of living quarters should be businesslike, and there the city may appear in its work-clothes. However, major plazas and thoroughfares should wear their 'Sunday best' in order to be a pride and joy to the inhabitants, to awake civic spirit, and forever to nurture great and noble sentiment within our growing youth. This is exactly the way it is in the old towns'

The situation could be saved, in other words, if at critical points there can be designed urban spaces that conform to a number of age-old principles that would make even a country cousin feel 'at home'

Sitte states his purpose clearly in the opening pages of his polemical little book: 'It is only in our mathematical century that the process of enlargement and the layout of cities has become an almost purely technical concern. Therefore it seems important to remind ourselves once again that this attitude solves only one aspect of the problem, and that the other, the artistic aspect, is of at least equal importance'

He felt that plaza design lay at the basis of city building because it had been in public plazas that community life had always transpired. The pre-occupation with street design – straight or wriggly streets, etc – was a concern of his followers, not of Sitte; he worried more about the heartbeat of the city. 'Nowadays plazas seldom harbour great popular festivities, and they see less and less daily use. They often serve no other purpose than to allow for more air and light, or to bring about a certain interruption in the sea of houses, or, at most, to provide freer view of a large building and thus to add to its architectural effect. How different in ancient times! In those days the main plazas were of primary importance to the life of every city because such a great deal of public life took place in them; today not an open plaza but closed halls would be used for such purposes.' Of ancient Rome he remarked: 'the forum is for the whole city what the atrium represents in a single family dwelling: it is the well-appointed and richly furnished main hall'; and of later times he reminds us, 'in the Middle Ages and the Renaissance there still existed a vital and functional use of the town square for community life and also, in connection with this, a rapport between square and surrounding public buildings'

He explains at great length how the closure that transforms the raw material of an open space into a finely designed plaza is obtained:

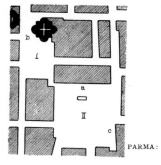

PARMA:

'This cohesion of the vista, so contrived that one cannot see outside the plaza, is achieved by such a variety of devices that one cannot speak of it as a matter of pure chance. It may often have happened that the circumstances were already favourable when the plaza was about to receive its final shaping. However, that such circumstances were exploited and preserved was not in the end an accident. In the same situation today one would completely ignore these fortuities and would knock fine wide breaches into the wall surrounding the place, as, indeed, is actually happening wherever nicely enclosed old plazas are being enlarged and modernized

'Also it certainly is no mere accident that in all the old plazas we see streets opening into them in a manner exactly the opposite of the modern system. Today it is the rule to let two streets intersect each other at right angles at each corner of a public square, probably to enlarge the break in its confines even further and to make each block of buildings stand out as isolated as possible, thus preventing any coherent total effect. Precisely the opposite rule was followed in former days: if possible, only one street opened at each point, while a second one would branch off further back on this street out of sight from the plaza. However, there is more to it. Each of the three or four corner streets enters the plaza at a different angle. This remarkable feature occurs so often and with such a range of variations, that it, too, must be considered to be one of the major conscious or subconscious principles of old city planning. On further reflection, one realizes that by leading the streets off in the fashion of turbine blades, the most favourable condition results, namely, that from any point within the plaza no more than one single view out of it is possible at a time, hence there is only a single interruption in the enclosure of the whole. However, from most vantage points within the plaza its whole framing is seen as an unbroken continuity, because buildings at the openings of streets overlap when seen obliquely, and, owing to this mutual covering, no offending gap is left

'The whole secret consists in the fact that entering streets are laid out at an angle to our lines of sight instead of parallel to them'

Sitte's empiricism succeeded in putting city planning, for a while at least, on to a visual, architectural basis that it sorely needed. For example, he considered that everything in civic design depended ultimately on the viewer: 'What counts in this is the position of

the spectator and the direction in which he is looking.' Or again: 'Only that which a spectator can hold in view, what can be seen, is of artistic importance'

His most eloquent description, perhaps, is of his favourite set of plazas in Venice:

'One of the most magnificent combinations of plazas is that which forms the heart of Venice: the Piazza S. Marco and the Piazzetta. The first is a deep plaza in relation to S. Marco, and a broad plaza in relation to the Procuratie. The second is a broad plaza as regards the facade of the Doge's Palace, but, more importantly, a deep plaza with regard to the splendid view across the Canal Grande towards S. Giorgio Maggiore. In addition, a third, small plaza lies alongside S. Marco. So much beauty is united on this unique little patch of Earth, that no painter has ever dreamt up anything surpassing it in his architectural backgrounds; in no theatre has there ever been seen anything more sense-beguiling than was able to arise here in reality. This is truly the sovereign seat of a great power, a power of intellect, of art, and of industry, which assembled the riches of the world on her ships and from here exercised dominion over the seas, relishing her acquired treasures at this, the

loveliest spot in the whole wide world. Not even Titian or Paolo Veronese could invent anything more magnificent for the imaginative city views in the backgrounds of their large paintings of weddings and other occasions. If we were to examine the means by which this unexcelled grandeur was achieved, they would, indeed, prove to be extraordinary: the effect of the sea, the accumulation of superlative monumental structures, the abundance of their sculptural decoration, the rich polychromy of S. Marco, the powerful Campanile. However, it is the felicitous arranging of them that contributes so decidedly to the whole effect. There is no doubt that if all these works of art were disposed separately according to the modern method, straight in line and geometrically centred, their effect would be immeasurably decreased. Imagine S. Marco isolated, with the Campanile set on the axis of its main portal in the middle of a huge modern square – the Procuratie, Library, etc, standing about separately in the modern "block system" instead of forming a tight enclosure – and to top it all, a boulevard of almost 200 feet in width running past this so-called plaza. One cannot bear the thought. Everything would be destroyed, everything! After all, the two things do go together: beautiful structures and

monuments, and the correct placement of them. The grouping of the Piazza S. Marco and its adjoining squares is really perfect in the light of all the rules mentioned so far – and particular note should be taken of the placing of the Campanile to one side so that it stands guard at the juncture of the larger and smaller plazas

'In conclusion, one should keep in mind the special effect that results from walking about from one plaza to another in such a cleverly grouped sequence. Visually our frame of reference changes constantly, creating ever new impressions. What wealth of effects these plazas harbour can be judged from photographs of the Piazza S. Marco and the Signoria in Florence. More than a dozen different photographs exist, each taken from another point and each showing another view, so that one can hardly believe them all to be of the same plaza. This should be tried just once with a perfectly rectangular modern plaza! Not even three views of different artistic content can be eked out, because the set shape of modern squares, laid out with a ruler, has no spiritual meaning at all, but is only every-so-many square yards of empty surface'

Sitte was particularly scornful of those who planned primarily from the point of view of vehicular traffic and made plazas into street junctions:

'Yet what shall we say about traffic intersections where as many as six or more streets run together from all sides? In the centre of a populous town at certain busy times of day a smooth flow of traffic is actually impossible, and the authorities have to intervene, first, by stationing a policeman who, with his signals, keeps the traffic precariously moving. For pedestrians such a place is truly hazardous, and in order to eliminate the worst dangers, a round piece of sidewalk is raised in the middle – a small safety island on which a beautiful slender light rises like a lighthouse amidst the stormy waves of the ocean of vehicles. This safety island with its lamp is perhaps the most magnificent and original invention of modern city planning! In spite of all these precautions, crossing the street is advisable only for alert persons; the old and the frail will always by preference take a long detour in order to avoid it

'These, then, are the achievements of a system that, relentlessly condemning all artistic traditions, has restricted itself exclusively to questions of traffic. Its monstrous street junctions are called "plazas", yet in them everything is avoided that would make for character in a plaza, and at the same time everything seems to be accumulated that is impractical and ugly. These are the consequences of design based on traffic considerations rather than, as it should be, on the arrangement of plazas and streets'

He was aware that at the root of the present evil was the factor of the immense and anonymous character of modern cities and its consequence – the retreat of public life from the streets and plazas:

'The life of the common people has for centuries been steadily withdrawing from public squares, and especially so in recent times. Owing to this, a substantial part of the erstwhile significance of squares has been lost, and it becomes quite understandable why the appreciation of beautiful plaza design has decreased so markedly among the broad mass of citizenry. Life in former times was, after all, decidedly more favourable to an artistic development of city building than is our mathematically precise modern life. Man himself has become almost a machine, and our frame of reference has shifted, not only on the whole but also in detail, since the changed conditions of our time imperiously demand many modifications

'It is above all the enormous size to which our larger cities are growing that has shattered the framework of traditional artistic forms at every point. The larger the city, the bigger and wider the plazas and streets become, and the higher and bulkier are all structures, until their dimensions, what with their numerous floors and interminable rows of windows, can hardly be organized any more in an artistically effective manner. Everything tends towards the immense, and the constant repetition of identical motifs is enough to dull our senses to such an extent that only the most powerful effects can still make any impression. As this cannot be altered, the city planner must, like the architect, invent a scale appropriate for the modern city of millions. With

Right: Vicenza, the Piazza dei Signori by Gustav Bauernfeind, ca. 1876
 Some of Sitte's ideas about the form of Italian squares and the activities with which they were once crowded may have come not only from his own extensive voyages, but also from the popular travel prints, like this, with which he illustrated his book

such an extraordinary concentration of people at one location, real estate values also increase exorbitantly, and it is not possible for an individual person or the local administration to escape the inevitable effects of this increase in value. Everywhere, as if spontaneously, lots are divided up and streets are broken through so that even in the old parts of town more and more side streets result, and something of the obnoxious building-block system surreptitiously takes over. This is a phenomenon which is naturally connected with the current value of real estate and the value of street-frontage lines; hence it cannot be eliminated by decree, least of all by aesthetic considerations. All these elements must be reckoned with as stated factors that the city planner has to take into account just as much as an architect must consider the strength of materials and the laws of statics – even if they impose the most disagreeable and petty limitations

'The regular parcelling of lots based on purely economic considerations has become such a factor in new plans that its effects can hardly be avoided. In spite of this one should not surrender quite so blindly to the consequences of this universal method, because it is precisely this that has led to mass slaughter of the beauties of city planning. These are the very beauties which are designated by the word "pictorial". In a rigidly uniform arrangement where do all the picturesque street corners end up? These are a delight in old Nuremberg and anywhere else where they have still been preserved, because of the originality of their appearance: the street panoramas at the Fembohaus in Nuremberg, at the Rathaus in Heilbronn or the Brauerei of Görlitz, at the Petersenhaus in Nuremberg, and elsewhere. However, they are unfortunately diminishing in number from year to year because of constant demolition'

Our modern procedures in planning always fare rather badly when Sitte compares them with the ways of old:

'Laying out a city is certainly a vast and difficult task. Whenever one peruses the chronicle of a famous old town, it becomes clear what tremendous sums of intellectual capital have been invested therein and still continue to bear dividends in the form of its noble legacy. On closer scrutiny one observes that, as in material things, here also the payment of dividends is in proportion to the capital invested. The enjoyment of the effect of these dividends depends upon the astuteness of the original invest-

ment. To think about the level of intellectual investment in any modern grid-layout is literally embarrassing. Size of the block and width of the street are invariably determined by the decision of some board. After that the parcelling of the new town section can be carried out by the lowliest copyist or clerk unless delicacy of execution of the drawing is considered important. The artistic values invested here certainly amount to zero to start with, and so the resultant effects also amount to nil. As a consequence of this, the pleasure that the inhabitants take in their city in turn amounts to zero, and for this reason their attachment to it, their pride in it, in short, their feeling of belonging, amount to nothing, as one can in fact see among the dwellers of the artless, tedious, new sections of cities'

Also:

'We ought to consider the impression we receive upon returning home from Venice or Florence – how painfully our banal modernity affects us. This may be one of the basic reasons why the fortunate inhabitants of those marvellously artistic cities have no need to leave them, while we every year for a few weeks must get away into nature in order to be able to endure the city for another year'

In the decades that followed, many a romantic absurdity was perpetrated in the tradition of Sitte's reverence for the past. We find little basis for this, however, in the writing of Sitte himself:

'Modern living as well as modern building techniques no longer permit the faithful imitation of old townscapes, a fact which we cannot overlook without falling prey to barren fantasies. The exemplary creations of the old masters must remain alive with us in some other way than through slavish copying; only if we can determine in what the essentials of these creations consist, and if we can apply these meaningfully to modern conditions, will it be possible to harvest a new and flourishing crop from the apparently sterile soil

'An attempt should be made regardless of obstacles. Even if numerous pictorial beauties must be renounced and extensive consideration be given to the requirements of modern construction, hygiene, and transportation, this should not discourage us to the extent that we simply abandon artistic solutions and settle for purely technical ones, as in the building of a highway or the construction of a machine. The forever edifying impress of artistic perfection cannot be

dispensed with in our busy everyday life. One must keep in mind that city planning in particular must allow full and complete participation to art, because it is this type of artistic endeavour, above all, that affects formatively every day and every hour the great mass of the population'

And again:

'Nature and art, historical wisdom and a fresh effervescent life should always go hand in hand, so that dry tedious patterns may be dispensed with and once more each town can achieve a unique character in its layout and architecture, in keeping with its location and ethnic idiosyncrasies. Every new town the world over need not end up with the identical monotony of appearance, as if stamped out by the same mechanical mould'

Sitte's words, dated as they may be, can still be read today with profit, as is true of any great classic

CURVILINEAR SPACE FORM

STEPHEN GILBERT

The development of pure abstract knowledge is to a great extent independent of evolutionary change. The influence of this dual movement in the life of man has led to a technological civilization in which we tend to think in abstract terms, and in art to conceive a visual expression from an abstract idea

Abstract forms of visual art date from the beginning of this century, and have developed on a broad front from formal to informal expression in two, three and four (kinetic) dimensions. It is difficult today to visualize a new art-form which could be figurative: such an art would seem like a spiritual devaluation. (However, it is a fact that, for ideological reasons, a time-lag exists in certain societies)

The various aspects which the abstract idea in art presents to us can be considered as visual situations, which for periods of time evoke correspondences between the life of forms and the developable idea. The artist, more than ever before, is compelled to a process of continuous revision. The materials he uses even are various, inventive and untraditional. Technical inventiveness becomes an important creative factor

It is with this situation in mind that one must consider the creation of the art-object today. The abstract idea renders two-dimensional form non-objective: in three dimensions one searches as well for the elimination of mass and the means of des-

cribing space-form. Since all visual art needs material supports, space-form in three dimensions cannot be produced in its pure state (except by coloured light). However, the artist is not so much concerned about this, for he relies on his intuition to convey to us the quality of space-form. Its properties become apparent in, one might almost say, collective efforts of research, from which this qualitative content emerges. In this way an art-form is created which transcends, and is at the same time a synthesis of the artist's attempts to envisage space-form

This art-form is a signification. I do not think an artist proposes to do more than this, and it seems a process common to all art. There is perhaps one difference today: instead of the figurative notion of many subjects and one style, art has many styles for one subject. The means are multiplied–from microcosm to macrocosm. Kinetics, 'trompe l'oeil', acoustics, light and disassociated colour are important factors in the creation of an art-form, where space is the real preoccupation

I have written the above notes to explain why I have personally felt the need for participation in the technical developments of present-day life. My painting became abstract in 1948–informal first and then formal–and in 1954 I started to make formal space constructions using flat planes of colour to animate space within an armature. At the same time I worked on projects for the integration of pure plastic theories of colour and space-form into architecture

In 1958, however, I went back to personal work, and developed a free-standing type of structure in curved radiating planes, using at first anodized metallic surfaces in colour; later uncoloured and highly polished ones. In the latter, the curvilinear forms develop in reflecting surfaces, which also pick up ambient colour and light. This changing colour and light, by its fluidity and movement, cut across by shadows, partially masks and sometimes completely transforms the original structural elements. An extremely mobile and complex system of tonalities is built up from reflections, in the composition of which elements of colour and light are brought forward, which escape control and appear disassociated. These visual metamorphoses of the material structure multiply to infinity the means of describing space

Opposite: Structure 14 C, 1961. Aluminium and duralumium. Height not given on original
Collection: The Tate Gallery, London

Below: Structure 20 B, 1962. Aluminium and duralumium. Length approx 6 ft. This work, for which the sculptor received the Gulbenkian Award, is owned by the University of Leicester, England. Photo: Bertrand Weill

Reproduced with kind permission from Architectural Design, April 1962

TWO PROJECTS
FORT WORTH TEXAS 1956

VICTOR GRUEN

A   50 Story Apartment Tower

B   30 Story Apartment Buildings

C   8 Story Apartment Buildings

D   Town Houses

E   Ferry Landing

F   Park

G   Existing Bridge and Service Access

H   Existing Bridge Widened for Bus Stop

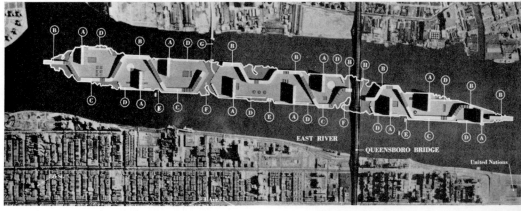

DO NOT SEGREGATE PEDESTRIANS AND AUTOMOBILES

JANE JACOBS

Solicitude for city pedestrians slips easily and naturally into preoccupation with the problems of traffic-separation. From this preoccupation, it is only a step to infatuation with tour de forces of gadgetry on a grandiose city-centre scale. The pedestrians, having somewhere along the line become metamorphosed from whole and various human beings into abstract 'pedestrian traffic', become an excuse for a showy but fake, inflexible and limited pretence at city environment

This shift in emphasis, and its deplorable outcome, can be seen not only in the drift of ambitious pedestrian and town-centre schemes as a whole, but can

be followed even in the work of specific planning groups or firms. As an example, note the 1956 pedestrian scheme proposed by Victor Gruen Associates for Fort Worth, Texas; then compare it with the same firm's scheme, five years later, for East Island, a proposed development for an underused piece of land in New York's East River. The initial conditions for the two schemes greatly differed, of course; East Island presented a virtual clean slate, and more freedom for the designer

The Fort Worth scheme, for all its huge garaging and traffic service arrangements, subordinated these devices to the city centre as an intricate, pluralistic,

Schematic Section: Section of East Island Project

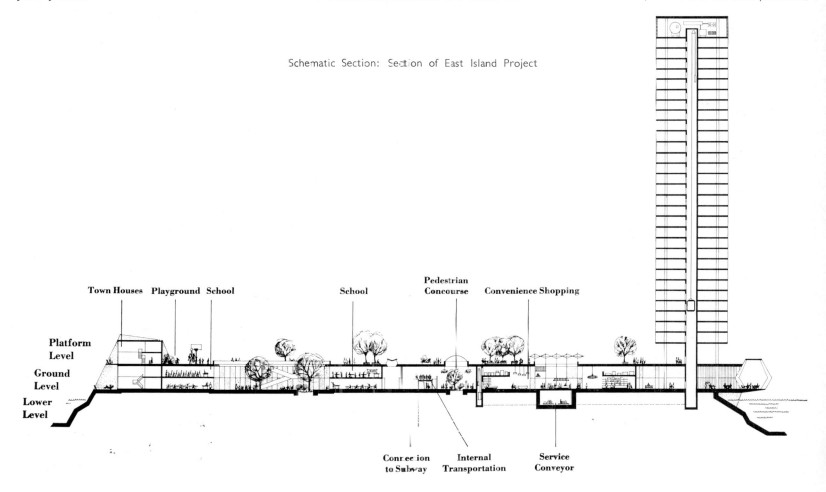

Town Houses   Playground   School   School   Pedestrian Concourse   Convenience Shopping

Platform Level

Ground Level

Lower Level

Connection to Subway   Internal Transportation   Service Conveyor

flexible collection of enterprises and establishments. The object was, quite literally, that the pedestrian was to inherit a busy bit of the earth (paved and unpaved) and it was to be a relatively various, adaptable and free piece of the earth at that

In the East Island scheme, the gadgetry of circulation and of precinct separation has become an end in itself. Not only the pedestrian, but all of life is subordinated to it. The bit of earth under the sky which the pedestrian inherits as his purest precinct is a cold and dreary platform, little different from the monotonous promenades without promenaders that have become all too familiar in existing housing projects. The putative ingredients of a town centre, along with the schools, are underground where they may be served by transportation in arrangements of endless ingenuity and perfect lifelessness. Nor is this a unique aberration. Much the same philosophy governs the long range planning goals of centre Philadelphia, for example, or the Golden Triangle centre in Pittsburgh. The idea is to put underground as much as possible of what the pedestrians use, and this is called providing the pedestrians with more light and air (where they will not be). In Philadelphia such an ideal must be compromised because of what exists already; and here we may venture a law about elaborate city pedestrian schemes: the more flexibility permitted the designer, the more inflexible the product

There are other means than the tunnel of arriving at similar impasses in the name of the pedestrian. Among the most celebrated and unworkable were Le Corbusier's mid-floor shops and roof playground in the Marseilles apartments. Other means are to cut the whole city into series of unrelated islands. The Fort Worth scheme depended on the island approach, but excusably, because all of this settlement which operates at all like a city was contained in the one island. This is the approach much used in town centre schemes, but for cities of big size it is most unpromising and artificial. The most extreme subordinations of all other functions of the city to the gadgetry of traffic and precinct separation are probably the theoretical studies by Louis Kahn, which are enormously influential in U S schools of design today

This drift from humanism to gimickry reflects a difficulty that afflicts architectural design as a whole today: the decline of respect for function, and consequently lack of interest in it. Perhaps it is not surprising that urban design should share this serious flaw, for the two fields of architecture and urban design draw on the same reservoir of unconscious

assumptions and conscious ideas, and often on the same practitioners

Almost unnoticed, the word 'function', and the idea of function, have taken on a different sense from that understood in the formative years of modern architecture. Function, which form was to follow, then meant primarily the uses for which a building was needed. The structural methods and building materials were to abet and express these uses, free them in a sense, rather than warp or conceal them. Various building types were analyzed and understood in those terms, and some were revolutionized, such as the elementary school and the single family house. Architecture is still living off this inheritance of analysis of function, but it is a very incomplete inheritance and, except in the case of hospital design, remarkably little has been added to it for a generation

Instead, in the meantime, 'function' has come to mean, not use of the building, but use of its structure and materials. It is possible now to write about form following function and confine oneself entirely to discussion of structure and materials; indeed it has been done. Architecture with a capital A has become more and more interested in itself, and less and less interested in the world that uses it. (Hence we get a term with connotations of functionalism, like 'universal space', meaning great undifferentiated areas that are an excuse for using dramatic trusses; such space, far from approaching universality of use, works out badly for almost any kind of use other than big auditoriums, and is less adaptable to a variety of needs than a row of old brownstone houses!) When architecture concentrates ever more narrowly on its own devices, and gets farther away from interest in the world that uses it, it becomes narcissistic, and that shows. Like all things that get far from the truth, it has to begin saying sensational things – about itself, because it has nothing else to talk about

In a very similar way, the more elaborate and ambitious pedestrian and town-centre schemes inform us insistently about themselves and their own novelty and cleverness. But they do not inform us about the variety and vitality and intricacy and opportunity and adaptability of prospering cities. They ignore – and even warp and thwart – the means by which cities generate the diversity that we call urbanity. Insofar as most of these schemes do draw upon the world outside themselves, they depend heavily on assumptions drawn from two very limited themes: suburban shopping centres and parks. There is a great hollowness where there should be a rich

store of understanding about the complex functioning of cities and their streets

I suggest that the way out is, first, to admit that we are not yet ready for grandiose or very radical schemes for rescuing city pedestrians. We have not done our homework. To do it, and simultaneously accomplish something, we should start quite humbly. We should start simply by giving direct, very functional and obvious consideration to pedestrians. And this should be done in precisely the places where pedestrians already appear in large numbers in spite of the inconveniences they meet and the impositions to which they are subjected. Some of these humble improvements which immediately suggest themselves are: more frequent places to cross the streets; widened sidewalks (i.e. a bigger share of the road bed); more sidewalk trees; niches for standing outside the line of foot-traffic. To be sure, all such immediate, direct, functional aids to city pedestrians compete with convenience for automobiles. This is one of many truths about cities which have been too long evaded, but it cannot be evaded. Nor is it so terrifying a truth, even from the point of view of the automobile, when we realize that automobiles themselves are victimized direly by their own redundancy and that this redundancy feeds on the very palliatives conventionally intended to accommodate and relieve it

As for visual help to the pedestrian, the most direct and sensible guidance of which I know comes from Gordon Cullen's book, 'Townscape'. As Cullen demonstrates to the respectful mind, the most interesting visual ideas are suggested out of the unique reality that already exists, but needs pointing up. The Cullen approach is the very opposite of design narcissism, because the loved object is the place already existing and the purpose is to enhance its nature. The variety of visual observations and ideas in Cullen's book is astounding, and yet even this is only a beginning of the possibilities, because the variety and intricacy of real city is endless, and the means for clarifying and celebrating it are infinite. Conscious attempts at this could not possibly look like the tiresomely repeated shopping-mall cliché nor like scenery for 'The War of the Worlds'. And wouldn't that be a boon

PITTSBURGH NORTHSIDE

JOHN ALEXANDROWICZ

LONDON

ROGER MAYNE

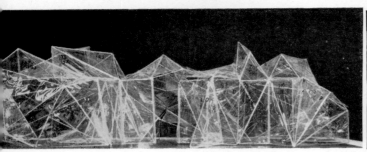

LIVING CITY

WARREN CHALK
PETER COOK
DENNIS CROMPTON
BEN FETHER
DAVID GREENE
RON HERRON
PETER TAYLOR
MICHAEL WEBB

116

PART I

Architecture is only a small part of city environment in terms of real significance, the total environment is what is important, what really matters. Our object is to determine the effect this total environment has on the human condition, the responses it generates; we are trying to capture, to express, the vitality of the city, a vitality we must perpetuate, or the city will die at the hands of the hard planners and architect aesthetes

'LIVING CITY' is not so much a display of data on city planning as a happening, an experience. It is not a blue-print for a city, architecture is not in evidence here, our aim is to capture a mood, a climate of opinion, to examine the phenomena of city life, to condition the spectator into an awareness of himself, his attitudes, and the significance of the throw-away environment around him

'LIVING CITY' takes the form of a complete structure, an organism designed to condition the spectator by cutting him off from the everyday situation, where things are seen in a predictable and accepted relation-

Part I of LIVING CITY describes the exhibition—experience of the same title at the Institute of Contemporary Arts, London, July/August, 1963. Many of the illustrations are from the same exhibit

ship. This city simulator is a conditioning chamber, like the corner of some giant brain or analogic computer, and has compartments we have called 'Gloops'. Each gloop defines an area of basic constant and reasonably predictable fact. MAN, SURVIVAL, CROWD, MOVEMENT, COMMUNICATION, PLACE, SITUATION. All contributing and interacting on one another and sum totalling to 'LIVING CITY'

MAN GLOOP—City is an organism housing man, man made, for man. We have tried to determine the characteristics of man in the future. What will his ultimate development be? Presumably he will still be in control to operate the mechanism, to activate the switch, he will still be at the centre of things

Because of the difficulty of expressing the unknown we depict man pushed to the extreme limit of known advancement in one particular sphere—the astronaut. At the same time we trace man's preconception of this area of advancement. The robot figure that opened 'This is Tomorrow' at the Whitechapel Gallery 1956 has been superseded by today's spaceman, the nearest man has yet come to realising the ideal SUPERMAN dream, the ultimate in physical and mental development

The presented images are however only significant as ideas' generators at a moment in time; ideally the images would constantly change, clocking up every conceivable permutation, a visual ideas indicator, an awareness stimulator, subject—man in living city

SURVIVAL GLOOP—Cities have been laid down by man since the beginning of time in order that he may survive. Survival in-city is big business, conditioning man pays dividends—buys speed, horsepower, happiness. Each man to his own survival kit, the artifacts of adjustment and escape and it's all throw-away, nothing matters any more than anything else, importance shifts key at every step. Man in-city will always have a survival kit—food, drink, sex, drugs, clothes, cars, make-up, money, in order to live, and survival conditions the living city

CROWD GLOOP—An indication of the kaleidoscopic coming together of all manner and types of man and the way in which they interact upon each other in the shared experience of living city

Crowd gloop indicates the importance of recognising the social whirl, the cosmopolitan scene, the structure of community, the influence of 'family' and 'togetherness', of commuters and consumers, of man as individual, as groups or as anonymous crowd. There is a continual feed-back process going on in terms of social patterns, occupation index, organisational and group activity that must condition the packaging of these activities, shape up the space in a specific way, providing significant city environment

MOVEMENT GLOOP—Here is an attempt to examine the significance of the conceptual sense of movement in-city, which gives a certain kind of form and value to otherwise vacant and static spaces. Our contention is that a knowledge of and interest in the movement of people and things is essential to an understanding of the nature of living city

Human movement is determined by biological

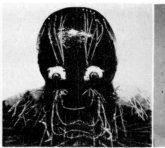

factors and depends on the structure of bones, joints and muscles. An individual's age, sex, height, weight and other constitutional factors determine to a great extent the duration and speed of the movements he can make. On analysis, body movement is an enormously complex mechanism allowing for spontaneous movement. Gesture, the free action of walking, running, jumping, climbing, help to determine patterns of action in the city

Climate, emotions, physical circumstances or the impact of other people, influence human movement in-city. The point of origin or destination, direction, speed and route taken by individuals or crowds are informative in determining objective movement-cycles

Objective movement cycles can be classified; ie directed movement, purpose movement, multi-directional movement and psychological movement etc. The overall configuration of mass movement is also significant in predicting the behaviour patterns of man in motion. These patterns have the effect of splitting and isolating known city environments in loosely defined but distinct areas and movement between is limited or changing. We have become increasingly dependent on motivation in the city. The flow, high speed/medium/slow speed, stop-go

movement of traffic is an exciting aspect of the living city, and important in determining its future mood and appropriate form

COMMUNICATIONS GLOOP – One of the outstanding characteristics of our time is a deep and pervasive concern with communications. It is communications as a social dynamic, as experience rather than physical fact that concerns us here, as a basic concept in formulating ideas of future city

The foreseeable rapid rate of change in transportation method may eventually make invalid the concept of a rigid mobile communications network as the main urban structure, as the framework for laying down the pattern of city. A whole area of study is open for experiment on expendable systems and more flexible technology in terms of communication networks. Static communications are becoming increasingly important in so far as they may be exploited to produce new concepts in city planning. Large organisations will control their own visual communications network allowing for a city centre control with satellites dispersed in constant touch with the communication centre no longer dependent on physical communication. This may result in a revaluation of the accepted city centre format and allow for greater spread and integration of disparate

'use classes' easing the commuter problem, making feasible a 'work-at-home' situation

PLACE GLOOP – The intelligibility of built environment, the content, use and arrangement of space in the city is the theme of 'Place'. In the city as centres tend to become more and more similar to each other so their success and identity will be lost. Architecture alone cannot achieve this feeling of 'place', it is the total environment that is important and we are concerned with capturing the mood, the special quality that identifies one place from another

The built environment and the manner in which it is manipulated can define certain kinds of space but this alone is not enough to give it identity, it is the content and the use that is important

SITUATION GLOOP – Situation concerns the state of change and unpredictability within city environment due to the fluctuating come/go of people and things over a time scale. Situation – the happenings within spaces in the city, the transient throw-away objects, the passing presence of people and cars are key factors in creating a solution which is of the living city

Below left: Plan of Exhibition
Below right: Section of Exhibition

117

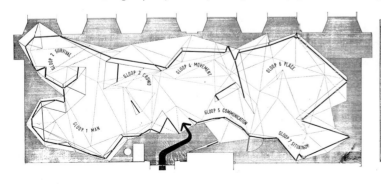

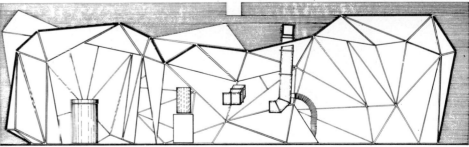

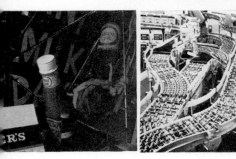

THE NATURE OF THE LIVING CITY

What have cities been doing over the few thousand years in which they have existed?

They have provided society with a physical centre – a place where so much is happening that one activity is stimulated by all the rest. It is the collection of everything and everyone into a tight space that has enabled the cross stimulus to continue. Trends originated in cities. The mood of cities is frantic. It is

all happening – all the time. However decadent society may be, it is reflected most clearly and demonstratively in the metropolitan way of life

In old cities, however, there comes a time when the cycle of interaction and regeneration has become so established as a pattern that the true reason for their existence is clouded over. There is the obvious aggregate of a metropolis: palaces, places of government or control, monuments, symbols of an established centre; but these are not the vital part of cities. They can go on existing despite the latest tendencies in the development of the rest of the place. The thread connecting the city state of Athens with present-day New York is not that they both possess such monuments, but that they share the coming together of many minds, and they are vital

We are seeking the living city

When we try to continue a city in physical terms, we tend to start from the assumption that there are certain basics of living, and that there is a single way of providing for these at any one time. Our cities extend and regenerate spaces by way of bricks and mortar and roads and sewers; and people are inside somewhere. We hope that the city will catch up somehow. If we build into this brief 'qualities' or provision for things beyond, it becomes a forced or deliberate environment. Architects, particularly the better ones, attempt to feed their buildings into the culture that holds them – into the symbolic hierarchy of palace – church – workplace – community – street – house. They attempt to perpetuate a lasting culture and yet they use the vocabulary of the moment (or possibly the just previous moment). It would seem that buildings must last even if their methodology will be unable to

'Fashion' is a dirty word, so is the word 'Temporary' so is 'Flashy'. Yet it is the creation of those things that are necessarily fashionable, temporary or flashy that has more to do with the vitality of cities than 'monument-building'. The pulsation of city life is fast, so why not that of its environment? It reflects rise and fall, coming and going . . . change, so why not build for this?

A pattern of ways and means has to exist: communications, services and facilities must be there as a form of ground base to the city that spreads over them, but they should be as physically capable as possible, not tied to standards produced by outworn

scales or values. The living, vibrating crust of the city must regenerate in its own terms. The only way to create cities – or within cities – is to stop pretending about the significance of 'Architects' Architecture'; for by hanging on to the comfort of such a context for recreating the living city we are opting out of the struggle to maintain it. We shall find instead a vast suburb without any cities, and in it the odd pocket of architects building their own houses – no longer involved

Whatever else it has been, the work on 'Living City' is a first laboratory experiment in the analysis of a very elusive subject, with a communication about the experiment (the exhibition) and a summary at a staging-point (the necessity to define and explain the exhibition by a fixed date). The process so far has been to dig beneath the normal planning-theory paraphernalia in order to capture and recreate a mood – the key mood of the vitality of cities

The definition so far is that man is the ultimate subject and the principal conditioner, so that the exhibition is a mirror of man himself. Cutting across normal hierarchies of what is 'rated' by planners and intellectuals, the objects and images used to convey the idea tended more and more to reinforce the designers' first viewpoint: that cities achieve their

unique spirit through the interaction of people, once those people have a vital, perhaps even frantically vital, background

PART 2

The next phase is a move outwards from the definition to a much larger study: that of city regeneration. A series of investigations into regeneration patterns, building and timescale, movement and interchange, conditioned environments, expendability, population impulse (all of which link back to the exhibition as a baseline), is under way. This stage is recognised as being a much longer process. The investigation is an outward-moving thing leading perhaps to a series of physical proposals, almost certainly to a series of idea proposals; but of what? Almost certainly patterns will emerge. So far the suspicion is that there may be a city-type-unit or organisation that might apply equally to regenerating existing cities and to finite cities that will have real vitality from the beginning

Preliminary to further study, schemes are shown which relate back to the outlook at the moment of the group. Of these COMEGO II and INTER-CHANGE are to some extent complementary

COMEGO II illustrates several principles:

Basically, that the city is a dense crust throughout, in which family life and 'centre activities' – quality shopping, work, shows, meeting-places – are able to go in the same district – in fact at exactly the same place

Timescales are an important factor: the lifespans being:

Housing-group organisation	50 years
Housing-unit organisation	20 years
Housing-appliances and components	5 years
Centre activities organisation	50 years
Shopping groups	10 years
Shops	3 years
Commodity handling	daily

This results in the provision of a 'plug-in' system of housing and shop units. These need permanent cranes and crane-ways in order to function. These are also a primary servicing element

Movement is three-dimensional – diagonal and on several different (and changing) levels, it is then not only able to segregate, but is flexible and able to absorb user-change

The conditioned environment for this project is put over the 'centre-activities' only. The actual level at which conditioned environment is really needed will be one of the principal studies

Local enclosed open space is another topic, in this project it is towards the top of the housing groups, but the whole problem of 'local' and 'non-local' as an idea needs much more investigation

The shop units are seen as an extension of the packaging system of today

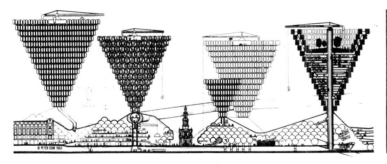

Far left: Comego 2-Project: Peter Cook
Left: Plastic unit

119

CITY INTERCHANGE–PROJECT

Communication interchange – first step to Living City. The knot – node point for static and motivated communication complex

Rail – public transit interchange – long distance and inter-regional rapid transit using linear induction motor propelled trains
Inter-city electric underground ring
Sub-underground inter-centre links and outer metropolis commuter services

Road – north/south – east/west communication cross-over and interchange for feeder roads off express trunk routes skirting metropolis

Mass transit express bus turn-about
Car and bus long and short term underground parking

Air – heliport and hovercar station connecting to supersonic air travel port on perimeter of outer metropolis
Services – service line control station for inter-regional distribution
Pedestrian – high speed vertical lift interchange links within interchange station amenity arena
Horizontal low speed travelator and escalator arteries radiate out to periphery
Static communications control centre
Towers – suspended from central masts containing services
Tower groups contain electronic data transmission, traffic control and administration, radio-telephone tower, communication and news service relay station, inter-commercial closed circuit television hook ups, public television and telstar rediffusion centre

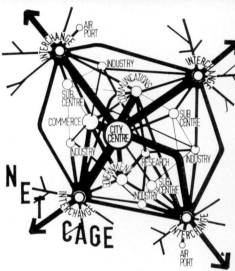

NET CAGE

120

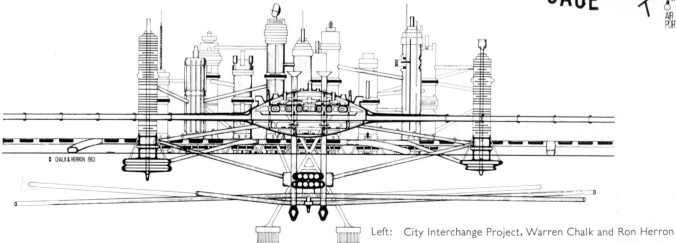

© CHALK & HERRON 1963

Left: City Interchange Project, Warren Chalk and Ron Herron

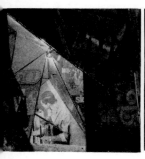

SPIDER WEBB SPECIAL

Chemcor: a glass sheet as flexible and as strong as steel yet considerably lighter. Glass produced by treating outer surfaces so that 'prestressed' layers are formed. 'Whiskers' of silicon nitride used to reinforce aluminium. Plastics which can resist a 10,000°F flame, twice as long as a comparable piece of steel

Crashing world population exceeding 5,000 million by year A.D. 2000 perhaps curtailed by nuclear war simulating the results of over population in any region. United States Air Force to spend $49,000 on research into a technique for growing plastics structures in space. Scientists have found they can make articles thirty times greater in size than their ingredients by adding two reactive and foaming chemicals together. When in space the capsules, fired by rockets, could be sprayed into a pretreated plastics mould and left to react by age, solar rays or even cosmic rays. Space platforms including meteorite

bumpers, bridges and solar power collectors could be made from a few cylinders of material

Development of Tensegrity structures: systems whereby compression members are held apart from each other by means of tension wires that redirect stress along the axis of the member. Research suggests use of tension membranes which theoretically allow length of compression member to be reduced to molecular spacing of membrane particles

I have given you some facts and pictures which have illustrated the social and scientific developments of the middle of the twentieth century and I shall ask you to correlate them into producing your own idea of the future environment rather than accepting mine

In your mind you were doing that, while reading the facts and looking at the pictures. If you read a novel a mental image is built up of the heroine which is far more beautiful than any illustrator's feminine ideal

The vision you need to realize what ought to happen (as against what will happen) is of far greater complexity than when Sant Elia and Le Corbusier set down their dream cities of the future. The unknowns of social and political events were similar, but the rate of scientific discovery and development is multiplying at a vast pace owing to world wars and the space race

I feel it is essential for designers to do this; to sense the nature of the things to come so that they can orientate themselves accordingly. The demands of scientific understanding, of thinking on a world scale and of the pooling of mental resources imposed on the designer by the new materials, new techniques of mass production of components and the revolution of social ideals will never be met with the present organization

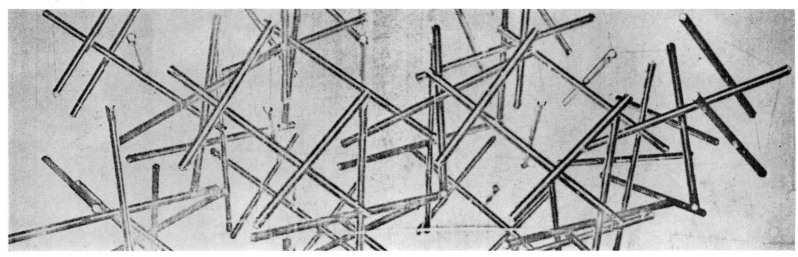

THE HISTORY OF NOTHING

EDUARDO PAOLOZZI

Four stills from 'The History of Nothing 1961/62'
A 12½ minute 16 m/m film made with the facilities of
the Television School of the Royal College of Art,
London

1 Monopoli

2 Polignano al Mare

3 Andria

4 Brindisi Kastell

124

MATMATA

HERMAN HAAN

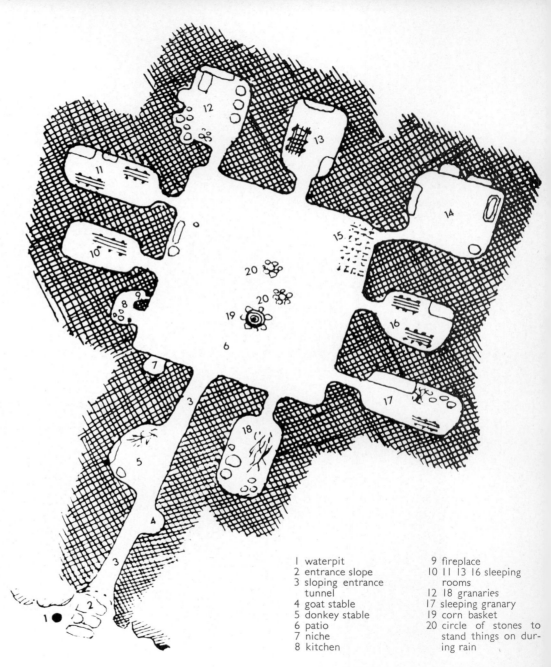

Matmata, a tableland of the northern Sahara, a plateau covered with a deep hard layer of clay, a hot desolate place where only a few drops of rain fall each year, or none at all

The Matmata people say: only once in about seven years will enough rain fall to fill our waterpits: and sometimes it happens that, even after seven years, the rain will still stay away. When this happens the Matmata people have to move, and wait for the blessing

Then they move back again, and stay because their forefathers did, and because they love the place and their ancient timeless homes

When you approach a Matmata hamlet on the desert plateau you see nothing but small elevations at the bottom of an excavation some 40 ft long, wide, and deep, a negative cube. Several of these cubes, interconnected, form a village. The cube is the patio of a house, surrounded by dug out underground spaces, somewhat in the form of bottles

These spaces are sleeping rooms, reception rooms, granaries, stables, and a kitchen. Each of these hollowed out and vaulted cave spaces is covered by some 30 ft of clay, which gives the best protection

1 waterpit	9 fireplace
2 entrance slope	10 11 13 16 sleeping
3 sloping entrance	rooms
tunnel	12 18 granaries
4 goat stable	17 sleeping granary
5 donkey stable	19 corn basket
6 patio	20 circle of stones to
7 niche	stand things on dur-
8 kitchen	ing rain

against the almost unbearable summer heat of the desert. Each Matmata family has a patio dwelling of this kind, with its sequence of rooms, as well as workshops and even oil presses, and most of the dwellings have underground intercommunication tunnels between them. No wonder this region was one of the important places of resistance in southern Tunisia during the struggle for independence

The photograph above shows a series of rooms opening on to the patio of a Matmata house. In the shadow on the left is a doorway into the kitchen, and the small round hole in the wall beside it is the fireplace. The opening in the corner goes into the food granary; in front of it, in the soil, is a hollow for pounding spices. Between the kitchen and the granary is the area for corn grinding and sieving. Directly in front of us is grandfather's sleeping room, and at the right is an upstairs granary with a raw palm tree trunk as its staircase

It is good to be in such a simple, effective house. In the photograph on the right above we see the main entrance to the patio with its upward sloping tunnel. The clay has an olive colour which contrasts wonderfully with the brilliant blue ceiling formed by the sky

Aisha is posing beside the corn basket standing on flat stones which will protect it from rain, and water draining through the sloping tunnel; a crazy idea, for there is almost never any rain – but you never know

In the desert plain beneath the Matmata tableland you find the Gorfa villages. These villages have been built by the Matmata people to help solve their food problems. Long ago they found on these sites deep water veins, and they dug wells to the water level, sometimes 200 ft below the surface of the earth, and began drawing up the precious liquid by means of leather watersacks (guerbas) tied to a long rope pulled all day and night by camels. Gardens have been laid out in the desert, an artificial oasis made fertile by a careful system of irrigation channels (sequias). As might be imagined, the harvest had to be protected against nomads who lived in worse conditions, so these people built fortified villages near the gardens

There was no timber to speak of, so they built with clay and water, making cells of loam with arches and barrel vaults, opening on to a central square. Thus the closed outside walls formed a defence

Within the square, the lower vaults or cells are used as dwellings, and the upper ones are granaries, reached by steps and landings. Understanding the structural strength of the eggshell and the honeycomb, they built during centuries more and more cells superimposed one above the other to form a veritable fortress with the minimum of material

The round hole beside each entrance door is at once a window, a chimney, and a keyhole through which an arm must be inserted to get the big wooden key into the wooden lock. Clay stairs go up, but it is impossible to reach every door, particularly the doors to the food granaries, so you have to jump from stair to small balcony, and from there to perhaps another small stair; not always too comfortable an experience, but its a clear recognition of a primary condition of defence. After all, where before there was just a piece of desert, now there are gardens and a village, thanks to water and clay and to the Matmata who used them

THE DOGON AND THE TELLEM

HERMAN HAAN

THE HOUSE IS THE BELLY OF THE MOTHER

on the southern border of the saharan desert
some 200 miles south of old Tombouctou
the flat african soil slopes upward
the eastern end of this rocky plateau
sheers down some 1,000 feet
or more
an inhospitable high cliff
more than 100 miles long
in a barren hot country

looking up from below
the rock is densely perforated with
caves often forming horizontal galleries
now look closer
and discover geometric forms
in many of these caves
look closely and everywhere you look you will
find them
near the foot
near the top

these conic structures
belong to the tellem
so say the dogon, the people who live here

in the beginning of the world
the soil belonged to the yeban spirits
who live in the earth
small people with big heads and red hair
normal men can't see them
the yeban taught the tellem
how to build a house
preparing clay and then making bricks and
throwing a rope in the air
they strapped up the bricks
and they climbed and clambered as termites do
along the ropes to the caves

thus the tellem
made houses
in a conic form
which is a particularly strong form
related to the little clay they could afford
the walls are never thicker than 2 or 3 inches

cabinets and granaries have circular entrances
doors did not exist in the time of the tellem
openings were locked
by filling them up with clay

the main buildings are sometimes covered with
a thin layer of fine wet clay
and in this wet layer they made with their fingers
structures and symbols the meanings of which
are still a mystery to us
if we cannot read their language
we can read the size of the hollowings
which is the size of their fingers
they are very small

on the floor of the cave in the rock
are sometimes other very smooth and deep hollowings
here the tellem ground their corn for generations
patiently over centuries

other caves were necropoles
where they buried their dead
in squatting posture

dead?

no say the dogon
the tellem are still alive
but you cannot see them
they can make themselves big and small
and they can enter their caves in the cliffside
with one enormous step

sometimes they come back
mostly in the night
and when you find a foreleg of a goat
and some millet pap on a rock
it means the tellem were back
and the harvest will be bad this year

looking down from the tellem caves
you find scattered along the foot of the cliffs
the dogon villages
built on the pyramid of blocklike stones
which came down by erosion

on one side of the village the endless
central african bush
on the other side the precipitous protecting rock wall

metropoles of clay and stone protected
by the sometimes 240 feet of overhanging rock wall
a dwelling place consists of a cluster
of granaries and stone walls surrounding
a more or less circular patio
beyond which are a small kitchen
and the sleeping houses
only used in the short rain period
for the dogon living–sleeping–cooking room
is the patio
shadowed by the rock

the first building in a dogon village
is the 'togu na'
this is the old men's palaver place and

situated on the best location for
overlooking the whole village it
integrates old age in the community rather
better than we do

the roof is covered by a thick layer
of millet branches
ensuring the best possible insulation
for old age is not only integrated
in communal life by the 'togu na'
but also in mind

the dwelling is the belly of the mother
said good old 'pangam-say'

of the village of 'pegué'
and so it is

tell me something about these round clay forms
I asked my friend 'diankouno-dolo'
of the village of 'ogul-dounyou'
round forms? he asked
yes round forms, I said
now I don't understand you, diankouno said

well, I said, look at that house,
those are not round forms, diankouno said
they are all square forms
for what you see are tender forms

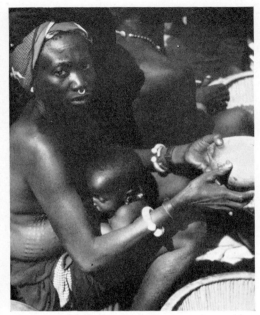

this is the shape of clay
and it is the shape of a hand
and a hand follows the shape of clay
and clay follows the shape of a hand
hands can't follow a rectangle

tender forms
water is tender
clay forms are tender
water can follow tender forms
tender forms accompany water

that's why tender forms are good forms
and nice

why should you caress your tender wife
and not your home

home is the belly of the mother
pangam-say said
home is for babies

home is for children
home is for women
home is for men

there is also a home for the spirits
the spirits of ancestors
inside there is food and there are oil pots
and small ladders carved in wood
giving access to the atmosphere

round the door are painted symbols
most of them are symbols of the serpent
which is the symbol of 'Lébé'

Amma the creator of all things
the earth heaven animals trees ghosts
last of all created a man and a woman
the man was Lébé, the ancestor of humanity

they had children and grandchildren
there were eighty men, eighty dogons
the eighty patriarchs of humanity
they lived in a country in the very south
the country of Mandé
where life was good
because nobody died
old people changed into Yéban spirits
one day a woman saw the mask dances
of the 'Andoumboulou' ghosts
shortly afterwards Lébé died

Lébé was the first man and the first dead man
life in Mandé got worse
the dogon decided to leave the country
but not without the corpse of Lébé
they opened his grave but they did not find his corpse
they found there a living serpent
the reincarnation of Lébé
who followed the exodus of the dogon
to the far high cliff

since that time people have died
and every man gets his obsequial ceremony
during three nights and two days
bang the shots of the old guns
one hundred times repeated by the echo of the cliff

some months after the burying
the spirits of the deceased
swarm around the village
he is in danger now

specially his 'nyama'

nyama resides in a man's blood
nyama is his best part
nyama is why he is specially he
it is what makes him
different from all others

perhaps the dead man had enemies in his lifetime
certainly he was a hunter
he killed animals for food
but animals also have nyama
and after death the body is gone
and there are differences in size
between bodies
but no difference in the size of nyamas
no not at all
a nyama of even a sparrow
is equal to one of a man
so his nyama is in danger

but then comes the day of the 'dama'
and the masks come out of the secret caves
and dance a wild dance
to save the nyama of the dead
against the other nyamas
and to bring him to the world of his ancestors

the mask of 'kanaga' the bird of prey
is an important one
he hovers and dives

often the symbol of kanaga appears
on the facades of granaries
and sanctuaries

the symbol of kanaga
is one of the most powerful symbols
in the dogon's world of myth

the mask 'sirige'
is the mask of 'the' house
the house of the first eighty
ancestors of humanity
the mask is twenty or twenty-five feet tall
and holes in the mask represent this house

he dances and turns and bows over
the participants of the dama
the house of the first ancestors of humanity
covers the whole world

the 'ginna' house
is the house of the patriarch
a sacred place
and its facade represents again
the eighty ancestors of humanity

inside there is the altar of Amma, god
often the altar of both good and bad

the sanctum of magic rituals
witnessed by statues carved in wood
which have their own secret forces
and can heal illnesses or revenge injustice

ginna houses sometimes have carved wooden doors
representing the sun
ancestors
millet seeds distributed to the clan by the patriarch
are breasts
but these breasts do not represent fertility
or femininity
they represent the cover of the heart
the heart of the patriarch
who remains always in the ginna

THE HOUSE IS THE BELLY OF THE MOTHER
said old pangam-say of the village of pegué
yes yes

TWO SCULPTURES

WILLIAM TURNBULL

142   **RITE**
1955/62 bronze and ebony
height: 58½ in (148.5 cm)

HANNIBAL
1955 bronze and rosewood
height: 58 in (147 cm)

143

FOUR RELIEFS

BEN NICHOLSON

1   Relief. May 56 (Ioy)

2   White relief, Aegina January 63
$33\frac{1}{2} \times 40\frac{7}{8}$ in (85 × 102 cm)

3   Relief. January 62 (Arahneon).
Project for rel ef wall

4   Free Standing relief wall at Documenta III,
Kassel, Germany, 1964. 4 × 15 metres

145

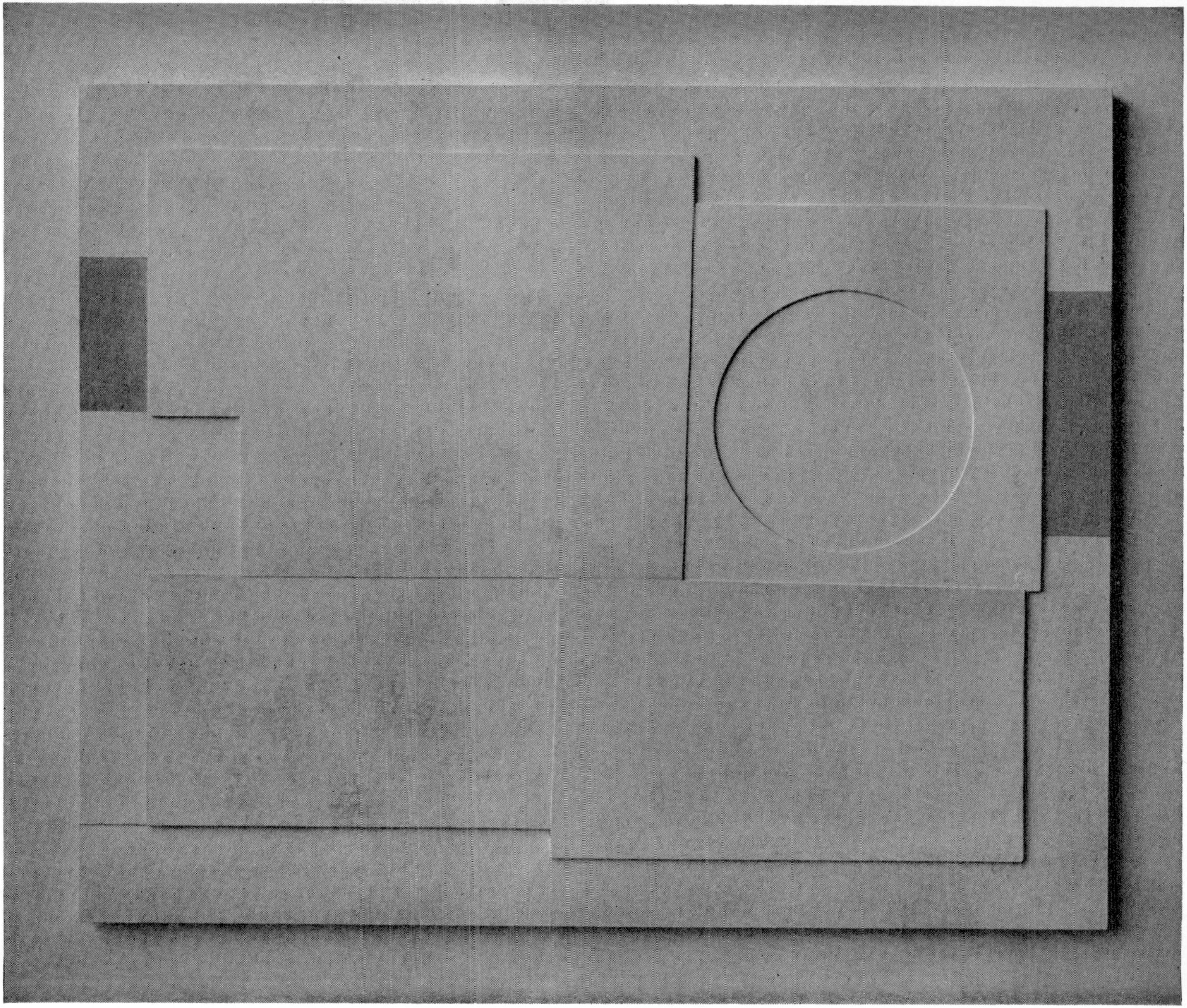

TEPOZTLAN:
NATIVE GENIUS IN TOWN PLANNING

ELEANOR SMITH MORRIS

We have become more and more aware of the maturity of indigenous architecture, but not enough aware that this maturity is very often carried over into popular town planning. Some of the few remaining examples of native genius in the building of communities are found in isolated villages of countries where the rural population is relatively unaffected by the demands of the twentieth century. In the province of Morelos, Mexico, lies such a village, Tepoztlan, which has preserved its special character from its Aztec beginnings through the Spanish Conquest to the present day. Anthropologists[1] and others have long travelled to Mexico just to study Tepoztlan's almost static nature, as Tepoztlan is both typical and yet outstanding among the many

[1] See Robert Redfield, 'Tepoztlan–a Mexican Village', 1930 (University of Chicago Press). My account is based on the study done in 1951 by Oscar Lewis, 'Life in a Mexican Village: Tepoztlan Restudied' (University of Illinois Press), and a visit to Tepoztlan in 1960, when the photographs were taken

Right: Built by the Dominicans in the sixteenth century the cathedral and convent are sited off the Main Plaza

self-sufficient Mexican villages tucked away in their isolated mountain valleys

Tepoztlan lies about sixty miles south of Mexico City, surrounded by rugged mountainous countryside whose cliffs hang over Tepoztlan. The village sits on the edge of these cliffs, about 5,000 ft in altitude, and commands magnificent views both up to the spectacular peaks and out over the bowl. Sited on a slope, the upper part is several hundred feet higher than the southern part

TEPOZTLAN: CLUSTER PATTERN

In urban form Tepoztlan is typical of the many Mexican rural communities making their living from agriculture. About two-thirds of the inhabitants of Mexico live in communities having less than 2,500 inhabitants. Most Mexican farmers live in a village and travel back and forth between the village and their farms in order to carry on their agricultural activities. Hence almost every morning there is an exodus from the village to the fields, and in the afternoon a reverse migration. Since a Mexican village consists principally of farm families, a community of 2,500 inhabitants usually will not contain more

than a half-dozen families who are completely divorced from agriculture

The village pattern of settlement thus consists of clusters of dwellings, as against a linear-village pattern found in some rural settlement patterns of other countries, such as Japan. The advantages of the Mexican cluster villages are mainly for social and security purposes. The cluster form has its origins in the Aztec tradition of the land-holding village owning land communally. A tribe consisting of a number of clans lived closely together in a village. The area of communal land surrounding the village was known as the 'town land' (alterpetlalli), and included agricultural land, timber land and hunting grounds. The village also owned the water rights, as well as land set aside for public purposes. Land for the town and land for farming was governed by the angle of the sun and the slope of the land. Sunny hillsides were reserved for agriculture; while the shady spots were set aside for public lands and clusters of dwellings Clusters of large walled courtyards housed the extended families or clans of Aztec society. These courtyards were distributed upon a regular system of intersecting streets which, when the topography allowed, became a complete grid-iron pattern. This intention is apparent in the plan of Tepoztlan

URBAN CHARACTER

The village is about one mile and a quarter in length by almost a mile in width. It contains roughly a population of 4,000 people living on 662 house sites, whose houses are separated by low walls enclosing the courtyards. The walls are low enough both to see on to the street and be seen from the street. Very few of the houses are contained by high walls in the Spanish manner

The Aztec intention of rational development and orderly communal life is still reflected in the division of the village into clan areas. There are seven self-governing precincts of the Aztec village, called barrios. The Spaniards cleverly did not disrupt this physical organization, but merely gave each barrio its own church in addition to the main cathedral in the central plaza

The streets, running north and south, slope steeply and when it rains these streets become full streams. Thus it was to avoid erosion that the Aztecs evolved the system of terracing with stone paving in a series of inclined ramps and platforms. The east and west streets are left as rough footpaths with streams and gorges cutting across at irregular intervals. The main road from Cuernavaca is paved, and the central plaza

149

Above: Tepoztlan on slope

Left: The cobbled Aztec streets and pavements rest below the mammoth cliffs

Next page: The Aztec inclined ramp leads on to its platform and then to another ramp. These ramped streets are valuable as ancient prototypes of urban forms now being used for new pedestrian areas and upper-level decks

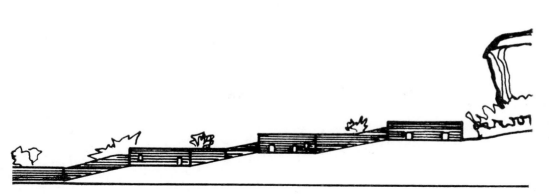

The better type of Indian house is the adobe dwelling, roofed with red tiles, but still with earthen floors or occasionally brick ones. The adobe dwelling contains one or two rooms, of solid walls except for the single opening of the doorway. Each door opens on to the patio, where often the kitchen has been added as a kind of lean-to. A sleeping porch across the front of the house is usually made by extending the roof and supporting it with brick columns

The jacales are more congested than the adobe houses. Each occupied jacal hut room will have on average, five persons, while the adobe houses contain two persons per room or four or five in two rooms

The few Spanish houses shield themselves behind high outer walls protected from the street by iron-work and heavy shutters. These houses are of brick or stone covered with plaster and are whitewashed

has been flatly laid out by the conquering Spanish colonists

It is the Aztec cobbled streets which give the village its special interest. The inclined ramps require some effort for the pedestrian but certainly not even half the effort that steps would demand. The street becomes a sequence of energy and rest, energy and rest. Visually the ramps are extremely exciting. When one is at the bottom of a long ramp the views from the next platform cannot be seen and therefore the platform's view comes as a pleasant surprise

The vertical incline of the ramp forces the eye to see constant variations in the village scene, much as a slightly curved road shows off the changing horizontal view

The Hispanic conquest left its imprint on Tepoztlan. First the Spaniards laid out the traditional square plaza around which are grouped the important civic buildings. These include the court house and the school house. A small public park adjoins the plaza and encloses its own bandstand beneath shade trees. Between the civic buildings and the plaza is the shopping street or Portales. The shops are in an arcade affording protection from the sun and rain

As was their custom, on the plaza the Spaniards built a large sixteenth-century cathedral and convert, a handsome Baroque building, with walls more than 13 ft thick, sited on high ground overlooking the village

Since the Spaniards, services have been the main addition to the village. In 1902, public street fountains were carefully placed at important street corners. These numerous public fountains are now serving a few of the dwellings. Many of the fountains

are covered by beautifully curved clay and cement vault roofs topped by a cross

TEPOZTLAN: HOUSES

Houses in Tepoztlan are of three kinds – the primitive jacal, the adobe house and the Spanish style house near the plaza. The jacal and the adobe house both are Indian. The jacal is made of cornstalks (Mexican bamboo) tied together with vines in a somewhat flimsy structure with a thatched roof and a dirt floor. There are no windows and the only opening is the doorway. The jacal structure usually is gabled in contrast to the adobe house where the one long sloping roof is preferred. The jacal is the indigenous answer to the problem of living in a hot and wet climate. The thatched roof sheds the rain, while the vertical cornstalks allow cooling breezes to blow through the hut

The jacal, in many parts of southern Mexico, provides housing for more than half the population. Very often the jacal is part of a compound of cornstalk dwellings, each unit serving a particular purpose. One jacal is the kitchen, another is the storage dwelling, another is the sleeping quarters for the parents and the young children, while others may be sleeping units for the older children. The entire compound is surrounded by a cornstalk fence. In the kitchen jacal, moulded low adobe tables serve as the cooking hearth while stone three-legged metates of pre-Columbian designs are used in grinding the corn. A decided advantage of the compound of huts is its flexibility. When one sleeping hut is outworn, another hut is built nearby and the old hut burned to the ground

TEPOZTLAN: FUTURE

Although Tepoztlan is on a cul-de-sac from Cuernavaca, modern services are appearing more and more in the village and can't help but slowly change its character. We would hope that the Aztec ramped streets would remain. These ramped streets are an important form for modern urban planners to study, and to reconsider as ancient prototypes for new pedestrian areas

Native genius has indeed shown itself in Tepoztlan, in the Indians' choice of a sloping location with magnificent views, a well-organized plan and most interesting of all, the use of the stone cobbled ramps

Above left: Aztec system of ramps

Below: Public fountain

151

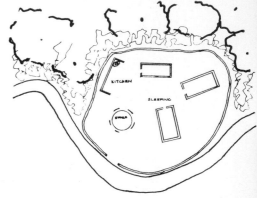

152

Left: This dwelling compound contains the kitchen on the left, storage in the centre, and living quarters on the right

Above: Plan of jacales

Below left: The flimsy kitchen jacal of Mexican bamboo shelters the moulded adobe hearth

Below: The cuescomatl, plastered inside and out with clay, is used for storing corn

Above left: The main sleeping jacal is the largest dwelling in the compound

Below left: A new jacal is freshly thatched

Below: The roof structure of the jacal is held in place by knotted twine

153

Above left: The worn-out sleeping jacal has been burned and is replaced by this new hut with its Latin cross of thatch

Below left: Diego Rivera designed these guest houses deriving their forms from the cuescomatl or storage dwellings. Note that the tapered form prevents rodents from climbing in while the thatched roof sheds rain

Below: Tepoztlan is 60 miles south of Mexico City in a mountainous region some 5,000-6,000 ft in altitude

154

MARGARET GRENFELL
DIEGO ROBLES RIVAS

155

The industrial revolution has come to Peru. It has created an economic and social unbalance by forming highly industrialized pockets within a country which is poor and underdeveloped; and because of this unbalance, the population is quite literally on the move. People are leaving their home communities where they have houses but little else, and are travelling, sometimes for hundreds of kilometres, and on foot, to those urban centres which they think can provide them with work and a living wage

Migration from the hinterland to the large coastal cities is traditional in Peru, but the almost total concentration of economic and political power and opportunism in the coastal cities, particularly in Lima, during the last twenty or thirty years has touched off vastly increased migrations. For example, probably 50 per cent of Lima's population of 2 million are migrants, and huge squatter settlements are developing along the Rimac River and up the hillsides overlooking the city

Above: Workers at a fiesta. Coastal hacienda of Paramonga

Below: Workers' housing: hacienda of Torres Blanca

Seventy-eight kilometres north of Lima, the capital, and bordered to the north and south by the coastal desert, lies the fertile valley of Chancay, which has a population of about ten thousand. This is a valley of sugar cane, orange groves and vineyards, where in the past the haciendas, or large agricultural estates, were served by the small port of Chancay, and by the market town of Huaral, eight kilometres inland. However, changes have occurred in the valley, and these are typical of what is also happening elsewhere in Peru

Within the valley the standard of living varies a good deal. Some of the haciendas are degenerating and in these the employee families live in row upon row of neglected, windowless hovels. Each house is composed of a single room with a door at one end, and with a portion of the roof missing at the other end in order to provide light and ventilation. As a result, the families tend to live in the space around their houses, rather than in the houses themselves

On other haciendas much recent building has taken place. Schools and playing areas are now provided for the workers' children; and new housing has been built which, although very minimal in standard, at least provides electric lighting and a piped water supply. In spite of these improvements, the workers continue to drift away, looking for work in the industrial areas, though not to such an extent as from the poorer haciendas of the valley

Huaral, the market town, is linked to Lima by railway, by macadamized road, and by sea. Because of this, it continues to flourish as a centre of trade. The shopping area is alive with hotels, and has a new and very ugly fountain in the square, and new brick housing is springing up on the outskirts. The town possesses a large covered market; and in addition to this, on market days, its streets are lined with brightly coloured stalls selling pots and pans from Lima, sandals made from old tyres, and lamps made from old tin cans, besides traditional clothing, earthenware bowls, and the produce of the valley

In the port of Chancay itself, a new industry began to develop about ten years ago. This is the preparation of fish-meal fertilizer from the anchovies which abound off the Peruvian coast. In 1957 the total anchovy catch was 43,364 tons, and by 1963 it had grown to 122,647 tons. Thus Chancay has become a

156

Above: Children on a coastal hacienda

Below: Barriada of Chancay: invaded, March 1963

boom town where there is plenty of work and where wages are high. As a result, in March 1963 the desert areas around the town were invaded by squatter settlers. Squatter settlements of this kind are common and extensive in Peru today, and are termed 'barriadas'

At the time of the original invasion near Chancay, it was claimed that 5,000 people took part. Members of the United States Peace Corps, including an architect, moved into the zone and helped the squatters to build and run a temporary school, while the squatters themselves built a church. Government architects drew up a development plan for the area, allowing a plot of land of approximately 2,000 sq ft to a family, and making provision for shopping centres, parks and schools. Garbage was collected from the zone by the Chancay municipality, which also provided deliveries of drinking water each day. Shops and restaurants appeared on the site; and yet by the end of 1963 there were only about 100 families living there

The main reason for this apparent failure of the scheme seems to be that the majority of families in tha Chancay barriada came, not as one would expect from the valley itself, but from the slums of Lima. Their chief interest was to obtain a plot of land on which to build in the future. The distance from Lima was too great to allow them to commute to and from work, and leave time for the building of a house on the site, so that once their claim to the land was established they were prepared either to return home and wait until the zone was more developed before settling there, or else they hoped that in the future land values would rise and they would be able to sell their sites at a handsome profit. At any rate the area is now almost deserted

This desertion of the barriada at Chancay after invasion is exceptional, but the pattern of the invasion itself was typical. In other districts of Peru the people invade the land, and the people stay. In 1960 the squatter population of Peru in barriadas was already 950,000. This figure has been massively surpassed in the last four years, and rapidly is still rising

Above: The barriadas of San Martin and Mirones with Lima in the background. Photo: John Turner

Below: Close up of San Martin. Houses built by the people themselves, and nearly all requiring roofs. A Government sponsored reservoir is under construction. Photo: John Turner

157

The invasions are taking place throughout Peru, around all the major towns, particularly around the coastal cities; and, to a less extent, on to rich agricultural land as well. They are highly organized—often by people in search of political power, who establish one invasion, and then move on to direct another. The pattern is for each invasion to be carefully and secretly planned beforehand by committees of invaders, who intend to become, themselves, a kind of invasion task force

Each family brings its own cane-straw mats and poles for the erection of its own hut, aboard shared trucks and taxis. The provision of mats and poles is, in fact, now a minor industry, and intending invaders can buy them, instead of having to make them themselves. Plots of land, usually about 2,250 sq ft in size, are planned, usually on a grid system; and as soon as the invasion occurs these are laid out along streets, which are demarcated with stones. Government property is usually the target of invaders, as it is easy to see that the government cannot close down barriadas without political embarrassment, to say nothing of creating worse overcrowding problems in the slums. Once the family's straw-mat shack is up, and plots and streets are laid out, the most urgent task is to build a brick wall around each 'property'. The shack, within this courtyard, is then gradually reconstructed, in stages, in brick, concrete and timber, from its straw-mat origins, over a period of perhaps five to ten years, several families often teaming together to help each other

Barriadas grow quickly in population from these beginnings. The Pampa de Comas barriada outside Lima was first invaded in 1957 and already has a population of over 30,000. At first the government turned its back on the problem. But the proper housing of these people has now become a major issue. Before 1961, the unaided self-help of these people, mostly very poor, was remarkably courageous. Since 1961 the government has begun to take some steps to rectify the pathetic situation in which no amount of self-help could, in fact, produce properly co-ordinated electricity, water supplies and sewage, or prevent disease. The present policy is now to integrate the barriadas into the towns they surround, by the building and completion of houses, and by provision of both public services and facilities such as schools, shopping areas, churches, and paved roads

Architects and planners now face the problem of developing to the standard of acceptable environments, large areas of land already carrying high-density populations. One of the great disadvantages of this system – invasion, followed by organization and consolidation – is the difficulty of achieving a creative planning scheme, since squatters are unwilling to move from the actual site they occupy for fear of not obtaining another one. This fear is aggravated by the fact that squatter sites tend to be smaller than the minimum size acceptable to a planner, so that unless the barriada zone is capable of expansion some squatters must inevitably lose their land. A successful solution to these problems has been attempted at Tahuantisuyo outside Lima, where the site plan was drawn up, and the building lots marked out, before the invasion of the area occurred. In other zones any development still tends to be accompanied by tension between the developers and the land occupiers

Much the largest problem however is how to produce the number of houses required, using the extremely limited money and resources at present available. Peru is a poor country. It possesses only a small number of craftsmen and technicians, and has not the facilities to set up the highly-organized building industry required to provide any large-scale production of prefabricated housing systems. In addition, the traditional reputation of South America as an unsettled continent does not encourage foreign investment. Thus though the Government can afford, with the help of foreign aid, to give a certain number of housing loans, each house is ultimately paid for by its owner

Any barriada has a very varied population. This is what makes working in one so surprising and enjoyable. A few of its members may be first generation professionals. When we were working privately as architects with owner-builders in barriadas outside Lima, we had a lawyer, a dentist, and two obstetricians among our clients and some of these were probably earning about £60 a month. Certainly some of them had servants. The majority however were bus drivers, cobblers, policemen, domestic servants or shopkeepers and were earning small wages. Others were unemployed and penniless, and had given up any hope or attempt to improve their circumstances. At present a monthly income of £20 is the minimum on which a Government loan may be obtained

The plan on the left is typical of houses whose owners have applied for Government loans to make possible their completion. Sometimes one encounters this plan completed – i.e. a string of rooms down each side of the site, against the outside walls, with a narrow corridor between. And once this has been completed,

it is difficult to convert it to any sort of fluid plan with adequate standards of lighting, unless parts of the roof are left open. During the construction of these houses, it is difficult – when wandering through a series of sunlit roofless rooms – to make people realize what they will be like when roofed over, and almost impossible to explain the difference between a room having a window, and having adequate cross-ventilation

Most of the self-help house designs built in the barriadas are based on such a plan type, and this inability to visualize appropriate form for a building is a cause of many faults in design. Spaces left for bathrooms and stair wells tend to be too small and no account is taken of where the stairs will emerge at the upstairs level. They are also nearly always in a single flight of up to twenty steps, with no allowance made for landings. Outer walls are built substantially, but all internal divisions are in single leaf brickwork, so that these must be reinforced in order to provide economical spans for roofing

For the purposes of producing mass housing, unskilled labour is the greatest resource which Peru possesses, and the Government is now making use of it. For years the people of the barriadas have been building their own houses around their original squatter

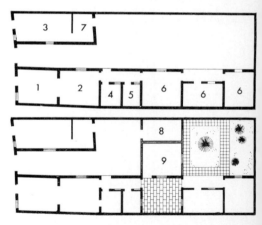

The first plan (above) is typical of barriada self-help house builders. The second plan (below) shows changes that might be made as part of the barriada improvement plan. A garden patio is at the rear of the plot
1 living; 2 eating; 3 shop; 4 kitchen; 5 bathroom; 6 bedroom; 7 store; 8 proposed henhouse; 9 proposed bedroom

158

huts. In the evenings and at weekends, they can add a little more to their houses, because they use their own labour, and bricks are cheap and can be bought a few at a time

Recent Government policy has thus been to install public services, and to give people loans for the connection and installation of the services into their homes, and for the completion of a basic housing unit for each family. A series of bye-laws has been drawn up, giving minimum standards to which a house must conform for the grant of a Government loan, though alterations to make the houses conform to these standards can be included in works executed under the loan

In this way a large number of housing units is being completed quickly and for a small capital outlay. The system has limitations which are particularly obvious to the people handling loans and giving technical assistance. But until money and technicians are available, it continues to be the only solution — and a solution it is, however modest — to the enormous housing problem which now exists

159

Right: Squatters' invasion of Chancay, showing sites and streets marked out with stones. The Peruvian national flag symbolises ironic patriotism

DEREK COUTTS
RICHARD DOUST

161

The fundamental character of the Moroccan market has remained unchanged for centuries. Although they differ from place to place according to local customs, their commercial and social functions remain the same everywhere. The market has no typical form or location – it simply occupies an area which has been found to be convenient by those buying and selling

Broadly speaking there are three types of market in Morocco. To be found in every large town is the central market which has a permanent walled and gated site within the town precincts. On one recognized market day each week people come into town from outlying country districts to buy, but the market is often open throughout the week for regular trading. Since these central markets frequently have fixed stalls for the use of traders, it is easy for areas of specialization in fish, meat, fruit, leather, etc, to be established. Thus despite apparent lack of order, the location of stalls selling different types of produce may be quickly identified by the buyers

Opposite: central market. Above: carpenter's shop

A second common and traditional form of market is the 'souk', which may be held, weekly, monthly, or perhaps even yearly, on any large space of open ground in or just outside a town. More complex commercial transactions are likely at the souk since people come both to buy and to sell – something in bulk – and since trading involves exchanges of both money and of produce

The larger and less frequent souk, known as a 'moussem', will often specialize in trade in only one commodity – for instance, dates or livestock. Certain cultural activities such as local singing or story telling contests frequently take place at the moussem, and more than any other markets they are occasions for entertainment and the performances of poets, singers, jugglers and dancers. The square of 'Djma El Fna' in Marrakesh, once a market place, has now become famous throughout Morocco as a centre for such performances on every night of the week. Here innumerable magicians, animal charmers and story-tellers are to be found, and here one can buy anything from a love potion to an ointment to cure warts. Here also prostitution and vice of all kinds flourish. For a few years after Independence the Djma El Fna was turned into a car park. The authorities in Marrakesh decided that its reputation had become so

unsavoury that it must be closed as a public meeting ground. But the attempt to transform the square was only temporarily successful, and gradually the performers spectators and vendors drifted back to the traditional site

The narrow streets of the 'medina' around the central markets are lined with tiny cubicles built of mud bricks, the folding doors of which open to reveal the interior, which is often both shop and work-room. Where these little shops take the form of a group in an arcade – a bazaar – the shopkeepers sometimes agree to be jointly responsible for the upkeep of the bazaar area, but this is generally the limit to group enterprise in the markets. The average trader is either incapable of grasping any concept of such enterprise in buying, selling and market procedure, or unwilling to adopt new methods. Banking and investment services are little used or understood by Moroccan market traders

These traders rely on their personal reputations to bring them custom, and also to a great extent on display. The Coca Cola sign is one of the most evident graphic symbols in any market place, together with various advertisements for European products such as detergents. Apart from the patriotic display of

162

the Moorish flag and photograph of the king, to be found in every bar and in many private houses, there is a singular lack of signs of Moorish origin, and even identifying shop signs are rare. The shopkeeper knows and is known by his customers, and is not selling in any direct or fierce competition with other traders. If the element of competitive trade were stronger there would obviously be a greater need for positive graphic identification and the use of advertising. The government is introducing a system of price control which requires that prices be displayed on all goods, but until the time of writing price marking had been completely haphazard

Market gatherings are obvious occasions for public announcements and are much used for the purpose by the civil and religious authorities. Government announcements usually take the form of small printed notices, but since some 50 per cent of the population is illiterate the people are often informed of impending religious festivals by a 'berrah' – the equivalent of a town crier. Many of these festivals do not fall on a fixed date but depend upon lunar conditions, which are watched by the religious authorities. When the lunar phase is correct for the festival the berrah is informed and he then proclaims the date

Moroccan traders rent their stalls and shops from a local authority; private ownership is rare. The central markets and the majority of shops were built by the government, but whatever planning there was originally in the allocation of market areas within the medinas, it has since proved totally inadequate to the volume of trade conducted. All available spaces in the market area and in the narrow streets surrounding it are crammed with shops and stalls. The convenience of pedestrians in the market has never been considered nor has any attention been paid to the flow of traffic from one part of the market to another. A space is usually reserved in the market for tethering mules or camels. Bus transport to and from the markets is in general well organized as are communications all over Morocco. In most towns where bus services operate, the bus station is situated near the market, and the buses are used extensively by traders and customers for transporting produce. A journey in one of these heavily laden buses is an uncomfortable, and sometimes an alarming, experience

Since every Moroccan town will have several mosques there is likely to be one either close to the market or actually within it, its intricate carvings and decorations contrasting strongly with the

basically functional architecture of the surrounding shops. The 'muezzin' – the call to prayers – which is heard at least three times in a working day, is sounded from a parapet high up on the mosque, often amplified eerily by a loudspeaker. Those who are strict in their observance of religious duties will then leave their shops for ten or fifteen minutes, sometimes tying a piece of string across the open entrance, or chalking up a notice to the effect that they have gone to pray

The mosque and the market are among the most typical manifestations of Moroccan life, greatly contrasting but equally characteristic. The ornate beauty and the peace inside the mosques indicates a cultural tradition with a quality of permanence that perhaps explains the very slow adoption of western commercial practices in the markets

Opposite left: central market

Opposite right: trader at a souk

Above: a story teller

Right: Djma el Fna at Marrakesh

Over: babouche seller at a souk

CITIES STASIS OR PROCESS

GUNTER NITSCHKE

165

πάντα ρεῖ = all is change, all is moving

This is the pre-Socratian view, according to which the world is seen as a process or a series of events rather than as substantive. Having been eclipsed for several centuries, it has been reborn in post-war years through the character of modern scientific research, through recent developments in painting, sculpture, music, literature and architecture, and perhaps to some extent through the infiltration of eastern philosophies

In architecture we stand at a crossroads: it is easy to discern two different attitudes

The first, a sort of extended Renaissance principle, tries to preplan and prefix a whole new town or city in all its major parts as a single genius-act of design – the Ideal Plan in the Renaissance, or the Master Plan in the twentieth century – and to implement this preconceived idea to the prefixed shape and size. If you look at the early days of modern architecture you will see that the Hilberseimers and the Corbusiers and the Gropius's were designing these Ideal Cities in the Renaissance sense, in the sense that their aesthetic was the classical aesthetic, one of fixed formal organization. Such a city, however, is bound to be an unfinished product up to the very moment it has reached its preconceived target and the 'ideal plan' is bound to turn into a straitjacket for the future life of the city from the very second it has reached its target population. In this sense the Ideal Plan in the end becomes a sepulchre; but life will always outgrow its dwelling-place and will express itself in changing forms

The second attitude basically introduced by TEAM 10, sees the city as an organic process which is constantly flowing and changing, a process which can never arrive at an end, an ideal destination. To quote Peter Smithson, the motor behind the development in this direction –

'Planning is a problem of going on, rather than starting with a clean sheet. We accept as a fixed fact that in any generation we can only do so much work, and we have to select points at which our action can have the most significant effect on the total city structure, rather than try to envisage its complete ideal reorganization, which is wishful thinking. Our current aesthetic and logical aims are not "castles in the air" but rather a sort of new realism and new objectivity, and a matter of acting in a given situation'

This means, applied to the design of a New Town, fixing only a sort of 'infra-structure' along which development can take place, a structure based on our new patterns of society and movement and on an awareness of the different life-cycles of the fairly transient and the more permanent objects, out of which a new discipline of architecture and environment and town-building can be developed related to cycles of constant change

This change in ideology is supported by the influence on contemporary thinking of eastern countries like Japan. In a recent copy of Kenchiku Bunka on the philosophy of new cities, this awareness is compared with the philosophy of Zen which finds order in 'chaos'. Just as Louis Kahn stresses 'realization' as the medium to link inner order to design, so does Zen stress 'associating moments' to link form (reality in Zen) to shape (phenomenon in Zen). In modern terms 'associating moments' could be expressed as the always new factors of development. Therefore, the problem of chaos in the contemporary city is not in its design but in its order. Louis Kahn sees this relationship very clearly:

'Order is:
Design form-making in order
Thru the nature why
Thru order what
Thru design how

Order is intangible
It is a level of creative consciousness
forever becoming higher in level
The higher the order, the more diversity in design'

Let us compare the two attitudes

FIRST

1. As a symbol for the form-images of geometry the cube, the dead stone, had first place. In ancient times the cube was used as a symbol of the earth under the aspect of death, not of life

2. Matter, approached from outside to inside, reflects a world whose elements may carry apparently individual characteristics, but their individuality is in fact ordered and subdued by the unifying powers of geometry

3. 'Unity in form' is the result of image-forming power of geometry; the question of beauty is therefore aesthetic

4. Turning to design, in the form-realm of geometry the laws of form are prefixed; design is disciplined by the problem of how a building programme can be accommodated within the structural principle of geometric figures

5. The form-giving power of geometry demands, if not uniformity, at least unifying (anonymous) factors; in the realm of geometry society is regarded as a matter of population

6. The 'Weltbild' is static—a world of crystals

SECOND

1. The genesis of the north creates the human being out of a tree, symbol of life, a manifestation, on which birth and death takes place every year

2. Matter, seen from within as energy and growth, reflects a world in continuous process

3. 'Unity in attitude' allows each element to be in the process of perpetually creating its own inherent form; the question of beauty is therefore ethical

4. In contrast, form is not preconceived nor its discipline prefixed; form is allowed to emerge from the multitudinous factors within the programme necessitating its birth and evolution

5. The process of individuation in the social and political sense is fostered; for social form is seen as additive and changing, the amalgam of perpetual interaction

6. The 'Weltbild' is of change and becoming, a world of process

A SOCIAL/ECONOMIC APPROACH

At the present stage of economic development, the stage of high mass consumption which many regions of the world have reached, with the United States in the forefront followed by Western Europe and Japan, Adam Smith's liberal concept that the freedom of the individual would bring about the order of the whole is replaced by the Keynesian concept according to which demand – i.e. consumption plus investment – determines supply. An even greater accomplishment of J M Keynes was to make it possible to group the national economy, not in terms of Smith's 'guidance of unseen hands', but in terms of 'perceptible structure'

An electronics expert made it clear that the complex organization and movement of the national economy can be analyzed as an analogy in an electric feedback system. The national economy can now become a matter of continual prediction. In our age this finds expression in high organization, and in the importance of the Government as an intermediary in stabilizing the national economy. At this stage a new awareness becomes necessary, an awareness that the prosperity of the national economy can be attained not merely by increasing production to maximum proportions within the entrepreneural framework, but rather by the organized activity and dynamic balance of the economy. The Keynesian theory of effective demand comes from this background

A large proportion of investment is in construction. At this point construction comes to be regarded not simply as a means to house and implement production, but as a factor itself determining production. The vast amount of building activity under way is changing the living environment of the human being. Its speed of growth accelerates in proportion to the growth of the national product and to the rise in the rate of investment. The cycle of ever more rapidly changing the usually long-life objects of our environment, and the metabolical replacement of short-life everyday objects, caused by increasingly intense consumption and extinction, has confronted planners with the task of reflecting this contemporary situation of construction and consumption, growth and rapid change, in their projects

Among all the other changes, I would refer particularly to the changing character of labour and employment, and the continually increasing growth of urban populations. Metropolitan urban areas of 10 million people are now not uncommon. In such cities the proportion of population which has charge of the productive system has greatly increased during the course of the 'second industrial revolution'. These organization men call for highly effective systems of communication, and therefore there has been a revolutionary leap forward in the means of communication to satisfy the increased organizational activity in our pivotal cities. This is effectively changing the relationships of man with man, of man with environment, of man with nature. Without mass transport facilities and individual means of transport like the automobile our present day mammoth cities would be unthinkable. Mass communication has changed the radial concentric pattern of circulation into an open and fluctuating organization. We understand communication as an economic or technical life factor, but we still have hardly any vision of communication as a physical structure, or as a spatial theme in our urbanized society. Although the question of balance of social and private investment, of infra-structure and element structure in the city is normally considered now from an economic point of view in terms of distribution of capital, we have not yet found a method of reflecting it in physical form. Among architects and planners there are few signs of a reflection in fundamental design thought of intense economic investment and consumption, of accelerated construction and obsolescence, and in connection with that of the dynamic of growth and change

A SCIENTIFIC APPROACH

Werner Heisenberg, speaking at a world conference of atomic energy in Geneva, showed that large areas of phenomena cannot even be approximately described by the concepts of classical physics. And not only the applicability of the concepts and laws of classical physics, but the whole representation of reality, which has been the basis of the exact natural sciences up to the era of today's atomic physics, has been recast. By the phrase 'representation of reality' I mean here the old concept that there are objective phenomena taking place in a definite manner in space and time, whether they are observed or not. In atomic physics observations can no longer be objectified in such a simple manner

The concepts of classical physics are in many ways similar to the 'a priori' forms of perception in the philosophy of Kant. Just as Kant explains the concepts space, time or causality aprioristically because they already formed the premises of all experiences and could therefore not be considered as the result of experience, so the concepts of classical physics form an 'a priori' basis for experiments in a quantum theory, because we can conduct experiments in the atomic field only by using these concepts of classical physics

Planck's action quantum was the beginning of a revolution in physics. While the laws of the former physics e.g. Newtonian mechanics, should basically be equally valid for all orders of magnitude (the movement of the moon around the earth should obey the same laws as the fall of an apple from a tree or the deviation of an alpha particle that grazes the nucleus of an atom), Planck's law of radiation shows for the first time that there are scales of operation in nature, that phenomena in different ranges of magnitude are not necessarily of the same type. In addition, the work of Born, Kramers and Slater contained the decisive concept that the laws of nature determine not the 'definite occurrence' of an event but the probability that an event will take place

This concept – that events are not determined in a peremptory manner, but that there is the 'possibility' or 'tendency' for an event to occur – is our new reality. An indeterminate layer of reality, halfway between the massive reality of matter and the intellectual reality of the idea or image, is formulated quantitatively as probability, and subjected to mathematically expressible laws of nature. These laws of nature formulated in mathematical terms no longer determine the phenomena themselves but determine the possibility of happening – the probability that something could happen along these lines. The apparent inner contradiction between classical and modern atomic physics is thus overcome by the application of the so-called 'Uncertainty Relationships' by which the classical laws of physics are restricted; or better, extended

The last twenty years in the development of atomic physics also showed that the smallest particles of matter, the so-called elementary particles, are not eternal and unalterable but can be transmuted into one another, and that according to the theory of relativity mass can be converted into energy; and the elementary particles to which huge accelerators have given a large amount of kinetic energy, can with the help of this energy be converted into mass and generate new elementary particles. This means that all elementary particles are the various forms which energy must assume in order to become matter. Here the pair of concepts 'content and form' or 'substance and form' from Aristotle's philosophy reappear. Matter originates when the substance energy is converted into an elementary particle.

Energy is not only the force that keeps the 'all' in continuous motion, it is also the fundamental substance of which the world is made

It is absurd to say that this has no relation to architecture or to planning, since this new knowledge about the physical structure of matter exists in our consciousness. The uncertainty principle, the interrelation of energy and matter, are part of our reality or Weltbild; we are working with them, maybe often unconsciously. I would like to mention here some of the latest explorations for New Towns made by Candilis and Woods, with their systems STEM and WEB; systems which seem to be an application of this new vision to town design. The system STEM, which is illustrated here by Candilis and Woods' project for Toulouse le Mirail, originated in considerations of mobility, in other words in form/energy interrelations. Its dimensions are no longer given in measures of length (Renaissance Principle of Planning) but of speed (measure of energy): $2\frac{1}{2}$ miles per hour, 60 miles per hour. STEM attempts to provide a relationship between these measures of speed; it also attempts a relationship between measures of validity (5 years, 25 years). Thus STEM evolves an urban structure based on mobility, growth and change—deliberately forming a planning language within which future development can be designed. STEM becomes not only a link between additive cells, but the generator of habitat, inviting the possibility or tendency of urban events ('uncertainty relationships') to take place within an established grammar, and not within an Ideal Formal Plan

AN APPROACH THROUGH PAINTING

Today, as in the past, the key to creative work is symbolic transformation, the translation of direct experience into symbols which sum up experience in a communicable form. At the same time the traditional concept of an image as a mirror held in front of nature is now obsolete

Would it not be feasible, in order to realize the full potentiality of his available resources, that the contemporary planner should draw on this understanding of creative transformation and combine it with his new scientific or metaphysical knowledge?

Modern painters and sculptors have sought to express inner events without aids taken from the outside world of objects. In fact, with new visual patterns and structures they are able to suggest a deeper understanding of the hidden movements of phenomenal outer reality

167

Looking at Jackson Pollock's painting world, which seems to turn upon a new principle of indeterminacy, one finds a world remote from the closed and intelligible universe of post-Renaissance art where man cut space to his own measure. It belongs to the vast free spaces of modern science; and reveals the limits of the modern individual's rational powers by opening up glimpses of a nature essentially irrational

The work of modern painters like Pollock or Robert Motherwell could be explored for new image systems, for an order with a structure where every piece is correspondingly new in a new system of relationships. In their work one seems to discover urban and landscape references—not in any descriptive way, but analogically by means of painterly rhythms, a space generated by the gesture, the act of painting, and by the properties of colour. The paintings may have started completely at random, with a splash, a series of whiplash lines; but as the work progresses the artists improvise order on the basis of their discoveries as they work. In his approach to order through the act of painting (rather than through some previously accepted standard of composition) Jackson Pollock admitted that his 'methods may be automatic at the start but they quickly step beyond that'. The repeated decisions become crucial factors. Unlike the traditional concept, paint is not the slave of the painter, passively administering his wishes; on the contrary, paint characterizes everything the artist does or can do in his art. Once the artist begins to work the emerging painting influences him profoundly, so that the present experience of the work of art outweighs other factors, such as the emotions the artist started off with or a clearly conceived state of finish at the end. The central issue of this art is one's ability to learn from the creative act itself, and to arrive at a point which one recognizes as an acceptable formality, but which one could not predict at the beginning

This process of painting, expressed especially by American action painters, seems to be reflected in the statements by Peter and Alison Smithson about patterns of growth concerning New Towns. They are aware that Municipal Planning – official planning – as it exists now attempts to create a pattern in advance of circumstances; it lays out the form of community as a finished object. Yet (as with the action painter) form is generated in part by response to existing form; every addition to community, every change of circumstance, will generate a new response and a new definition. 'The realization of the actual

town,' Smithson has said, 'should be in the hands of the builders of the parts, who, understanding the general intention, must at every stage assess what has gone before and by their activities – the action of pouring or splashing the paint, as it were – mutate (and if necessary redirect) the whole'

AN APPROACH THROUGH PHILOSOPHY

Philosophy today is, I think, quite aware of the revolution in the natural sciences – that matter has resolved itself into energy, whether it be systems of radiations (Heisenberg) or systems of waves (Schroedinger)– that all phenomena have ceased to be objects of substance, but are evalued as successive events in a space/time continuum, in perpetual movement and transmutation. Thus we find that the conscious 'human being' is in reality a cause-effect continuum flowing through space and time, and his existence in a moment of conscious awareness is a cross-section of an eternal process. The ego is shrunk – in a slow evolution starting with the Renaissance – to a conditioned subjective phenomenon, and psychic life to a series of mental events. In a manner that foreshadowed the trends of the present-day dynamic psychology of C. G. Jung, very old Eastern ethico-psychological systems like the Adhidhamma spoke about these states of mind unattached to any concept of a persisting entity. There we find thought without a 'thinker' and action without an 'actor', both thought and action being no more than aspects of the life-flux of consciousness, just as they are in the philosophy of Henri Bergson

If the real term of a being's conscious existence is no longer than the duration of one of these moments of consciousness which are strung, as it were, on the thread of cause and effect to give the illusory sense of self-identity, this problem of identity-in-change can only be understood by viewing identity as a relationship of cause and effect. Identity can derive solely from the progression of this causal relationship, as it does in a single life-course when the child becomes an adult and the adult becomes an octogenarian. This new feeling of identity as dynamic and relative rather than static and self-supporting is brought into city design by the post-war tendency to create a new architectural language of change and relativity by visually expressing themes of progression and interrelationship. Aldo van Eyck defines the new attitude by saying that the identity of the whole should be latent in the components, whilst the identity of the components would remain present in the whole.

That does not imply, however, that these identities need or should remain constant in the face of mutations. On the contrary, it is exactly this potential to face change without losing identity which should be brought into our city designs, embracing a hierarchy of superimposed configurative systems multilaterally conceived. And this new 'aesthetic of change', paradoxically enough, would generate a feeling of identity and security, because of our ability to recognize the pattern of related cycles, the pattern of interdependence, of identity in relativity

TOWARDS PROGRESS

Le Corbusier's Ville Radieuse was an early and profoundly important step to introduce a new awareness of mobility into architecture and the city. In his Plan for a City of 3 Million Inhabitants, 1922, Corbu recognized that the automobile would be fundamental to the infra-structure of our contemporary society. Even at that date he realized that the automobile was certain to transcend its role as a mere means of transportation and become a communication symbol, unifying the open society as a new kind of organic unit

He invented the piloti-system for the purpose of separating the pedestrian from the automobile: and to Corbu this was really more than a functional concept in his design. It was an organizational concept in the sense that it was a new and basic structuring element in the design of cities. Nevertheless the Ville Radieuse concept as a whole, of which Corbu's Moscow plan is a good example, reveals that his concern was a clear and formal beauty, and his means were the classical means of geometry

Forty years later we clearly recognize the construction of this geometry. And this helps us to recognize that the C I A M Athens Charter of 1929 fundamentally gives advice on the technical organization of cities— but none on their FORM

KAHN'S PHILADELPHIA

In his suggestions for the dynamic renewal of the Philadelphia city centre in 1953 Louis Kahn tried to relate architecture organically to types of movement. 'Architecture is also the street

'There is no order to the movement on streets at the moment. Streets look alike, reflecting little of the activities they serve – Carcassonne without walls, cities without entrances, indiscriminate movement

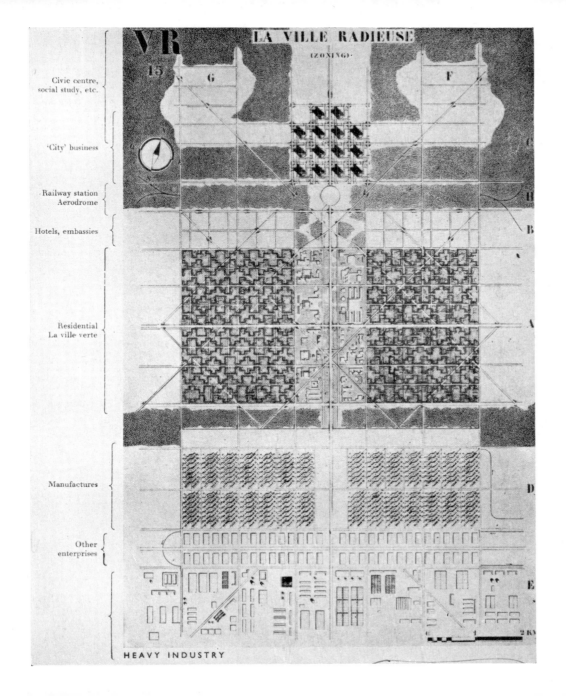

without places to stop. The design of the street is design for movement'

By designing specific streets for the staccato movement of buses and trolleys, specific streets for go-traffic, and others as terminal streets for stopping, etc – Kahn creates an orderly discrimination of traffic of varying intentions, and thereby increases the efficiency of street movements. And thus, zoning grows naturally out of the type of movement of a particular street; and the architecture tends to be related to the type of movement

Kahn introduces the concept of the 'port' as a connection between the highway and the architectural cluster – forming an intermediary step between the two dimensions – the highway-speed of the urban motorway (55-70 m.p.h.) and the much slower speeds to which he intends to have the centre restricted. Thus the architecture of the centre responds functionally and visually to the time/motion scale of restricted vehicular speeds and pedestrian freedom of movement – gaining a specific and organic unity and identity of scale

The location and design of these parking terminals becomes in fact an integral part of the design of in-city expressways – since it is to the expressways that the terminals are linked most powerfully in

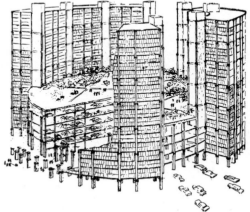

Left: Ville Radieuse – a plan by Le Corbusier for Moscow, c. 1926

Above: 'Port'. A 1956 drawing by Louis Kahn showing a parking garage, with offices, shops and hotels on its periphery

Above: Louis Kahn. 1956 study for Philadelphia

Right: Hauptstadt Berlin by Alison and Peter Smithson and Peter Sigmonde-Wonke. Hierarchy of vehicular routes

terms of fluent movement and of engineering. Indeed in Kahn's Philadelphia plans it would seem that this theory of the mass transportation terminal as a major structuring element is not only justified but is his most cogent and basic contribution to post-Ville Radieuse post-CIAM thought

'The tower entrances and interchanges, wound-up parking terminals, suggest a new stimulus to unity in urban architecture, one which would find expression from the order of movement. The location and design of these entrances are an integral part of the design of the expressway. At night we know these towers by their illumination in colour. These yellow, red, green, blue and white towers tell us the sector we are entering, and along the approach, light is used to see by and to give us direction'

At the same time, in the remainder of his plans for Philadelphia it seems to me doubtful whether Kahn has yet found the structuring answer to the central areas – where the desire of individual automobiles to move from door to door is impossible to achieve whilst retaining a traditionally grid-city form. In cities like Philadelphia, the radial centripetal flow of traffic has already brought the central sections to a point of suffocation through the overloading of in-city communications. And this only underlines the

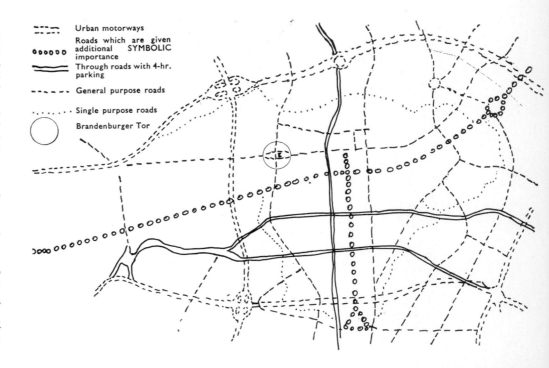

- - - - Urban motorways

oooooo Roads which are given additional SYMBOLIC importance

——— Through roads with 4-hr. parking

- - - - General purpose roads

· · · · · Single purpose roads

◯ Brandenburger Tor

fact that the organic thinking based on movement which led Kahn to his concept of 'ports' has now to be applied to the structural reorganization of the whole

SMITHSON'S HAUPSTADT BERLIN

The 1958 plan for the centre of Berlin by Alison and Peter Smithson and Peter Sigmonde-Wonke was primarily based on a study of mobility – both physical, and in its social ramifications – went somewhat further than Kahn's

'Mobility has become the characteristic of our period', wrote the Smithsons in Uppercase 3, 1960. 'Social and physical mobility, the feeling of a certain sort of freedom, is one of the things that keeps our society together, and the symbol of this freedom is the individually owned motor car. Mobility is the key both socially and organizationally to town planning, for mobility is not only concerned with roads, but with the whole concept of a mobile, fragmented community. The roads (together with the main power lines and drains) form the essential physical infra-structure of the community. The most important thing about roads is that they are big, and have the same power as any big topographical feature, such as a hill or a river, to create geographical, and in consequence social, divisions. To lay down a road therefore, especially through a built-up area, is a very serious matter for one is fundamentally changing the structure of the community

'Traditionally some unchanging large-scale thing – the Acropolis, the River, the Canal, or some unique configuration of the ground – was the thing that made the whole community structure comprehensible and assured the identity of the parts within the whole

'Today our most obvious failure is the lack of comprehensibility and identity in big cities, and the answer is surely in a clear, large-scale road system – the URBAN MOTORWAY lifted from an ameliorative function to a unifying function. In order to perform this unifying function all roads must be inte-

Top right: Smithson/Sigmonde-Wonke, Berlin 1958 The pedestrian circulation net in its setting of urban motorways

Bottom right: Smithson/Sigmonde-Wonke, Berlin 1958. Detail of the southern section with hotel cluster around the Bahn Hof, commercial, printing areas and the flower market, with a surrounding 'wall' of office slabs

171

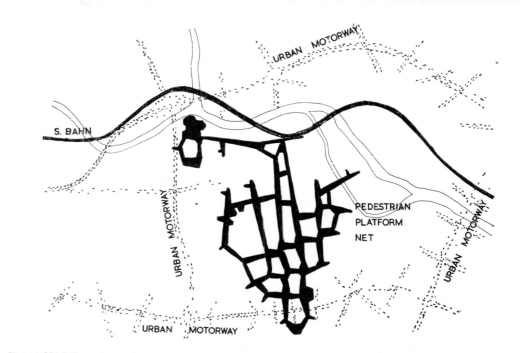

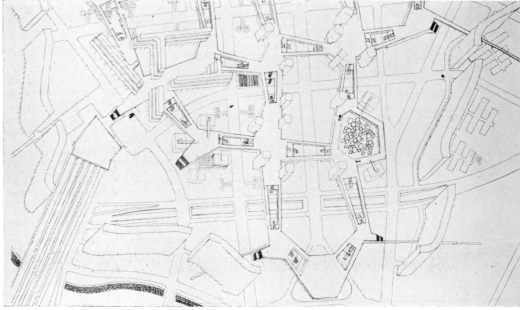

grated into a system, but the backbone of this system must be the motorways in the built-up areas themselves, where their very size in relationship to other development makes them capable of doing the visual and symbolic unifying job at the same time as they actually make the whole thing work

'To be physically positive the roads must run in a neutralized zone of green planting or constructed landscape (whichever does the job best)'

In planning the horizontal road-net, the Smithsons have drawn through-traffic away from the central areas by means of tangential urban motorways; and the in-city local traffic, moving at lower and more leisurely speeds, is then able to use a road-net which often follows existing streets, with stop lights at intersections, controlled crossings, and frequent and convenient arrangements for parking

Pedestrian platforms are designed as irregular but not unsystematic paths expressing a much freer choice of routes, running above low-spread buildings on the ground – the cinemas, trade centres, markets and so on. This pedestrian net serves high-level shops, roof gardens and restaurants; and tall buildings, such as blocks of offices, are entered at this level by pedestrians, as well as from the ground

At points midway between each road intersection, continuously running escalators are situated to connect the ground with the pedestrian decks. These escalators, together with additional elevators, make it easy for the pedestrian to go from one level to another, and encourages the use of the platform level which bridges the roads at the escalator points

Where this design goes further than the previous designs we have considered is that the two nets, vehicular and pedestrian, are conceived as one problem leading to a positive structure uniting the whole by a common scale and form-language – which is NOT static, but is extendable, uncompleted, enabling variation and growth, decay and regeneration – without destroying the basic concept. The open structure reflects the designers' fundamental acceptance of the steady interior growth (metabolism) and steady exterior growth (additive) in our cities. And the work of the designers is then seen to have become the establishment of a growth-structure, a dynamic theme for development and change – an architectural parallel to the 'uncertainty' factors we spoke of in relation to recent physics and mathematics

One key to establishing a growth-structure is through differentiating objects whose cycle of change is slow, from those objects existing within cycles of more rapid change and evolution. 'The

structure needs "fixes" (fixed in the sense that they are changing over a relatively long period) by means of which things changing in a shorter cycle can be valued and identified. With a few fixed and clear objects, the transient ones – housing, drug stores, shops, and in the shortest cycle, of course, people and their extensions, like clothes, cars, etc – are no longer a menace to sanity and sense of structure, but can uninhibitedly reflect short-term need and justification. If this need of distinction between changing and relatively fixed objects were observed there would be less need for elaborate control over things for which no good case can be made for controlling, and legislative energy could be concentrated on the long-term structure'

By developing this theme of related cycles of change into a new discipline of planning and architecture, an 'aesthetic of change' would generate paradoxically a sense of security, stability and order

SMITHSONS NITSCHKE MEHRINGPLATZ BERLIN

A more recent competition (1962-63) for Berlin, this time the area around the Mehring and Bluecher Platz, gave the Smithsons (team: Alison and Peter Smithson and G. Nitschke) an opportunity for developing further the theme of 'aesthetic of change'

We were given 'official' road proposals but we found that the remaining areas for buildings were too small for the sort of development in which detailed traffic handling can be considered as part of the act of city-building; and from the start we conceived our task as one of total integration, and not that of designing buildings to fill in gaps

Following the previous theme of fast movement along the Berlin southern tangential motorway, we perceived that a powerful rhythm was being generated which had to convey a sense at once of orientation and yet an identity of parts. The essential problem as we saw it was how to sense an 'event' at any place; and thus following the line of the motorway, what we proposed in essence was that the new Mehringplatz (replacing the old Mehringplatz of Baroque Berlin, the Belle Alliance Piazza) should become once again but in a wholly new way an 'event' in a chain of 'events'. These events are related to, and would become to some extent symbols of, the zones through which the line of the motorway passes. For example, related to the formerly huge Anhalter Bahnhof there is an interchange with mass-transit facilities; related to the

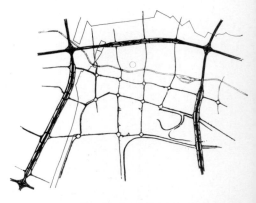

Top: Mehringplatz Berlin. Official road proposals

Bottom: Smithson/Nitschke, Berlin 1962/3. Macro- and Micro-structure of traffic movement applied to competition area

172

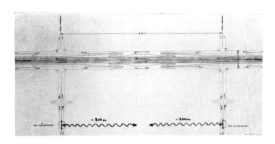

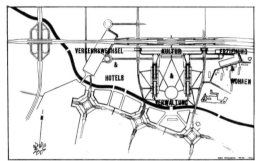

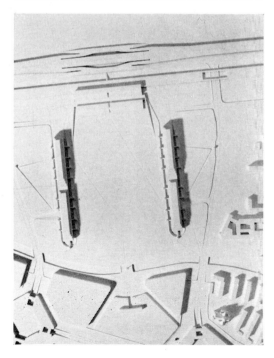

173

'Rund um die Kreutzkirche' housing area there is a technical school complex; related to the open space of the Mehringplatz there is a cultural and administrative centre

But we did not try to build up these events along the 'chain-centre' into a unified linear architectural composition: rather they are based on systems of connection, and use-intensity zoning

The first step, then, was to split the complex vehicular movement in the Mehringplatz part of the city into macro-, micro-, and service traffic according to speed, volume and destination. The macro-structure was formed by the motorway grid, with identical junctions, and elevated so that the changing character and massing of the city can be visually experienced in movement. The smaller grid of roads—which follow in the main the old existing routes—form the micro-structure. The spacing of the micro-structure and nodes is based on a maximum walking distance of 300 m. Clarity and orientation is created by sinking the system half into the ground wherever possible. Service traffic, branching off the micro-structure to individual buildings is left as flexible as possible, and is always below ground level though not necessarily covered

The transition from the high-speed movement of the macro-structure to the lower speeds of the micro-structure is expressed in the basic rhythms of the take-off geometry. These take-offs are at approximate intervals of 650 m, following the standard American practice for downtown areas of three take-offs to the mile (which, in turn, is the minimum that the geometry of the take-off requires). In addition, of course, this produces a pattern giving a maximum walking distance of 300 m between the principal routes of the micro-structure

The maximum intensity of traffic is naturally along the motorway and at the nodes of the micro-net; and this sets up the basic design discipline for the growth-structure of the area. Here are placed the car parks and service areas as shields against traffic noise. The car parks are of two kinds. Along the south tangential urban motorway on both sides runs a continuous parking strip, varying in width and number of floors to suit the need, a 'linear garage'. At the junctions of the routes of the micro-structure a circular multi-level parking strip encloses the actual roundabout, a 'nodal garage'

Arriving by private car from the straight high-speed motorway, the transition from auto to pedestrian movement is experienced as a step by step process spatially, and enforced structurally and architectur-

Top left: Smithson/Nitschke, Berlin 1962/3. Take-off geometry of urban motorway

Centre left: Smithson/Nitschke, Berlin 1962/3. Chain of 'events' experienced along motorway: mass-traffic interchange—hotels—culture and administration—housing and schools

Bottom left: Smithson/Nitschke, Berlin 1962/3. Model showing culture-administration hooked to linear garage and motorway take-off

Above top: Model showing the transition from vehicular to pedestrian traffic, in this case from bus-stop of micro-grid to the 'porticos' of administrative block

Above bottom: Model showing take-off and slowing down process from high-speed motorway to linear garage and pedestrian routes leading to buildings

Below: Smithson/Nitschke, Berlin 1962/3. Perspective sketch of central space

Bottom: Smithson/Nitschke, Berlin 1962/3. Final layout for Mehringplatz

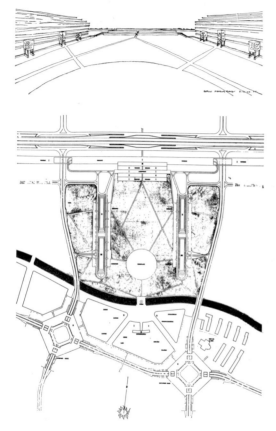

ally. As you leave the motorway via the take-off ramps you enter curved routes which slow your speed until by means of the micro-grid you arrive at a linear or nodal garage–from where you are a pedestrian. If you arrive by bus at a stop on the micro-grid, you walk towards the office blocks in a continuously decreasing ditch and enter your building on the ground floor through a 'portico' via a bridge. A limited number of official cars may reach individual buildings – since the office buildings stand on stilts, as it were in a waterless moat – by driving to

'portcocheres' at moat level, where there would be parking bays for official cars (on the inner side) and service bays (on the outer side)

The patterns of pedestrian movement form one of the main keys to the architectural solution. The rondel, the former Mehringplatz, lying between the banks of office-tracts like a large gramophone record, a shadow only of a former reality, is one of the points of origin of the footpath system (emanating from the 'Hallesches Tor' U-Bahn station); the other points of origin being the bus stops on the micro-grid and the elevators on the linear and nodal garages. The geometry of pedestrian movement is kept approximately diagonal to the rectangular micro- and macro-grid traffic movement. Inside the area enclosed by the buildings there is no vehicular traffic at all–and indeed there is no traffic at surface level anywhere within each block defined by the road net; the two systems do not meet on the same level

The three buildings, marking the 'event' of culture and administration, are hooked on to the linear garage building; together with the two administrative office tracts they enclose a green space, calm and urbane, in a manner similar to the Louvre, and like the Louvre, they would be realized serially in a phased process of construction. In fact the growth-structure for the whole areas is consciously evolved to allow elbow room for buildings and services to develop and change, like a growing tree whose boughs instinctively spring from its trunk in such a manner as to allow ample space about them for subsequent growth, without compromising the initial theme and discipline of growth

TANGE'S TOKYO PLAN

Kenzo Tange's Tokyo Plan results from his interpretation of the new characteristics of the pivotal cities of the second industrial revolution, some of which we have already discussed

1. Cities in the 10 million population class have now arisen in which administration/organization (as distinct from production-processes) for the age of consumption are concentrated

2. In these pivotal cities an open organization results from the invisible network of communications, an open organization in which any combination of function and function is possible

3. The population which lives in these cities enjoys average per capita incomes and consumption far beyond their basic need

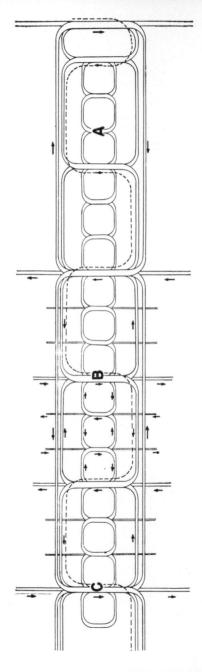

4. The vast increase in speed-range and volume of various forms of mobility, together with the increasing complexity and differentiation of social structure is in fact revolutionary, for it leads to a freer, more spontaneous city. Meanwhile the centripetal structure of the closed city forms we have inherited from the middle ages cannot stand the strain put on it by the permanent flow (movement of daily commuters, repeated at definite intervals) and the highly complex variable flow (indefinite spontaneous movements of traffic) which are characteristics of the open organization of cities of the 10 million class

Kenzo Tange therefore defines the task facing him as follows:

To find a new urban spatial order which will reflect the open organization and increasingly spontaneous mobility of contemporary society;

To find means of bringing the city structure, its transportation systems, and urban architecture into graphic unity;

To get away from the existing centripetal system of transportation which if improved merely works to increase the demand for more traffic, leading to a vicious circle creating more and more confusion in the centre

In his proposals for Tokyo, Tange rejects the concept of the metropolitan civic centre in favour of a new concept which he calls the civic AXIS. This takes as its point of departure the present metropolitan centre of Tokyo, and gradually extends out over Tokyo Bay. In effect he proposes that the existing concentric structure of Tokyo is changed into an axis which develops linearly, a symbol of our open organization

The organization of the axis in distinct units with a cyclic transportation system makes gradual development possible; in fact at each stage of development the system is complete, but it is continually possible to add another unit. The highways are so designed that there is no limit to the number of lanes at the points of interchange, and thus from the bigger (9 km) to the smaller (3 km) or the smallest (1 km) cycle Tange's transportation system is capable of handling from ten to thirty times as much traffic as the high-speed highway system now in existence

Within this cyclic system Tange replaces the zonal planning methods of urban planning today by organized spatial planning. He takes the piloti-system of the architectural pioneers of the early twentieth century, which constituted spatial links between private areas above ground where man could live and work, and public areas where the flow of pedestrian and automobile traffic, and the flow of public space, meet with stable architectural space, and he combines this with the core-system according to which the internal circulation of buildings is linked to urban arteries. In his Tokyo plan he devises means by which the cores of buildings take the place of columns, creating 'columnless' piloti-areas under the buildings, and these cores are unified with the cyclic transportation system. Architecturally speaking, the cores are laid out on a grid of squares of approximately 200 m; and on these cores

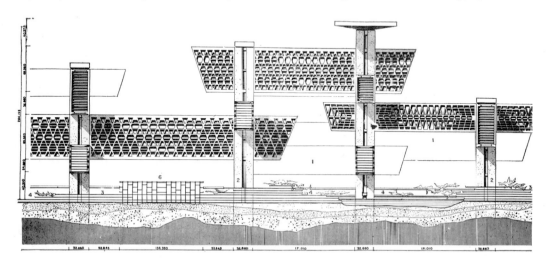

175

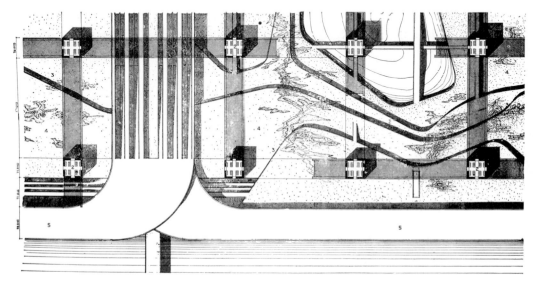

Left:
1 Office space	4 Plaza
2 Vertical shaft core	5 Highway
3 Parking floors	6 Interchange

1 Residential space
2 Public facilities and public square
3 Square and kindergarten, etc
4 School
5 Shopping centre
6 Parking space
7 Monorail station
8 Highway

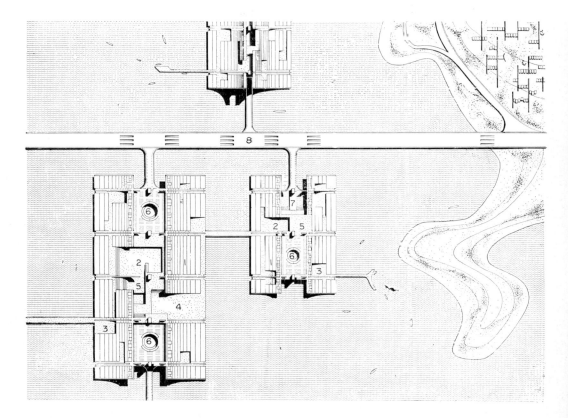

177

ten- or twenty-storey office buildings would rest. In the units themselves large areas of land are released for pedestrian use, and these are designed to continue the city's traditional human scale with small shopping streets, large piazzas for crowds, auditoria, etc. Tange is also deeply aware of the different life-spans of various constructions – the longer life-cycle of large-scale constructions like the communications infra-structure, compared with the life-span of the houses and articles of our daily lives which are gradually growing shorter as a result of our enormous consumption of modern consumer goods. To unify these conflicting extremes Tange suggests vast triangulated structures for the housing areas, based on concrete platforms, in which it would be possible for each individual to construct his home to his own taste from the available manufactured building materials

THE METABOLISTS OF JAPAN [1]

The highest shrine of Japan and of her own original religion Shintoism, is today far removed from our hectic metropolitan life and our industrialized progress. All the same it enables us to feel distinctly the former familiarity of oriental man with the eternal mutation of all things. Here Shinto faith has built a poem on the theme of the eternal in the changing. Every twenty years the symbol of the 'Eternal' changes the symbol of the 'Transitory', namely the transient earthly shrine building. A second identical sacred domain, lying close, is always established as the symbol of divinity in a newly erected shrine: as a result of the transitoriness of all earthly things, the old crumbles. Thus the continuity of the eternal in the transient is guaranteed

The same awareness is expressed in Kanji, Japan's adopted Chinese script, the ideographic roots of which are not pictures of abstract things, i.e. of nouns, but of actions. The majority of the original Chinese ideograms are shorthand images of natural processes and operations. There is no such thing in Nature as an isolated, abstract thing, corresponding to a noun. Things are always only the end points, or rather, the intersecting points of events, the intermediate stages of processes, comparable to a snapshot. An abstract movement, corresponding to a verb in grammar is impossible in Nature. For the Chinese, the substantive and the verb are the same: things in movement, movement in things. As things are in Nature so are words in the Chinese language. They remain living and flexible, since thing and function are not formally divided. Suddenly we understand: the Oriental mind saw things not only in their aspect of things as they are, as was primarily the case in the West, but also as the movement of things in their continuous mutation. Change, growth, interaction and the simultaneity of functions are integrated components of their thinking and writing. The third spiritual source of perennial change in man and in things derives from India, and from Buddhism. In Japanese Zen, Chinese pragmatism, Indian metaphysical speculation and Shintoistic sensitivity towards Nature are fused together in a philosophy of active creativity. Zen contains, on the one hand, the Buddhistic principle of the phenomenality of all existence, which proceeds analytically and resolves existence into its ultimate constituents, into mere shadowy phenomena, both spiritual and physical; while on the other hand Zen also postulates the principle of the

relativity of all existential phenomena, both physical and spiritual; this principle proceeding synthetically and seeing all phenomena in their conditionality, their interrelation and interdependence. Buddhistic vision thus conceives of the manifestation of objects or forms as events and not as isolated static substances; consequently it perceives in them the essential characteristics of every form of energy, namely, movement and continuous transformation

In the Japanese tea-house, Zen created and translated into architectural terms, a room which strove to express the transience of all things in this world, the world of forms; therefore the demand for assymmetrical compositions, and for only what appears as unideal, incomplete; still in the process of living and therefore unfinished, i.e. asymmetrical in respect of form. Similarly, in the Japanese dwelling, life expresses itself in terms of the dynamic of our existence. It provides a space that is eminently changeable; and therefore functionally flexible. The Japanese house possesses in fact all the qualities for which we strive in modern architecture. These qualities are present, moreover, in the proposals of the 'metabolists' with their prefabrication of structural elements, which when modularly co-ordinated provides for the complete flexibility of the space-enclosing parts and thereby for:

(a) susceptibility of change between rooms;
(b) flexibility of functions in rooms; and
(c) reciprocity between inside and outside

Thus the Japanese dwelling can fulfil, for us, the inconsistent requirement: inexhaustible individual variation within a common, higher, formal whole

That which at a small scale the Buddhist spirit breaks up according to an established rhythm, Nature has permitted on a large scale to occur to the creations of Japanese man. A cycle of comparatively small earthquakes daily, of larger ones yearly and of catastrophic ones at longer intervals. Indeed a cycle of devastating fires to the wooden constructions is still preponderant today. In the truest sense of the word, the ground is cut from under the human ego – all too prone to erect monuments with the intention that they shall last for ever. The consciousness 'Eki' or 'I' of change, which with sureness and ease is enacted in all the phenomena of life, is the theme of one of the oldest Chinese texts: of the 'I Ching' or the Book of Transformations

In Japan Nature tends to constrain the eye away from built, from the fixed elements, from the house itself, from the town as something settled, towards perpetual change and transformation

For this reason a group of Japanese architects and planners who understand human society as a living process and who propose an active 'metabolistic' development of our society through their projects call themselves 'metabolists' (change, mutation, revolution, transformation in cycles). At the International Design Congress in Tokyo in the spring of 1960 the group came for the first time collectively into prominence through a presentation of their draft projects. They believe that they, as a group, are subject to the same metabolic process which they make the basis of their proposals

NORIAKI KUROKAWA AND ARATA ISOZAKI

Two members of the metabolist group are Kurokawa and Isozaki. The new tasks facing city planners are to secure a working system of communications and thus to organize a super-collective life for a city of 10 million people without neglecting the needs of the even more isolated individual. This means seeing open space and built-up area as a unit, safeguarding the varying life cycles of the composing elements and mastering the increasing mobility of both man and his constructed elements. These new tasks have led Kurokawa to new structural solutions

His system of 'metabolic cycles' take the form of 'helicoidal towers', which result from a screw rotation of one or more straight lines, create a stairlike artificial ascending ground. This provides a large-scale 'infra-structure' into which various small-scale 'element structures' (both in respect of volume and use, and length of life) can duly be inserted and incorporated. Every ten storeys these towers are connected with each other on the same level. In this way, an adequate network of horizontal and diagonal connections guarantees a three-dimensional development of traffic within the towers

Below: Noriaki Kurokawa. Model of helicoidal towers based on a screw-rotation of straight lines

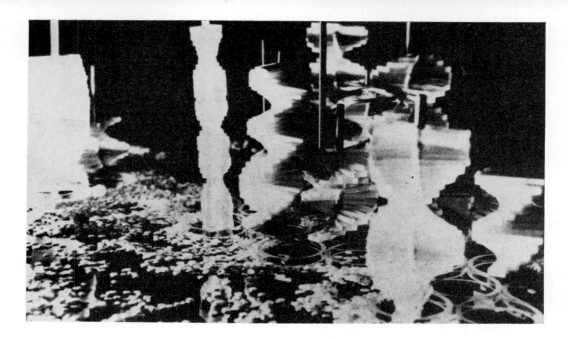

Left above: Noriaki Kurokawa. Helicoidal towers massed into clusters in a 10 million population city

Left below: Noriaki Kurokawa. Drawing of helicoidal towers as an infra-structure showing connector systems and inserted 'element structures'

Below: Traditional Japanese roof construction is a source of inspiration for Isozaki's clusters-in-the-air

Next page: Arata Isozaki. Infra-structure for clusters-in-the-air, based on 12 metre masts, for a sector of Tokyo

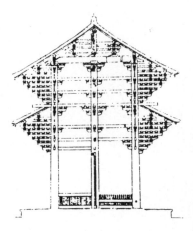

Isozaki compares his proposals with the art of kimono making: a very simple system has produced for centuries an inexhaustible wealth of diversity and beauty. So in his proposals he derives a simple system which will permit a variety of spatial formations. It consists of vertical poles, some 12 metres in diameter, which are the supports for the horizontal elements spanning between them, and which serve at the same time as vertical communication and service shafts. Urban arteries (horizontal streets) and structural arteries (vertical streets) are connected. The basement level is a parking and service level; the ground level is a grid of 80 metres forming a mesh to serve local traffic. Above this are the cultural and communal levels which are developed according to the conditions of the terrain and the will of the community. And once again above this rises the infra-structure into which, like Kurokawa's, a variety of 'element structures' may be inserted

COLLAGE BLACK AND WHITE

KATE LEWIS

182   1963 paper
       29½ × 22 in (74·9 × 55·9 cm)

GEORGES CANDILIS
ALEXIS JOSIC
SHADRACH WOODS

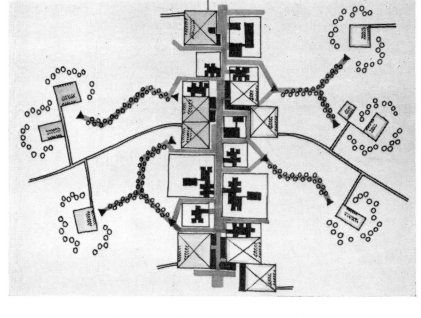

183

Today we are involved in mass production, mass distribution, mass consumption, mass housing, mass education, mass leisure. We are especially concerned with the relationships between these mass activities. We have to define the use of public and private transport, from rocket ships to bicycles, and to relate their different scales of speed to each other and to man as he continues to be, despite these hurrying marvels. These problems are most acute when populations are greatest, i.e. in our cities and urban regions

The constant and rapid evolution of our society will not allow the stratification of cities. The question is not to build flexible buildings but to establish an environment in which buildings appropriate to their function may occur, and to encourage an interaction between these buildings and their environment. It is clear that no formal composition can provide an answer to this problem; for the nature of all formal composition is static, precise, and fixed. Buildings which formerly took fifty years to fail, now fail in five. We assume that technology will solve the problem of the five-year economic life by considering the total economic context. Our problem is to seek a way of allowing the five-year building to occur when and where it is needed. The object is not to make the building flexible but to make the urban complex flexible enough to foster short-life buildings as well as long lived ones

Town planning and architecture are parts of a continuous process. Planning is the correlating of human activities; architecture is the housing of these activities. Town planning establishes the milieu in which architecture can happen. Both are conditioned by economic, social, political, technical and physical climates. In a given environment thorough planning will lead to architecture. Planning remains abstract until it generates architecture. Only through its results (buildings, ways, places) can it be. Its function is to establish optimum conditions in which the present becomes future. To do this it must seek out, explore and explain the relationships between human activities. It must then bring these activities together so that the whole of life in the city becomes richer than the sum of its parts

Town planning and architecture today must reflect the image of an open society. New techniques of planning must be developed. We propose

1 To distribute ancillary activities throughout the domain of housing instead of localizing them in certain fixed places, to bring together as many activities as

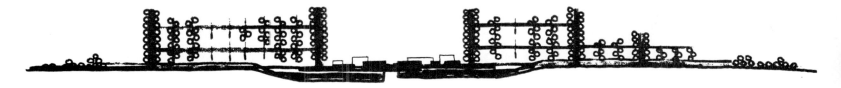

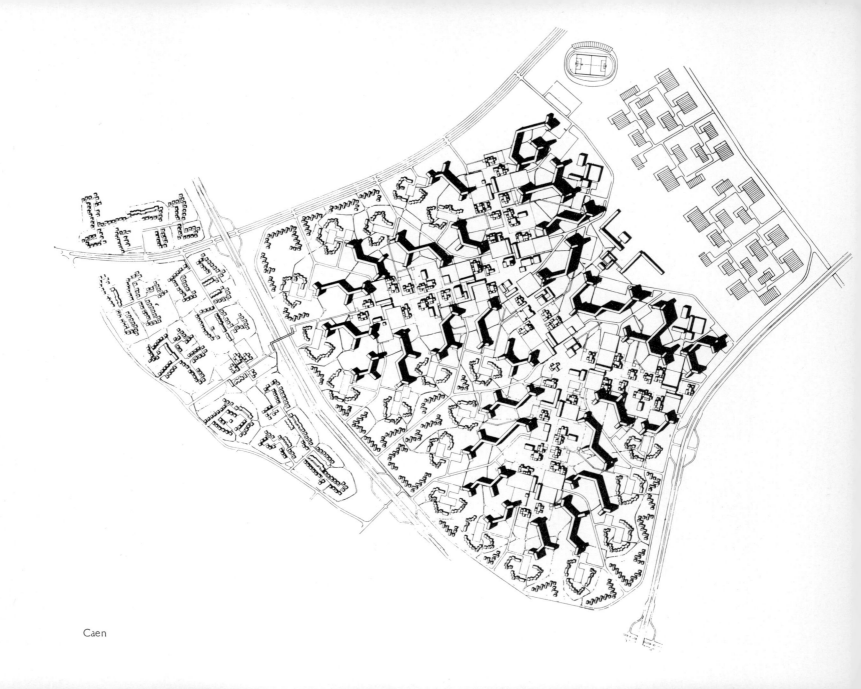

184

Caen

possible, to bring the sum of life to all parts. A linear organization (a line has neither shape nor size) is the truest reflection of an open society

2 To define the use of the automobile which, covering greater distances in shorter times, enables us to imagine a totally new organism in which vehicular and pedestrian traffic is entirely independent

3 To determine points of contact between transportation and dwelling as a way towards the realization of a collectivity and hence to the identification of the individual

4 To re-establish multiple access in collective dwellings, to have more than one way into one's house

The important question is not 'how?' but 'why?' or 'what for?'

Town planning, like architecture, has to help society to achieve its ends, to make life in a community as rich as possible, to aspire to a present utopia. We have no quarrel with the past except insofar as it is used to compromise the future. The past can guide us but past techniques (composition) are of little avail. Present techniques and present means must be used to open as many doors to the future as possible

Candilis, Josic and Woods Le Carré Bleu, No. 3, 1961

I STEM

As it became clear to us that the scale of human relationships is now such that they can no longer be expressed solely through architectural composition, we have sought new, or at least other, ways of organizing these relationships

Our assumptions were:

1 All of our problems are problems in urban design. The city, the highest expression of the society of men, is the natural habitat of man in society

2 The city is, of necessity, oriented towards public mass transportation rather than towards private mobility. The city is the domain of man on foot and seeks to respect his scale. The engines of private mobility have another scale – which is suburban

Our first approach was to consider two families of components—Dwellings and Ancillaries—and to organize these on a linear system. All the servants of dwellings were to be organized into a system of activities and services, to which dwellings might attach themselves

The stem would correspond to a pedestrian street – not a road – composed of commercial, social, educational, and leisure activities and including those

elements of administration and industry whose size and character will allow them to be closely associated with dwellings. The stem would be served by public transportation, service roads and service yards, and could be reached by private motor car at points where this seems desirable and practical

Dwelling complexes, of different types, could be associated with the stem ('plugged in' to it), as the need arose and in measure with the collective equipment provided

The stem, then, provides a total organization within which various forms of human association occur with considerable freedom and spontaneity. By its linear character, it retains a high degree of flexibility. It is by nature open-ended, allowing therefore maximum possibilities for growth, whilst remaining valid at all stages of development

This theme is illustrated here by our three consecutive competition projects for Caen (above), Bilbao, and Toulouse Le Mirail

2 WEB

Further research into systems for human associations led us to consider the possibilities of forming a web of interconnected stems. This generally led to a more intense organization, using multi-level grids of services. The web, as a structuring device, has a higher degree of order than the stem, although in both the form is not a preconception but a result, in fact an unknown, which is assumed to be constantly changing or at least capable of change. We feel that both approaches are valid, possibly each at a different scale

In a web composed of interconnected stems, including all forms of human association and activity, it is supposed that some functions would tend to generate more intense activity than others. The web itself is non-centric by nature and through these peaks of intensity it becomes polycentric, reflecting the life of the society it serves. Like the stem, it is open-ended and can grow and change

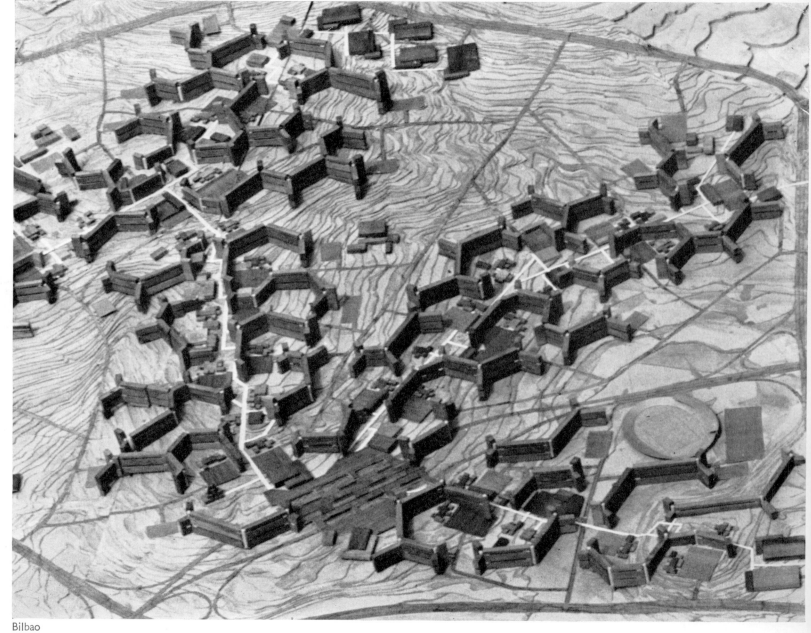

186

Bilbao

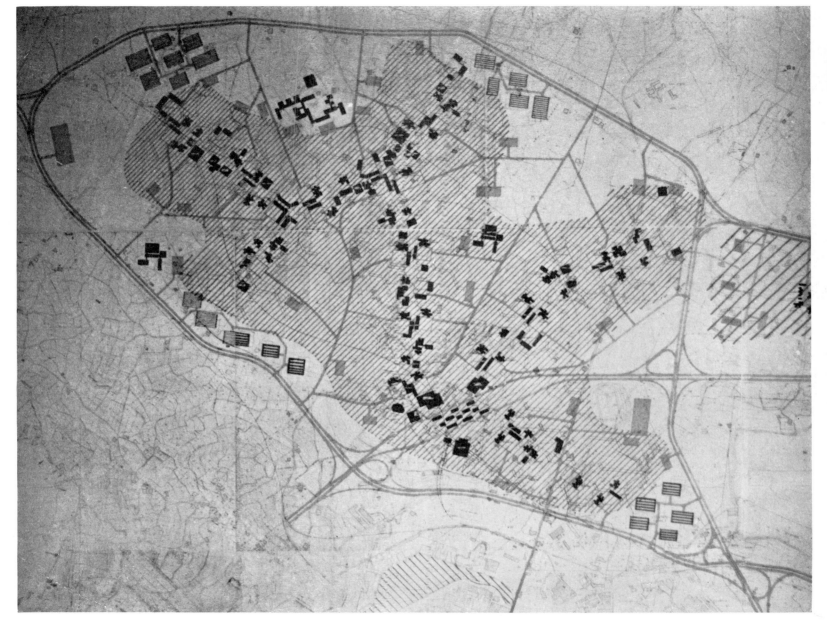

Bilbao. Stem of ancillaries

The web is illustrated here by our project for the centre of Frankfurt

Shadrach Woods 1963-64

WEB

Architecture and planning, which are each a part of the other, are concerned with the organization of places and ways for carrying out man's activities. The architectural process begins with a way of thinking about organization in a given place/time, then establishes a system of relationships and, finally, achieves plastic expression

This process has as its object the integration of specific activities into a total social context. Ideally the result is functional, in the same way that all art must be: it illuminates a society and prepares it for the next step along the way of its progress

As long as societies are evolving within the limits of perceivable human groupings (villages and towns, classes, castes and sects), so long could architecture operate within the limits of purely visual disciplines. With the breakdown of these limits and as man evolves towards a universal society, the need is felt to discover a clear framework for planning and architecture at the new scale. The visual group and its disciplines continue to operate but are no longer adequate to the scale of human relationships today. New systems of architecture are required to illuminate these relationships. The approach can no longer be only visual; we must call upon the whole range of sense, intellect and emotion to elaborate an architecture consonant with our aspirations

Today space is total and society is universal. These realities must be reflected in our planning and building

The rediscovery of continuous total space is the chief non-technical contribution of modern art and architecture to the social phenomena of the twentieth century. The world is one: a continuous surface surrounded by continuous space

Total space and universal society are interdependent; the one engenders the other

In order to reflect these realities of total space and universal society in our planning and building, and to deal with these problems of space and society at today's scale, we try to set up systems (intellectual frames) which can relate activities to each other and which can be understood. Understanding must come through the perception of the parts, as the whole system can never be seen. We try to discover

processes which will lead us to the realization of our society as surely as the visual groups gave clear expression to the societies which they served. In this search, it seems clear that we must dispense with the use of symbols and monuments, for this century has cast aside these crutches of authority. Indeed if authority can be said to exist it can only be through consent, and has no need of formalism or of allegories to impose itself

In Carré Bleu 3, 1961, we illustrated parts of one system for the organization of new housing development at large scale. The essence of the system is a linear association of those activities which serve the housing: shops, schools, social services, etc. . . . The system extends into the housing groups so as to form a continuous collective circulation

The idea of continuity in the organization, so that no parts of it are in danger of isolation and none are subject to an a priori over-densification, is essential to our thought about what systems can be suitable to the evolving total society. Chains of relationships and circulations are continuous, cyclical and tend towards the infinite

When we predetermine points of maximum intensity – centres – it means that we are freezing a present or projected state of activity and relationships. We perpetuate an environment where some things are central and others are not, without, however, any competence for determining which things belong to which category. The future is thus compromised

Given the disciplines of a continuous frame system, functions may be articulated without the chaotic results which we obtain when we pursue only the articulation of function without first establishing a total order. Indeed it is only within such a frame that function can be articulate. The parts of a system take their identity from the system. If there is no order, there is no identity, but only the chaos of disparate elements in pointless competition

The purpose of any putting-together, to create a whole which is greater than the sum of the parts, is only possible if we can guarantee a whole – a total synthetic order of all the functions

Point = concentric (static, fixed)

Line = linear (a measure of liberty)

Web = non-centric initially, polycentric through use (a fuller measure)

Although we do not know where the search for system in planning will lead, we can already recognize

some of the conditions to which these systems will conform. Among these are, principally

The systems will be such that man can, within them, contribute to the creation of his own environment, and in so doing, ameliorate the total environment. This condition holds at all scales, from man in general to each particular man. It is the reason for the systems

The systems will have more than the usual three dimensions. They will include a time dimension

The systems will be sufficiently flexible to permit growth and change within themselves throughout the course of their lives

The systems will remain open in both directions, i.e. in respect to smaller systems within them as well as in respect to greater systems around them

The systems will present, in their beginning, an even overall intensity of activity in order not to compromise the future

The extent and character of the systems will be apparent, or at least ascertainable, from the perception of parts of the systems

We feel that Web, by which word we mean to designate Stem to the next degree, may provide a way to approach the search for systems and, hence, for a true poetic discovery of architecture. (It is ridiculous and infantile to seek out the forms or techniques of the past, for their moment has gone with their society and can never return)

Web is not primarily a circulation system, but an environmental one. It is a way to establish a large-scale order which by its existence makes possible an individual expression at a smaller scale

In its circulation, it intends to find ways for men on foot to associate without inflicting hardship on other men in machines. It seeks to re-establish the human scale in planning. In relation to speed, the measure of which is distance, the human scale is the pedestrian who moves at about 4 km/h. This speed must be accorded with that of automobiles and other mechanical devices. If the human scale is to survive, it must subjugate all the other scales in the places where it is to be conserved. A pedestrian on a throughway is just as ridiculous as an automobile in a casbah. The web must have, as one of its dimensions, the time spent going from point to point, at those various speeds which range from man on foot to man in machine. It is clear that the measure of speed is distance and the measure of distance is time

Web must be a highly flexible system in a rapidly changing world. At the scales at which architect-planners are operating today, it is not possible to conceive of any long-range plan based on fixed spatial or compositional relationships. Even as the first part of such a plan is realized, it modifies the conditions which govern the second, and by continuous feed-back, the whole plan. The non-centric, open-ended web seeks to respond to this life process

Openness is guaranteed by the initial even intensity of activities over the web, so that it can be plugged-into at any point and can itself plug-in to greater systems at any point. These connections provoke points of greater intensity but the original flexibility always remains and the points of density which occur, as the web becomes polycentric through use, retain a non-fixed character

Shadrach Woods Paris August/December 1962

CAEN

In 1961 a competition was organized by the Société pour l'Equipement de la Basse-Normandie, an agency sponsored by the city of Caen, the Département, and the French Government, for a comprehensive site plan to develop a new quarter of the city of Caen. The present population is around 110,000. The proposed extension was to house 40,000 inhabitants with some light industry. The site assigned for the extension covers about 750 acres, of which 125 were to be set aside for industry. The land slopes towards the east and south-east about 3 to 5 per cent and looks over the valley of the Orne. The development was expected to extend over a period of ten to fifteen years

Our proposal was based on the principle of a linear association of all the ancillaries, excepting the industry which was accommodated as requested along the north-west side of the site. Schools, shops, social services, churches, administrative functions, etc, were disposed along pedestrian ways so as to form a continuous stem of activities

The plan was to be developed in five stages of 1,500 to 2,000 dwellings

The basic organization of dwellings was to be in six, ten and fourteen storey buildings plugged into the stem at those points where parking and services were provided. The buildings were to be served by banks of lifts at these entry points connected by 'streets in the sky' at convenient levels, as in Alison and Peter Smithson's Golden Lane proposal of 1952. Automobile access could be controlled and a continuous collective pedestrian system would be provided, which meets but does not follow the

automobile. The distinction between street and road is established

BILBAO

A proposal similar to that for Caen, on a hilly site of about 1,000 acres, provided dwellings for about 85,000 inhabitants. In this scheme, the light industry was more intimately associated with the other activities which support and serve the dwellings. As in the Caen scheme a peripheral road was proposed, collecting all the secondary access roads. The linear centres of activity were proposed along the ridges in the site, and automobile access was to follow the valleys. Industry would be established at the ends of the stems, along the peripheral road

This sector was to be served by an underground rail transit system, connecting it with Bilbao and with the beaches

The pedestrian systems all come together in a central plaza from which the entire scheme can be comprehended. This plaza bridges over the main road from France to Portugal, overlooks the railroad and the new port being built at the conjunction of the Asua and Nervion rivers and lies directly on the axis of the airport's main runway. From here one might see and understand all the transportation systems which link it to the rest of the world. Luxury shops, cafés, and entertainment would be placed here

Dwellings are organized on the same principles as in Caen, without, however, the low-density infill which had been required in that scheme

Toulouse Le Mirail. The shaded area shows the situation of the new city in relation to Toulouse

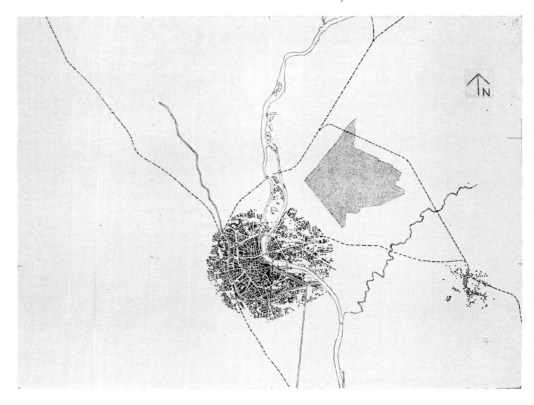

189

Top left: Toulouse Le Mirail.
Basic green structure

Top right: Pedestrian ways

Bottom left: High density
housing and stems

Bottom right: Roads and
parking. Hatched areas represent parking under the
pedestrian ways and plazas

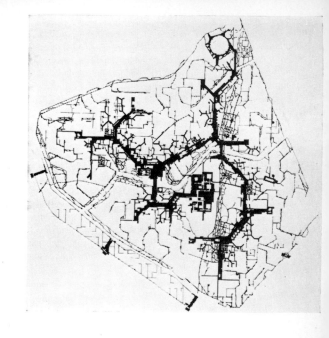

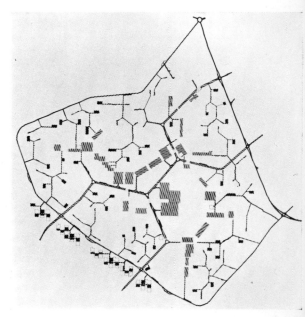

TOULOUSE

Le Mirail is an extension of the city of Toulouse, to house 100,000 inhabitants. Our project illustrated here won first place in a national competition organized in 1961 by the Mayor of Toulouse, Louis Bazerque, through an interministerial agency working in collaboration with the municipality

The present population of Toulouse is around 350,000. The increase in population reflects industrial development as well as the attraction the region holds for settlers returning from North Africa. It is estimated that the realization of Toulouse Le Mirail, which will include light industry and offices as well as housing, will extend over a period of ten to fifteen years

The site for this new sector comprised 2,000 acres of semi-agricultural, semi-residential land, about five miles from the centre of Toulouse. It consists of two relatively flat plains, the alluvial Garonne to the east, and the Blagnac terrace, separated by a 30-50 ft bluff, running north-south through the site. The upper plateau is again divided by a ravine running from west to east. These natural conditions have created a heavily wooded natural green system on the site, which we proposed to retain and to use as a basis for a structuring system

The plan is a further application of the linear centre as a servant and generator of habitat and as a structuring device for the city. Human activities, ancillaries and services are organized into a linear system of relationships into which housing units are plugged. The stem will contain commercial, social and cultural activities, and traffic will be completely separated, with automobile parking and service roads and courts being sunken so as to leave the pedestrian completely free in his movement. The dwellings along these stems are organized in interconnected buildings of six, ten, and fourteen storeys with streets-in-the-air—continuous horizontal ways through the buildings, linking their vertical circulations and various entry points. This facilitates the localization of automobile ways and parks, establishing a harmony of pedestrian and mechanical circulations. Roughly 75 per cent of the dwellings will be organized in this fashion: the remaining 25 per cent being arranged in typical low-density infill patterns around the dense, central core. The embankment and a small stream running from west to east through the upper terrace determine a natural linear park which is retained in this scheme. The stream feeds an artificial lake in the centre of the project, bordering the regional administrative and cultural centre. The linear centre, which follows this

191

natural greenway, contains shops, markets, social and cultural centres, places of entertainment and of worship, parks and gardens, etc. The origin of the linear centre is an administrative complex which is intended to serve the region (radius about 125 miles), and will contain public buildings, offices, theatres, a shopping centre, meeting halls, exhibition halls, a museum, etc

The high density housing plugged-into these linear centres is in continuous six- to ten-storey buildings, as we have said. All apartments have double orientation and all have outdoor space in the form of either balcony or loggia. Maximum distance to the nearest elevator is 250 ft

Shadrach Woods 1963, with acknowledgments to Architectural Design, London, April 1963

THE CENTRE OF FRANKFURT

The city is the expression of human associations and activities. It exists to stimulate and encourage human intercourse. It is the realm of man in society

Men create cities in order to conjugate their efforts and co-ordinate their activities in such a way that the whole of their life together may become greater than the sum of their lives apart. If the city is to fulfil its promises it must be able to adapt itself constantly to the changing forms and intensities of human exchange. The city cannot be the result of either a land-use diagram or a composition of spaces and volumes, since the first tends to dissociate the various functions of the city and to ignore the relationships between them; while in the second, the most perfect manifestation will be that which is the least adapted to change and growth, which is life. The city expresses life; it is a living, changing organism, formed by man and his activities for the development of his society

Any event in the city relates in some way to every other event in the city

The problem of the construction or renewal of cities lies in the discovery of these relationships and may be resolved by the invention of systems which enable us to put them into harmony in a total, organic order

These systems or organizations can not only harmonize present functions; they should also take into account change and growth, and the evolution of the city. They must organize the present, while opening the way to the future

The problem of the centre of Frankfurt is not to make a museum of it, but to discover a system which the

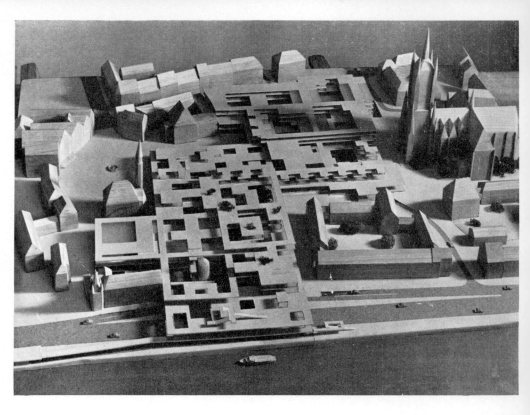

citizens can use to create their own environment and which they can evolve parallel to their own evolution

The needs of such a centre are so diverse, the activities so different, that if each were to be considered separately the result would necessarily be chaotic. The only way to proceed is to consider them all as parts of a single organism, containing or supporting different functions, keeping a valid scale for both the site and the people using this complex

Our proposal was made as a result of an invitation to participate in a competition to determine how the centre of Frankfurt, destroyed by fire-bombs in the second world war, should be rebuilt. This was the second competition; the first, held in the early fifties, was fruitless

The cathedral, the town-hall (Römer), the Nikolaikirche, and some gothic houses around the site had already been rebuilt and restored. Some new buildings with a historic (pseudo-gothic) flavour have been built, notably some medium-rent apartment housing along the Main Quay between the site and the river

The programme given by the organizers of the competition called for a commercial and cultural complex, consisting of two libraries, a youth centre, a historical museum, a school of music, an art gallery, exhibition spaces, a bus station, shops and stores as well as restaurants, snack bars, cabaret, cinema. It was left to the discretion of the competitors whether to include office space for the city's technical services or to leave these in an existing, quite ugly building in the north-east corner of the site. We chose to include them

Since such a variety of accommodation was required, we sought to discover an organization in which all these different functions could integrate in a total order. This was felt to be preferable to housing each function in its own building – each building expressing its function – and the whole being sprayed with neo-gothic paint to avoid chaos. Our approach was through a multi-level web system, scaled to the pedestrian and to the immediate environment, into which different uses and functions could be plugged

The proposal therefore consists of a system of multi-level distribution grids containing the mechanical services and corresponding to a circulation net of horizontal or inclined ways. This organization serves as a basis for the determination of areas to be built up on a secondary structural grid, inserted into the main grid. Parts of the distribution grid are executed only as they are needed; if they do not serve any immediate building, they exist only as possibilities or as 'rights-of-way'. As more accommodation is needed, more of the web can be built. Presumably, if parts of the complex were removed, the corresponding parts of the web could be disconnected. The system, then, retains a certain potential for growth and for change

The lowest level of the complex is the service area containing direct access for trucks, lorries and other service vehicles, storage space and the heart of the mechanical systems. Above this level a network of horizontal and vertical ducts, and of pedestrian ways with level changes by escalators or travelators, is established. The dimensions of this network are determined by the known needs as well as by manageable building sizes. In the present scheme the basic dimension is around 100 ft square. The net is composed of 12 ft rights-of-way, leaving free areas of about 11,500 sq ft. The 110 ft dimension was found to correspond approximately to the size of the existing net of pedestrian ways in the immediate vicinity of the site. Within this net, there is a system of construction based on bays of 25 ft 5 in and 15 ft 8½ in. These dimensions are not arbitrary but are based upon the relationships between man and the

193

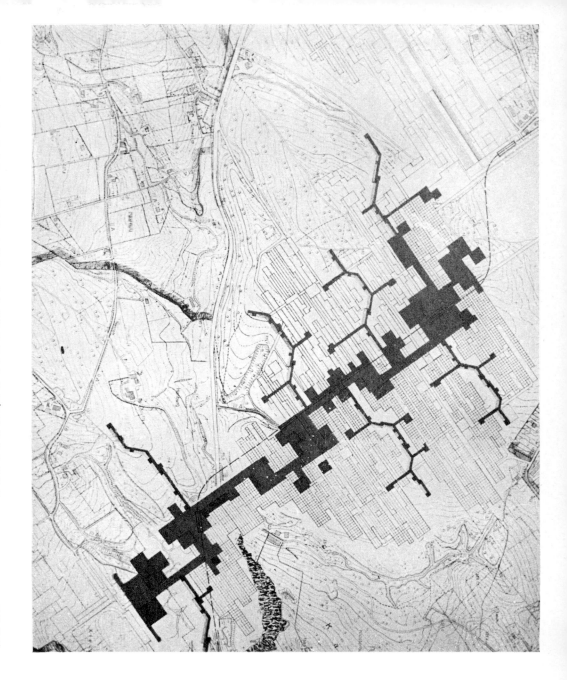

Right: Bochum University. Plan showing pedestrian routes and central spine. The dotted line indicates the elevated monorail route, and the cranked blocks on each side of the central spine are the student housing suspended above the faculty wings

194

space through which he moves as put forth in Le Corbusier's Modulor

It was felt that any project whose purpose was to revitalize the centre of Frankfurt should not be separated from the Main by a block of apartments. We took the liberty of demolishing some thirty apartments, to bring the centre out over the Main Quay to the riverside where excursion boats now dock. These apartments would be replaced by dwellings at the upper levels of the new construction

An attempt was made to re-establish the conditions of scale and space in which the cathedral was built, so that it could retain its vertical validity

(All the prize-winning schemes in this competition created large open spaces in front of the cathedral, a form of architectural assassination which delighted Viollet le Duc and Baron Haussmann!)

Candilis, Josic and Woods Le Carré Bleu, No 3, 1963 Bauwelt No 34, August 1963

PROJECT FOR BOCHUM UNIVERSITY

The project illustrated here was designed for the international competition for a University of the Ruhr at Bochum in 1963. The competition programme called for 'an arrangement of relatively small departments which are brought together into the closest possible contact'; yet the design for the projected 10,000 student enrolment must also be capable of expansion in numbers and facilities

The solution illustrated shows a linear university organized along a stem or 'backbone', running northeast south-west, which is both open-ended, and extendable sideways. The architects have placed large lecture rooms, restaurants, libraries, auditoria, administration buildings and other important common facilities along this central stem so that a dense pedestrian-oriented central thoroughfare will act as a spine for the University as a whole

To the east of the stem are buildings for technical, natural and applied sciences. To the west are the human and social sciences, philosophy, religion, languages, economics and law. Student housing accommodation is in the cranked blocks which rise above the faculty buildings and extend outwards from the central stem. Indeed, in common with the University as a whole, extension outwards is the principal means of growth

The south-eastern end of the stem links with Bochum itself, and at this end the architects have sited the largest of the University auditoria, the theatre, the sports stadium, and some library facilities. At the north-eastern end of the stem are the medical school with a 2,800-bed teaching hospital. Although the stem is entirely pedestrian-oriented, an overhead monorail links Bochum with the hospital, and on to Wissen

The site is extremely hilly, and along the length of the site as a whole there is a level change of over 200 ft. These level changes are used to interpenetrate buildings and segregate pedestrian and automobile circulation

BERLIN FREE UNIVERSITY

This proposal was designed for the competition for the Berlin Free University in September 1963 and emerged the winner. The Berlin Free University was formed by professors and students who left the university located in the East Zone of Berlin, and settled in the Western Zone, re-establishing themselves in old mansions and some new buildings financed by the Ford Foundation

The competition was not for the university as a whole, but for an extension of about 3,600 students of the faculties of arts, philosophy, literature, and psychology, physics and organic chemistry. Like most universities, it is assumed that the Free University will continue to expand, and in fact much of the land surrounding the site is already being acquired for this purpose

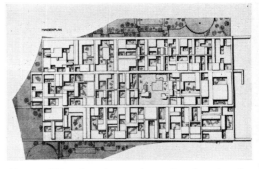

Above: This plan shows the web of pedestrian circulation within the University, the four main spines and the cross connections linking faculty buildings and quiet courts

Previous page: This view of the model from the southeast shows the University extending from the stadium and the town of Bochum on the lower left to the teaching hospital complex on the upper right. Note the dramatic changes of level, and the spread of the University outwards from the central spine

Below: This site plan of the Free University of Berlin shows its relation to the parklands (shaded areas), the U-bahn and the S-bahn. The dotted lines indicate the main pedestrian routes through the University complex

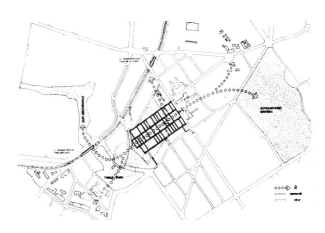

The orientation of the site is again north-west south-east, and is related to two small parks. Its direction is roughly parallel to the main rapid-transit facilities, U-bahn (subway) and S-bahn (elevated); by U-bahn, the site is about thirty minutes from Berlin Centre

This proposal is based, not on one, but on four parallel stems, 200 ft apart, and oriented in the main direction of the university. The design is thus capable of expansion, in the main orientation by the extension of the stems, and also a further bay-size of 200 ft on each side. Like the Frankfurt project, the stems are interconnected by secondary ways at appropriate intervals, transforming the total design into a web

Along the main stems are situated those functions which serve the whole university and encourage easy contact with people in other disciplines—auditoria, libraries, exhibition spaces, restaurants, meeting rooms, plazas, and lounges, etc. Those places and functions—private workrooms, laboratories, seminar rooms and studies, offices and so forth—which require privacy and tranquillity are located away from the main stems, and yet are linked to them by the comprehensible structure

The thematic advantages of this structure are enormous in terms of flexibility and formal subtlety, ease of access to all parts, multiplication of contacts (which is one of the chief functions of a university), comprehensibility and compactness, and the rapid transition from public areas to buildings and courts of absolute quiet and privacy. The present stage of the design shows three levels; an underground service and storage floor, a ground floor on which most of the public activities occur, as well as the tranquil courts so traditional to university life, and an upper floor of offices and lecture rooms, seminar rooms and private studies. Most of the roofs are made accessible as public or private terraces. Localized third and fourth floor levels of student and faculty housing accommodation may be added as the programme progresses

The architects have been careful not to impose a hierarchy of importance on certain parts, or buildings, or faculties, in their design of the university. To the contrary, the design is deliberately non-centric, in the belief that buildings should be places in which men may locate importance through their work, activity and association—and that these, within the discipline of the overall structure or web, will create the more important evolving character of the university as a whole

196

Below: Model of the University from the south

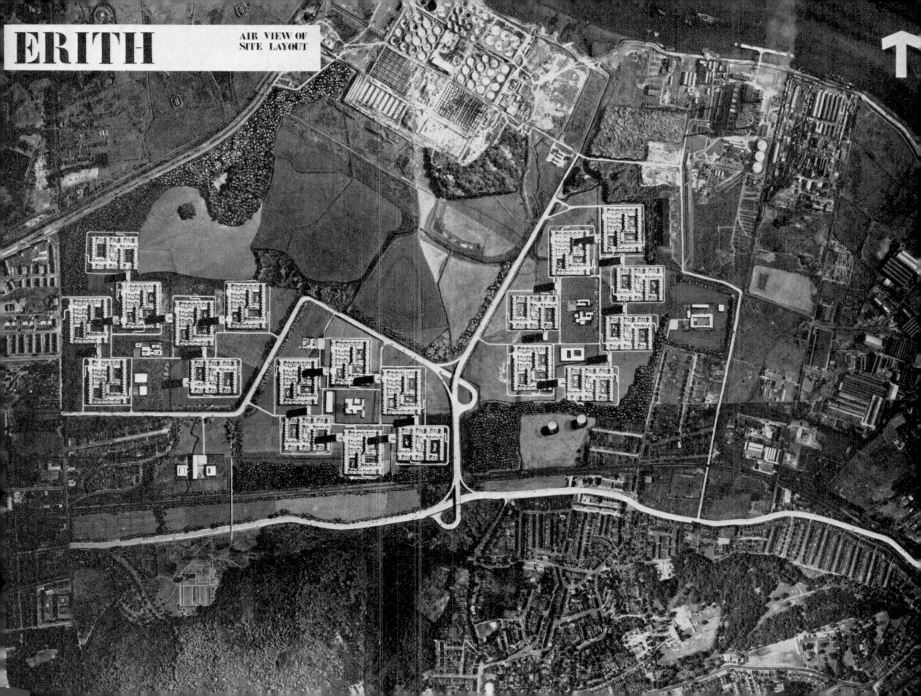

ERITH

AIR VIEW OF
SITE LAYOUT

ERITH

KENNETH CAMPBELL

LOCATION

Ten miles down river from the Pool of London, where the eastern boundary of the County divides it from Kent, the Thames makes a considerable loop to the north. This loop, running by Gallion's Reach past False Point and Old Man's Head through Halfway Reach, encloses a great expanse of level, marsh-like land bounded on its southern edge by the low hills of North Kent which fall here in a sharp escarpment facing north. At the west and east ends of the loop lie the towns of Woolwich and Erith respectively and on the high ground between and to the south are several former villages—Plumstead,Welling, Bexley-heath—joined together by speculative development during the 1930's. This development, however, is not continuous. It is broken by commons, ravines, and woods, which give the whole area a remarkable character of its own, almost unique and little known by the majority of Londoners

CHARACTER OF SITE

The level lands within the loop itself, running some four miles from east to west and over a mile from north to south, were hardly encroached upon until the nineteenth century. Then the great naval and military arsenal at Woolwich spread over a large area at the western end. The southern outfall works of the London drainage system were constructed on the river's edge and in the far eastern end the Erith industrial area began to develop after 1945. The greater part of the land, however, still lay open and untouched between these encroachments, wide pastures of coarse grass intersected with water courses and with pools and reed beds here and there

Over the blowing grass the cloud shadows run in the summer with a loud singing of larks and in winter the north-east winds cut across from the North Sea and the Essex flats beyond the river

RECENT HISTORY

In 1950 the London County Council, as part of its post-war housing programme, decided to develop that part of this land which lay within its own boundary and this, the Abbey Wood housing estate, was begun in 1955. Its character is conventional for its period. At a low density—some twenty dwellings to the acre—it is composed mainly of two-storey cottage terraces with some three- and four-storey flats and one tall block of ten storeys to mark its main shopping centre

It was not built without difficulty. Its subsoil, where many centuries ago the river ran sluggishly in wide lagoons, is largely wet and spongy peat with little bearing capacity and foundations even for two-storey houses were deep, difficult and expensive. Higher buildings had to be piled deep down to the London clay beneath the peat and even the sewers had to be supported on similar piles

The experience of these costs and difficulties were fresh in the minds of the architects when the new scheme came to be considered in 1961

By this time practically all the open spaces and bombed sites of any size at all within the County had long been built over and the County Council was finding it increasingly difficult to find land on which to build the housing so desperately needed for the long waiting list, the homeless, the slum-dwellers and those displaced to make way for the equally necessary new roads, parks and schools. A very large part of the marsh lands at Erith outside the County boundary, which divides the whole area roughly in two, were in fact in the Council's ownership. This had been designated as 'barrier land' to the main southern drainage works bordering the river. When under the pressure of land shortage the Council's eye was turned towards this area it appeared that some 500 acres could well be made available for housing and the ancillary uses which should go with it

POPULATION

After deducting the necessary sites for these uses—schools, public open space and so forth—and applying the 100 persons per acre density which the Kent Planning Authority when approached were prepared to allow, it appeared that housing could be provided for some 25,000 people (about 8,000 families). This would be a very substantial contribution to the housing supply, equivalent to nearly two years of the Council's normal house building programme and involving no demolition of existing property

PRELIMINARY INVESTIGATION

The Valuation Department of the London County Council and the Housing Division of the Architects' Department with the help of the Town Planning Division of the same department began the necessary consultations with the interests and authorities involved. Of these the principal ones were the Erith Borough Council in whose area the site lay, the Kent County Council and the transport authorities – British Railways and the London Passenger Transport Board. At this point two of the major problems connected with the site became clear. The first was that of communications and transport; the second the physical nature of the ground

At first sight communications appear to be satisfactory. Running along the southern edge of the site, parallel with each other and immediately under the escarpment of the hill are a main east-west road and an electrified railway line running into termini in the centre of the city. Unfortunately the rail line already serves an enormous commuting area of the south-east of London and in spite of nose to tail running and double-decker coaches it is loaded to, and almost beyond, capacity. The road system for buses into Woolwich and beyond into town is in a similar condition

It soon became clear therefore that it would be essential to provide employment either in the area or further to the east and south (against the peak traffic flow), for the wage earners in the new development. On the face of it this appeared to be reasonably possible. Erith Borough Council itself was already planning a major redevelopment and expansion of its commercial centre, which would provide some office employment within a short distance, while ample land was available in the Erith industrial area and in the Council's own industrial estate next to Woolwich Arsenal to take a very considerable number of industrial firms to provide both skilled and semi-skilled jobs. In addition the opening of the

Tilbury Tunnel under the Thames provides access to the important area north of the river which is scheduled for considerable industrial expansion

In spite of these potentialities, however, the actual organization of the movement of industry particularly to the industrial areas near the site presents great problems of legislative powers, administration and finance. These are being attacked by the Council with considerable vigour and in the meantime the parallel technical problems are being tackled by the Architects' Department

The major technical difficulty as stated earlier lies in the nature of the ground itself. This is composed of deep peaty strata overlying London clay, intersected with many water courses which act as a partial reservoir for storm water between tides and the whole lies well below Thames high water level. The flood defence system along the river has been greatly strengthened since the disaster of 1953-54 but understandably the whole area is subject to an Erith bye-law stipulating that the floor level of all habitable rooms must be at least 8 ft 6 in above Newlyn Datum, i.e., about 10 to 12 ft above the existing ground level

Below: Erith: Section through the Platform

199

GENERAL SOLUTION

It was the combination of these two factors—the nature of the ground and the existence of the bye-law—which first gave the architects concerned the idea of the 'platform-town': that is, the idea of establishing an independent pedestrian level for the entire area, some 12 ft above the ground, which would carry the whole of the housing, its ancillaries and its associated circulation. From this many important results began to flow. It established immediately a vertical segregation of pedestrian and vehicular traffic, not artificially but arising out of the nature of the solution itself. It enabled all garaging and car parking at a ratio of one garage per dwelling to be placed at ground level under the pedestrian decks and thus avoid the waste of surface use which normal garaging presents. The space under the platforms could also comfortably accommodate areas for electricity sub-stations, maintenance workshops, refuse collection, incineration plant, pumping stations, covered play spaces and, if required, tenants' workshops. Architecturally also the platform idea gave the possibility of defining the actual building forms into three-dimensional groupings which could relate in scale with the wide flat landscape, the dome of the sky, the powerful industrial

buildings in the background and the high level pylons carrying power from beyond the Thames. Any conventional ground level groupings of small dwellings would have been dwarfed and made practically meaningless against such surroundings

To achieve this modelling it was necessary to divide the total development into units of suitable size and volume; moreover it was strongly felt that social reasons demanded that the total number of 8,000 dwellings needed to be subdivided into more 'human' and intimate groupings. Here the research carried out a year or two earlier on the abortive Hook New Town project gave useful assistance. In the publication 'The Planning of a New Town' it was suggested that a community of between 400 and 1,200 persons provided the basis of a comprehensible social unit. A 'platform' carrying some 400 dwellings was therefore taken as the basic design unit. Each would include a full cross-section of family sizes and types. Since such a platform by itself would be too small to support adequate shopping facilities or schools, clusters were proposed, each of some six or seven platforms and each containing for example a primary school or schools, a shopping centre, community centre, surgeries or clinics, and perhaps a library. Three of these clusters made up the total scheme and in the

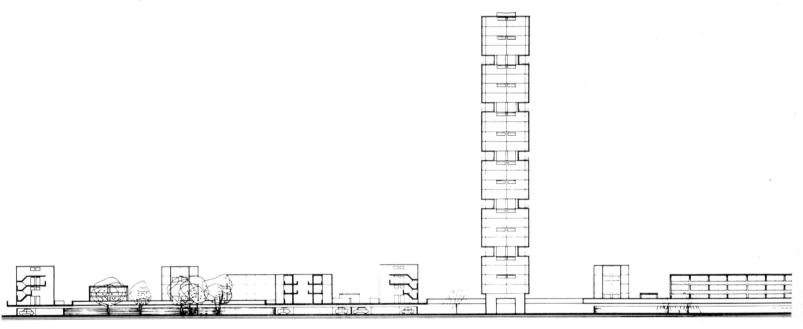

wide spaces outside provision was made in the plan for two secondary schools and defined public open space at the ratio of seven acres per 1,000 population

COMMUNICATIONS

The overall picture therefore is of three 'star' clusters each of about 2,600 families composed of six or seven platform units of some 400 families. The clusters are linked by a ground level road running up on a viaduct over the railway line and connected to the main east-west road beyond (scheduled for widening) by means of an over and under junction. In addition a high level pedestrian way running past the secondary school site south of the clusters spans both rail and road to connect directly to the open slopes of the Abbey Woods close to the ruins of Lesnes Abbey

The platforms in each cluster are linked together by bridges at platform level. From the ground level ramps will bring milk and bread floats, ambulances, etc, up to the platforms

DISPOSITION OF DWELLINGS

Between the platforms, slender towers of some thirty storeys straddle the pedestrian bridges. Their elevators which travel down to ground level provide access from ground to platform for the aged, infirm and overburdened

These towers contain two and three room dwellings only, the larger family dwellings being disposed in one, two, three and four storey buildings on the platforms. These would have 'patio' type gardens which would depend on boxes, tubs and specially recessed parts of the platform slab for a modest amount of planting

The present proposal is that heating should be by recirculated warm air units and the possibility of using waste heat from the adjacent Belvedere Power Station is being considered for this purpose

STRUCTURAL DESIGN

The platforms are not to be thought of merely as enclosures for garages since they form an important part of the foundation system. By relating the dimensional organization of the superstructures to that of the garages below, the latter with their dividing walls form a sort of 'egg crate' box raft linking the pile heads together. This idea sets a dimensional discipline which provides the basis for a fully developed system of Industrialized Building for the whole scheme. Since the co-ordination of building with the provision of employment would

200

appear to indicate a total construction period of, say, ten years an economic basis exists for the erection of a fully mechanized factory on the site for the production of all the necessary structural units. An output of some 800 dwellings a year would on present techniques be provided by four production lines

LANDSCAPING

It is intended to exploit the special 'Fen' like character of the site by retaining and controlling certain of the existing water courses, lining them with willows and similar trees together with carefully placed belts of 'shelter' planting. This would link with more intimate groupings of trees and water within the clusters. The idea would then be carried down still further in scale by penetrating each platform with openings down to ground level providing protected leisure and playspaces within the platform itself

It is also suggested that the greater part of the surface water storage in the area should be concentrated in a large shallow lake occupying the reedy and marshy north-western corner of the site. This could provide all kinds of water recreation including perhaps a modest 'marina'

Generally speaking the areas of flat land round the clusters would be regarded as informal recreation and walking space, the grass scythed rather than mown, and providing for the more energetic activities and ball games for the older children. This would, of course, be separate from the more formal and controlled public open spaces and playing fields required by the Planning Authority

FURTHER DEVELOPMENTS

The foregoing sets out the scheme as illustrated and as presented to the County Council and other authorities in its first form. Since then further structural and design studies combined with continuing research into the physical characteristics of the area indicate that certain modifications may be necessary in the visual build-up of the scheme. It is too early to be specific on these changes and in any case they have not yet been submitted to or approved by the committees concerned

The general trend, however, leads towards a breaking up of the present rather stiff repetition of formal rectangular shapes for the platforms in favour of greatly increased modelling of their outlines on plan

This in its turn is leading to a lessening of the individual identity of the individual platforms which

will be much more closely related and towards a much increased organic shaping of the cluster as a single unity

With this is developing a more controlled and strongly modelled vertical shaping of the buildings on the platforms leading again to a greater architectural unity in each cluster

Further consideration of the tall blocks has also produced some doubt of their role in the overall landscape. Certainly they seem to be too closely clustered. However, in any case there are several serious technical difficulties connected with them, not the least being the fact which has now emerged that their upper levels would be subject to a layer of noxious gases from the stacks of the adjoining power station

Nevertheless nothing has yet emerged to invalidate the basic conception of the scheme as a whole and, given a solution of the employment and town planning problems, it remains a valid architectural and social answer to the challenge posed by a difficult but, in its own way, magnificent site

202

CREDITS

The Erith scheme was designed in the Architects' Department of the London County Council, County Architect – Hubert Bennett, FRIBA

Principal Housing Architect – Kenneth Campbell, FRIBA

Senior Planning Officer – John Craig, ARICS, AMTPI

Original design team – E. E. Hollanby, ARIBA, AMTPI, Dip.TP(Lond); A. C. C. Jones, ARIBA, AA.Dip

Present design team – D. Groves, ARIBA; T. M. Leitersdorf, AA.Dip

Chief Engineer – The late F. M. Fuller, OME, BSc(Eng), MICE, MIStructE

Valuer to the Council – The late W. Webb, FRICS

Director of Housing – R. J. Allerton, FRICS, AMIMunE, PPI.Hsg

Perspective drawings – Norah Glover

BRASS SCULPTURE NUMBER 32

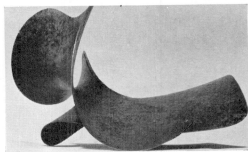

KENT BLOOMER

203

When a hand, in order to investigate an object, touches, it does so with the whole hand, not just the fingertips. Nor does the enquiring hand remain in a fixed position; it moves over the surface, tapping and pulling

Eyes which stare at space do not see space. Only by a visual reaching out and grabbing at, turning upside down, and shaking of space does accurate perception begin; permitting meditation

The brass in my sculpture is something for the eye to dig into. It is the hand performing a probing action. It does not try to trap space, for space confined is space lost

I compare my sculpture to an open hand. I am investigating, not asserting

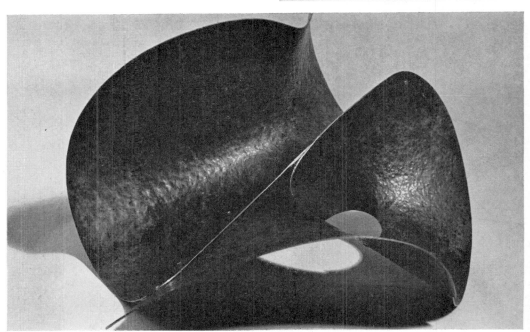

Right: Brass Sculpture Number 32, 1962. Forged brass. 20 × 11 ins. Collection: Paul and Dorothy Schweikher, Pittsburgh, USA. Photo: James Cook

THE LINEAR CITY

GEORGE R. COLLINS

It would appear that if man in his capacity as a pedestrian is to survive this century, he must be able to insulate himself physically and psychologically from the beaten path of vehicular traffic. But he must, at the same time, have quick and easy access to every type of transportation. These two apparently irreconcilable necessities have been a major concern of planners since their profession came into being. Nearly every planning blueprint of the past 100 years has been put forward with this dilemma in mind; the suggestions have been varied and numerous

Some of the most comprehensive schemes have been what we call 'linear'. Linear plans tend, by their very nature, to be regional rather than merely city-wide. For the linear planner, arteries of transportation are like the backbone or the circulatory system of the body – his desire is to obtain the most efficient, the most organic relationship that can be devised between these arteries and the other functions of our living and working

In laying out his arteries the linear planner is not usually concerned with slashing through the internal blockages of our cities as would a Haussmann or a modern traffic engineer; but is more interested in arranging lines or nets of routes 'between' existing cities that can be flanked with future settlements,

and thus draw off the pressure on the metropolis. For instance, to a linear planner the dread ribbon development, city-spread, and overspill are normal processes, natural dwelling patterns of mankind; as such, then, these tendencies should be rationalized and exploited rather than legislated against. How?

As we shall see there have been many solutions proposed, differing widely in character, but all of them opposed to perpetuating the centripetal, centrifugal metropolitan hives to which we have accustomed ourselves. Most linear plans are decentralist in intent, but decentralize along some sort of structured 'route' – unsatisfied with relieving a congested centre by merely throwing off of a planetary system of satellite communities. Behind all linear planning lies the conviction that the staggering scale of our future can only be met by a schema that allows for infinite and integrated expansion of both the core and the periphery of our communities simultaneously, ie, the LINE

This idea was first expressly stated in the early 1880's by a Spaniard, Arturo Soria y Mata:

> A single street of 500 metres' width and of the length that may be necessary – such will be the city of the future, whose extremities could be Cadiz and St Petersburg, or Peking and Brussels

> Put in the centre of this immense belt trains and trams, conduits for water, gas and electricity, reservoirs, gardens and, at intervals, buildings for different municipal services – fire, sanitation, health, police, etc – and there would be resolved at once almost all the complex problems that are produced by the massive populations of our urban life

> Our projected city unites the hygienic conditions of country life to the great capital cities and, moreover, assumes that the railroads, like today's paved streets and sidewalks, will carry free or for little all citizens

This suggestion appeared on March 6, 1882, in a column that Soria was writing for a Madrid newspaper about aspects of municipal reform. The elements of his future city seem rather primitive by modern standards, but the vision was there

Soria's Ciudad Lineal, as he called it, was based on a now extinct form of locomotion – the tramway – powered by a long forgotten method of traction – the horse. At night these 'rapid' transit vehicles were to give way to goods trains chugging along the central boulevard of his 500 metres wide settlement. To a generation that no longer derives solace and inspiration

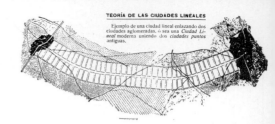

TEORÍA DE LAS CIUDADES LINEALES

Ejemplo de una ciudad lineal enlazando dos ciudades aglomeradas, o sea una *Ciudad Lineal* moderna uniendo dos *ciudades puntos* antiguas.

Top: The regional layout of a Ciudad Lineal connection between two old 'point-cities' as Soria termed them

Below: Bird's eye view of a Ciudad Lineal laid out in the later manner with a buffer zone of vegetation along both sides. A boulevard 40 m wide, tree-lined, and with double car tracks, forms the axis of the community. At 300 m. intervals were to be 20 m. cross streets forming superblocks of 40,000 to 60,000 sq m. From the beginning, Soria proclaimed 'for every family its own house, for every house an orchard and garden'

from the clicking of the rails these arrangements are not happy ones, but for that day – in Spain at least – they were utopian. Soria was a businessman and a public servant with political leanings of a democratic sort; he had pioneered in the development of tramway lines in the capital, and was campaigning for subways, telephones, telegraphic warning systems, and other modernities which Spain was not yet prepared to accept

During the years 1882-83 when he was writing about civic problems in Madrid, he referred on several occasions to his plan for a Ciudad Lineal. It becomes clear, on reading these articles, that the common notion that Ebenezer Howard's was the first regional plan is incorrect. The scale of Soria's thinking was large; from the beginning it was his intention to include in his local Ciudad Lineal all the outer villages in the Madrid area. 'Ruralize city life, urbanize the country,' he said, 'Linear cities will make on the map of Spain an immense triangulation.' The growth of linear cities is simple, he noted, because the line itself can go on to infinity and at any point a new community can shoot off like the branch of a tree, the tributaries of a river, the veins of the body. He constantly stressed the organic

The remarkable thing about Soria is that he actually launched such a project on his own. In 1892 he published the details of a stock company designed to establish around Madrid the ring of linear cities that he had proposed in the newspaper as an answer to the growing problem of internal congestion. Although he won the support of those Spaniards who had studied urban problems and housing, he never succeeded in extracting the slightest concessions from the 'authorities'; his Ciudad Lineal, financed largely by the savings of little people and its own residents, never achieved more than a tenth part of its purpose. Madrid, naturally inimical to industry, did not provide the manufacturing basis that Soria had hoped for, and the Ciudad Lineal ended up as an independent residential suburb with sports, weekend recreation, and the Spanish movie business for its major assets. As a commercial venture it almost went bankrupt (ca. 1918), mainly because of Soria's herculean effort to bring in a proper aqueduct, and not be dependent on the bureaucrats who would unpredictably turn off his municipal water supply from time to time. As an active movement it succumbed in the 1930's to the political vicissitudes of the Republic, the Civil War, and world-wide economic depression, but not before it had been illustrated in nearly every textbook on city planning

The way in which this bucolic little suburb is being destroyed today by the incursion of high-rise buildings, by the cutting of its precious trees, and by general dilapidation is a crime that will someday weigh on the conscience of 'madrileños' when they discover that they have allowed one of the historic monuments of city planning to suffocate to death

There seem to have been no precedents for Soria's ideas. He was acquainted with Spanish writings on municipal reform and housing – a substantial literature – but they contain no prototype for his scheme. In assembling his arguments he was more inclined

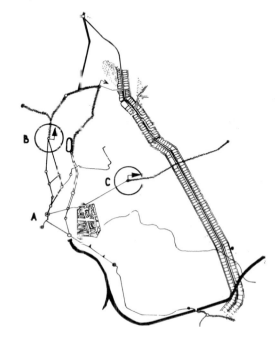

Below: A diagrammatic map of the Ciudad Lineal as finally laid out. This is only a fifth part of the circuit originally planned to surround Madrid; and only the upper third of it was actually constructed. Arrows indicate the starting points of the Company's own tram lines which were part of a circuit through the centre of Madrid. This route was completed in 1904, electrified in 1909, and functions in part to this day. A–Puerta del Sol; B–Cuatro Caminos; C–Ventas

to quote from philosophical writings; Darwin, Spencer, and Henry George were favourites of his. Perhaps he had been attracted by some technological gimmick, now forgotten, that appeared in the literature he consulted for his transportation business: Spanish engineering periodicals frequently reported on city planning developments in those days. The Great Victorian Way which Paxton had proposed in the 1850's is the type of project he might have read about, although that circumvallating, arcaded crystal palace had little in common with the concept of the Ciudad Lineal

Although the Ciudad Lineal was only a limited success in itself, its theory permeated the consciousness of the international planning movement as a result of the untiring publicity campaign of Soria and his associates. In 1897 he founded a house organ, 'La Ciudad Lineal,' which by 1902 had developed into a city-planning magazine – our first such. More familiar abroad, however, were the company's numerous illustrated booklets that explained the theory, reported on the progress of the little community, and described linear projects elsewhere in the world. The breadth of interest of these publications owed much to two of Soria's collaborators (and successors), Hilarión González del Castillo and Georges Benoit-Lévy

González del Castillo, a lawyer and free-lance writer in the foreign service of Spain, was a resident and director of the Ciudad Lineal. Well informed about architecture and city planning, he suggested many elaborations of Soria's original idea in order to meet special needs. Most important, perhaps, was his effort to counter the common criticism of linear planning: that it is too strung-out a form to possess civic character, to have community centres, etc. In 1919 González del Castillo proposed (at the Reconstruction Exposition in Brussels) a regional plan consisting of a series of wider strip cities, each only long enough to accommodate 60,000 residents and zoned for various activities. These would have Imperial Roman type forums at the intersections of their cross-avenues, the main such transverse boulevard connecting up with airport and major railroad lines that were now to run outside the city proper instead of along its central axis

His also was the proposal to add buffer zones of greenery to separate the linear city from its countryside – an idea obviously taken over from the Garden City. In fact, González del Castillo considered there to be two classes of garden city: the English satellite type and the Spanish linear type. One of his most

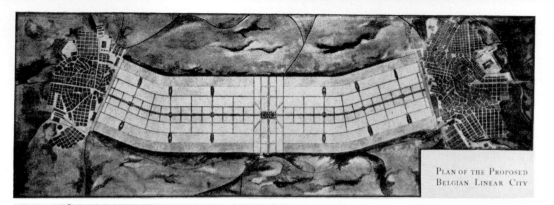

Left: A typical unit of the 'Belgian Linear City' which Gonzalez del Castillo designed in 1919. It is zoned into a central residential and administrative band with boulevard and plazas, two flanking industrial zones, and two outer farming belts, all bordered by a continuous forest belt. A series of these units would be used if the point-cities were more than 10 km apart

Left below: Plan of a Saharan rail-city by Jean Raymond, 1931-32

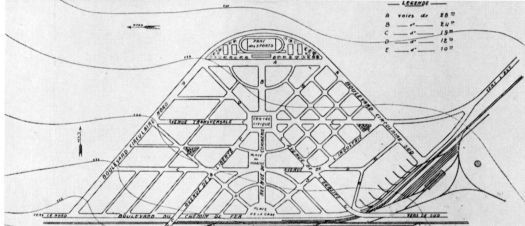

206

prophetic suggestions, that the two be combined in regional webs, will be discussed below

The English Garden City movement has always been the linear city's greatest rival, although at the same time the major contact abroad of the Spanish group. Soria had taken almost immediate notice in 'La Ciudad Lineal' (1899) of the appearance of this younger competitor to his ideas, and from about 1913 his company's literature always carried a long comparison of the two theories, pointing out the advantages of linear planning

One of linearism's greatest exponents, Georges Benoit-Lévy, was recruited from among the ranks of the Garden City movement. Benoit-Lévy, leading French protagonist of the English theory, was quite critical of the Ciudad Lineal when he translated the

company's brochure for the Ghent Congress of Cities in 1913. However, he, like González del Castillo, decided that the rival theories were actually only two different varieties of the same idea. He became – and is to this day – the major propagandist for the Spanish invention outside the peninsula. During the 1920's he promoted it at meetings of the League of Nations, founded an international association for linear planning, represented the movement at international planning conferences, pamphleteered, and reported regularly on the world-wide progress of linearism. Of his many international contacts, perhaps most significant were those with Miliutin (the Russian linear planner), with ELCA (the English linearists), and with his correspondents in the U S A. An interesting variant of the Spanish plan was proposed by him for the expansion of Paris in 1927. His

approach to this latter problem was a regional one. He wanted a belt of open space to be left around the present city, run through by linear settlements of fixed density, all connected by rapid transit to the centre. These linear extensions of the city would have two axes: one would be a residential strip like the Ciudad Lineal of Madrid but with community centres at intervals along its length; the other, parallel and a good distance away in the countryside, would consist of industries laid out along a service railway. The idea of running industrial and residential zones parallel and buffered from each other is common to much later linear planning

Since 1900 many suggestions have been advanced for plans of a linear nature, some affected by knowledge of Soria's Ciudad Lineal, others of apparent independent invention. Their forms have been so heterogeneous, their ultimate purposes so different, their geographical distribution so haphazard that it is hard to decide how to classify and describe them. I shall try to do so here in terms of the particular needs of twentieth-century life for which they appear to have been designed

First, regardless of their particular form, a large group of the linear proposals were intended primarily for the colonization of land, viz the resettlement of abandoned internal areas or the exploitation of unused territory abroad. For instance, both Soria and González del Castillo had, during the period of greatest crisis in Spain's Moroccan territories (1911-29), repeatedly suggested the deployment there of linear agricultural colonies to serve as a peaceful alternative to the disastrous colonial war. Benoit-Lévy reported that a similar project had been suggested for the 250 miles from Brazzaville to

Pointe Noire in the French Congo. An even more ambitious scheme was proposed in 1931-32 by Jean Raymond, French writer of handbooks on city planning, for a series of 'rail-cities' along a 1,600-mile trans-Saharan railway running from Algiers and Oran in the north to Timbuktu on the Niger River

The most persistent campaign to achieve colonization by linear planning was that of the Chilean engineer Carlos Carvajal Miranda. Carvajal heard about the Spanish linear city in 1906 when, as Inspector-General of Architecture in the Chilean Department of Public Works, he was overseeing the reconstruction of earthquake damage in the agricultural south of his country. From this time on regional planning, civic beautification, and low-cost housing became his life work, and, under the tutelage of Soria and González del Castillo, he became one of the most effective advocates of linear planning. His major interest was to improve rural and urban workers' housing and to increase the efficiency of Chilean farm production by arranging workers' colonies along transportation routes. He obtained sufficient support from his country's progressive political parties almost to make his suggestions official government policy on two occasions, 1924 and 1939. Except for certain modifications owing to the nature of their proposed sites, his settlements were to be constructed quite like the Ciudad Lineal of Madrid

A considerable number of linear plans have been characterized by technological adventurism, verging occasionally on science fiction. This class of project is based on a core element of exceptional efficiency — usually a highway, street, or rapid-transit system

A completely mechanized street is what Milo Hastings, an American inventor and free-lance writer, used in his 'Solution to the Housing Problem', a project that in 1919 was premiated and illustrated by the American Institute of Architects. Hastings' desire to obtain a park-like residential community of greater efficiency than the English Garden City led him to arrange his dwellings along great U-shaped road loops that extended from highways far out into the countryside. These loops were not thoroughfares but rear service roads with underground pipes, cables, central heating, vacuum for house cleaning, etc. The houses were to face in on a central park which contained community buildings, schools, and recreational spaces for the neighbourhood. In more rural areas where the service loops were not warranted, houses could be placed, in alternating fashion, on either side of the highway

Edgar Chambless, a friend of Hastings and also an inventor, had proposed an even more radical type of linear core some years earlier. Called Roadtown, his proposal was for an endless house made out of poured concrete, with three levels of monorail transportation underneath it and a continuous promenade on its flat roof. This 'house' core was to be two storeys high, constructed according to the Edison concrete patent. Markets and public buildings would rise at intervals along the core, and certain subsidiary buildings would flank it at intervals. Chambless' plan was described in great detail in a book he wrote in 1910 and it evoked considerable interest at the time. Although mechanistic in appearance, Roadtown was actually an agrarian plan intended to bring people into contact with the land and to cultivate it, thus serving as a form of agricultural colonization. Insofar as possible, Roadtown would run through open country, and its residents were expected to tend their own gardens nearby. The trains below ground were to be smokeless and noiseless. All manner of mechanical aids would be available to liberate the women from housework. Every home would include a workroom in this new freeholding, handyman environment. Hastings, who may have contributed some of the ideas, assisted Chambless in the promotion of this project for many years. It came closest to fruition in the 1930's when a modernized version — essentially a skyscraper lying on its side — was proposed as a Federal project to be built from Washington to Baltimore; this appears to have elicited interest in government departments. Chambless died in 1936, but in recent years a friend

Above: The Roadtown of Edgar Chambless, 1910

Below: Richard Neutra, 'Rush City Reformed', 1923-30. Residential neighbourhoods can be seen in the background

207

of his, Harry Singer, has updated and kept alive the Roadtown idea

The sense of speed and streamlined life in Roadtown – as well as its date of invention – qualify it to be called Futurist in the sense that we use the term architecturally. Other schemes to which that label could be applied are those that lay out cities along multi-lane arteries which whiz through them in sunken culverts. Many cities today have been hacked open by such thruways, but rarely if ever has the city actually taken its form from such a spine. Richard Neutra's project 'Rush City Reformed' (1923-on) would appear to be the first example of such a modern high-rise city plotted out longitudinally. Neutra's dramatic superstructure of raised overpasses in the business core and his relegation of residences to the fringes show him to be part of the planning tradition which we associate with Sant 'Elia and early Le Corbusier. Neutra's residential sections are in plan, if not in technique, strikingly similar to the loops that Hastings had proposed. One basic purpose of Neutra's Rush City Reformed was to avoid cross currents of traffic – an idea which, as we shall see, is fundamental to much linear theory

A sunken roadbed also formed the basis of the arrangement by which Stanley Freese hoped to redesign the English countryside in the interests of better living and more efficient transport. In his novel 'The Ten Year Plan' of 1932, Freese described a great cutting which would allow railways to cross English rural districts out of sight and, on entering towns or cities, become the multi-level system illustrated. A subsequent plan by Freese, co-founder of the English Linear Cities Association (ELCA), was less Futurist in character and more like the Spanish Ciudad Lineal which he had become acquainted with in the meantime

The last word in this type of technological linear plan seems to be Metrolinear, designed by Reginald Malcolmson of the Illinois Institute of Technology. Devised about 1956, Malcolmson's theory has, as a programme, attracted considerable attention in recent years. It has been illustrated frequently in architectural literature, has been exhibited at New York's Museum of Modern Art and elsewhere, and has formed part of a television documentary about the metropolis of the future. The core of Malcolmson's system is made up of a combination of transportation arteries and continuous buildings. The former include central rail and truck routes as well as flanking automobile highways. The buildings of the core are alternatively administrative-commercial and light-industrial, in eight-mile sections. Administrative-commercial units contain the rail and truck transport in two storeys below ground, above which is built a continuous four-storey parking building. The roof of the latter serves as pedestrian promenade and is laid out as a sequence of public squares; at half-mile intervals it is surmounted by higher commercial structures. At similar intervals, out past the auto highways, stand tall office buildings of star plan. The latter are joined to the core building by overpasses (not indicated on model), the different levels of freight, car, and pedestrian traffic being interconnected by elevators, escalators, and ramps. Flanking this in the countryside are residential areas, arranged in groups that include low- and high-rise residences and public buildings. Then come park and farm lands. Heavy industry is ranged along its own arterial belt about six miles out, connected to the core at eight-mile intervals. This schema, which contains reminiscences of Chambless, Neutra, and Benoit-Lévy, has been continually modified and refined by its inventor, who has proposed its use for Manhattan, San Francisco, and elsewhere

Above: Stanley Freese, 'The Ten Year Plan', 1932. Express transport runs along the bottom; local carriers range up the side. Wind driven power stations can be seen in the distance

Below: Reginald Malcolmson, Metrolinear, 1956– . Scale model of a 175 square mile section

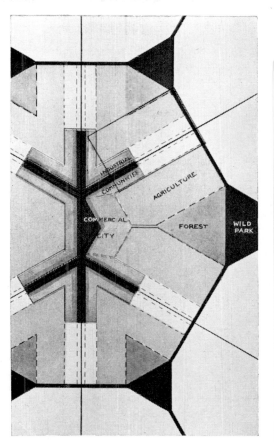

Above: Diagram of the cardinal arterial system of a nation. Arthur C. Comey, 1923

Above right: Diagram of a large city-state developing in strips along cardinal arterial routes. This is element '4' in the centre of the drawing on the left

Linear plans like these based on high-speed arteries lead logically to our next category of plan – the regional net of superhighways or thruways. The idea of nation-wide transport systems is, of course, ancient in origin, but it underwent a special modern theoretical development over the turn of this century. At that time it was thought (in America at least) that the future of transportation lay in the expansion of inter-urban rapid transit (trolleys) on a national scale. The Chicago-New York Airline Railway which tried from 1906-13 to develop such a tram line between those two centres is a case in point; it succumbed finally to the intransigence of the railways and mountains it had to cross, as well as to the unexpected popularity of the automobile. At about the same time (1902) H. G. Wells in his 'Anticipations of the Reaction of Mechanical and Scientific Progress upon Human Life and Thought' predicted accurately what has actually come to pass: the national highway system of mid-century. 'Through the varied country the new wide roads will run,' he wrote, 'here cutting through a crest and there running like some colossal aqueduct across a valley, swarming always with a multitudinous traffic

of bright, swift (and not necessarily ugly) mechanisms . . .'

The vision of H. G. Wells only began to take form after World War I when the United States embarked upon its first phase of automobile highway construction. One of the earliest to catch on to this new dimension in planning was Arthur Comey of Harvard who suggested (1923) that by laying out industry, business, and residence in a rational relation to regional transportation networks we could overcome the shortcomings of Garden City planning, then in vogue. The cure for what he considered the basic fault of the English theory – holding the community to a theoretical size – was built into his plan which, because it was linear allowed infinite and innocuous expansion along the various branches of its network. Comey's schematic presentation of his theory was based on the triangle as being most efficient and direct for routing; the corners of the triangles do not meet, however, but leave short synapses on which to structure the cities. Such a network of triangles builds up to hexagons, and the outer limits of each community on the network are marked by a slightly elongated hexagon. The manner in which growth was to be directed along the branches and lesser twigs of the net is quite ingenious, as is the simple and yet integrated system of zoning that Comey's schema permitted. A study of his proposal reveals a number of preoccupations typical of this class of planning. One is his fascination with the mechanics of multi-level traffic interchanges; this became almost an obsession with regional planners in the 1930's: e.g. Frank Lloyd Wright and the designers of the General Motors Motorama, as can be seen by examining their models. Also, Comey's dependence on a pattern that combines triangles and hexagons is a tradition in itself. The American architect Charles R. Lamb had prepared such a system about twenty years earlier in a plan that was not actually linear but did seek to zone a city by placing its different functions at the conjunctions of a grid of hexagons and lining up related activities along the radial streets that connect any two points. The most complex analysis of this type would appear to be the 'Central Place Studies' of the German Walther Christaller in the 1930's – seemingly linear in implication. Such triangular webs were predicted in the writings of Soria and his Spanish associates: 'The best way to combine the point-cities of the past (in which land-values drop concentrically from centre to suburbs) with the linear cities of the future (in which land-values decrease in bands parallel to the railway of the main street) is to interconnect the actual point-cities of today by means of linear cities; thus there will result in time in every country a vast net of triangulations, in which the area of each triangle that is formed by the vertices of old cities and the sides of the new cities will be dedicated to agricultural and industrial exploitation'

The outbreak today of national highway construction all over the world fulfils, in a sense, the predictions of Soria and Wells and seems to be one of the factors that has contributed to current interest in linear planning. The many publications which, since World War II, have pointed out the disastrous effect of highways and thruways on our countryside have, in fact, framed the question. How can our living and working and even walking be intelligently related to routes which are no longer theoretical in the Wellsian sense, but are actually taking over the surface of the globe, breaking down national barriers, etc? Jellicoe's 'Motopia' arose out of this predicament. Those who now look at the thruways in cities as examples of 'civic sculpture', who sketch 'Stadtbilder' of the city from moving vehicles on the thruway, and who make the interchanges into shopping centres, are beginning to face this reality. A recent study, 'The Motor Road: Forerunner of the Universal City' by Theodore Larson of the University of Michigan is an example of shrewd analysis of the potentialities of thruways as a structure for settlements

Below: Miliutin's schematic plan for Tractorstoi at Stalingrad, 1930

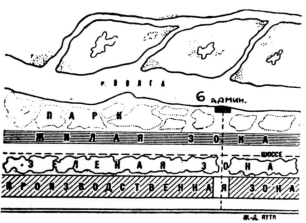

Volga River

Park, with Palace of Soviets at (6)

Residential zone

Arterial highway in green-belt buffer

Industrial zone

Railway

It requires only a slight mental step to move from considerations of planning based on regional traffic arteries to another class of linear plans derived from the flow-efficiency of a linear layout – what we might call the production-line metaphor. The theoretical background to this type of planning would be the Taylor System of industrial analysis and the assembly line procedures in which Henry Ford pioneered. In fact, Ford appears to have produced the archetype of this sort of regional plan. In 1921 when Ford (then a presidential aspirant) was offering to take the wartime electric and nitrate installations at Muscle Shoals off the government's hands, he suggested that this was only a first step in the electrification of the entire country, the harnessing of 'every creek and brook' that crossed a farmer's property. At Muscle Shoals, which Senator Norris succeeded in saving for the TVA, Ford would have used the Tennessee River dams for power to manufacture fertilizer and tractors in a series of small industrial centres stretching for 75 miles in a continuous city. Giant industry could thus decentralize, Ford theorized, the broken down city would be abandoned, and each family would have its own acre in a community of houses and gardens (cf Soria). The small industrial units would employ the winter time of farm workers, who could in turn construct their own homes bit by bit from the most modern materials produced by the Ford quantity production lines. The plan was a 'package' like his $5 day and his Fordson-truck-flivver combination. Precise details of Ford's scheme are hard to come by since it was never carried out and was reported mainly in newspaper interviews

Although there does not seem to have been an industrial town or model workers' settlement laid out in the United States on Ford's model, he may have had influence abroad, in particular with regard to one of the most significant linear plans of all – that suggested for the Russian complex of new industrial towns at Stalingrad (also for tractor manufacture). This well-known scheme was worked out by N. A. Miliutin, professor of the Communist Academy, in a book on the planning of socialist cities. Miliutin approached the problem of the industrial town as if he were designing or analyzing a well-planned large-scale steam operated power plant. Each element of our living, working, and movement was carefully weighed in relation to every other and to the overall productive purpose of the town. One of his most important contributions to the history of linear planning was his parallel arrangement of elements, buffered by strips of greenery in a way that presages certain parts of the later Athens Charter of CIAM planners. As for prototypes, there is evidence that Russian architects and planners were acquainted in a general way with Soria's ideas, at least our first illustration. However, Miliutin's is an 'industrial' town plan and, as we have seen, was based on theories of industrial assembly lines which have nothing to do with Soria. Miliutin emphasized many of the same elements that Tony Garnier had dealt with in his Cité Industrielle of 1901-04. But Garnier, although much concerned with the trajectory of his various means of transportation, did not arrange them in a relation to each other or to his residences and industry that could properly be called 'linear'; his highway-boulevard axis that bisects the town its entire length was, in fact, a catastrophic bit of formalism even before the impact of the motor car. The Russians could hardly have heard of Benoit-Lévy's Paris plan of 1927. An influence of German theory of the time is more likely; Arthur Korn's first essay in linear planning, a Collective for Socialist Building, had been exhibited in Berlin during 1928-29. Once phrased, the logic of Miliutin's reasoning and city-form seemed indisputable to many. The most obvious adaptation of it was a schema for industrial areas put forward by Renaat Soeteway, a Belgian, at the International Housing and Town Planning Congress of 1935

One of the most sophisticated examples of linear planning theory based on the assembly-line metaphor was that of the Reverend William Drury, co-founder with Freese in 1933 of ELCA, the English Linear Cities Association. Drury, a retired army chaplain with a strong social conscience, had evolved an

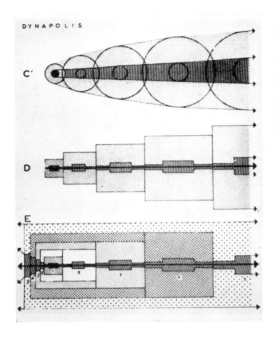

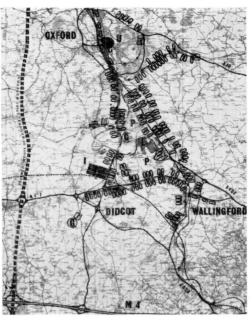

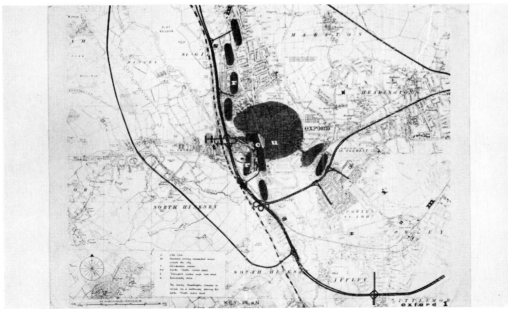

Far left: Constantinos Doxiadis, Dynapolis, 1960. Centre I will not be sufficient for the left-hand part, nor for those sectors developing above and below Centre I; therefore Centre I must be able to expand as one large centre in successive phases, unlike the l neal development on the right-hand side which develops as a series of centres on a lineal corridor

Left: The Oxford-Didcot-Wallingford Linear City (Tom Hancock, 1964). Spine is a combination of highway and monorail. Ovals are housing, dark rectangles are industry. G, atomic energy research establishments; L, lagoon; P, parks

Below: Tom Hancock, the linear redesigning of Oxford, 1960. C, city core; u, university; r, residential areas; s-s, north-south spine road; t, transport centre and core road; m, monorail serving outer residential areas

interesting thesis about the significance of transport in the production of wealth, which is a bit too intricate to go into here. The crux of it, for our purposes, was that the cost of transportation can be reduced by straightening out lines of communication; as a city is essentially a mechanism by which people and goods are kept in close communication, a single axial route with a minimum of cross currents of traffic was the most efficient means of organizing it so as to avoid over-production, unemployment, and other economic ills of that era. Drury came in contact with Freese as a result of seeing a review of Freese's 'Ten Year Plan', and for more than a decade their ELCA group campaigned for linear planning by means of articles and leaflets and kept in contact with other protagonists such as Benoit-Lévy, the Spaniards, etc. Among their publications was a linear plan for London

This rather general idea that the linear plan is peculiarly adapted for infinite growth and for the unimpeded flow of goods, traffic, and processes has received increasing acceptance among architects and planners. Constantinos Doxiadis would appear to be of this school. An explicit statement of his position was contained in his R I B A address of 1960 on 'Architecture in Evolution'. On this occasion he demonstrated the futility of all types of centric plans for settlements, because they inevitably throttle their own core. In his schematic 'Dynapolis' plan he showed how by linear extension the core could expand harmoniously along with the city periphery

As we shall see, the British seem to have been

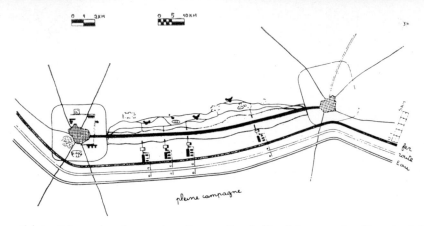

especially partial to this mode of reasoning. For instance, the architect Tom Hancock considers himself to have been influenced by Doxiadis' point. Hancock's statements about his own development towards a linear analysis of architectural and planning programmes are interesting, in particular his discovery that Venice, eternal source of inspiration for the English, is essentially a linear city with the Grand Canal as its 'spinal cord'. With Hancock as with many, linearism is as much a mode of analytic reasoning as a form of layout. We illustrate his group's suggestion, published in 1960, for the expansion of Oxford along linear principles (page 211). He has recently developed this concept into a triangulation of linear 'connector' cities between Oxford, Didcot, and Wallingford, in order to obtain a regional balance of industrial, cultural, recreational, and research activities in the area. The interior of the triangle will include a large complex of parkland and artificial lakes

The most widely publicized linear plan in recent years, Le Corbusier's 'Cité Linéaire Industrielle' is, in part, a product of the same type of reasoning, but subsumes enough other categories of planning theory to be considered a distinct, albeit rather eclectic, theory. Formally, its outstanding feature is the variety of types of transportation on which it is structured. It is a part of Le Corbusier's latest planning ideas (regional in scope) in which he predicates three types of human activity and settlement: his diffuse and decentralized 'Radiant' farms; a centre-city of commercial, political, social, and intellectual interchange; and these 'connector' cities. The last are potent cells of industrial produc-

tion 'bridged' to currents of transportation (water, rail, truck, auto) that run in parallel fashion, and connected to footpaths that meander through the residential areas. The scale of these linear arrangements is continental (Soria, Christaller), their layout and isolation by greenery recall in part Miliutin, in part CIAM. Le Corbusier's secure position in the company of linearists is thus obvious to anyone who has read this far. That his message falls on deaf ears is also evident. His speech of acceptance of an honorary degree at Columbia University in April of 1961 was devoted exclusively to a presentation of his linear regional plan; not one of the news media covering the event mentioned this fact although he had decorated metres of paper with his drawings of it and the visit itself was reported at great length

Many of the categories of linear plan we have examined have had a good deal in common, differing mainly in detail or perhaps in the portion of the plan emphasized by the author of the scheme. Some planners are more concerned with basic processes than with specific parts of the layout; others emphasize the media of transportation or speed and efficient hook-up; others (especially the Soviets), the benefits of rural-urban confrontation; and some, like Le Corbusier, the mode of segregating or integrating the various activities of their inter-urban complexes

This last concern, which Soria dealt with on a rather primitive level eighty years ago, has led to a large number of what we might call 'composite linear plans', complex arrangements that usually incorporate planning theories other than the purely linear. Some of these attempt to adapt themselves to

the natural radial growth of cities; others are based on a circumvallating 'Ringstrasse' (as was Soria's). A variety of devices have been suggested to give the attenuated and essentially decentralized linear plan a sense of civic or residential cohesiveness; this has generally been sought through some compromise with classic Garden City theory or with modern neighbourhood planning. Plans that look in the abstract like clusters, strings, snowflakes, branches, twigs, and even leaves have resulted

Perhaps the simplest 'composite' plan was that of González del Castillo in 1919 which articulated the original Ciudad Lineal into a string of separate units, providing each successive one with its own centralized civic centre as in our fourth illustration. Cullen and Matthews' recently announced ALCAN Linear Circuit Town is in this tradition – a necklace of beads, loosely strung, that can adapt itself flexibly to any type of terrain or pre-existing constructions. 'The key to the dilemma,' they write, 'is the car/man

Above left: The industrial linear city of Le Corbusier and ASCORAL, about 1942

Below: Radial corridor plan for Washington D C, 1961, 'for the year 2000'. These corridors will not be linear cities of the Soria type, but will be a series of urbanized areas, each with a new town centre, connected together by transportation routes. The next drawing (overleaf) shows diagrammatically a series of such urbanized areas; their distance from each other depends on the widths and positioning of the controlling open spaces

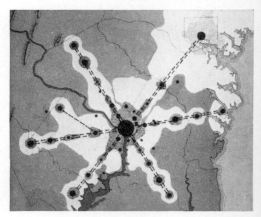

212

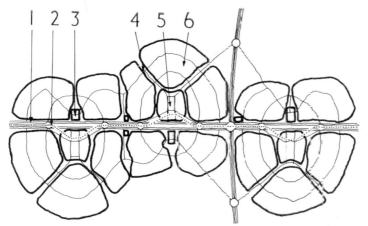

Left: Mode of attaching suburban communities to the radiating arteries in the Washington corridor plan 'for the year 2000'

1 freeway, 2 rapid transit, 3 intensive industry, 4 controlled open spaces and parkland, 5 shopping and administration, 6 residential

Below: Bird's-eye view of a commercial area laid out by Ludwig Hilberseimer in linear form, c. 1944

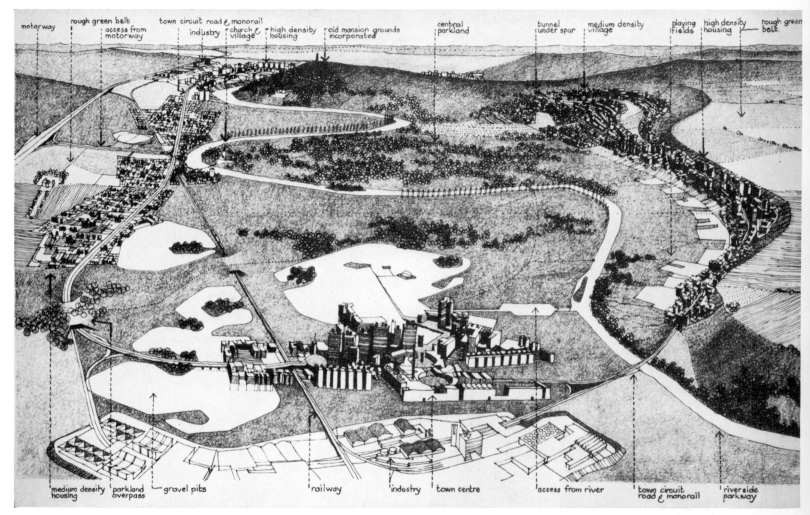

motorway | rough green belt / access from motorway | town circuit road & monorail / industry | church & village | high density housing | old mansion grounds incorporated | central parkland | tunnel under spur | medium density village | playing fields | high density housing | rough green belt

214

medium density housing | parkland overpass | gravel pits | railway | industry | town centre | access from river | town circuit road & monorail | riverside parkway

Above: Bird's-eye view of the theoretical linear town designed by Gordon Cullen and Richard Matthews for Alcan Industries, Ltd. Units of high-rise and low-rise building are threaded on a circuit of road and monorail that hugs the contours of the landscape

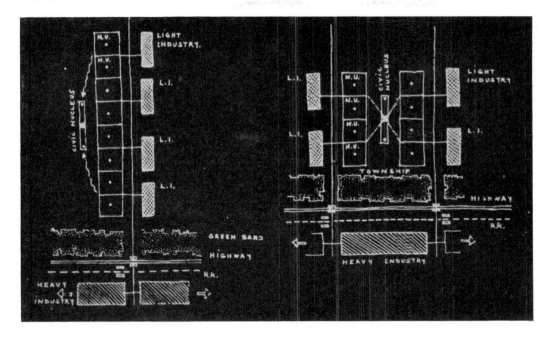

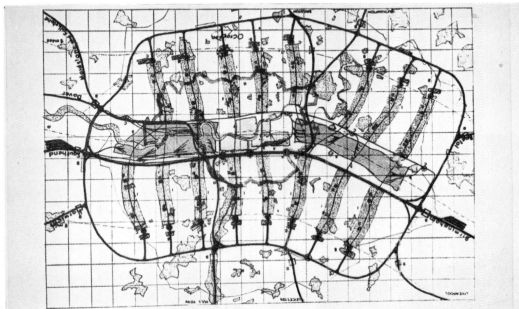

Above left: Modified linear plan, José Luis Sert, 1944. 'If neighbourhood units extend at great length along a road (see left diagram) the distance of some of them from the social services forming the civic nucleus and also the distance to the main industrial area may become too great. As a result, the civic nucleus of the township would have to be split in different sections, and these townships could no longer function socially as one unit. This is the main objection to the lineal pattern

'By grouping the neighbourhood unit as shown in the second diagram, the civic nucleus of the township occupies a more central location and its services are more accessible. Also the distance to the main industrial area is considerably shortened'

Below left: Plan for London by the MARS Group, 1938

relationship which has not yet been really resolved.' Their answer is to scale their plan laterally and vertically to the pedestrian, longitudinally to the motor car and monorail. Latest of our linear schemes, this is one of the simplest in concept and, in plan, comes closest to Soria's original project for a string of linear settlements around Madrid. The distinction between man-scale and transport-scale had been one of Soria's basic contributions

A so simple is the snowflake form made up of arms radiating from a central city, as suggested in 1909 by Captain J. W. Petavel of England. Petavel believed in decentralizing congested towns by means of high-speed suburban locomotion. He pointed out that the slowness of transport in the past had required people to live in crowded proximity to each other, whereas modern rapid trains require only that we live close to a station. Four narrow 'limbs' of about a mile and a half in length were to radiate from the centre of the city. Each limb consisted of a central boulevard with shops, public buildings, and transportation lines, with streets for dwellings running parallel to it. Every house would be within a few minutes' walk of both boulevard and countryside. A suggestion of this type was made for Madrid in 1931, independently of Soria. The use of such a schema for the redevelopment of congested areas in existing cities has been proposed as recently as 1959 by a German, Wilhelm Seidensticker

A logical outgrowth of the plan with radiating arms is what we might call radiating satellites. This form derives from the satellite theory of Howard and Unwin: when a Garden City unit has reached its optimum size it flings off a new settlement in which growth could continue. When, in the 1920's, Unwin urged the establishment of concentric green belts around London with satellites outside, González del Castillo quite logically suggested that the connecting highways passing through the green belts be laid out as linear cities. This was a simple application of Soria's connecting linear city. The Copenhagen 'finger plan' is of this category, and similar schemes have been proposed recently for use in the United States. Portions of the Detroit plan by the Architects' Urban Design Collaborative (1958-59) have been described as linear, but the monorail connectors to the satellite suburbs in this case are merely transport, not linear settlements, and the 'linear' necklace of plazas in town is nothing but a hackneyed (fifteenth-century) 'Ringstrasse' arrangement. The recent Washington, D.C. plan ('for the year 2000') is, however, of radiating satellite design with corridor towns connecting the satellites to the core. By the year 2000, however, such a simple schema cannot, as critics have pointed out, accommodate the population pressures that will build up around the central area where the corridor towns have their origin

Co-ordinated neighbourhood units can be obtained in a rather elementary fashion by making loops of, or adding loops to, the linear artery, thus giving closure and compactness to the area within each loop or bow. Examples of this are to be seen in the residential planning by Hastings and Neutra, already discussed

More complex forms – probably the most intricate examples of linear planning – are achieved by attaching bunches of residential units to belt arteries along which industry is ranged. O. E. Schweizer's plans would appear to be the earliest of this category; he has given much study to variations on this theme in a series of publications stretching over many years. It is difficult to judge how much influence a particular individual may have had on the ideas of others, especially as regards these composite plans which have attracted the attention of a number of 'names' in planning. Ludwig Hilberseimer, for example, since adopting a linear format in the 1940's, has done much in his teaching and writing to gain acceptance for linear methods of analysis and design. For instance, he considerably startled and perplexed a number of Madrid architects who were visiting Chicago in 1959 by asking them, 'How goes it with the plans of Soria?' Blissfully unaware of the implications of their suburb the Ciudad Lineal, the Spaniards assumed he

was referring to the sleepy little Romanesque town of Soria in northern Spain, which is of no significance whatever to modern planning. They looked up Arturo Soria's writings on their return home and published an article that seems to have contributed substantially to interest in the matter among young Spanish architects today. Hilberseimer arrived at his branched type of linear plan after a careful study of the traffic problems that render centralized cities impossible in our day. The resultant form has certain analogies to the Russian system of segregating residences from industry, but is considerably more advanced in its accounting for prevailing wind directions and the like

Among others who have used branching neighbourhood units in order to preserve some of the human scale that we had in old towns are José Luis Sert and the Goodman brothers. Sert, as is clear from the illustration, organized his settlements in a criss-cross manner so as to make their parts easily accessible to each other and to make the civic complex – not the arterial axis – the crux of the plan. The Goodmans in Communitas plead for the efficiency of the linear plan and for the humanism of a Camillo Sitte at the same time; their suggested scheme for Manhattan island is of the type we have been describing. The linear arrangements proposed by Michel Kosmin for Tunisia in 1952 are also of this category

Perhaps the most studied, detailed analysis of a specific planning problem by linear methods was that carried out by the MARS group (of CIAM) with regard to London in 1938. A team headed by Arthur Korn, whom we have seen was already a linear planner, analyzed the metropolitan region in the manner of Patrick Geddes and came up with a pattern that would allow continuous, uncongested expansion, would conserve the old heart of the city, and would relate the whole more efficiently to existing national arteries. London's industry, commerce, and administration were retained along its primary east-west artery of Thames and railroads. Residential zones would be laid out along a series of secondary axes arranged perpendicular to the primary artery in a herringbone pattern of sixteen ribs (each a city district of about 600,000 residents). At their outer ends these secondary ribs might contain industrial units and would be connected to a great railway freight line that encircled the entire complex. Each of these parallel city districts would be about a mile wide, separated from the next one by a two-mile band of countryside that penetrated right into the fringes of the main artery of the city (as is not

possible between the 'limbs' of the new Washington plan since the latter are all tied to a point instead of to a line). No dwelling would be more than a few minutes' walk from its feeder artery or from open country (cf. Petavel). National north-south highways and railways could run uninterrupted through the intermediate open spaces, hooking up directly with the major east-west artery at large central terminals. The plan was roundly criticized, of course, by all the traditional town-and-country planners and was pretty much squelched. However, the flexibility of its form as well as the adaptability of its scheme of ring road, internal herringbone, and arterial axis to the problems of modern transportation have apparently appealed to those who are today trying to make the New Towns work

The highly organic appearance of the MARS plan anticipates our last composite form: the leaf plan. Hans Bernhard Reichow's 'Organische Stadtbaukunst' is an example. Oddly enough, Reichow's flowing forms result not so much from a desire for organic shape in itself, as for efficiency in traffic routing. A safe and rapid interchange of vehicles is, of course, essential in the attachment of twig to branch and branch to trunk in all the composite plans we have seen; Reichow solves the problem without complex overpasses, using instead tangential intersections (merging traffic) that give him his leaf-rib

Below: A neighbourhood laid out by Hans Bernard Reichow on organic principles, 1948

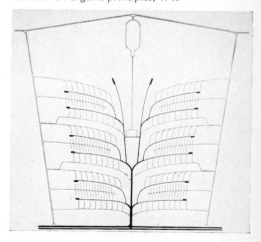

pattern. 'Leaf plan' is also the term that Matthew Nowicki used to designate a similar stage in his working out of Chandigarh

The inclination of British architects and planners to turn to linear methods of analysis in recent years is marked. Why this did not catch on earlier, in the times of Petavel or ELCA, is not clear. The innate tendency of the English home, if not semi-detached, at least to cling to its neighbours along a street instead of, as in the U S A, sitting on its plot like a duck on a pond would seem to make ribbon development a natural. A group of Spanish planners visiting the New Towns noted that the Sittesque type of European plazas with which they have been provided are not native to the Englishman, who seems to prefer a high street as the locus of his public life; they remarked that at Crawley where the new plaza and the old high street are close at hand it is the linear high street that has the life on it

Cumbernauld, Hook, and Meyer Hillman's Sussex plan are all examples of the way in which linear planning seems to be taking over from the old-line Garden City. As Peter Smithson remarked (1959): 'Urban motorways can be so designed that they form the structure of the community'. The recent report of the Ministry of Transport on traffic in towns seems to sidestep any discussion of linearism, but expresses admiration for the Cumbernauld and Hook plans. The examples cited are city plans, of course, but British regional planning has also become imbued with linear thinking, as evidenced by Derrick Rigby Child's recent proposal for chains of new linked cities and urban groups in his 'Counterdrift Strategy' and by the Cullen-Matthews proposal to 'redeem the landscape' by the introduction of lasso-like linear towns under strict regional control

It was probably inevitable that some planner would eventually propound a plan that has no form at all — complete decentralization. But since in our century even the most unstructured system must retain modern utilities and transportation, it seems natural that our most radically decentralized regional plans should be linear at root. The dissolution of cities, as Bruno Taut called the process, could come about only with the flexibility of modern motor-vehicle arteries, with far-reaching electric power grids, or both

The classic instance of complete decentralization was, of course, that proposed by the radical wing of planners during Russia's first Five Year Plan. In the late 1920's the extremists among Soviet planners 'called for the complete abolition of cities by

rearranging them in linear strips of indefinite length. Basing their plans on the transmission of electric power over great distance (as suggested by Lenin himself), these planners hoped to carry out the early revolutionary doctrines of decentralizing industry, mechanizing agriculture, eliminating domestic economy, and establishing the Russian population in collective dwellings. After extended discussion of these matters in professional circles, in 1931 the disurbanist point of view was officially condemned for practical reasons (the absence of the power grid and industrial capacity upon which the theory was predicated) and for the same ideological reasoning that was to put an end to all progressive artistic activity in Russia

Incongruous as it may seem, the successor to the Soviet decentralists was Frank Lloyd Wright. In the very years when Marxist linearism was being stamped out as a deviation, Wright began to formulate his regional plan, Broadacre City, predicated on that most American and bourgeois element, the automobile. Wright's plan, well known, has only one structural element, a twelve-lane car and truck route on which all else depends. The City was damned in his estimation, and 'the stems for the flowering of the new City . . . will be the great topographical road systems . . . ,' he prophesied. This agrarian utopia, based philosophically on Henry George's land theory, outfitted for Henry Ford's tinkering farmhands, and scaled to the man at the wheel of a motor car, has attracted little serious attention or study. During the thirty years that he wrote and lectured about Broadacres, Wright embroidered the issue with so much political and social mythology, and, finally in the 'Living City', with such improbable Vernian drawings, that everyone took it as a joke. But boiled down to its essentials it may be the clearest vision of them all: nothing but industry, residence, commercial buildings and civic centres laid out in relation to superhighways (under the direction of an archi-

tect) and stretching out over the horizon. 'If you can see the extended highway as the horizontal line of Usonian freedom,' Wright said, 'then you will see the modern Usonian city approaching'

Who knows?

BIBLIOGRAPHICAL NOTE

For more details, illustrations, and documentation of the plans discussed here the reader is referred to other studies of linear planning by George L. Collins: in the 'Journal of the Society of Architectural Historians', XVIII (May and October 1959), pp. 38-53 and 74-93; in the 'Architectural Review', CXXVIII (November 1960), pp. 34 -5, added note in January 1961, p. 6; and an extended analysis of Wright's Broadacre City in 'Four Great Makers of Modern Architecture', Columbia University School of Architecture, New York City, 1963

Much information about the Ciudad Lineal of Madrid and other linear projects depending on it is contained in the report presented by Soria's Compañía Madrileña de Urbanización to the International Housing and Town Planning Congress at Berlin in 1931: 'La Ciudad Lineal fórmula española de ciudad Jardin como sistema de arquitectura de ciudades y de colonización de campos', Madrid, 1931. General discussions of Linear Planning will also be found in Percival and Paul Goodman, 'Communitas, Means of Livelihood and Ways of Life', New York, 1960; Ludwig Hilberseimer, 'The New City', Chicago, 1944; and Arthur Korn, 'History Builds the Town', London, 1953

For a brief and amusing presentation of the concept of 'Postcivilization', ie, the possibility that cities will, in the age of cybernetics, decentralize to the point of disappearance, see Kenneth E. Boulding, in 'The Historian and the City', Cambridge, Mass., 1963, pp. 133-145

ASSOCIATION NTERNATIONALE DES CITÉS-JARDINS-LINEAIRES

CLYDE CITY

GEOFFREY COPCUTT

THE PROBLEM OF INDUSTRIAL DECENTRALIZATION

Since World War Two, the decline of heavy industry in Scotland, affecting particularly the shipbuilding yards along the river Clyde, on which the city of Glasgow is situated, has been a source of concern to Britain as a whole

At the heart of Scotland's anxiety lies, not political ideology, but the renewal of her whole social capital. With accelerated redevelopment of slum areas, modernization of communications, and extension of education facilities—the vast industrial strength of the country can re-emerge, uniquely equipped for a European role

One of the key factors is that of communications—and crash programmes on public works, accompanied by long-term plans for attracting science-based and mass market-conscious industries, will not be maximally effective unless all the authorities concerned in the region's major economic unit, the Clyde conurbation, can together reassess the network of communications, and the elements to be linked by it, in their fifteen-year-old regional plan

This plan remains a seminal study, undertaken on behalf of the nucleus of an administrative structure correlating land and water policies with control of air pollution and metropolitan, district and new town developments, aimed at producing a unified central industrial region for Scotland. Now there must be reconciled the conflicts between dismembering the city to the benefit of minor neighbours, and competing with them for new growth; between random overspill, which could overload and unbalance communications, and rational decentralization; between the concept of economic survival manifested by 'Industry-on-the-move', and the need for economic renaissance through a planned and centralized power-house policy

At a time of peak male unemployment the city cannot equably anticipate the voluntary loss of one-fifth of its manufacturing industry together with a substantial displacement of population. The economic repercussions of compelling 1,000 firms to leave Glasgow over the twenty-year period of the plan could be crucial, with the prospect of the Channel Tunnel connecting the south-east of England and the London area with France and the Common Market countries, adding attraction to the south

In theory, Glasgow emigrants would travel with their decentralized firms to relieve serious industrial congestion, and to thin out high population densities. In practice, industry is reluctant to forego the proximity of transport and marketing facilities, technical colleges and supplies of trained labour, in exchange for the imagined market value of their premises plus the inducement of subsidized factory space. The postwar influx of lighter trades into the new industrial estates is unaffected, but not all older Clyde-based industries are easily able to move. Nor are companies, at their optimum size in their own established factories, likely to be interested in being transplanted to a reception town

If the conurbation is a still valid product of waterway, mineral deposit, and industrial technique, then sensibly the maximum houses should be built outside but related to the existing urban apparatus which can be unravelled. Britain, a recent Government report states, cannot lapse back into working-class poverty, and the report evidences inter alia the trend to suburban home ownership and the quintupling in the number of personal incomes between £500 and £2,000 a year over the past decade. By what anomaly then, with already a little over one-tenth of the land surface of Britain built up, is it justifiable to proceed with a plan which offers as an index of its idealism the belief that few families with children

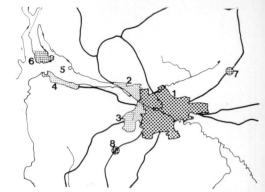

1 Glasgow, 2 Clydebank, 3 Paisley, 4 Greenock, 5 River Clyde, 6 Site for Clyde City, 7 Cumbernauld, 8 East Kilbride

need to be housed above a fourth floor?

It is doubtful, now that 40,000 acres of the Clyde Basin are populated over twice as densely as the capital, whether for most people the city has ever been less convenient, or more hideous. The dilemma of geographical constraint to peripheral growth, confronted by the need for commercial expansion, of course cannot vindicate building on municipal parks or golf courses. Likewise the still substantially intact green belt, which defines the city's ultimate areas, must continue as a bastion against further spoiling of some of the most north-westerly first-class agricultural land in the country

The disturbance could be hazardous if labour skills are critical. A company may be compelled to shift, but not made to settle elsewhere. With the dissipation of a commercial complex would come the loss of job mobility; and smaller communities inevitably mean that employees would lose much of the opportunity to advance their careers without disrupting homes or family relationships. By tending to tie their future to a single company, they would be exchanging environments, certain only of being deprived of the stimulus of the metropolis and of the challenge of a great industrial centre

Within these parameters the two-part remedy of gap-filling and redevelopment in Glasgow, together with new towns and reception areas over the edge of the basin, can be only partially effective and may be socially perilous. Fragmentary implementation of Comprehensive Development Areas is slow, expensive and gives no guarantee of completing a satisfactory environment. Gap filling is almost at an end—wasteland, bounded by canal or railway, and flanked by factories, should never have been pressed into residential use. New and expanded towns provide, so far, the best opportunity for those families who can be accommodated by this means; but there is not yet even a new town's housing consortium after a decade

In twenty years East Kilbride, Cumbernauld and Livingston may contribute 50,000 to 60,000 new homes, of which 80 per cent will be for occupation by emigrants from Glasgow. Taken together with other components of the overspill programme, they may just succeed in containing the housing pressure. Introduction of industry, however, must be the springboard of this form of relief; and industry cannot be directed commensurate with population requirements. To stem, then decentralize, the build-up of commerce within sectors of the city is to attempt to turn back the economic tide

The combined monumental housing shortfall in the major industrial cities can be relieved only if it is treated like an operation of war. One in every four of the human beings of the Glasgow conurbation is living in the worst of nineteenth-century conditions and many of the remainder in the worst of the twentieth century. To the vast bulk awaiting decent living conditions in redevelopment areas, new towns and reception zones, the Government must seem to be sitting with the blinds down playing Chopin

While Scotland is being steadily defaced by mediocre community planning and architecture, land is being sterilized, extraction of minerals hindered, communities disintegrated, and her principal city rundown, without satisfying the housing shortage or renewing obsolete stock or making provision for future increase in households, on anything like the scale required

Essentially the problem is a technical one of urban logistics, and the quantity production of a high standard of flexible dwelling. Pointing out last year that councillors, responsible for an annual net expenditure of £40 million, were being obliged to surrender their authority because functions they had to carry out were too complex – one of their number argues that if the local authority is to succeed there must be full-time paid councillors. He makes unknowingly a stronger case for a city manager, for under the right leadership, there exist resources of energy, skill and invention which harnessed to these tasks could initiate a chain reaction of national consequence

A RESIDENTIAL TWIN CITY

When the whole Forth Clyde axis is re-examined, only one solution to the problem of humanely disengaging a quarter million people from Glasgow is now economically, socially and technically possible – the establishment of a wholly residential twin city located in the exhilarating surroundings of the Clyde Firth, the most beautiful estuary in Europe

Current methods of dispersal, including attempts to establish self-sufficient communities, have been shown to be inadequate quantitatively, and tending to perpetuate existing living patterns with their struggle to duplicate impoverished versions of central city services. Their distribution and rate of growth have so far failed to provide either the necessary consumption for the employment of flow-line building production, or to free the congested area of the city

If these efforts were co-ordinated and concentrated on the development of an all-electric fireproof city of 300,000 people, it could be fabricated in the ship-yards in five years, and assembled to form a gigantic artificial isthmus, more closely connected by really rapid transit lines to its complementary urban base than are the scattered suburbs to the principal destinations in the parent city today. Since no vast new metropolitan facilities are required, industry, relieved of its admixture of tenements, and existing central foci, can be encouraged to stabilize and expand the economic future of the conurbation

By 1975 it has been estimated there will be 45 per cent more young people and 25 per cent more old in the population, in which 15 per cent fewer hours will be worked, 50 per cent more holidays taken, and 60 per cent more disposable income available. This kind of prediction emphasizes the major underlying need to commence planning now for a completely different pattern in which inevitably, work as normally understood will decline until it occupies the minor part of man's day. This challenge, so far obscured by the enormous need for any kind of accommodation, cannot be met by historical forms of organization, nor will the urgency of the situation permit the continued acceptance of the handcraft building methods. On grounds of physical health alone, the conventional city type has long ceased to be a sensible principle. One expert attributes over one in every three deaths due to lung cancer to 'urbanization', the action of atmospheric pollution more corrosive though less concentrated than tobacco smoke

The only sane solution to this social problem, which does not invoke the equally undesirable alternative of breaking kinship ties responsible so often for the loneliness and rootlessness which is a major cause of 'new town neurosis', is to aid the evolution of highly specialized elements within the conurbation, rather as the new town was grafted on to the mediaeval trunk of Edinburgh. The mental and physical climate of the valley could be changed by the construction out into the Clyde Firth of this twin city, free from ancient burdens, designed for leisure, and enriched by a centre of learning which is yet the very means of existence for the old. A great modern settlement would be an architectural inspiration, prevented by its nature from coalescing once more into that amorphous mass that passes for environment, rejuvenating riparian development and enhancing land and waterscapes

THE SITE

With 22,000 square miles of highlands and islands to the north, this site has considerable potential for expansion. Greenock would be a link in a chain of communications, supremely well placed as an international terminal for Atlantic shipping, hovercraft, coastwise vessels and the Clyde steamers which already carry 4 million passengers a year. Proximity to resorts would promote new tourist and convention hotels in an atmosphere of tranquillity, unattained by the people of Glasgow who today battle through unsegregated streets to a soulless tenement. Glasgow's world-wide reputation for a virile, tough people, inhabiting a drab slum, would be replaced by an image of a people able so to order their lives as to discriminate between optimum environments for different activities and vocations

Power and water, essential preliminaries, are abundant here on a scale which would permit the economical introduction of such services as universal space and water heating, centralized vacuum cleaning, pneumatic goods distribution and water-borne waste disposal. Functioning as a gigantic immersed heat-pump, the base deck of the development itself would make the city self-sustaining

The principal cultural influence can be, to its own benefit, the presence of a fifth science-based university, the only means of satisfying that proportion of 10,000 new places which cannot be provided by existing universities or double-shifts, coupled with the establishment of Government research agencies. The Glasgow area, which already has a relatively larger number taking full-time day courses than any other city in the Commonwealth, together with 60,000 evening students, set up the first chair of Engineering in the world, and could now provide in the continuity of her tradition and institutions a significant force in promoting a university city

In addition, Civil Service Departments, whose transfer, except for a nucleus of ministerial aids to maintain links with the Government, has been advocated to relieve overcrowding, staffing, housing, discomfort and high costs, could be offered unique facilities where their presence could not but react favourably on the whole region

The projected Clyde barrage, comprising a dam and lock system from Greenock to Ardmore Point, eliminating within the harbour the tidal range of 12 ft, permitting large ships to navigate up and down at any time to make best use of the £20 million port investment, is here suggested as a boundary (incorporating road and rail link and hydro-electric station) of the reclaimed site of the twin city. The unified Clyde authority, suggested by the Rochdale Committee, would be the ideal body to consider the effect of the twin city on the whole estuary, since the site of the proposed city is outside the seaward limit of the Clyde Trust's jurisdiction. Greenock's imaginative bid to become a trans-shipping centre, and her intention to increase her 15,000 liner passengers a year by improved pier facilities, will, with the dry dock under construction, further assist and be assisted by the total development of the area

RAPID TRANSIT TO LINK GLASGOW AND THE TWIN CITY

Accessibility is clearly the crux of urban planning. The relative decline of public transport, accompanied by the enormous expansion of private vehicle usage, has generated more vehicles to the square mile in this country than in the United States – on one-tenth of the motorways of our main trade competitor, West Germany, while centres are congested by the driver who occupies more room in his car than in his office. In these circumstances, the speed of public transport must become high enough to exert a compelling attraction

A twin city will generate principally simple shuttle trips which can be met ideally and cheaply by captive rapid transport making maximum use through automation of the route-space made available by a given capital outlay. The second prototype monorail in the world, erected on Clydeside thirty years ago, needed only the opportunity to point the way for mass transit in tidal flows. Even the conventional railway which at 60 miles an hour has a capacity seven times that of a motorway, has been shown to be capable of speeds in excess of 200 m.p.h. when segregated from normal traffic and operated under full automation. The only feasible answer to the urban and suburban transport problem, it could take the form here of a linear-motor train running through a fully submersible tube on the bed of the Clyde, providing a shuttle service of enormous capacity and rapidity without points, crossing or inter-running. It could terminate in the transportation node from which passenger distribution could be assisted by the installation of pedestrian conveyors; these need only move at 8 miles an hour to rival the average speed of cars in Glasgow's centre at peak hours and 2 miles faster than bridge traffic. A trunk link service of this kind to carry 30,000 seated passengers per single track per hour along the main corridors has been designed for the San Francisco conurbation to compete successfully with the private car

The system, which will be self supporting in ten years, will be controlled by a central digital computer, programming 80 m.p.h. trains operating at ninety second headway during rush hour. Road, rail, air and river transport can thus be integrated into a balanced system, in which the physical and social repercussions are fully considered

TWIN CITY TO BE CONSTRUCTED IN THE SHIPYARDS

The twin city itself could be constructed as an extension of the south-facing Roseneath peninsular, extending across the shallows of the estuary to 500 ft above sea level. Hydraulic engineering know-how exists on our door-step; the Dutch Delta Plan for example is winning thousands of square miles from the North Sea. The twin city's superstructure would exhibit an aesthetic derived from a planning and constructional system remote from the compositional Rennaissance concepts that have invested our thinking in city planning right into this century. Once tooled up, incredibly complicated artefacts are capable of rapid industrial mass-production and,

The George Bennie rail plane, 1928. Pioneered in Glasgow, and now demolished, it was the second prototype monorail in the world

like a car, are able to be built in a few hours – unlike the average unsophisticated house which still takes one year or more. The Ministries of Transport, and of Public Building and Works, are at last considering how to employ the spare capacity of shipyards and the obviously sound economics to harness these. Since the British Merchant fleet requires replacement orders of no more than a million tons a year, compared with the total capacity of half as much again of our shipyards – the traditional shipping cycle of slump and boom cannot obscure our permanent over-capacity, in common with the rest of the world. In the last five years the shipbuilding labour force on Clyde-side has declined by a third, and like mining, must continue to contract. The solution suggested here, however, is not made to mop-up labour pools,

but because the yards are the right places and have the right tools for the job

Diversification into other fields already accounts for 15 per cent of the work of British yards, and a few fitting-out tradesmen are producing mobile dwellings. But by the end of 1962, 23 000 men in the marine and electrical engineering and constructive groups were without work. If this reservoir of skill and equipment can be tapped before it is dissipated, a unit system of construction for the twin city, permitting many combinations within the kinds of formal discipline apparent in the traditional Japanese house, could be devised, fabricated in the yards, and erected by the city's direct building labour force. No other solution offers such possibilities at such speed. Its precedent exists in the export from the Clyde of prefabricated cast-iron building components in the nineteenth century. The real cost would be far less than the money cost as a large part of the development would be undertaken by men and resources otherwise idle

SIMULTANEOUS RENEWAL WITHIN THE CITY

If it is true that quite a large increase in national production may do little more than offset redundancies now in the pipeline, leaving little extra employment to divert to the north, the only positive policy of self-help is to abandon the rescue service on a wide front, and concentrate solely on a growth point which can remain the self-sustaining centre of attraction for an entire area

By a continuous process of fission and mutation cities displaying organic characteristics of society rebuild every hundred years, and that process is being manifested in the centre of Glasgow, principally in the comprehensive renewal of twenty-nine housing and mixed use areas, and the feasibility study for the construction of the central orbital motorway

A third factor is now present in the need to make adequate provision for functions only barely accommodated in the former St Andrew's Hall built for a city one sixth the area. Not since the nineteenth century has the opportunity existed on such a scale to stimulate and steer development. Yet never has planning been so suspect among the democrats of Glasgow Corporation – 'if a plan is inflexible it is incompatible with democracy and if it is flexible, it is not a plan'. While it is certainly unsatisfactory to straight-jacket redevelopment in three-dimensional envelopes, it is equally shortsighted to accept random speculation. It is the duty of planning to ensure that the sites favoured by a rise in value are those whose redevelopment can best serve the needs of the community. This is not to be achieved by disposing of sites by tender, with the superficial attraction of replacing outworn areas with little trouble, capital outlay or risk on the part of the local authorities. The ultimate increase in rateable value could prove a poor insurance

Economic trends should be harnessed rather than thwarted by the instrument of land use, which should be concerned with nothing less than the promotion of conditions for growth, and the integration of circulation and habitation towards the evolution of a multi-grade city. The commercial locus of a nation must rate an exhaustive analysis of all the circumstances of urban renewal, not merely a search for a convenient piece of land of about the right size; for the real dynamic is not physical planning but economic purpose. Legislation by itself will merely deter visitors whose mobility brings them the power to discriminate between centres unable to discharge their transportation responsibilities. It is wrong to resist the vitality of the community in pursuing its everyday activities, and to meet with prohibitions its ability to include in its economy a costly form of transport

Man and motor, personal and mass transport, are usually presented as irreconcilable rather than incompatible; a major city cannot continue to exist in anything like its present form without public transport and pedestrian access. The problem is thus to devise that complementary system of highways and transit lines which will most effectively promote and serve a functional pattern of land use. Except for the quarter million who must be dispersed by 1980 from Glasgow if urban conditions are to be improved for the remainder, there need be no flight from the city. Its present geographic shape may be retained – comprising essentially a high value core half-a-mile square containing civic, commercial, banking, cultural, entertainment and transport uses; a twilight zone of mixed uses, isolated from the business centre by the line of the proposed inner-ring and the presence of steep slopes, the river and railway land, ringed in turn by pre- and post-war housing schemes, subsuming, where they encounter, existing settlements; but its form needs drastic redefinition. Using a brilliantly conceived inner-ring road as an economic tool, the Corporation have begun to alleviate this terrifyingly classical case of conical density distribution which produces congestion at the core and inadequate social amenity on the periphery

But air, rail and water-borne transport all involve the vehicle, the right-of-way and the terminal; and the great new motorways must feed parking and passenger interchange facilities on a similar scale, for when car ownership rises to the inevitable three cars to every two families the central area will seize-up or be dismantled, producing social debilitation and poor rating economics

Unless the highway system can be designed as one component of a comprehensive transport plan, which relays the full economic cost of travel to the user, and embraces road, rail, air and pedestrian, no part of the apparatus can function efficiently. Until a parking policy is announced as a constituent of a central land use pattern, the ring road consultants must continue to base their trip assignments on an extrapolation of the existing, with consequent redesign as political winds blow. The magnitude of the task should not be underestimated. A

£60 million new town developed by 100 professionals over twenty years recreates an area equivalent to only 7 per cent of the land surface of the City of Glasgow

THE INFLUENCE OF AUTOMOBILES ON NEW URBAN FORM

Now that decentralization thinking is being implemented with a transport plan based on feeder services to railheads, plus urban motorways, the

Right: This view shows Glasgow in the foreground with Greenock and the new Clyde City in the distance. The multi-deck terminal project at the base of the picture integrates road, rail, air, river and riverbed transport systems in a single urban structure

Below: This view of the multi-deck terminal project shows its relation to the city, the river, the railroad, and the new in-city highway ring

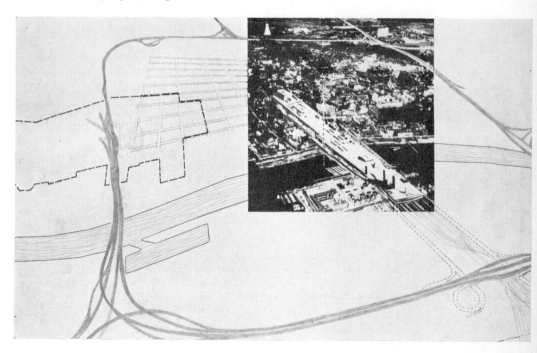

222

focus of a city region for 2½ million people must provide corresponding services. The transport department, which lost 30 million passenger journeys in two years, would like privileges for its surface vehicles and its £500,000 fuel tax rebated. If the former were given through the conversion of multi-purpose roads to specialized gyratory patterns, the latter would not be necessary. The acceptance of uni-directional principles would reduce decision and accident points and eliminate conflict areas together with crossing streams. Access would be less restricted, since only merging and diverging manoeuvres would arise, capacities would be raised and where, as here in the impressive central business grid, land use and communication patterns can be integrated its message would immediately be comprehensible

The adoption of superblocks, with freer running public transport and convenient parking terminals, would permit the introduction of pedestrian malls capable of being linked to form a separate pedestrian network. The realization of this potential hinges on storage provision for the vehicle right at the preferred zone of destination. It has been calculated that the city of the future will require 100 extra acres in the designated central area – half might be provided by steering away certain non-conforming uses, but this effort may be nullified if the vehicular problem has been underestimated. In the wealthiest nation in the world, one family in five own two cars, yet some traffic facilities, already absurdly high by British standards, are proving increasingly inadequate

Twelve months ago, over one in three of the 7,000 cars and 2,000 goods vehicles in the centre were illegally parked. Yet the level of vehicle ownership in Glasgow is only half the Scottish average, itself less than that of the U K, which is in turn half the still rising level of the United States. It is accepted that the number of vehicles registered in Glasgow will at least treble in fifteen years, and it has been estimated that 18,500 parking spaces will be required. This load cannot be imposed on the grid-iron even if 50 per cent of the trips now made through Glasgow prove by-passable

Universal ownership of the motor car, and the introduction of the structural frame, coupled with the ability to service vast complexes, must lead inevitably to an era of vertical multi-use of land in a new urban form. Its characteristic will be flexibility in response to social and economic pressures, rather than preconceived notions of form. Parts will be devoted to individual and mass transport, parts to

internal and external activities. Servicing will be analogous to the bodily nervous system and must itself be adaptable

The day of the individual identifiable building on a separate site at grade is, in general, over in central areas. Projects of the scale necessary to bring back coherence and unity into our cities can be achieved only by a union of government, nationalized undertakings, and private enterprise from which will flow new management and funding concepts

MULTI-LEVEL USAGE OF AIR RIGHTS OVER GLASGOW'S CENTRAL STATION

Exactly at the peak property value intersection in the city exists a providential vacuum – the air space over the Central Station rail tracks. This is the only point in the city where all components of a transportation system converge, where the opportunity exists for civic functions, and where their presence can reinforce the high value core and stimulate development in the declining area on both sides of the Clyde

A calculated investment here complementary to, rather than disruptive of, the existing shopping centre would create a new highly accessible focus in the city centre – outside the grid-iron yet served by a spur from the inner-ring road. Associated with the river – the source of the City's greatness – the establishment of this centre could aid its transformation into a priceless amenity

The sterile prospect of a rates-borne 'Arts Centre' that has been canvassed, enshrining art as a separate hot-house activity, will ensure the perpetuation for the masses of a world in which art is either irrelevant or historical. Here is both the opportunity to demonstrate the fruitful interaction of all aspects of urban society and to create the very means of its enhanced existence. St Andrew's Hall, which was burnt down three years ago, was not ideal for some who used it, and there were many needs it could not meet. This is an occasion to remedy some of Glasgow's deficiencies with the provision of a great concert hall and public forum, and to satisfy the needs of the amateur and professional for small and medium-sized halls

The construction of a comprehensive Auditorium Centre, combining in different areas skating, concerts, exhibitions, bowling, spectacles, political meetings, dancing, lectures television studios, drama and hotels, under a great umbrella of office space, would generate activity by day and evening through-

out the year, encouraging not merely spectatorship but participation. The inclusion of prestige offices with large-scale entertainment interests at this fulcrum in the city could serve to promote this development to the benefit of the Transport Commission, who would profit both from leasing air rights, and multiplication of traffic. The impact of the whole will be greater than the sum of the parts, for one use would activate another, and events generate events, in an environment in which the welfare of the clerk is as important as the quality of the acoustics. The presence of one makes the other possible. New stores could be associated with this facility. There are some 14,000 retail outlets in Glasgow, but few are modern purpose-built establishments on a scale suitable for efficient vending techniques. One component of a multi-occupation structure, the hotel, already exists: extended, this could handle, at different levels, catering for the whole centre

Two use groups, however, which have been linked with the relocation of St Andrew's Hall should be excluded – major outdoor sports functions and the Burrell art collection. Each is important enough in itself to promote separate growing points in the city, while a gigantic nucleation of all these in the Auditorium Centre would deprive other areas of activity of a communal kind, and upset the economic aspects of the proposal. Similarly, at a time when urban authorities everywhere are desperately trying to increase the marginal amount of open space to be found at the heart of our industrial cities, it must be quite wrong to encroach on existing parkland for any of these uses

While the use of air rights is new to Scottish Law, there are no technical problems present here that have not already been solved in other cities involved in building over existing transport centres. The cost of building over rail is greater, though less demolition is necessary, as the permanent way makes the movement of heavy construction machinery difficult, and supports must be arranged to avoid obstructing track planners, but as the price paid for purchase or lease of air rights is lower than for other desirable sites, the total cost can be about the same. The creation of an all-weather centre in the heart of the city with magnificent views, without hazard or distraction for the pedestrian, could be achieved, not at the expense of the motorist, but to his advantage, for this is the only point in the city where, too, a transportation centre accommodating 3,000 private cars could be integrated with a new bus station (replacing the five stations in the vicinity), connected

223

Above: The concept has basic similarities with air-craft carriers

Right: The multi-deck terminal project is a city within the city, combining office blocks, shops and department stores, auditoria, galleries, hotels and entertainment in one gigantic urban structure

to main line and suburban rail services and all linked by travolator to the subway under St Enoch's square. To this node would then gravitate air and sea passenger terminals and tourist agencies with access to taxis and cushion-craft below and helicopters above

MULTI-USAGE TRAFFIC CO-ORDINATION IN A SINGLE STRUCTURE

The co-ordination of private and all forms of mass transport, including a low-level link with long-distance Blue Trains, possible on this site, would simplify park-and-ride systems by providing complete passenger interchange for visitors, and a proportion of the 150,000 commuters. A parking facility of this capacity could be of real significance, connected to the coming ring road, yet probing right into the only potential multi-use vacuum that exists in the centre. On this scale the parking decks would be readily identifiable, and accessed by grade separated inter-changes where the inner ring overpasses the rail to

give free-flow conditions into the heart of the central area. No cross-town flows would be generated; it would be quicker to park using the ring road

The grouping of uses within one fabric lit by a single beacon-like artificial sun will ensure the economic use of passenger-handling and parking facilities which could be offered as a concession to a consortium of petrol companies and accessory interests. Coupled with a ban on long-term kerbside parking this could be operated without subsidy on a commercial basis A future parking programme should involve the construction of two further major terminals incising into the centre, equipped with highway systems, and on a scale again large enough to generate development within and on their edge, plus a distribution of 500-car garages, and the retention of 3,000 on-street, metered short-term places. The alternatives are ad hoc provision which will be more expensive, less efficient and disruptive both of the uses and flows in the vicinity, or fragmented continuance of the in-city basement garages demanded by city ordinance for new development

Other cities have derived social and economic advantage by creating new metropolitan assets from a largely untapped source of space, ranging from the forty-one-storey Prudential Plaza built over the Illinois Central Railroad in Chicago, to the Ponte Vecchio in Florence

The Clyde has always fertilized imaginations, but related to the property void at the high value core in the context proposed here, has never offered a more useful medium for urban improvement at a time when its generative properties could play some part in the long-term prospects of the Scottish economy

URBAN RENEWAL
AND CENTRAL AREA REDEVELOPMENT IN GREAT BRITAIN
THE PARTICIPATION OF PRIVATE ENTERPRISE

COLIN HUNT

Urban renewal has, of course, been continuous since the dawn of cities when men first congregated to form social units and rationalize production. During the past few years history has speeded up; technological and social changes have accelerated, in some ways predictably and in others in a manner that could not be foreseen, with the result that in the immediate future the shape of cities and the conduct of life in them will alter more radically and more profoundly than at any time in our past

Because of this there is a greater need than ever for care and forethought in planning. In fact planning has become the key profession, basic to the very survival of cities. Already it is only too tragically plain that lack of understanding and obsolete thinking, caused by unconcern and little social conscience among some planners and architects, have solidified into huge immoveable lumps of buildings in our towns and cities which now will remain with us for a century or more

Behind the need for renewal lies considerably more than decay and obsolescence. Obsolescence is physical, functional and environmental – and is to some extent built-in to every new building. But the need for renewal is more radical and wider than this.

The central areas of many cities throughout Britain, the USA, and Europe – their nodal points or fulcra of citizen-use – have evolved from street patterns traditional of the middle ages, and are now absolutely archaic, incapable of adaptation to the complexity of modern usage and traffic flows

Radical solutions are needed if new environments are to be built that are sufficiently flexible to meet today's needs as they evolve into tomorrow's. And the planner's approach will be successful only if it is aimed at reappraising the physical fabric of urban life as a whole – not merely the threadbare patches

There have been isolated moments in the past when whole cities, or parts of cities, could be planned or replanned in terms of unified and comprehensive vision. But our century is unique in that for the first time it does seem as though an overall view of planning may be achieved in many different cities simultaneously, by means of the general adoption of an administrative structure in which private enterprise and local government can work together towards agreed common goals for the good of the community as a whole. Already in Britain some 350 towns and cities, including most of the major industrial conurbations, have announced comprehensive plans for the redevelopment of their central areas; and in many of these the public and private sectors of the economy will work together. Perhaps the best way of understanding how such a situation will work in practice is to review the last fifteen or so years historically

The large-scale destruction of property during the second world war was followed in Britain by the creation of a system to compulsorily coalesce land ownership. This was the Town and Country Planning Act of 1947. It allowed the various local government planning authorities to designate 'Areas of Comprehensive Development', and as a result they were given legal powers to redevelop large areas of our cities, previously in private ownership, in terms of overall design. But in principle these were to be areas of war damage, bad layout, or obsolete development

The 1947 powers were based on the premise that the land would be acquired at existing use values, and in the areas of blitz and blight, use values were not high. But as the need to redevelop large areas of cities on a more comprehensive basis became year by year more and more pressing, particularly as a result of the enormous growth in traffic volumes and also changes in the patterns of industrial expansion and commercial trading, various cities began to use their

powers of compulsory purchase more widely than the 1947 Act envisaged. But existing use values are often far below market values, and pressure for a repeal of the Act began to mount up

The 1959 Planning Act made a fair current market price the basis for land acquisition, and returned to the individual the benefit of a profitable planning consent. This has meant in practice that cities now have considerable difficulty on limited budgets in gathering together sufficient pieces of the jigsaw of land ownership to fit them together into a site suitable for comprehensive development

The key to proper redevelopment of cities is unified land ownership. Under existing legislation the only machinery to achieve this is by public acquisition— plus redevelopment by the city itself or private enterprise, or both together combining their resources, under suitable controls. There are enormous difficulties involved in this. The cumbersome and time-consuming process of proposal, enquiry, designation and implementation of Comprehensive Development Area powers backed up by compulsory purchase orders is still the only tool available to the Local Authority. And the pressures for redevelopment are today too great and too complex for these rigid and time-consuming procedures

Private enterprise, on the other hand, without being allowed to have within its sheath the Sword of Damocles of eventual compulsory purchase, often finds itself paying excess market value and can in the end be prevented from a clean site by one or more unwilling co-operators. At the same time it is obviously unwise to publish what it is proposed to do with the land until all the relevant property is bought – for this would cause land costs to soar. As a result proposals are not brought to public notice soon enough for creative discussion and participation on the part of citizens. Some simple and quicker procedure is urgently needed

INFLUENCES

Yet the public itself is gradually becoming aware of the importance of the urban environment in which it lives and all the benefits of attractive and amenable surroundings. It has been proved over and over again that office workers are happier and work better in new buildings designed to suit the work they do. New trends in retail marketing, the growth of mailorder buying, discount systems, and the growing numbers of married women working, have furthered the acceptance of one-stop buying, resulting in the rapid expansion of turnover taken by multiple shops at the expense of the small trader. Increasing private car-ownership, the demand for greater leisure with new ways of enjoying it, and more money to spend, are all changing the traditional way the citizen uses his town

In the past urban renewal has been carried out by a number of different agencies. The private individual has always had, and in part he still retains, the right to redevelop his real estate interests. But this results in that scattered and piecemeal renewal which has been only too evident in so many cities in the recent past

The trend today is the gradual usurping of individual rights for the common good. New skills of organization and control are being learnt by developers, and gradually a salutary rationalization is taking place among the rush of property development companies which sprang up in the boom years. The graph of development profitability has levelled off, and in contrast to the machinations of the property speculator the serious developer accepts that urban renewal is a long-term business, and that he is in that business to stay

THE LOCAL GOVERNMENT CATALYST

A few cities (Sheffield, Coventry, Liverpool, the London County Council are examples of this), faced with enormous areas of blitzed or blighted property, courageously seized the opportunity to carry out urban renewal on a large scale on their own without the aid of private enterprise. Their massive achievements have, however, been the exception rather than the rule – and in the face of considerable difficulties. And it is by no means established that such methods are appropriate to meet our present complex needs. The amount and type of money available to local authorities is a permanent problem under the present system which relies on an annual budgeting of income and expenditure, and does not sustain a grant specifically for urban renewal purposes

Before 1955 and the Local Government Act of 1958, a Government Grant of 50 per cent was available for land acquisition and development by local authorities within any Comprehensive Development Area. But these specific grants are now payable only in areas of war damage; and since these areas have virtually all been rebuilt, work on comprehensive redevelopment is obliged to compete for a share of the general grant with all the other local government functions

A further budgeting difficulty is the unremunerative period before a development is complete and working. Development is a long-term process and may occupy several years before returns are made, and a heavy initial capital expenditure on land acquisition involves a continuing burden of interest charges for servicing and developing the outlay

MONEY

The interest of private enterprise in urban renewal has sprung, of course, from the profit motive. Profit derives from being able to anticipate or create changes in the trend of demand and thus value, and to take advantage of the special structure and nature of the investment of money

There has in the recent past in this country been an increasing momentum to the long-term swing of emphasis in the investment of insurance monies in property, away from British Government securities and Commonwealth stock. This trend of investment policy has been continuous since the first world war, in a changing concept of security in relation to income yield derived from prudent investment. The investment of insurance funds in property prior to 1939 was mainly in well secured ground rents. The book value of investment in real property by insurance companies at the end of 1962 was £730 million, representing 9.5 per cent of total investment. The trend of investment in property by insurance companies continues at about 10 per cent of an annual investment figure in excess of £500 million

Real property in fact fulfils most of the principles for the investment of insurance funds. Experience of the devastating effect that depreciation of currency can have on the capital value of long-term investment on fixed rates of interest, together with the current view that further inflation is inevitable, emphasizes the need for investments to be tied to the inflatory spiral. Equity shares and property admirably fulfil this function

Nevertheless there is even yet a great variation in the amount of property investments held by insurance companies, and a recent survey showed that of forty-three offices, no less than forty-one had less than 10 per cent of their total investments in property, and only one had in excess of 30 per cent; the average is about 10 per cent

The investment policy of Pension Funds has also helped to sustain urban renewal by making available long-term finance on suitable terms. Their property

holdings at the end of 1963 amounted to £53 million representing 26 per cent of their total investment. Pension Funds are in fact showing an increased interest in property investment

Another source of money has been by new public issue of shares, sustained by increasing prosperity and more diffuse methods of tapping the private individual's money

Such fiscal methods backed by a growing confidence and proof of their ability have enabled property entrepreneurs to raise adequate finance, and to amass the expertise and experience necessary to carry out large-scale property development, in contrast to the difficulties facing local authorities. Many of the private fortunes created since the war have been through development and speculation of property. The process has been relatively simple; but market conditions have now changed. With the trend to larger redevelopment units, the solution of development problems has become more sophisticated

PARTICIPATION

In the past, the property developer has tended to take all current and future profits accruing through his anticipation of demand and inflation. This situation is now changing. The developer in effect supplies his skill, entrepreneurship, expertize, experience, little personal cash, carries a major portion of the risk, and makes use of a considerable number of consultants. But today the financier has come to realize that no development can proceed without finance; and, in return for his mortgage debenture solving, on a fixed interest basis, the long-term finance problem – he now insists on participating in the equity accruing from the use of his monies as a hedge against inflation. This is generally achieved by the purchase of ordinary shares of the development company at an agreed price

Alternatively, where the finance is for a specific project and there is less 'spread' with greater risk, or where there is no pre-letting or guaranteed income prior to commencement of outlay, then the financier maintains that he effectively carries risk and his money should earn risk profits. In this case he requires an increased proportion of the equity. Equity shares equate with risk or cover to the monies involved, and thus the financier gives up some measure of one criteria to earn another

At the same time the private and the public landowner has now similarly realized that by disposing of property permanently, all rights to share in future value are lost. Land owners who have amassed or inherited suitable properties for large-scale redevelopment are now tending to convey only a limited interest in the property by the leasehold system, which has itself been a vital historic factor in keeping intact the great estates of Central London

Terms now being imposed tend to require an annual sum to be paid for the site on the basis of a proportion of the income that may derive from what can be put on it, either on an assessed basis prior to commencement of work, or on the actuality of the first letting. As a hedge against inflation and in order to participate in the outcome over the term of the lease, a review of the ground rent is being required at increasingly frequent intervals, such as every thirty years. The developer in turn endeavours to pass the impact of this demand on to the occupier by similarly requiring the full rent payable for the use of the building to be reviewed periodically, preferably at a shorter period than the ground rent

Occupiers have been prepared to some extent to acquiesce in such an onerous burden due to competition for prime locations, and in expectation that the trend of an increasing volume of turnover would continue. This has so far proved justifiable, but in certain peak locations a maximum capacity of turnover on present marketing systems can be estimated for specific trades. This latter realization has therefore resulted in first, a certain measure of hostility to what are termed 'uneconomic' rents and secondly, a firmer attitude to bargaining based on the contribution or betterment value that essential key multiples bring with their drawing power

TOWN CENTRES

The intolerable conflict of traffic, consumer demand and high land values tends to produce a vicious circle, strangling the achievement of an ideal city centre that works from every aspect. Demand for sites, and the competition of numerous developers backed by ample finance, merely aggravates the situation

The high rents of new central area redevelopment, deriving from increasing building costs, land and finance terms, tend to drive out the local and small traders. Care must always be taken to ensure a proper balance of facilities, and for appropriate off-peak positions for local and specialized traders who are unable to sustain the turnover necessary to be near to the shopping fulcrum. In fact a great

difficulty of shopping balance is that traders must regard rent as part of running costs, and it is thus directly geared to volume trading and mark-up. And so a further factor that has to be considered is that to make one pound gross profit some traders have to take five pounds, others fifty pounds

In addition, higher rental quotients mean other overheads must suffer, such as labour costs and customer service. More sales per square foot of ground floor space become necessary

Some schemes have endeavoured to resolve the demand for ground floor space by two-storey shopping. In general this has proved to work in this country only where there is an absolutely natural flow of pedestrians to either floor, each possessing similar status; deception is the key

American experience proves a valuable indicator to the problem of downtown central areas, and a test-bed for various practical remedies. There, a development has been the successful creation of suburban, fully enclosed, comprehensive shopping centres sustained by a traffic solution. They have proved to be convenient, appropriate and acceptable – but they are not a contribution to urban environment

Proposals for similar ventures in this country have encountered hostile reactions from both planners and established retailers within the trade catchment area. A feasible solution in this tight-knit residual garden city of a country seems to be the fully enclosed shopping centre with environmental facilities, located in dense urban areas and sustained on a nodal point of both public and private transport systems. Examples are the Bull Ring in Birmingham and the Elephant and Castle scheme in London, although each of these is open to criticism from other points of view

New thinking and bold ventures are required, one of the most important of which is variation of traditional shopping hours. In American centres, where they conform to what the public wants, 60 per cent of trade is done after 5.30 pm

In the three years 1959-62, per capita income in Great Britain increased by 20 per cent while the cost of living rose only 12 per cent. This is the indicator of the retail trading potential, and by projection, means a considerable expansion of vending facilities.

Shopping, however, need not be a fight for survival or a worrysome process of physical and mental attrition. It can be an enjoyable and pleasant pastime, compensating the effort of earning money by the pleasure of spending it

DEVELOPMENT METHODS

However, all novel and adventurous solutions must be examined in the cold light of financial appraisal embracing not only the curtilage of the comprehensive site; but also the impact which the development makes on the neighbourhood, on public services, and on other non-profitable elements of the urban scene provided and maintained by the ratepayer

Many of the schemes at present proposed co not stand cold analysis, and in fact a Ministry examination in 1962 of six central area projects revealed that only one was properly viable

There is need for the greater use of scientific method in the assessment of demand; and the techniques of market analysis and motivational research, long used for consumer good marketing and advertising, are gradually being employed. Plenty of useful data is available, such as traffic counts, age and family grouping of population, spending power, car registrations, etc, and further breakdown of trade statistics is proposed. The skill lies in the analysis of data, the projection of it to prognosticate future trends, and more particularly in its translation into a comprehensive architect's brief

The central approving body of the Ministry of Housing and Local Government is at the moment the only source of assessment of the impact which individual town centre proposals make on a region. It is not sufficient to shelve the responsibility and burden of over-provision or duplication of facilities on to the interaction of the market. This could mean unwise and wasteful employment of capital investment. Analysis and assessment of the overlapping spheres of influence is essential to allow valid policy directives to be made. The planner and the architect tend to operate far too much on an ad hoc and empirical basis

In contrast to this, the urban economist must be brought into a central position during the period of planning and architectural briefing, and he must examine the economic base of urban and regional land use, the legal and economic policies and institutions affecting land tenure, analyze price and rent problems and examine the economics of location, spacial patterns and trends

The developer's new role becomes one of depth, for he has to marry these new disciplines to the old, and to employ a feed-back of responsible critical information and instruction from analysis of completed schemes, to see how they tick; whether and why they tell the hours successfully

PRIVATE ENTERPRISE AND THE LOCAL AUTHORITY

Urban renewal involves redevelopment and renovation, and includes twilight areas as well as town centres

Town centres have greater potential for organic change due to commercial values. However, a city must be seen as a whole, and the statistics on housing are alarming, in that by 1975 we shall have to find room for 3 million more people – equivalent to fifty new towns. Furthermore some 850,000 houses in England and Wales today are unfit for human habitation and more than one in six are over 100 years old

The dynamism of private enterprise, bolstered by the profit motive, has enabled it to take the lead in urban renewal and force the pace of the reconsideration of town centres, their use and value structure. Local authorities – handicapped by cumbersome acquisition procedure, budgeting and finance difficulties, together with their difficulties in attracting suitable staff – have lost ground as leaders. Private enterprise can mobilize the cash, and buy the skills. Local authorities possess the last-resort powers of compulsory purchase, but have, of necessity, had to use their town planning in practice to administer the complicated provisions of the Planning Acts, rather than positive action

It is now recognized that the complementary contributions of the local authority and private enterprise must be brought properly together; the former supplying the skilful planning background, local concern through the agency of their democratic structure, and the final unification of land ownership; the latter aiding and implementing the agreed proposals by means of their financial resources and commercial expertise, experience and ability to take risks

The objective would then be to secure unified control over a sufficiently wide area to enable commercially profitable development to bear the cost of what is socially and aesthetically desirable. The difficulty has been to determine the most appropriate way of achieving this objective

The Royal Institute of British Architects in September 1960 circulated all local authorities with a memorandum on 'Competition by Tender', pointing out the dilemma of choice in inviting a combined architec-

tural scheme and a financial bid – one or the other often suffered. A further Joint Memorandum was prepared by the Royal Institute of British Architects and the Royal Institution of Chartered Surveyors in January 1962, endeavouring to distinguish and separate competition based on design, and competition based on evaluation of commercial potential; and methods of allowing the local authority to participate in the outcome were suggested

It was followed by a Ministry of Housing and Local Government Planning Bulletin, 'Town Centres–Approach to Renewal', which clarified the problems involved and indicated a Ministerial policy strongly in favour of partnership. As an aid to comprehensive land acquisition it suggested that the local authority would define a Comprehensive Development Area (CDA) and prepare development proposals in consultation with a development company. The company then acquires as much land as possible by private negotiation, and the local authority can back them up if necessary with their powers of compulsory purchase. The freehold of this development unit is then transferred to the local authority in exchange for a long lease to the development company with upward rent review clauses attaching to the payment of ground rent

The disposal terms under the ground lease are calculated to take into account the betterment accruing from new road patterns, car parks and other socially desirable but non-profitable elements at charge to the local authority, as well as non-commercial facilities required and the long-term prospect. This practical method of solving the administrative problems which exist under present legislation is now increasingly being used

THE DILEMMA OF CHOICE

Partnership by negotiation introduces the dilemma of choice. If it is appropriate for the local authority to work from the beginning with a single developer, which one should be chosen out of the dozens of applicants sending bouquets of tempting glossy brochures? The availability of money and the increase in the number of property companies during the share boom years have meant an increase in the pressure on the local authority. Those companies who have carried out one or more developments in association with a local authority have some wares in their basket

The choice must be made very carefully since once an association is formed it is very difficult to break,

and the wrong developer can lead to permanent urban disaster. Buildings last a long time. Town councillors seem more prone than the rest of us to folie de grandeur; and the bait of hotels, ice rinks and vast shopping centres may lead eventually to a small row of shops profitably developed by private enterprise, while the burden of over-ambitious civic amenities and road improvements is left to be carried by the taxpayer

Unbiased and independent professional advice and analysis are needed for every proposal, with overall ratification by the central government

The trend might well be towards even greater amalgamation, under a single agency, of all the various components of urban renewal. The builder/developer is emerging into prominence in a way historically parallel to his past. New agencies for development of commercially non-viable schemes of urban renewal – covering the immense problems of 'twilight areas' or soft rings of obsolescence around town centres – may well come into being on a 'package deal' approach

Rationalization of both development companies and builders has already occurred, giving better stability and synchronization, and providing greater resources. Schemes embracing much larger areas, allowing industrialized building techniques, and the subsidizing of non-profitable elements by the profitable parts, are almost certain to be a trend in the immediate future, possibly on some generalized control basis, or on a carefully defined programme, or perhaps a consortium of implementers

The solution of the twilight area problem along such lines may well pose re-examination of exchequer grants, rates, funds, subsidies, rent equalization schemes, sale of housing by the local authority, variations to control and accounting of local authority expenditures, and other political questions

THE DEVELOPMENT TEAM

The developer's role becomes every day therefore more crucial. Development can only proceed under a team that brings every appropriate skill to the task; and the architect is a leading member, but not the leader of this team. The leader must always be the developer, the man who carries the responsibility, not merely for the first success of the project – and success is measured by cash in a capitalist economy – but throughout the life of the buildings

The two principal advisers to the developer are the

architect and the estate consultant. Aiding each of these members is the data and analysis of research into relevant problems. The architect is concerned with functions, planning, materials and cost. The estate consultants will make use of market analysts to assess demand, potential turn-over, trade area, the dangers of over-supply and duplication of facilities. He may also employ physicists, geographers, sociologists and psychologists to undertake functional research, and an urban economist to synthesize this information and advise from historic studies upon future trends

Under the architect and in direct consultation with the estate consultant and his team will be the planner, the civic designer, the engineer and other technical consultants, the specification writer, and the quantity surveyor. Liaison from the earliest possible moment in the scheme will be maintained with the prospective contractor, his estimating, supervision and design staff. Use will be made of modern management tools of critical path programming and method study practices, introducing new plant and handling techniques

The estate consultant's team will contribute regular economic appraisals of the evolving proposals against the background of the terms on which money is being raised, and the local authority lease proposals. The lawyer and the tax consultant will advise on their specific aspects and the letting agent, and possibly key or multiple pre-let tenants, will contribute their experience

Implementation will only result from viability. A continuous check on the balance between the viable and non-viable elements and assessment of their contribution to the totality is necessary. This means evaluating in an empirical way their hidden contribution – in a similar manner to invisible exports and the balance of trade

Continuous co-ordination of this amalgamation of skills and talents is the developer's role. At all times there must be dovetailing with the local authority and its staff, who become in effect members of the team

The cross currents of information necessary to be fed into the machine to produce a successful physical product mean utilization of cost/value and cost-in-use techniques. The value consequences of design decisions must be analyzed to give more precise limits and thus greater freedom to the architect in finding the most beneficial form of design

Higher first cost versus lower maintenance and other aspects of cost-in-use mean close co-operation between the quantity surveyor, the valuer and the architect

THE ARCHITECTS' ROLE

Indeed, a new sort of architect is required. There is a danger that this very large scale of development means only a limited number of firms capable of such work and the talent becomes more and more disseminated. Good architecture is very difficult to produce by a committee. The role of the co-ordinating architect is becoming fashionable, though it is difficult to measure its contribution. One needs to live with a scheme from inception to completion, tramp the streets and hear the pleas of displaced traders, feel the draughty winds and dust and be unable to park one's car. There must never be compromise to barren and dull mediocrity

A heavy burden is thus placed on the developer; he must recognize a social responsibility and be educated in assessing and assembling the talents of others and above all he must care about buildings and environment

The new architect must be a humble man and of choice, as well as necessity, come out of his ivory tower of design. His work is an end-product of the contributing skills of the whole team. He must synthesize all the myriad of conditioning factors and ensure that the end-product is humanist, has scale, dignity and delight, is functionally efficient, and adaptable to changing trends of use. In this almost impossible task, he must guard against built-in obsolescence of old ideas and invalid techniques

Too often it has been the architect who for want of a definitive brief has been the subjective interpreter of the current mores of society, its sociological needs; and by personal alchemy produces admired architecture of form but an inappropriate answer to the problem to be solved. To cite two examples; the Hunstanton Secondary Modern School of Peter and Alison Smithson is rightly admired as an excellent example of architectural form and design; but in practice, apart from technical defects in the juxtaposition of materials, its functional requirements are not adequately achieved by its plan. A further case is the much admired Bethnal Green cluster-block by Denys Lasdun, where the vertical terraced streets are intended to recreate a sense of community. A recent survey by the Institute of Community Studies suggests that in practice the opposite is the result. The new architect as a member of a team can avoid the past mistakes of subjective personal interpretation through good analysis and thorough briefing; but equally essential is the need to ensure that teamwork does not stifle the individual

Excellent solutions to functional needs and rational use of materials still need the delight and quickening of the senses which a building as architecture can bring

The slur of 'developer's architecture' is often levied as just criticism because the developer's evaluation of the result has been on a user/cost ratio basis and the meeting of an anticipated demand. Yet fundamentally this is the only successful criterion possible in a capitalist society. There is rarely any other implementer than money, and where there is – if the result is a delight – it is generally someone's folly. Given this basic factor, the nettle should be grasped. Yet looking at the problem the other way round – what will homo sapiens pay in rent or on-costs to retail prices for enhancement of the spirit? It can often be proved that the amount is considerable. Environment, amenity, space, form, art objects, can all stimulate and attract commercial demand. Given proper techniques the architect can be given more freedom within his discipline

In town centres where activity and colour and movement are great spending stimulators, the architect must be prepared to modify his formal interpretations of style and perhaps introduce a certain brashness; an American car look – General Motors has the largest turnover in the world. Architecture should relate to the human dimension and comprise elements possessing similar foibles and idiosyncracies. But remember it is the developer who actually bears the cost of the consequence – the cash outcome of rejection or acceptance

Form, style and art expressed through and as architecture are as necessary to the development of the spirit and personal 'growth' as painting and poetry. Architects need more lay criticism of their buildings, leavened by a commentary from other parallel and not opposed disciplines, instead of esoteric polemics. Not only poets read and criticize poetry

Architecture is not a pure art like music – notes have no use by themselves but they solace the spirit when in harmonic arrangement, and delight the mind by counterpoint. The terms are transferable. Architecture is like poetry – words have other uses, such as asking the way, and communication is in one sense more difficult and in another more easy

Architects should also be poets

230

PLANNING AND DESIGNING THE CENTRAL AREAS OF CUMBERNAULD NEW TOWN

GEOFFREY COPCUTT

BRITISH PLANNING POLICY

Britain, one of the world's most densely populated industrial nations, with about two and a half times the density of France and about ten times that of the United States, cannot afford to waste either space or manpower

British planning policy basically results from the need to recognize that, while unfettered enterprise may produce anarchy, the real dynamic is nonetheless economic. In a word, if the national product is to continue to rise, a way has to be found, in this geographically small country, for this dynamic to be canalized but not thwarted. The Government has to make its moves within this contradiction

Thus there is, at the present moment, Government reluctance to inhibit the multiplication of jobs in the south-east quadrant of England. At the same time the Government wishes to renew the infrastructure of other regions, notably in the north of England and in the industrial areas of Scotland, which are suffering from redundant mineral and engineering capability. A combination of land use controls and fiscal measures helps the British to plan. These have been many since World War Two and I will not enumerate them here, other than mentioning that the most recent trends

call for the 100 per cent transfer of ownership of land to the State (30 per cent of the land surface of Britain is already under some special protection as national parks, green belts or areas of outstanding beauty – and a further 10 per cent is occupied by towns and cities)

At the same time Britain is growing rapidly. Her urbanized population is expected to increase by 4 million by 1980 and rise at a rate of 1 million a year thereafter for the next twenty years. But her cities will increase in size somewhat larger in proportion to population than these figures suggest – due to a faster rate of household formation, rising prosperity and increasing mobility (40 million vehicles by 2010). Up to the present, physical planning has been largely controlled by local authorities working within electoral rather than economic areas. However, continued migration into the conurbations, and the excess of births over deaths, demands more comprehensive areas of control – for the present system of local authorities makes no sense for the discharge of modern functions. The trend towards regional government is, however, gathering momentum because it deals most effectively with the difficulties associated with overload at the centre and breakdown at the periphery. Regional management in the State-owned service industries (gas, electricity, railways, etc) has become the established pattern; and recent Government White Papers have made significant moves towards regional development planning

BRITISH NEW TOWNS

A particularly British contribution is the creation of wholly new towns, planned and built as self-contained communities, providing, in addition to houses, employment, shopping, education, recreation and culture. Towns will always grow where industry establishes itself, and the choice is only between the planned and the unplanned. In a small and overcrowded country, sites of the right size and facilities are long since taken, and if they are not to consist of first-class agricultural land, it becomes a matter of finding a location with the least objection

At the time of writing seventeen new towns are under construction in Britain, of which the first two are at a point where development can be left to natural growth. These new towns have already been occupied by half a million people with a full complement of jobs. By the year 2000 they will reach a million inhabitants. But even including the further three new towns now in active planning and design,

1 London, 2 Bristol, 3 Cardiff, 4 Cambridge, 5 Birmingham, 6 Liverpool, 7 Manchester, 8 Leeds, 9 Carlisle, 10 Newcastle, 11 Glasgow, 12 Edinburgh, 13 Crawley, 14 Bracknell, 15 Basildon, 16 Harlow, 17 Welwyn, 18 Hemel Hempstead, 19 Hatfield, 20 Stevenage, 21 Cwmbran, 22 Corby, 23 Skelmersdale, 24 Newton Aycliffe, 25 Peterlee, 26 East Kilbride, 27 Cumbernauld, 28 Glenrothes

there remains a considerable shortfall from, say, the Town and Country Planning Association's call for 100 new towns after the first world war

Twelve new towns have a 'decentralization' function; eight in the London ring, three around Glasgow, and one for the Liverpool overspill. Three further new towns are now being built close to industrial concentrations, to which workers may travel daily. Two new towns, Peterlee and Glenrothes were designed as mining towns, to provide better conditions for miners living in scattered miserable villages over the coal fields. Glenrothes, however, has suffered considerable crises and change of intention. This new town was originally designed and built to serve the newest, most modern and probably the largest deep coal-mine in the world. Unfortunately the mine was never worked, as it constantly flooded to an extent that could not be controlled. The development corporation had therefore to look for other industries to provide employment. A diversity of light industrial companies have been most successfully introduced to the town, some of them from the USA, making use of site grants and machinery concessions made available by the British Government. The population, drawn largely from the Scottish lowlands, which now inhabits the town, has been successfully trained to the new skills required. The flooded mine is now used as a reservoir of water for industrial processes

The great majority of people going to new towns are weekly wage-earners, either moving with their firms, or to fill vacancies in firms already there. They are younger, more skilled and better paid than the desperately needy families at the top of the city's huge public housing waiting list, or the groups which predominate in the vast featureless estates which mushroomed on the edge of every large city after the war. More developed new towns have 300 to 400 social organizations, roughly equal to more settled towns; and, as rate resources grow, these are able already, although far from complete, to equip their towns better than many long-settled towns of similar size. In fact settled towns show an annual turnover of population of 10 per cent, twice as high as the rate in the new towns. However, considerable difficulties arise with the very high child population; and efforts are being concentrated on getting employment which will provide for adolescents; similarly the effect of severing family ties with relatives left in the older cities is recognized as undesirable, and attempts are being made to meet this by enabling retired people to move with their married children and other relatives

Each new town begins by being governed by a corporation which is appointed by the Government and financed from the Exchequer, paying throughout the sixty-year period of loan the rate of interest appropriate at the time of borrowing. They have power to buy land compulsorily within areas designated for this purpose, but at a price which excludes value created by development of the town itself, and the corporation retains the freehold in interests of good estate management. Most have accumulated debt at the moment in respect of early heavy expenditure on water and sewerage, but the whole operation is moving into credit

Police clearing passage during a non-violent anti-Polaris demonstration in Scotland

That each new town can be a profitable investment in the long run has been expressed by one official thus: 'their abundant industrial success has shown that public planning investment can set up conditions in which private initiative and capital can combine with it to produce outstandingly beneficial results to the community. The entrepreneurial success of the State appointed and financed development corporations charged with building is beyond doubt. There is no other agency so powerfully equipped to lift the quality of life of a region or one better able to withstand the buffeting of a fluctuating economy. A development corporation can preserve the unity of freehold and retain the revenues for the nation. It is assured of capital advances to complete its work, with repayment of loans deferred until revenue is being earned. It is outside local politics and insulated from the pressure of shifting political opinion. It can carry through a balanced housing programme for all classes, and can lend on mortgages. It draws full Exchequer housing subsidies. It can build factories for sale or rent; or lend monies to firms to build themselves; and it can adjust terms to give aid under the Local Employment Act. Finally it can provide or assist local authorities to provide social and recreational facilities'

SCOTLAND: THE CENTRAL BELT

One-quarter of Great Britain in area, Scotland has only 10 per cent of the population, badly distributed over 22,000 square miles of highlands and islands, 8,000 square miles of industrial belt on the Glasgow/Edinburgh axis, and 2,000 square miles of fertile border country. Essentially a separate country with its own habits, characteristics, and culture, its tribes declined to join the Roman Empire, and its latter-day warriors took part in changing the Third Reich's plan of victory in six weeks to defeat in six years, but

through Polaris it has become a western arsenal, whether liked or not. This region, which has contributed as heavily in the past as any to the national economy, and which is today making herculean efforts to recover from its legacy of industrial imbalance, is nevertheless rich in terms of amenity – in uncluttered roads and incomparable scenery, in almost complete freedom from the tedium of industrial congestion, in excellent and cheap education, in a great variety of accessible sport, and so on. Within Scotland, the Highlander is considered by the Lowlander a rough creature, while the crofter has great contempt for the city slicker. Between Glasgow and Edinburgh exists a friendly rivalry (government–commerce) yet these are really both parts of a single conurbation – Geddes' bi-polar City Region

The British version of the California 'tilt' left this region a poor relation, with an unemployment rate of twice the national average, though by comparison with parts of the United States it is low, and in essential engineering trades there are in fact serious shortages. Again in the development of power, establishment of a gas grid and in preparation for a water grid, the central belt is particularly advanced. Two civil nuclear generating stations have been built with a send-out capacity of 800 megawatts – the Clyde provides cooling water and sites are adjacent to the industrial load centre. The north of Scotland, an area of great beauty and historic interest, reaching from the peninsula of Kintyre to the Shetlands, from the Outer Hebrides to the east coast, which suffered serious depopulation in the last 200 years, is served by a progressive hydro-electric board, which also collaborates in measures for economic and social improvements in the area. Its principal function is of course the distribution of electricity derived from fifty hydro stations, some fully automatic and others remote controlled

But 53 per cent of the insured population of Scotland lives in the Clyde Valley, employed mainly in industries of a basically heavy character, of which the output of one is the raw material of another. They are therefore particularly susceptible to large-scale unemployment in times of economic difficulty. The population and housing problem, however, dominates the scene: three-quarters of a million people live on 18,000 acres in and around Central Glasgow with a gross density of 400 persons per acre, rising in places to a net of 750 persons per acre, equalled in only a few of the most congested cities of Europe. One-seventh of the Scottish nation is compressed in 3 square miles of central Glasgow. On a smaller scale similar conditions exist in other towns in the region. Not surprisingly there are said to be 20 million Scots abroad. The city of Glasgow multiplied first during the Industrial Revolution, and such was its magnetism that it continued to attract ever-increasing numbers from central and north Europe even when there were 90,000 unemployed in the city (parish relief available), and major intra-regional movements will be necessary to ease the serious population imbalance in Scotland as a whole. Two hundred years ago Clydesider James Watt harnessed steam power and this area became the cradle of engineering technology. The greatest concentration of boiler making capacity in the world exists within 50 miles radius centred on Glasgow; it has the oldest shipyards in the world which before the war built one-quarter of the entire world's tonnage. It has a university five centuries old with 20,000 students taking full-time day courses. It has the second largest library service in the United Kingdom and a port which serves a hinterland of 8 million people

The acute problems of this area generated one of the best and earliest regional plans to be substantially implemented. In 1943, eighteen constituent local authorities of the valley set up a regional planning advisory committee and Professor Abercrombie undertook the preparation of a report. Nearly forty towns were involved besides Glasgow. These towns had hitherto tended to grow without regard for each other and had therefore accentuated each other's problems in transport, industry and recreation. Hence there was a real need for a comprehensive plan after the war if the local authorities were not to be competing for the limited amount of undeveloped land available

Even when all the ground available to the City of Glasgow is built-up, and when the congested areas are redeveloped, there will still be an overspill of 300,000 people, of which 100,000 would have to be found work well away from the region in other parts of Scotland. No powers of direction are held by Central Government or by any regional organization or by the people in industry. Each local authority is autonomous, and the regional plan is being put into effect as a result of voluntary co-operation between the major local authorities supplemented by an effective partnership with the Government. Seventeen industrial complexes have been built according to the regional plan and vast water and sewerage schemes completed

Since the plan more than 150,000 houses have been

General Manager

Industrial Officer (p.r.o.)	Secretary and Legal Adviser	Chief Architect and Planning Officer	Finance Officer (Accountant)	Housing Officer (+ welfare)
		Chief Quantity Surveyor (cost planning unit) — Principal (Housing) — Principal (Central area) — Principal (Industry) — Chief Engineer		
		Groups (territorial or use) — Groups — Groups — Deputy		
		Group Roads — Group Services — Group Structures		

Note: No sociologist or estates officer

Total number of staff–249 (including Clerks of Works, Model Workers, Draughtsmen, Clerical and Landscape staff: no direct building labour force)

---

built in the Clyde Valley, almost all on sites suggested in the regional plan. The City now proposes to redevelop twenty-nine comprehensive development areas in the next fifteen years and a measure of industrial dispersion has taken place. The roads programme is being worked up, railway electrification which takes account of changes in population is well on the way, and action has been taken to safeguard the recreation and scenic areas recommended in the plan, together with the preservation of sea coasts. Over 300 new schools have been built, more than 20 million square feet of factory space been made available at public expense and in areas recommended in the plan. As a result of new legislation further developments in the plan are being carried out. The local authorities in any part of Scotland may negotiate an agreement with Glasgow Corporation whereby Glasgow will sponsor the tenants of new houses and pay a contribution for the houses they occupy. In addition the Government will service the site and pay a higher subsidy for overspill. This is a city going into voluntary liquidation – by 1965 it will be dispersing 1,000 families a year and by 1980 the population will have fallen to 900,000

CUMBERNAULD NEW TOWN

The third in Scotland and the fifteenth in Britain,

Cumbernauld is designed to assist in the relief of Glasgow 15 miles to its south-west. The latest under construction, it will provide for a population of 70,000 people, four-fifths of whom will be nominated by the Corporation of the City of Glasgow. It is not therefore a university city, a spa, a coastal resort or an administrative centre but a small industrial town with no claim to functional distinction

One hour from major sea and air outlets to the Atlantic and European markets, it occupies a central position in the narrow waist of Scotland formed by the deep indentations of the firths of Clyde and Forth, contained to the north and south by upland areas. It is also close to raw material supplies of coal and fireclay and to the products of steelworks and foundries and attractive to industry based on these materials or products

ADMINISTRATION

The site was designated, a public enquiry held and the seven member Corporation under the Chairman, General Sir Gordon MacMillan, ex-Governor of the Rock of Gibraltar, and Chief of the Clan MacMillan, appointed by the Secretary of State for Scotland in 1956. It includes industrialists, ex-civil servants and representatives of the City of Glasgow and Dunbarton County Council who meet once

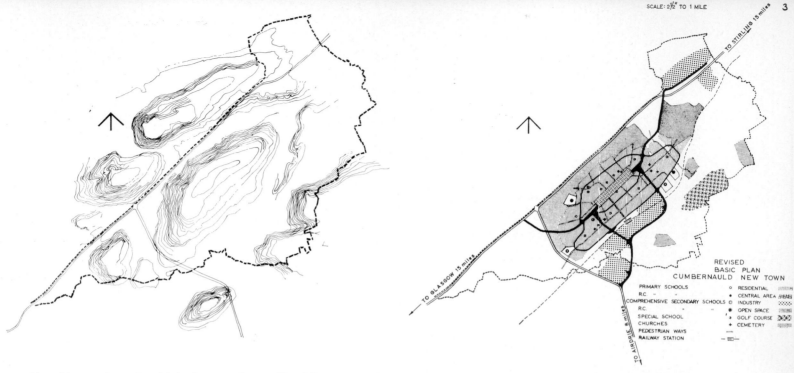

REVISED
BASIC PLAN
CUMBERNAULD NEW TOWN

PRIMARY SCHOOLS ○   RESIDENTIAL
R.C. " ●   CENTRAL AREA
COMPREHENSIVE SECONDARY SCHOOLS ◎   INDUSTRY
R.C. " ◉   OPEN SPACE
SPECIAL SCHOOL ◉   GOLF COURSE
CHURCHES +   CEMETERY
PEDESTRIAN WAYS
RAILWAY STATION   ─ ═ ─

monthly, with committees fortnightly. Its executive comprises three chief officers acting under a General Manager

CONSULTANTS OR ADVISORY BODIES

Road Research Laboratory
Building Research Station
Joint Fire Research Organization
Dept of Building Science, Liverpool University
Dept of Geology, University of Glasgow
Royal College of Science and Technology, Glasgow
Pilkington Bros
G. P. Youngman (landscape)
Meteorological Office, Edinburgh
Hillier, Parker, May & Rowden
Oscar Faber & Partners (Services and Structure)
Ove Arup & Partners

In addition a research officer, a materials library and testing laboratory are maintained and soil mechanics firms are employed from time to time. A punched card system for population statistics has been set up by Hollerith

The following agencies are also involved to some degree in the development of the New Town:

H.M. Treasury
Board of Trade
Ministry of Labour
British Railways
Secretary of State for Scotland (SDD, Dept of Health, etc)
Corporation of City of Glasgow
Hospitals Board
Central Area Joint Fire Committee
South of Scotland Electricity Board
Scottish Coal Board
Post Office
Scottish Bus Companies
Dunbarton County Council – (police, bye-laws, education, sewerage, library services, highways, water and rates)
Cumbernauld District Council – (public lighting, play spaces, community services and cleansing)

The following bodies have exerted influence in some way:

Trades and employers' unions
Church Boards
Traders' Federations
Tenant and welfare associations
Citizen and youth groups

There are more than sixty organizations active in the town at the moment ranging from the Communist Party to Country Dancing

In the first five years during which there has been a change of Secretary of State, Corporation, Legal Adviser, Chief Architect and Chief Engineer, Cumbernauld has grown from a village of 1,000 to a town of 11,000 people, a million square feet of industrial premises are operating, 15 miles of classified roads are under construction, 150,000 trees have been planted and a variety of community facilities are in use

It is worth remembering, however, that when all the sweat and headaches are over, when nearly 100 professional staff have spent twenty years and upwards of £60 million, the end product is equivalent to reconstructing only 6 per cent of the land surface of the parent City of Glasgow

THE SITE

The designated area of 4,150 acres is five miles long from north-east to south-west and 2 miles across from north-west to south-east at the widest point. The general topography, consisting of a series of similar hills determined by a glacial action, is dominated by a dramatic hogsback ridge which has dictated the whole concept of the town

The watershed of Scotland crosses this main hill which is highly exposed to the prevailing south-west winds blowing down the valleys of the Glasgow-Stirling road and the Glasgow-Stirling railway. The altitude varies between about 260 ft in the valley of the Glasgow-Stirling road to about 480 ft at the highest point on the hill-top. The other three principal elements comprise:

a steep and rather isolated hillside rising from the railway, south-east to Fannyside Muir with a maximum height of about 570 ft on the moor, outside the designated area;

a smaller hill at Condorrat rising to just over 300 ft; and

a plateau at the north end of the site astride the Glasgow road and comprising three farms whose levels vary between 300 and 400 ft

Building on the hill-top with the exposure to the rain and wind has unified the whole development; the existing windbreaks, and the new ones being planted, helping to provide shelter, with the compact form of layout and new and existing windbreaks. The site is subject to 200 rain days a year, six months from the first to the last screen frosts, and has the second highest driving rain index in the British Isles. It is an area of high humidity, limited hours of sunshine and within the smoke shadow of Glasgow. These conditions have produced particularly acute condensation problems, and a heritage of stunted timber

In many cases the poor ground conditions appear to be due largely to inadequate natural drainage of the more level areas, resulting in the presence of moss and soft patches of ground. Substantial areas of the site have been worked for minerals, and some areas are still reserved for this purpose

URBAN STRUCTURE

Cumbernauld's structure has earned it the title of a

Cumbernauld. View of the model of the New Town from the north-west

Mark 2 New Town but for all its particular distinctions, essentially, it perpetuates known urban forms and its vaunted absence of neighbourhood units is true only for the concentration of population on the hill-top where it must arise as much from topographical dictates as social objectives

The area of development on the hill-top is some 2 miles long and 1 mile wide, providing sites for houses, shops, schools, public buildings and some industry for 50,000 people, with the main industrial areas sited to the north and south, and the level land at the foot of the hill used for playing fields and general open space. It was clear from an early stage that the main hill-top, with a gross area of about 930 acres, would provide the most suitable site for the major development of the new town. This is the only section of the area capable of being used for a large-scale comprehensive project. The form of the hill-top, from which there are fine views in all directions and which in turn can be seen from many points outside the area with its clearly defined limits, leads to the general conception of the town as a compact urban centre with surrounding recreation areas, the whole set against the background of open hilly country. Beyond the peripheral open space system there is the countryside with its

existing walks; these will be linked to the town's open space system. The northern slopes are steep, up to 1 in 3 in places, but most of the area is to be used for development, with the lower slopes and the narrow floor of the valley up to the main road completely afforested. Later when these wooded areas have grown stout enough, rides and glades are to be cut out as walks and play spaces. The village, differentiated by a playing field area lying in the hollow between the steep escarpment on the northern side of the main hill-top area, and the rising ground to the south will be preserved with minor extension, for it has a pleasant vernacular character, although some of the properties need considerable repair

Elsewhere, sites are not defined for buildings such as schools until after the housing has been designed, and in some cases until after it has been built. Hence it is possible to formulate an integrated landscape pattern in which the common focus may be the children's play areas

Expansion to a population of 70,000 will be reached by the promotion of a series of satellite villages around the main hill-top, each with its own local centre but relying on the central area of the town for the main shopping and recreational facilities

EMPLOYMENT

There are two industrial areas, one at the north-east, completely clear of the central nucleus and on its lee side, and the other in the valley to the south. The third group is slightly more distant to the south-west where a group of standard factories occupies a plateau. Together with a distribution of flatted and single-storey workshop clusters on the main hilltop this completes the pattern of manufacturing industry. But the need, of course, is for a balanced population in terms of age, wage and occupational structure and attempts must be made to achieve a cross section of employment opportunity

The high rate of employment in manufacturing industry originally proposed was on the same level as the rate reached in other new towns, where it is now generally considered that offices have been too slow to develop and that the scope for employment is not as full as the second generation are likely to require. The new proposals envisage a much larger variety of non-manufacturing employment in Cumbernauld, not only to provide varied openings for the second generation, but also to attract from Glasgow a properly varied cross section of families. More of Glasgow's population is employed in shops, offices and a multitude of services than works in factories, and it is now proposed to move closer to this balance in Cumbernauld

Manufacturing Industry	45%
(13 per cent Retail and Service Trades, 25 per cent Finance Professional, Public Administration, Misc)	
Offices and Services	48%
(10 per cent Public Utilities, Transport, Wholesale Distribution)	
Construction	6%
Mining and Agriculture	1%
	100%

Preceding page, top: An early concept drawing of the multi-deck linear centre of Cumbernauld New Town from the south

Preceding page, centre: Central areas of the model of Cumbernauld from the south

Preceding page, below: Central areas from the south showing the first phase (now under construction)

This page, right: Aerial view of the model showing the town centre, the west-end enclosure, groups of peripheral uses, and the 'wall' of town houses

237

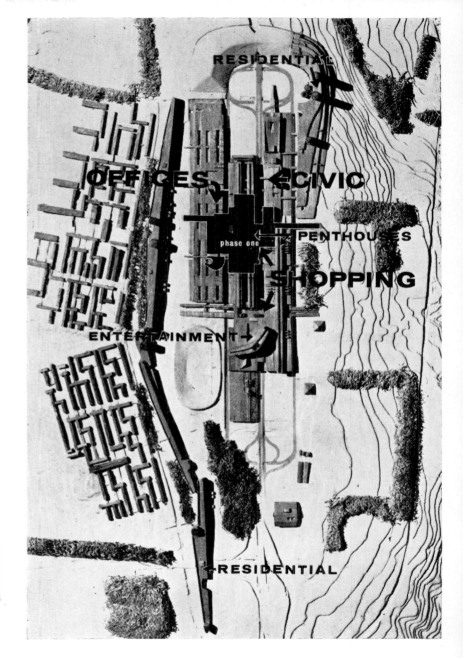

Because of the sex and age structure peculiar to a new town it is probable that in the early days of Cumbernauld, workers available will be predominantly male, and the 63/37 male to female ratio may not be approached until a later stage. On the basis of 225 square feet of floor space per worker and a plot ratio of 0.4 the density of a gross density of about 70 workers per acre of industrial land is obtained when allowance is made for service roads and communal facilities

LAND USE DISTRIBUTION

	(70,000 pop.)	
Housing	849	acres
Schools	167	,,
Central Area	110	,,
Industry	395	,,
Roads	288	,,
Railway	34	,,
Open Space[1]	916	,,
Unallocated	24	,,
	2,783	acres

Gross density—26 persons per acre

[1] Not including golf course and afforestation areas

EDUCATION

The total plan provides for three grades of education: primary, secondary, and further or adult education. Among the primary facilities there are twelve primary schools (eight Protestant, four Roman Catholic), each for 500-600 pupils, and each occupying 5 acres of site. In addition, a special school for 200 handicapped children with an occupational centre is provided on a site of 6 acres, and there will also be a child guidance centre. County education playing fields occupy 30 acres on dispersed sites

Five secondary schools are planned. The two Protestant junior secondary schools and the one Protestant senior secondary school, each for 750 pupils, are co-educational. But the Roman Catholic secondary schools are not co-educational; one is for boys and the other for girls and each has 500 pupils. Each secondary school is allotted 10 acres

Cumbernauld will also have a technical college, and four community and youth centres

CIRCULATION

A traffic analysis undertaken to test the correctness of the assumptions in the original plan included the assumption that 70 per cent of the families in the town would own cars in the future, that 63 per cent of the cars would be used at peak hour, and that 45 per cent of the population would travel to and from work by car, 42 per cent travelling by public transport and the remainder walking. The analysis was based on the number of cars travelling from each work area to the various housing areas, the most likely routes of traffic being assessed and the total flows arrived at for each of the junctions. It threw up one very major problem in and around the central area—in that there were likely to be uni-directional volumes of 2,000 to 3,000 vehicles an hour on certain sections of the road system and at least ten junctions around the centre where some form of two-level treatment would be necessary

The need to keep the functions of the various roads clear cut also became apparent; and instead of multipurpose roads there emerged a hierarchy of roads based on the following principles:

(a) local development roads to provide access to buildings either direct or by spur footpath;

(b) feeder roads to take traffic on to local development roads but to have no frontage development;

(c) main town roads in the form of radials or radial link roads to connect with feeder roads only at controlled junctions and to have no frontage development or other access;

(d) trunk roads to connect with main town roads only at grade-separated junctions;

(e) no car parking on any carriageway

The costs arising from the high standard of the town roads and interchanges are generally offset by the relatively low mileage of major roads required for this town of 70,000 people. Comparison with some of the other new towns shows that the total mileage of classified roads in Cumbernauld is about 40 per cent less than the average and in terms of cost per head of population Cumbernauld is only very slightly higher (4 per cent) than the average figure for the other towns, notwithstanding that the provision being made at Cumbernauld is of a very much higher standard to cater for traffic conditions which will arise in the very near future

The area of land required within the hill-top site for the main road system is 107.7 acres and the total length of principal town roads now amounts to 8.87 miles. The extensive provision of grade-separated interchanges represents a considerable advance in urban road policy; and before this was adopted a detailed economic comparison was made for a portion of the road system on the basis of grade-separated and normal single level junctions. This comparison indicated a very satisfactory rate of return of the order of 30 per cent to 40 per cent resulting from the better facility. The final road pattern evolved from a desire line diagram based on eight origins, five within the designated area and three outwith; fourteen destinations, seven on the hill-top, four satellite villages and three outwith the designated area and was rendered with 103 flows

HOUSING

Net densities will average eighty-five persons per acre, with each site taking its appropriate allocation of houses depending on conditions. Densities will vary within the overall figure from between 60 to 120 persons per acre. The general density and compactness of the town mean that privacy in the house is essential. On sunlighting the Codes of Practice Committee has recommended that the standard should be to provide one window in the principal living-room so placed that sunlight can enter for at least one hour of the day during not less than ten months of the year, from February to November. This standard, which has been accepted by the Scottish Development Department, has a very definite effect on the spacing of buildings, the distances varying with aspect and the slope of the land. Further possible controls on the size and layout of housing groups (together with road capacities, topography, and relative position) are the social foci. A series of orbits can be drawn based upon the number of people required to support a shop, pub, community room, toddlers' and children's play spaces, nursery and primary schools; some of these orbits will coincide and a pattern of social life emerge

PROPOSED INTERIM BALANCE OF DWELLINGS

Because the new town families are predominantly youthful and not yet at maximum size, there must be an attempt to forecast their likely development, so that the housing programme is designed to meet their future as well as their immediate requirements

The new fitting standards are an advance upon the crude rate of one person per habitable room assumed in the First Addendum Report to the Preliminary Planning Proposals which, if applied to all families, would cramp many smaller ones, and provide many

238

PROPOSED INTERIM BALANCE OF DWELLINGS

	1	2	3	4	5	6	Total
Bedroom types							
%	1.0 1.0	4.0 6.0	24.0 29.0	26.0 5.1	2.5 1.0	0.4	100%
%	6.0	30.0	55.0	9.0			100%

Bed-sitter	1 single	1 double	2 singles
1 single	2 single	1 single	2 single
1 double+	1 double+	2 double+	2 double+
1 single	2 single	1 single	
3 double+	3 double	4 double+	

families, with five or more members, with more rooms than they would require

Spare bed-spaces or spare rooms are allowed for over 70 per cent of the anticipated number of younger families, and for smaller percentages of middle-aged and older families at or past their maximum size. The most obvious effect of the new standards will be that the familiar but flexible three apartment four person (two double bedroom) dwelling – hitherto the most common of all – will be replaced by a more useful and satisfactory four apartment four person (one double and two single bedroom) type

A possible building pattern for Cumbernauld has been evolved thus: 18 per cent of one and two apartment dwellings, 19 per cent of three apartments, 54 per cent of four apartments and 9 per cent of larger sizes. While such a distribution may ultimately be right for Cumbernauld it seems, for the next few years, to lean too heavily towards smaller house types, for which demand is likely to be greater in the later stages of the town's development

House types built so far in both traditional, rationalized and semi-industrialized systems include one, two and three storey houses with private gardens; one storey with open and closed patio; two storey (split-level) with public open space; single storey over garages; three, four and five storey walk-up (or walk-off) flats or maisonettes; terrace and independent forms in stub block or slab forms

The Radburn system with road access and pedestrian access to all or the majority of houses in the scheme has been worked out at Cumbernauld with the use of about 70 per cent wide frontage single aspect houses and 30 per cent flats at a density of about

eighty persons per acre. This form of layout has many advantages giving convenience to the individual tenant in providing direct access to his house by car, in many cases with a garage adjoining. A meshed system of roads and footpaths, with motor vehicles entering the site from the periphery of the area by the use of culs-de-sac, with pedestrians moving towards the centre of the scheme by a series of spur footpaths linked to a main footpath, has been successfully used on the flatter slopes

The degree of control to pedestrian movement varies with the type of road. At the regional level there s complete separation; at the house, pedestrian and car meet. Within the housing group, movement is influenced rather than controlled. The pedestrian is focused inwards to the main town footpaths, shop, pub, primary school and play areas. This to some degree will control the width of housing groups in order to minimize diagonal movement and conflict with roads. Movement in areas of pedestrian attraction should be direct, but the object is to provide not only safe routes but safe areas for social life to develop. A pattern has evolved therefore, not of the purposeful group association of dwellings with windows and front doors facing, which would inhibit privacy, but the group association of outdoor functions arising from the footpaths and garages; indoor functions remaining private from noise and view. On the steeper slopes a form of layout has been evolved where 200 to 250 houses are sur-

Above right: Playground outside a church. Following five photographs in this sequence are of housing in various sectors of the new town

239

rounded by perimeter garaging, resulting in a longer walk between garage and house but keeping the residential area clear of permanently parked cars. Vehicular access to the houses and for visitors' parking can then be provided by a series of broad culs-de-sac running into the area from the peripheral road

A beginning has been made at Cumbernauld in the process of arranging a more flexible rent structure to allow schemes with greater amenities, of space, position or equipment. 10 per cent and 30 per cent (the latter is an exceptional figure) of better standard houses are provided already at selected points. With regard to the use of space within dwellings, attempts have been made within the limits imposed by the Development Department to achieve greater flexibility, by, for instance, siting the single bedroom on the ground floor where it can be used as a bedroom or an extension of the living space. At Ravenswood it will be possible to redistribute the space within the house at some time in the future to provide fewer rooms of a larger size, to meet the demands of an increased standard of living. At Carbrain the design of the house shell has been standardized with alternative room layouts within,

Below: Drawing showing the town centre with its groups of peripheral uses, central spine road, west-end enclosure, and urban 'wall' of housing

and the possibility of building an extra bedroom over the attached garage in some cases

THE CENTRAL AREA

The deliberate decision to build a town involves an equally clinical decision to build a central area. Our relative inexperience in shaping a complete packaged centre, is usually met by recourse to cosmetics of townscape in an attempt to compensate for the absence of the effects of time. The difficulty lies in discarding this fiction concerning the 'town centre'— in order that the real poetry of modern technology may be released

Cumbernauld's centre, while representing only the end of the beginning, is the world's first multi-level, multi-occupation structure to provide for all the functions commonly thought at the time of designing to be central area uses. After 1965 when the first phase of the centre comes into operation it will no longer be possible for developers in similar circumstances to argue that a full level of motorization cannot be reconciled with the absence of hazard or convenience to the pedestrian; or that the degree of amenity and the integration of non-profit making public functions cannot be achieved without making a loss. The development of a single envelope in which the whole is greater than the sum of the parts and wherein the citizen is encouraged to participate rather than to play a passive role, took some four years to bring to the contract stage. The result will

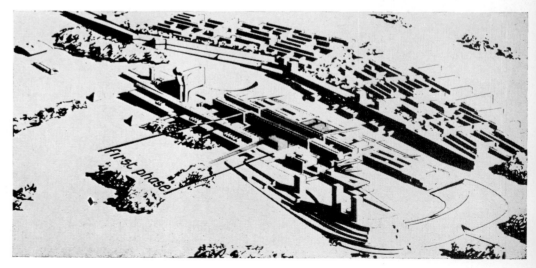

be a fragment of an elevated city within the traditional concentric town form compartmentalized by radial highways. Given these historical conditions stemming partially from the formal notion to build on a hill, I could only interpret the centre as a self-contained residential city within its own urban fence

The success of the resulting dense artefact is dependent upon the existence of a monumental external landscape

There is no point in attempting to disguise its size its very definition becomes a characteristic to exploit – one will go up and into the centre as specific experience. It does not display, nor would it be desirable so to do, the normal conical density distribution of a town wherein penetration is made almost by accident. Here the sheer size and character of the four components demands recognition. But size in itself is not a quality; the village of Cumbernauld is virtually a single building penetrated by nominal voids. Hook, for example, put back the clock by its failure to appreciate the new dimension In attempting to disguise the end-product of this line of thought, limbs were drawn out from the main body of the centre to provide familiar transitions. now take the view that the third school of thought which might argue the need for a single shell penetrated by air locks, provided with clothes lockers, and having a completely controlled environment within which all activities may take place in a totally unified interior, is probably the real next step

The very young and the very old, together with the domestic animal, have been designed out of our city centres, where they stray at their peril. At Cumbernauld, the ability to carry on town life to an extent independent of the weather, vehicular noise and fumes, together with the relation between public and commercial activities must generate fruitful contact. The proximity of uses and the absence of frustration should combine to extend the areas of interest and inter-action of those uses which in a conventional centre would be inhibited. Events should generate events and provision must be made for more multi-purpose trips of longer duration. The negative decisions arising from the necessity to park, unpark and repark cars, or from the reluctance to

241

Right: Two early concept drawings showing the central spine carriageway. In the lower drawing an inhabited 'umbrella' is on the left

Next page: Three views of the final model showing the first phase

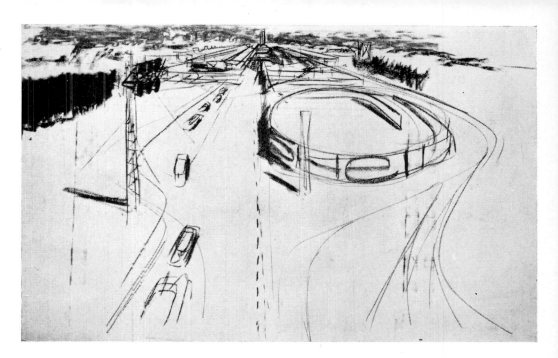

242

wait for a bus in northern weather to travel to another extremity will be replaced here by positive decisions influenced by simple proximity

PLANNING

The lower levels are devoted almost entirely to vehicular movement and storage, but they do not constitute a separate subterranean world from which the motorist emerges into the real world of light and activity above. The total work is so interpenetrated and consistently disciplined that equivalent messages are received at all levels from the arrangement of the structure and the services system

The Cumbernauld centre will function as a vast terminal facility incorporating its own vehicular system. The long flanks of the centre are presented

Centre. Aerial view drawing of an early version of vehicular circulation
Key: 2 Primary school, m.s.b., Library, Community Centre. 4 Retail and service trades. 8 Residential towers. 9 Service station. 10 Technical Institute. 11 Civic Square. 12 Entertainment square. 13 Bus station. 14 T.A. centre. 15 Fire Station. 16 Hospital

Below: Isometric drawing of ground level vehicular area for the final scheme

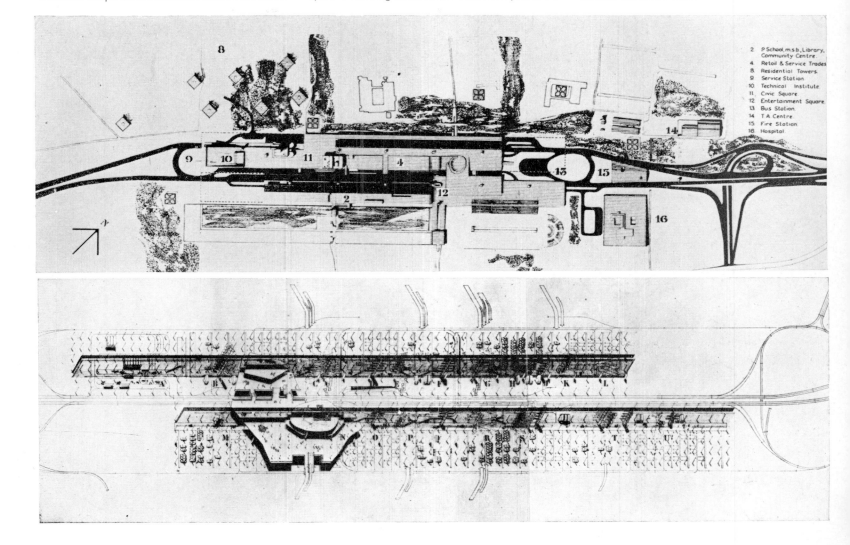

2   P. School, m.s.b., Library, Community Centre.
4   Retail & Service Trades
8   Residential Towers
9   Service Station
10 Technical Institute
11 Civic Square
12 Entertainment Square
13 Bus Station
14 T.A. Centre
15 Fire Station
16 Hospital

243

to the pedestrian to select his entry-points and ramps as he comes up hill from the residential areas, while the motorist by virtue of being mechanically propelled travels along the long axis. A system of signalling and signing will be necessary to reinforce the inherent significance of the formal physical arrangement

This consists basically of parallel decks, split in turn by secondary slots, constituting twin cores 15 ft wide, nine storeys high, and aggregating a mile in length. From these cores, which are sometimes negative and sometimes positive, sometimes solid and sometimes void, root services and the mechanical handling installations rise to feed laterally through the grid at 100 ft centres. The classical concept of master and servant grids has evolved from the necessity to reconcile the requirements of wheeled and foot traffic, public and private functions, group and individual activities, flexibility and minimum cost

There are three principal reasons for the adoption of a comprehensive treatment of functions. Firstly there is the necessity to do something more than pay lip-service to segregation of man and motor; secondly the climatic conditions at an altitude of 500 ft, on the same latitude as Moscow, are such as to inhibit social intercourse, unless some physical measures are taken to promote comfort conditions; thirdly there is the knowledge that the one absolute certainty about central areas is their proneness to change and growth

This is an attempt to create from a reinforced concrete carcase, a kit of parts, and a complementary rental policy, a form of development which will prolong the normal life-cycle of city centres. If central area functions, as we know them today, should decline, this structure can undergo considerable change of use. It would be inconsistent to claim the virtues of response to growth and change; and at the same time hedge the bet with the production of a jig-saw puzzle synchronizing infill with population growth. As the centre grows so will the passage of time be reflected

My original proposals for the whole central area (whose principal function was to act in the event as a catalyst for the first built phase) has four components. First is the decked structure of the town centre itself; second the vast hook-shaped protective mole at the west-end whose soft landscaping is continued into hard architecture; third the mile long wall of dwellings, the roof of which becomes a

244

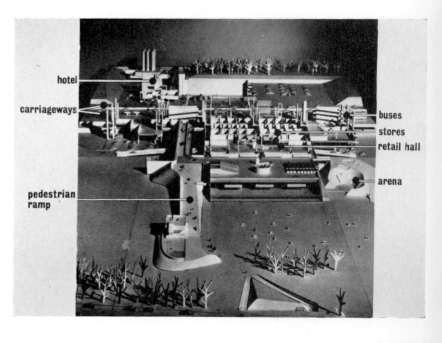

walk-way punctuated by twin towers at intersections of pedestrian routes; and fourth the group of peripheral uses, including places of worship and recreational buildings linked back to the main decks

The rampart-structure at the west-end, through which the entry road plunges, will be formed from material excavated for the construction of the two-level circus. It will be some 45 ft high and penetrated by 200 ft long culverts carrying the western radial link. Together with the associated terraces containing 550 dwellings with a drive-in arrangement served by spiral ramp from the western circus, it will change the climate of the hill-top and provide a massive natural bridge between the northern and southern slopes of the town. The decked development which flows from this will function as a great department store into which the citizen can walk or motor to find within the framework a kaleidoscope of urban furniture – commercial, public and quasi-public. Each activity can be reached under cover, though such journeys need not be exclusively so made. Within these spaces each functional element will give messages, not anecdotally but as a by-product of efficiency. Within this shell, essentially introvert in character, it will be possible to provide certain amenities which would otherwise be prohibitively expensive in a system of separate buildings at grade. These include an all-weather parking facility of great capacity, the integration of a variety of functions served by a heated network, the absence of hazard in the presence of environmental quality, the provision of parcel pick-up stations, the basic installation of fifty mechanical handling components including paternoster lifts, conventional electric elevators, inclined reversible conveyors, escalators and oildraulic elevators, closed circuit television surveillance and central security system.

Under a great entablature of penthouses (included not in order to lend credence to a third party claim for an 'active' centre, but because this is intrinsically

The two photographs on the previous page show the deck construction of the first phase, from the south. The photograph above shows the completed model of the first phase from the northern pedestrian approach and church. Note the entablature of penthouses, which rides above the city centre and commands superb views in all directions

Below: Detail from the east of preliminary concepts for extending the first phase into the second, with the construction of civic offices and auditoria over a terminal for eighty buses and a two-level passenger concourse

245

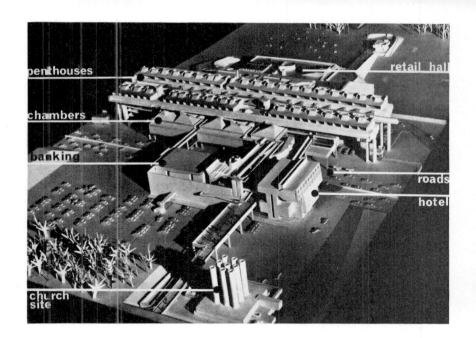

a good place to live for a proportion of the population), develops a series of forms and planes whose non-coincidence arises and is proven when the temptation to suppress functional characteristics is resisted

The third element in the central area is the southern terrace ('town wall') of 1,100 dwellings with integral garaging which opens on the inner side to the narrow central park

The remaining group of uses are accommodated in free-standing buildings nucleated around the decks. The decks themselves can, of course, undergo considerable extension and permit a variety of forms to erupt through the structure; they will also allow the adoption of increasingly efficient vending and storage techniques. Beyond a certain point, however, because of its geographic centrality, expansion could not take place; but since there are severe limitations to the ultimate size of Cumbernauld, the corresponding foreseeable demand can be met, and beyond this point the creation of a twin town or the adoption of some other device would be required

RETAIL AND SERVICE TRADES

The rising spate of central area development must be accompanied by an increasingly scientific analysis of the major land use, the principal source of employment and of traffic generation. But although the retail element is the largest spacewise, it is not therefore the most important socially. It does, however, along with the other commercial uses,

produce the revenue which makes all other activities possible

The common function of the real-estate agent has been the negotiation of tenancies rather than acting as a quasi-planner. However, this latter role is the growing practice. In this latter capacity, of course, he is forced to follow trends rather than foresee them, and to devise a jargon of 'units', 'establishments' and 'frontages', which tends both to freeze development patterns and preserve his place in society. It is notable that each step in the advance of shopping centre-practice – open fronts, canopies, pedestrian precincts rear loading, covered centres and finally multi-level, multi-occupation arrangements – was resisted in turn. Their success in this sphere is due not to acumen, but to the inherent difficulty of losing money in central area property in a society with a rising standard of living. Similarly the Retail Traders' Federation, in their 1949 blue-print for the new world, advised members to resist the living-death of pedestrian centres, while their 1963 statement acknowledges that only pedestrian centres will survive

With half the nation's factory production directly consumed by the public through retail shops (which exist at the rate of perhaps one to twenty families) and incurring wholesale and retail distribution charges of about a third of the selling price, an efficient organization is of prime interest to society. On the physical side the necessity for definitive planning is particularly acute at Cumbernauld where

Above: View of the model of the first phase, from the southern pedestrian access ramp, stripped down to the lower parking levels

difficult topography coupled with high densities leaves little room for manoeuvre. From a social and economic viewpoint, daily-need shopping facilities must be provided in step with population growth before shopping elsewhere becomes a habit; likewise mobile door-to-door delivery trades must be forestalled in seizing disproportionate custom and rendering more difficult the establishment of permanent shops

An acceptable method of calculating retail provision must result in both an economic and a physical planning tool and ultimately in a realistic forecast of floor space. Hence recommendations dependent on the term 'shop', 'establishment' or 'unit', as a quantitative measure of the kind which have been made by a number of authorities, are subject to a serious margin of error due to the inadequacy of their terminology and method. 'Retail outlet' for example can mean the itinerant trader or mail-order house, back street sub-marginal shop or department store. Its frequent use is aggravated by the apparent irrational distribution of premises

In the preparation of plans for the other towns in Britain, shopping requirements appear to have been related to similar existing towns in the region. These have been surveyed and the resulting information analyzed and applied, with various assumptions

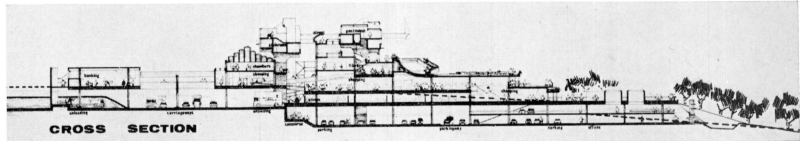

CROSS SECTION

and reservations, to the particular conception envisaged for the town, in nearly all cases a main centre with a number of neighbourhood units, each with its own subsidiary shopping centre. Surveys of existing towns nearly always show a disproportionate number of shops, many of them converted rooms in houses and held on low rents. It is very difficult, therefore, to apply these results to a new town. Elsewhere a number of investigations have been made with a view to determining the 'shopping population' or catchment area of different shopping centres but even this term is a loose one, difficult to define accurately except in relation to particular types of shop over particular times of the year

Until the publication of the 1950 Census of Distribution and other Services in 1953, the number and

quality of assumptions that would have been necessary to calculate shopping needs would have invalidated the results. Its publication with new data on the behaviour of the retail trades enables a method to be prosecuted based on post-war statistics corrected to present-day values. The result, which is qualified in the light of trends in techniques of retail distribution and Cumbernauld's own structure and hinterland, was expressed in areas by major retail and service trade categories abstracted and reclassified from the 1950 Census. Spending power, which is related to the income structure of the surrounding population will vary as between daily needs and consumer durables in a changing pattern as the standard of living rises

The general tendency to large-scale distribution,

Above: View of the first phase from the westbound carriageway

Centre: North-south section, banking to retail halls

with the decline in the proportion of retail trade handled by independent traders, must inevitably lead to fundamental changes in shopping patterns. Two distinct trends are emerging from the redistribution of income coupled with changing tastes and the marketing of new products. Stores retailing some consumer durables are increasing in number and degree of specialization, while in all other groups there is a tendency towards an overlapping between economic types of retail outlet as in the U S A. As income rises the proportion spent on food falls although the absolute amount spent increases

Trends of this nature have a fundamental bearing on land-use, since the multiples, co-operatives, departmentals and small private traders require varying frontages and depths for development. In order to meet the demands of the future though uncertain, it is clearly of first importance to avoid rigid terms of leasing and intractable physical enclosure

In addition to this movement, changes are occurring in the organizational structure of retail outlets and in the techniques of retailing itself, typified by the trend to mechanization and shopping habits which support prepackaging. The growth of the variety chain stores and the constant expansion of the multiples, often connected with wholesaling and even manufacturing, have been largely due to economies in distribution costs which they can show

While many small concerns only exist by virtue of resale price maintenance, technical advances themselves are pressing towards a greater mechanization in retailing. Sterilization of food, preservative packaging, branded goods, all contribute, for example, to the success of the self-service establishments which began in 1949

Many major variety chain stores appear to be coming full circle to 'general' stores on a vast scale while the trend of the larger supermarkets is to gain in sales and the smaller ones to lose. The movement towards consolidation and general increase in size in recent years, is lowering overheads by increasing efficiency; for competition is high, operational and staff costs are rising and profit margins are dropping

In addition to self-service, fully automatic vending is appearing in the U S A on a substantial scale and in Britain coin-operated food machines delivering anything from a cup of tea to a complete hot meal will soon have become a commonplace. Automatic catering is appealing to industrial management and public transport operators. Sales made through these vending machines are, of course, sales not made in certain other retail outlets

The final link in the chain of distribution is home delivery. The average working class family buys about 62 lbs net of foodstuffs each week. The fact that a 30 cwt van has the capacity of fifty such families' normal weekly purchases gives an indication of the quantity of goods involved

If then the effect of delivery is linked with the standing order, the roundsman, and the use of the telephone, it will be seen that the distance between home and shop may matter less and less to the customer. Delivery in fact encourages greater centralization with apparent advantages for the consumer. The frequency of shopping trips is reduced and the customer is enabled to shop further afield, since fewer purchases have to be carried home. Indeed it is conceivable that choice of certain goods by television could play a revolutionary part in the mechanics of distribution

The importance of qualifying any average calculation must by this stage be quite apparent. Allowances must be made for future spending patterns, changes in prosperity, trends in techniques and organization, population and employment movement and competing spheres of influence. The results which emerge from a fusion of fact and judgment give a picture of the retail and service trade requirements for the town as a whole from which must be deducted that proportion of trade carried on outside the central area in local shops, petrol filling stations, service trade groups, satellite village centres and by itinerant traders

The Final Report of the New Towns Committee argues against attempting to achieve a theoretical balance by apportioning total retail space as between department stores, multiples, co-operatives and independents. The landlord cannot successfully go beyond ensuring that sufficient floor space is provided in relation to the population, with the distribution of the floor space between economic types of outlet left to the market

The approach I have described was sufficiently objective to permit the analysis itself to be used in an aggressive sales policy to satisfy potential traders of the financial stability of plans and of the soundness of any investment. By calculating the risk, the opportunity has arisen for the Corporation to act as a developer to earn the maximum return. The private enterprise development companies which come in between the local authority and the tenants of shops may be a convenience to the former but probably result not only in the latter having to pay higher rents but in attempts to standardize terms of leases to an undesirable extent

Single ownership, it should be noted, can give to the owners social, visual and economic control, not to be achieved through any other form of organization

The calculation for the lettable shopping space alone will not by itself, of course, give a complete picture of facilities required for the retail activity. External customer circulation, freight handling and separate warehousing may require up to perhaps 50 per cent again of the area of sales and store

SUMMARY OF METHOD

Previous work has examined the relationship between the overall number of shops in existing towns and their populations. A refinement of this method is to break down the overall number of shops into their respective trade categories. This method was considered unsuitable mainly because of the unsatisfactory nature of the concept 'average number of shops'. Another method is to relate employees per square foot of shopping space to size in town's population and this was also found to be unsatisfactory on similar grounds. The method chosen was to calculate the probable sales, on average, for a town of 70,000 from 1950 Census of Distribution, for each trade category and by use of selected conversion factors (sales per square foot) to convert these sales into the area to be provided

1 A sample of 100 towns (population 25,000-100,000) was chosen, each town sited within a twenty-mile radius of one of the nine largest cities in Great Britain (excluding London). The object of this choice was to reflect the location of Cumbernauld close to a large city and the consequent effect on shopping within the new town due to this proximity

2 Scatter diagrams were plotted and coefficients of correlation calculated for each of the Census trade categories relating sales to population size. Sufficiently high correlations were found in each trade category to justify the use of this method

3 The average sales per head in each trade category for 100 towns was calculated from the Census for the year 1950. This was adjusted to 1959 values and sales per head were multiplied by 70,000 to represent sales in each category for a town of that size

4 Conversion factors to translate sales into area required where selected by empirical enquiry and applied to the results of Item 3 giving the area required in each category for a population of 70,000

5 This estimate was adjusted in the light of the conditions and circumstances of Cumbernauld

6 At this stage it was possible to examine the ratio of parking space to retail area to compare this with parking demand at peak periods. It appears that a minimum of 3,000 car parking stalls should be provided in the central area, for the use of shoppers and retail employees

CONCLUSIONS

1 On present calculations total floor area in the

town required for the retail and service trades is estimated to be 617,700 sq ft (14.18 acres) of which 411,000 sq ft (9.42 acres) is in the central area. 56,450 sq ft (1.31 acres) in the villages and 150,200 sq ft (3.45 acres) on the main hill-top outside the central area. A further 65,500 sq ft (1.5 acres) must be added for pubs

2 The only basis available for predicting retail and service trade area requirements in 1980 when the town should have been finally completed are present efficiency standards and U S retailing patterns. If these are used this would bring the total acreage required up to about 15 acres (excluding pubs)

3 Increases in the national income between now and 1980 will undoubtedly considerably increase retail expenditure. Whether or not the areas calculated for 1959 sales will be able to cope with this large increase is unknown. But there will be a considerable margin of safety in changing retail organization and methods (it is recommended that the estimate be revised from time to time to take account of new data as regards sales and retail method)

This summary of the method I evolved with Broady, Diamond and Gibb of Glasgow University, requires some qualification. The principle we sought to apply is not original and credit for its tentative introduction here belongs to W. Burns, until recently Planning Officer to the City of Newcastle, who despite rather unsophisticated sampling also appreciated the degree of inverse correlation between gross profit margins and turnover per unit area

That none of the fourteen new towns designated prior to Cumbernauld adopted this particular technique is evident, not that their shopping provision is unsatisfactory, but that this is one physical planning tool only, the absolute or finite quality of whose arithmetic ought not be deemed to lend credence to the hypotheses themselves. Many of the founding assumptions are of course by definition arguable, some of the reasoning specious, a few of the conclusions suspect and the field work critical

The principal reservation I have concerns the sales conversion factors; not simply their statistically unsatisfactory quality but their very nature

'Sales conversion factors' are the equivalent of the American 'business capacity per unit area'. They have no absolute value, for this would presuppose that a given area of retail space was the site of the maximum and constant rate of purchase of commodities by the

public that this space could bear. In practice this pursuit of the ultimate use by increases in efficiency is asymptomatic in nature – there is no foreseeable limit to the advance distributive machinery might make. Nor is it merely a question of more efficient retailing techniques. At present, shops in Britain on average vend goods for only a quarter of the possible number of hours a week. In the U S A, evening opening hours for shops are universal, and immensely fruitful, while holiday and Sunday opening in some lines is becoming commonplace. Even with the present restricted opening hours, however, the amount of sales made in a given space, if plotted at different times of the day or week, would produce peaks and troughs. The difference between the average slack day and the highest seasonal peak is the amount by which a current, so-called 'efficient' conversion factor could be increased without making any change at all beyond a more even loading by the public. This can be seen in the 'freak' turnover of shops in monopoly situations. But the exception today may be commonplace tomorrow. Furthermore a population with more money to spend, or more people to spend money, many not necessarily require more shop space as such. With or without the ceiling or saturation point or consumers' goods, increases in demand could be kept pace with by more credit, 'club' or 'check' trading, by an increase in mobile trading, mail order buying and other forms of retailing which do not necessarily entail conserving large stocks in central areas. Thus buying from catalogues or television is one way of relieving possible future pressure on central area space. Similarly branded articles like motor cars do not have to be bought out of stock, but can be supplied in order, perhaps from regional repositories. Yet another safety-valve exists with the possibility of more frequent replenishment of smaller stocks (cf. automatic vending machines) and a faster turn-round of goods

In order to assemble the material at all, the Board of Trade has had to attempt to define trade groups, then allocate returns under these heads. Now while this is satisfactory for some purposes, it is too arbitrary for physical planning since while it was true to a degree at the time, it is certainly entirely true eleven years later that retail trades with some exceptions do not fall precisely into these convenient categories. Thus while an overall estimate of retail area in terms of commodity groups can be performed, useful distribution within this in the only terms of any actual consequence on a drawing board, remain fugitive. The overlapping of retail outlets unfortun-

ately resists static classification, for like all manifestations of an organic activity, the pattern of retail trading displays characteristic of growth and change

I have now evolved to the view, that the technique for treating a problem whose answer, since it is concerned fundamentally with a money transaction, lies ostensibly in economic analyses, does in fact lie in the development of a planning and constructional system itself capable of responding to social and economic pressures. The adoption of this philosophy renders redundant the production of what must by their nature be short-term economic formulae. If it is accepted that the social sciences are less susceptible than some others to prediction in that they must deal essentially with human behaviour at some future date then from this flows the need for a new concept of urban means within which historical canons are quite irrelevant

In addition to the special degree of control over development in new towns as such, in Cumbernauld the centre occupies a monopolistic trading position. From this position of particular strength therefore, it becomes possible to canalize the energies of those interests powerful enough to wreck a delicately balanced operation. The absence of competing neighbourhood centres whose early establishment could work against the growth of a central area, ensures a captive population of 50,000 people who cannot shop elsewhere, plus a further 20,000 who must rely on the centre for principal services; the initial novelty which will attract some custom while the resident population is being built up but which should not be relied on beyond the point when the competitor towns become really competitive with the introduction of comparable amenities; the insurance policy that a further 30,000 people (allowing for migration in the area) who can reach Cumbernauld as quickly as any of her competitor towns; and the knowledge that an integrated centre includes associated amenities to reinforce the cumulative fact of one-stop shopping

The development under promotion here is a long way in intention from the three-storey facades flanking corridor streets, perpetrated for doctrinal reasons after World War Two. It does in fact approach the developer's dream of a single-storey commercial centre – for its multi-level character is more apparent than real. In this connection it has proved possible to calculate, in order to reassure prospective tenants, the capacity of the development to handle goods. This has been done by translating the value of the £10 million worth vended per annum into a cubic capacity and tonnage. By assuming the pattern of arrival for these goods at the centre, allowing for weekly and seasonal peaks, it is possible, on the basis of free flow conditions for vehicles, and a known time cycle for the mechanical handling installation, to predict the rate of delivery. As a by-product the amount of packing materials and waste may be guessed with some degree of confidence. Customer flows are of course arranged independently of servicing and both use-groups and levels are deployed in such a manner as to be activated by natural pedestrian movements

Traders will range from the largest supermarket in Scotland at 21,000 sq ft gross to automatic vending machines; from a few cheap units for second-hand dealers and others to branch department stores; from a variety store planned to double in size to two-storey exhibitions of electrical and gas equipment demonstration areas; from roof-top restaurants to a banking hall with note exchange and staff clubs grouped together with other desk type uses such as travel bureau and car-hire counter

THE SITE OF THE CENTRAL AREA

The centre which occupies the ridge and upper southern slopes of the main hill 200 ft above the re-aligned Glasgow-Stirling motorway at an elevation of almost 500 ft is highly exposed. The severity of the wind regime is being continuously studied by means of Beaufort Force diagrams in order that comparisons can be made with experimental work on the topographical models. A permanent electrical recording aremograph is being set up on an adjacent, corresponding hill site whose features are established from a pattern of cup-counter readings taken on the Cumbernauld hill-top. By this means it will be possible to study how the growth of the town affects the local climate in the long term, not from the point of view of structural stability but in its environmental aspects. The micro-climate which will develop within the centre proper can only be seriously studied on the basis of the first phase development. As a by-product it has proved possible to refine the normal classification emerging from C.P.114 by calculating the design wind speed rather than adopting the nearest of the specified classes

In area the central area site is 150 acres, including two grade-separated interchanges one mile apart. It has a cross-fall to the south of approximately 25 ft in the centre. Bores were taken early over the whole area, trial pits sunk and the rock head plotted with cores

taken to prove depths of sandstone strata. The sub-soil varies from soft brown clay to stiff boulder clay to a depth of 9 ft, from 9 ft to 12 ft soft weathered rock is encountered and below 12 ft firm sandstone with no bearing problems. The sandstone stratum lies in nearly horizontal structure and shows some laminations of varying thicknesses which are not removable by machine from above unless shattered first. They have, however, been worked from a standing face. Spoil from the self-draining excavations amounting to a quarter of a million cubic yards has been hauled to three tips including playing fields and road embankments. This accounts for about 50 per cent of the total excavation which will finally be required. Because of the weathering characteristics of the rock it is not possible to expose faces in the design

The corollary to the degree of exposure is of course the asset of the fine hillscapes of the north, from the Kilpatricks beyond Glasgow to the Campsie Fells– foothills of the western highlands – to the Ochils in Stirlingshire

EMPLOYMENT IN THE CENTRAL AREA

If the full employment potential of the centre is taken up, the structure could employ 9,000 persons before anyone goes into it for services, and discounting the 5,500 residents in the central area

The number of persons employed in retailing as a percentage of the total population of the 100 towns (after applying a 3.5 per cent increase in population and a 6.8 per cent increase in number of persons employed from 1950 to 1959), is 6 per cent which lies close to the Great Britain and Scottish percentages of 6.12 per cent and 5.8 per cent respectively or 60 retail employees to 1,000 of population. Applying 6 per cent to a population of 70,000 gives a total of 4,200 employees. This ignores the then national average unemployment figure of 2 per cent

From this total of 4,200 employees the number which will be employed in, (i) the Town Centre, (ii) the Village Centres and (iii) those employed in retail outlets in the New Town but not within the Town Centre was found by applying the percentage of total sales handled in each of the three groups to the total number employed (ie) 64.3 per cent in Town Centre; 21.7 in Village Centres and 14 per cent for other retail outlets

A separate assessment of the number employed in the Town Centre may be made by dividing the total sales in the Town Centre by the turnover handled by

one employee. This latter figure is obtained by dividing the total sales 1950 by the number employed in Retail and Service Trades 1950 for Great Britain and for Scotland; these are the same, namely £1,935 per employee per annum

Dividing the total sales in the Town Centre by the 1950 figure gives 2,800 employees

This closely corroborates the Town Centre figure of 2,700 employees gained from the initial calculation using the 1959 expenditure figures. It may be said with some safety then that the number of persons employed in the retail side of the Town Centre when completed will be between 2,500 and 3,000 employees, of which one-fifth will be part time and four-fifths full time almost equally comprised of males and females

PUBLIC ADMINISTRATION AND UTILITIES

Using the only comprehensive source of data, the 1951 Census of Occupations and Industries in Scotland, the 161 occupations listed for National Government Service (eighty-one) and Local Government Service (eighty) have been reduced by inspection to sixty-seven, eighteen male and female in NG Service and forty-nine male and female in LG Service as being the likely range of government occupations to be expected in Cumbernauld central area. Expressed as a percentage of the total group (itself one-sixth the size of the manufacturing industry group) the Cumbernauld fraction is 39 per cent of the whole public group. The revised figure for manufacturing industry in Cumbernauld is just over 14,000 persons. This bears a relationship to the total town population of a similar order as does the total Census group to the population of Scotland (Cumbernauld 1 : 5, Scotland 1 : 6). Thus that proportion of persons employed in this category likely to be accommodated in the town centre structure is 39 per cent of one-sixth of 14,175 which is 925

FINANCE, INSURANCE, PROFESSIONAL AND COMMERCIAL

Lettable office space for these uses is proposed in three forms:

(i) small suites, within decks for professional and related purposes, totalling 50,000 sq ft gross at 200 sq ft per person will accommodate ... 250

(ii) 250,000 sq ft gross arranged in an eleven-storey,

double-sided slab at 120 sq ft per person will accommodate 2,083

(iii) 300,000 sq ft gross distributed over three levels on the south side of the town centre at 120 sq ft per person will accommodate 2,500

This latter figure, while not as high as that revealed by surveys of certain existing office centres (which may often be the result of historical accident), is a good deal higher than the fire authorities' ratio of one person to 100 sq ft or the common scale adopted by elevator manufacturers of one person to 70 sq ft and reflects the likelihood that small separate offices will not be as economical of space as the larger open office users

In addition to these three principal categories certain persons will be working in medicine, religion, teaching and communications and a further group including parking attendants, porters and resident engineers will be generated by the building itself, totalling say 100

Thus total persons engaged in the central area exclusive of cleaning and maintenance staff ... 8,600

This is rather more than half the estimated numbers employed in Service Industry (15,120) and 36.5 per cent of 31,500 the total number of persons likely to be employed in Cumbernauld

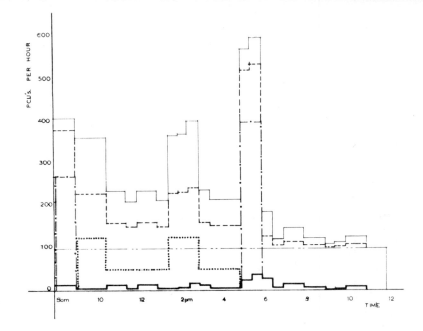

VEHICULAR SYSTEM

The technique of traffic analysis and the evolution of the highway pattern devised at Cumbernauld has become in a short space of time, not merely widely used, but superseded by more refined procedures. The Cumbernauld calculations were in long-hand and no computer programmes were available at the time. It was quite possible though to make a number of cost-benefit analyses

The approaches to the centre have been given prestige alignment and character involving high standards of design, which will promote safe travel at speeds around 40 miles an hour. They will in fact be extensions of the regional semi-motorway system, penetrating the structure at either end. Careful treatment will be required at the sudden change from bright daylight conditions at a major

Above: Through flows (not associated with car parks) Monday, Tuesday and Thursday

Below: Through flows (not associated with car parks) Friday

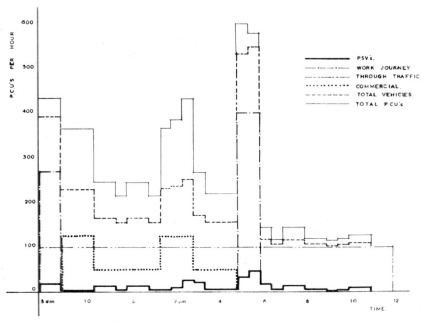

251

conflict point, where drivers will have to pay maximum attention to other traffic making lane-changes and a right turn. It is desirable, therefore, to introduce some physical speed deterrent outside the structure; this would have been best provided by a reversal of the alignment of the trumpet junctions, whereby the radial/link traffic passed uninterrupted, and radial/town centre traffic was retarded through turning ramps

Certain components of the resultant road works are under construction, while the grade-separated interchange at the east-end of the centre is now in use and ready for connection to its limited-access links. Owing to the rapid changes of thought at this time of transition, the whole system was designed on a car-ownership level of 0.7 cars per family, this was later revised to one car per family while the centre is designed for an ownership level of 1.4 cars per family. One aspect of this work which looks rather optimistic in retrospect, was the simplified assumption concerning the degree of proximity of house to work-place

Separate analysis, however, was made of the numbers of vehicles of all kinds likely to use the centre, the purpose and duration of trips, daily, weekly and seasonal peak flows; peak parking accumulations and daily parking stall turnover; goods vehicle generation, public service vehicle usage and maintenance and emergency vehicle needs. These total demands can only be met over the next twenty years by provision of ten lanes and the construction of crosslink tunnels (a little over 80 per cent of the journeys made to the centre will be shuttle movements and would have resulted in flows of the order of 3,000 v.p.h. on exit lanes)

The function of the vehicular system is of course to provide access to the town centre and related central areas use, and to accept limited through traffic. These movements will be compounded of:

(a) cars-through, stopping and parking (the latter including resident, visitor, shopper, staff, trade representatives and official cars);

(b) public service vehicles – local, regional, taxis;

(c) goods – through goods, goods delivery in, goods delivery out, and household removals;

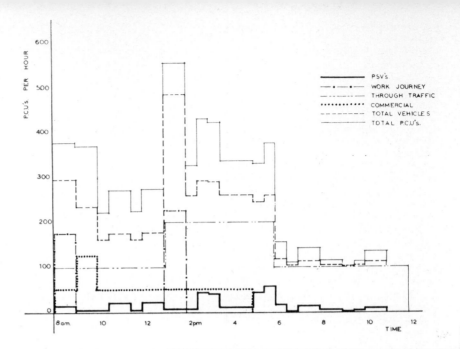

Above: Through flows (not associated with car parks) Saturday

Below: Approach from the west

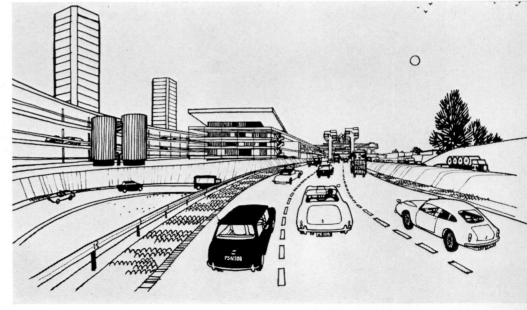

252

(d) service – fire fighting appliances, police vehicles, TA vehicles, ambulances, hearses, post office vans, cleansing and maintenance

In principle all running traffic is in the open, while all standing vehicles are under cover. Movements within the superstructure are comprised firstly of pedestrians – adults and children, old and infirm, and a major consideration is the perambulator. These movements will be made on foot or by escalators, conventional lifts, paternoster lifts, fixed stairs and ramps or motivated reversible conveyors (inclinec); secondly, goods – by hand trolley, powered truck, overhead rail, hydraulic scissor-action tables, portable conveyors, hand-operated hoists, packaged hoists and fixed oildraulic elevators. Pedestrians will have either walked in from the surrounding areas, be bus passengers or car drivers or passengers. The freight flows will include merchandise, office and household supplies, refuse. All these movements have a vertical component for which provision is made in the landlord's basic installation. The bus services will comprise regional, local through and internal town bus. Provision for an overnight bus garage and bus station as part of the fabric of the centre is made below the west-end for up to eighty buses. Bus stops within the centre will never be farther than 100 yards apart, and are designed to reinforce local nodes of activity. Attempts to calculate goods vehicle flows by land use generation proved to be something of a dead end. Too little work has been done on this problem. It proved in the end more accurate to estimate the number of goods vehicles required to service the centre from first principles, using the value of the commercial throughput of the centre as the basis

The car parking facility has been designed for the long-term, the short-term and the residential parker. Self park, mechanical park and joint systems were all investigated and a unidirectional self-parking system finally adopted. Mechanical parking systems, although the product of increasing ingenuity, suffered from the inherent defect (besides higher costs and psychological drawbacks) that the car cannot continue to be used as a convenient family base within the city, in that the vehicle is inaccessible in a pigeon hole. Were it, however, desirable to convert to an automated system, the most appropriate device, evolved after study of all types, including the horizontal adaptation of the vertical conveyor, would comprise a ram actuated dolly, controlled by hydroselector gear. The time cycle for this operation will be ten to thirty seconds depending on the

position of the bay for a cost of about £280 per car– this is lower than for any known fully automatic (customer operated) system

In addition to the variety of car sizes and types which have to be accommodated provision must be made for motor-cycles, motor scooters and motorized invalid carriages

The vehicular area as a whole is not seen as a throwaway space, but as an enclosure for an activity which has its own equivalent architectural discipline, met by a kind of radiused architecture. Wind tunnel studies indicated that there would be no natural concentrations of undesirable fumes, and that these could be dispelled in a random manner (assuming the worst case, ie, fog with no ambient wind and peak exhaust gas production). Exposed vehicular ramps will be equipped with heating cables and ice detectors. Stringent fire conditions have to be met, and a petroleum spirit licence is required, though there is no fuel for sale in the building. Provision is made for the installation of low-level extracts if conditions should exceed those predicted; and volatile liquids, in case of spillage, have special consideration

I know of no fatality within a car park, but the arrangement proposed here with pedestrian or parking fingers, makes it even less likely. Either a head-in or a reverse-in manoeuvre can be adopted for parking and this is likely to vary with the circumstances of the driver's arrival. A reversing manoeuvre is preferable for economy, safety and fatigue – although it is easier to reverse into a 20 ft aisle than into an 8 ft stall. The efficacy of the column grids was tested by a field experiment of one hour's duration. Statistical techniques can and have supplied information on which to base a number of recommendations; conflict and decision points, and general flow characteristics, can be determined by graphical means. This exercise therefore attempted to simulate peak and random flow conditions, so contrived as to produce the familiar difficulties experienced in car parks, using a variety of test vehicles of different lengths, and having different driver visibility and locks. The column grid spacing was found generally good, and it proved possible to reduce the planned circulation aisles and widen the footpath to allow end-opening vehicles to be used without obstructing foot traffic. A wheel check was obviously necessary, but had to be so arranged as not to prove a snare after the driver had alighted

PHASE ONE

The first phase comprises a little less than one-

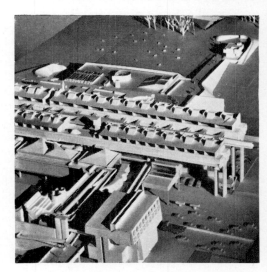

Aerial view of the model of the first phase from the north

quarter of the total planned cubic capacity. It is intended to come into operation in 1965 at which point in time it will serve about 18,000 people. Recognition of the factors of growth and change has been a major determinant in this development; and the general proposals, referred to earlier, were no more than the necessary means by which the definitive requirements for Phase I were evolved

The temptation to rest content and continue adding in similar terms to what will be a moderately successful system must be resisted if necessary by our masters who must force the pace in technical progress. For development, guided by certain principles and the services discipline, should proceed from this first component in response to social and economic pressures rather than formal planning notions. This first piece of construction, if it proves that in these conditions it is possible to provide this degree of amenity, does not begin to advance on the socio-environmental front. Nor is style the answer to our current urban anarchy, and the shorthand architecture in which I have clothed Phase I is merely a reflection again, of the extent of time consumed by non-architectural problems

The first phase of the town centre will make provision for those daily need functions which can be supported by this first relatively small element of the population. It can accept a number of permutations of tenancies and can expand on each face at its own rate: by pushing through the central concourses it is possible to leap-frog past areas already reserved for specific expansion

A pedestrian entering from the south side will be received by a series of small ramps approximating to the general grade of the existing hill. After passing the caretaker's lodge he will be elevated to the principal southern terrace by inclined conveyor. At this point on the roof of the office hall, designed to contain about 350 staff, he will be joined by people using the secondary ramp which functions also as a small protected arena strongly orientated towards the park. Within the shell below, a serrated mezzanine floor is to be constructed over the business equipment to provide executive floor space connected directly to the mezzanine car park

Entering on foot from the north the visitor will leave the wood, pass the low chamber of the Church of Scotland on his right and walk off a slightly inclined bridge on to the stepped civic square, over the first instalment of the entertainment centre. On his right will rise the municipal and Crown buildings, and on his left the small glass superstructure of the upper part of the Police Station. In front of him is a portal flanked by the hotel taking the form of an inverted pyramid, and the two-storey banking hall behind a Soane-like screen. The visitor who arrives below the centre will, if he is doing other than use the drive-in facilities, rise from cool concourses, into the heart of the complex

The unity and flexibility to be found by all arrivals could, however, be multiplied in later stages, by continuing the process of fragmenting conventionally excluding forms, and encouraging a much greater interplay of activities, in a vast tent of mass-culture. The current work would then act as a portal to a new world, complementary to, rather than competing with, the old. Connected by a mechanized tube, this would be a male and female centre. Concrete decks, however well manipulated, are no longer credible at one-half mile length. Their lack of unity, lack of flexibility and their relatively poor climatic conditions represent an advance only in political and economic terms. With these worlds it would be possible to choose or experience a sequence of environments in which 'pleasure' is not seen as a separate commodity to be retailed in a specific package, but as a characteristic of the whole mode

254

SERVICES IN THE FIRST PHASE

Servicing in general may be represented by an image, on the one hand a man in a cloth cap pushing a battered hand-cart, and on the other, by a man in a white coat accompanying a stainless steel trolley. The centre will be working twenty-four hours a day, and it goes without saying that servicing is not an undercover operation, and has to be as efficient and presentable as any other. The 'nervous system' of the building might well have been better arranged in duct walls of the external envelope, but because so much of the going had to be made from scratch there was not time to explore this possibility

The original intention to adopt a district heating system for the hill-top was abandoned, as a circulating system of this kind is inherently inhibiting to organic growth. The volume and nature of traffic required to fuel the installation, the necessary 200 ft high chimney, the disproportionate degree of capital equipment required for the first phase, the difficulty of accommodating storey-high heating mains, the extreme inflexibility of major pipe-work within the structure, together with a host of attendant managerial problems, were responsible for the decision to go all-electric. The tenant is responsible for floor, wall and ceiling finishes, certain boundary works, and his heating installation including charges for the meter and its connection (statutory undertakers accept their responsibility for taking supplies to the curtilage of each of the premises wherever placed). A variety of means of heating was considered, including heat pumps of various kinds and piping of surplus heat at present being dissipated from industrial installations on the Forth

Considerable problems, however, have been experienced in arranging, not heating, but cooling, and a variety of precautions have been taken. A certain amount of permanent supplementary artificial lighting is necessary which together with a load from the equipment, etc, is provided through three transformer rooms built in the rock but accessible from above. By switching, anything short of a grid failure can be remedied and in its event diesel generating sets come into operation to provide an emergency lighting system and certain elevators with fireman's control

Over thirty meetings have been held to resolve the fire aspects of the development, and some experimental work has been carried out. It has been necessary to consider this project from first principles in terms of access for appliances, means of

255

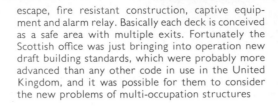

escape, fire resistant construction, captive equipment and alarm relay. Basically each deck is conceived as a safe area with multiple exits. Fortunately the Scottish office was just bringing into operation new draft building standards, which were probably more advanced than any other code in use in the United Kingdom, and it was possible for them to consider the new problems of multi-occupation structures

PHASE 2–SCAVENGING

A water-bourne or vacuum evacuated system is not economic in this form of layered development, hence each penthouse is to be equipped with chute from the kitchen delivering into a receptacle (hopper/paper-sack), stowed in a locker approached externally from the housing access street

Non-domestic refuse is to be collected by prime-mover with a purpose-built pick-up device from three refuse reception points, arranged at road level

P1

256

Most retail refuse will be generated at storage floor (loading dock) level and thence trolleyed to the receptacles at the collection points by any tenant outside the public circulation

STRUCTURE

L. G. Vincent of Stevenage speaking at a Town and Country Planning Association Conference stated that experiments with even newer and more costly types of centre (. . . than Stevenage!) in any new town were dashed by his figures of the cost of providing the space and facilities of the Stevenage centre in alternative two- and three-tier layouts. These suggested that the additional cost of a two-tier centre would have added on the average, £600 to the rent of the shops, and that the proposed Cumbernauld Centre (for a smaller population than Stevenage) is likely to be around £3 million more. He also made, he claimed, the very important point that the level of rents which shopkeepers can pay is somewhat lower in the north than in the London region, consequently the cost of a town centre may have to vary accordingly. For roughly similar accommodation as at Cumbernauld he gives the costs of a one-level scheme in 1961 money terms as £6,850,000: two-level as £9,700,000: three-level £11,500,000 (basic construction costs only)

Having seen his drawings one must be thankful his conclusions were so mistaken

The first phase of the Cumbernauld Centre is taking three years to construct and is being executed in four contracts. The first contract was for Civil

Engineering works for bulk earth moving and surface water sewers. The second contract was again Civil Engineering for central carriageways and foul sewers. The third contract was for the structural frame including excavation for and forming foundations, retaining structures, vehicle subway, shafts, columns, beams and decking. The final contract is a several works one, including specialist trades and mechanical services. Of these, the third contract is probably the most interesting in that offers were invited for the frame on a detailed design, supply and erect basis with the intention of tapping the resources of the industry, in design, construction and erection techniques. The exercise is negatived if there are too many limitations or arbitrary member sizes to fill out: hence the drawings were couched in terms of performance standards, i.e., the grid was fixed, the minimum head rooms which could be accepted was stated, the maximum deck depths

Below left: Photomontage of Cumbernauld's future central areas

On the right, three photographs of the model showing the preliminary project for three-deck extension, on the north side, of the first phase into the second

Above: Ground level showing terminal for eighty buses

Centre: Intermediate deck for bus terminal passenger concourses, public offices, and a bowling alley

Below: Aerial view of completed model showing, left to right, roof over auditorium; skylights over council and corporation offices; circular roof over council chamber; pedestrian plaza leading into hotel/banking complex. The small tiered building is the central police station

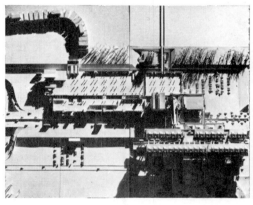

257

which could be permitted were given, all loadings were defined – superimposed, screeding, partition, snow, live; conditions and extensions by mechanical design were stated; where the presence of underfloor heating was known this was given (because of the tendency of certain shrinkable aggregates to behave badly in its presence): the fire characteristics were stated member by member; the various codes were stipulated: the design wind speeds were calculated and basic specification clauses were given: the bills had to be made up in a certain way and a number of extras–over were sought in order that permutations could be practised when prices were known. Continuous conferences took place with the contractors and designers during the tendering period and it was significant that every contractor submitted a bona fide tender. Four months were allowed for the bids, three months for global assessment (the cheapest structure would not necessarily mean the cheapest bui ding)

THE NEXT SCOTTISH NEW TOWN

At the time of writing there are twenty-two new towns at some stage of development in the United Kingdom. Four of these are in Scotland, and the latest is to be built at Livingston, 15 miles west of Edinburgh as part of an ultimate vision of a planned conurbation. Together with this town of 70,000 people, a wide scheme of regional redevelopment and rehabilitation will proceed simultaneously over 80 square miles. The limits of the region, largely following the remains of out-worked coal and shale industries, occupy an area 16 miles long grossly disfigured by spoil heaps accumulated over 180 years. The plan will provide an economic bridge between the main centres of industrial economy, and will promote new forms of industrial activity in the central belt. One of the mainsprings is already in production, the British Motor Corporation factory. In twenty years the entire region will provide homes and work for 170,000 people, nearly four times the present population

A striking feature of this area is the prominent oil shale bings or slag heaps, which lend the site a lunar aspect. On the productive side, they may have constructional brickmaking, pyrotechnical and an agricultural function (peat holds water, shale drains) and as stabilized bottoming. Certain of these slag heaps may be modelled in situ to offer protection from east winter winds, and to screen or contain industry

Livingston was selected because it is outside the congested Clyde Valley, but not too far from the city from which the majority of inhabitants will come. Special assistance will be available to local authorities under the Local Employment Act, Town Development Act and Planning Acts. The site cuts across local authority boundaries and requires the services of two of them

A PEDESTRIAN'S EXPERIENCE
OF THE
LANDSCAPE OF CUMBERNAULD

L J FRICKER

A visiting aesthete's opinions of Cumbernauld housing are not worth much. The town is designed for evacuees from Glasgow's slum clearances and no matter how well informed the visitor may be, it is the people from Glasgow (they will form 80 per cent of the total population) whose judgments are important. Cumbernauld architects have the best opportunity for assessing whether or not they have correctly predicted their clients' needs and wishes; yet despite his disadvantage, a visitor cannot but be impressed when he overhears, as I did, an exchange like this:

'How are you liking your new house?'

'Smashing'

Since for the duration of his stay, the visitor is a user in much the same way as the inhabitant, he has a better opportunity of studying the quality of the outdoor space. Provided he is not in a hurry—and if he is, Radburn planning soon puts a stop to that. In fact, given the problem 'design an urban environment which will discourage superficial criticism' one would be justified in turning in a Radburn scheme

Most of Britain's post-war New Towns have Radburn enclaves. Significantly tighter planning at Cumbernauld, leading to higher densities, has resulted in

footpaths
garaging
housing
gardens

Right: Housing in Cumbernauld, on Radburn planning principles, illustrating pedestrian-traffic segregation

enclaves of a very different sort – hard urban floorscapes, courts and pedestrian-ways. For the people from Glasgow these courts and ways may indeed be the most traditional aspects about Cumbernauld – for Glasgow's slum tenements are traditionally arranged around cobbled and paved courts often connected to each other by dark narrow alleys, forming a pedestrian network where almost all community exchange takes place, apart from in the public houses

In Cumbernauld pedestrian and vehicular traffic are almost totally segregated. Where footways do cross roadways, the road alignment does permit speeds of more than 15 m.p.h. and though I agree with Paul Ritter's claim that speed is not the main cause of traffic accidents, I still think that where segregation is not complete, slow traffic speeds do help

Few critics have applied the aesthetic theories of the media of mass communications to the fine arts.[1] And if, as I have already inferred, traditional fine art theories are of little use in judging contemporary environmental design, it might be useful to consider the ways in which the designer's intentions are communicated to the user – in this case, at Cumbernauld

Firstly then, roads. At 30 mph you are covering 60 feet per second, so, even at that 'safe' speed, information needs to be writ large and frequent. It is probably because advertisers' lives depend on it rather than ours, that their graphic displays get through to the moving viewer so much better than traffic engineers' information does

However, the logograms and pictograms[2] which are now being used in Britain are indicative of an awareness on the latter's part of successful advertising techniques.[3] But we still have not designed a language system for road transportation which is part of the road itself, even for a localized area, still less for the whole country. The traditional way of doing this in towns is well exemplified in a city like Edinburgh where the traditional surfacing material has, up to

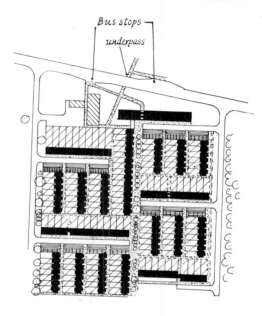

the present, been granite setts – blocks of granite, of sizes from 4 in square to 12 in square, in assorted colours: pink, dark brown, light and dark grey, black. They are laid in patterns, which informs the driver – and the walker – which is the major road, where the pavement direction continues, where parking is discouraged, and so on. It is something which was done far better in Edinburgh than is now being done in Cumbernauld (a matter which I shall return to further on). But although some of the details may be wrong, the road planning in Cumbernauld does show a way in which design can indicate the designer's intention and at the same time reinforce the users' proclivities

All trunk roads connect with the three main radial roads by grade-separated junctions only, and these connect in turn at controlled junctions with the feeder roads which go to buildings or footpaths. Except in a very few cases, the feeder roads are not fronted by buildings and car parking is not permitted on the carriageways, nor do pavements follow the main town roads

Traffic planning is based on the trend studies which predict that car ownership will reach a proportional figure of 1.4 cars per family before very long, that 45 per cent of the population will travel to work by car, 42 per cent by public transport and that the remaining 13 per cent will walk. These figures have been confirmed by the Road Research Laboratory and although predictions of this sort are notoriously fallible, it is clear that Cumbernauld is not working in arrears of current information

But while it may be the case that roads can only be justified in our present circumstances by sternly pragmatic transportation needs, this should not be – and in many cases is not – the only justification for walkways. In the eighteenth century Capability Brown enclosed the great private parks of his wealthy and sometimes aristocratic patrons by a tree belt within which ran a carriage drive. Status needs were often a justification, but the sensation of moving in a carriage over smooth-shaven undulating lawns and watching the flow of clumps of trees and serpentine lakes exemplified Burke's definition of the beautiful

But strictly pleasurable activities with voluptuous undertones were not the requirements of the nineteenth-century British municipal park. Parks for the general public were intended to educate the mind

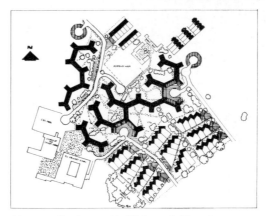

Above: Cumbernauld, Kildrum 5. Site plan

and exercise the body of the middle and lower classes. So the early parks were arboretums, threaded through by convoluted pedestrian path patterns[4]: and parks within towns were necessary for people who worked long hours and for whom a day in the country was no compensation for the money lost from taking time off work

The situation is very different now. Daily working hours are shorter, weekends are free, 'bus fares not exhorbitant. The town is sited on a hill; which means you see hills, farms and trees in every direction. That, as a reminder of rural life, is important. But compact development means that the town is only five miles long in one direction (NE–SW) and two miles in the other (NW–SE)

The town is immediately enclosed by playing fields and general open space, then by a forestry belt and

further farming land which gives way to the 1,000 foothills in the north and south. The close proximity of open landscape, the town's compactness and the segregation of foot and road users, means that the nineteenth-century municipal park per se, is an anachronism

You quickly find that the whole town is a park, even in the nineteenth-century sense of its being a place for education and physical recreation. And since there are so many more media through which these things are now available – we can accept the town as a place in which these two ideas are synonymous. It is within the scope of this definition that I shall discuss my experiences as a pedestrian at Cumbernauld. But firstly, to return to the matter of communication of information by textures and patterns

George Square in Edinburgh, which I walk round every day to work, is a typical eighteenth-century in-city Georgian square; a rectangular garden with trees in the centre, fenced off with railings, a road

Below: Details of pavement, George Square, Edinburgh

on all four sides, and the square itself finally and almost completely boxed-in by tall austere terrace houses. For months I have puzzled over something which, if my suggestion is correct, puts the pedestrian experience on a very different level from the walker-plus car level. On the left, the building. On the right, the garden. Art and nature. But how to link them? Well, the road must last and vehicles move easily—so pave with setts. Surface A paved with slate, contiguous with the building; urbane. But what to do with pavement B? It must be different both from A and the road, and be contiguous with the garden. Grass and gravel are useless, and they are both 'in' the garden. The answer: epitomize the country road for sophisticated townsmen! So they used knapped whin, the pieces clipped from shaping the whin into setts. They are laid dry and so grass and moss grow between the stones, something, of course, which does not happen in pavement A

When you are wearing stilettos, you walk on one side; wear brogues and you walk on the other. The railings are all spiked and keep out those who do not own keys. But they are fashioned like spears and characterize the way armies defended their camp with spears jabbed in the ground to form a fence. The gates are the same design and difficult to spot until you notice that the stones are laid in a different direction beside each entrance gate

The point of this digression is that most contemporary landscape architecture discussion centres round proper land use, and let's-educate-the-public attitudes, which is laudable. But if landscape design is an art as well as a science, then as an art it must communicate ideas about man's physical and emotional relationship with nature in ways unique to its own medium. This is exactly what George Square does. We know this is true of the great European gardens; but they were designed, in most cases either by the owner or by a designer for one man. What is important about George Square is that it is one of many of its kind, designed for an anonymous public; it works as well for us as it did for our great-grandparents; and it does so without ostentation and sublimely. But a lesson has been added to this experiment. Over one section the stones have been torn up and replaced by trowel-finished concrete. And you can feel something is wrong—not just untidiness or a revulsion against newness, but that the mood which was triggered has been snapped, and for no good reason

I saw nothing in Cumbernauld which communicated

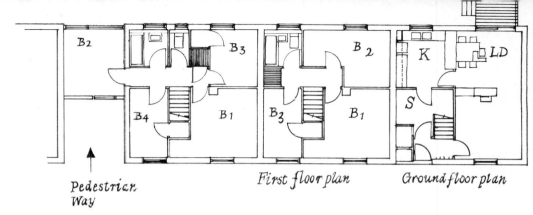

First floor plan   Ground floor plan

Pedestrian Way

ideas comparable to what I have just described. Yet the primary conditions are not so dissimilar, condensed urban situations with rapid transitions from hard surfaces to planting. Of course the shapes of the spaces are different, for Cumbernauld is based on pedestrian progression from one asymmetrical and non-repetitive space to another. Granted the Cumbernauld surfaces are durable and dry; but they should do more than that. In some cases they do. 1¼ in chippings set proud in concrete bump the breath from children pushed over it in prams. Whatever the faults of the picturesque aesthetic theorists, they never suggested we should physically experience the rugged or intricate in a well-sprung baby carriage

Why should that part of the path spell out 'walk here and you break your ankle'?

Are these railings to protect your fall as you stand, to look at the greens enclosed by the zig-zag blocks (in the Kildrum area), on what might as well be broken glass?

In buildings, it's the same. 'Stiletto heels cannot be permitted because of the condition of the floor.' Can we not yet make a floor on which people may wear whatever shoes they please? It is examples of such total lack of understanding such as these that lead people to say – as Lawrence Alloway once did say to me – 'Architects really hate people; it's the spec. builders who love them'

Communication at Cumbernauld is, in general, done better visually than tactilely, and this has something to do with the house plans and groupings. As many families as possible have their homes on the ground

Above and below: Cumbernauld, Seafar I

which means that most houses have back gardens approached through the house. The front doors of many houses open on to paved courts. Courts are, as we have said, traditional to the slums of Glasgow; and these paved courts at Cumbernauld are the most

261

successfully comprehensible areas, women stand at their doors and gossip, and small children play. Where, as in the house plan for Seafar 1, a bedroom is used on the second storey as a bridge, the footpath is thrown into patches of light and shade which make it appear shorter than it actually is. On the other hand to me, and probably even more to a child, an unrelieved footpath looks as long and intimidating as the Champs Elysées. I remember a footpath near my home when I was a child: it was just over half a mile long, 6 ft wide and boarded on either side by black railway sleepers 8 ft high. It looked interminable. As children we always went the long way round, it always seemed so much shorter though in fact the journey took five minutes longer. The lane was used most frequently by dog owners and it became a dog's lavatory. It always stank of urine

One gets little opportunity at Cumbernauld to see how gardens are used. Peeps through fences reveal motor bikes, prams, bicycles, vegetables, laundry, flowers bordering grass plots. Here, as in the earlier new towns[5], far more care is taken and cost spent on ensuring that gardens are not publicly seen than in dividing the gardens from each other. On the other hand, sub-division would encourage people to cultivate their own gardens; and if some are messy, they would still make little impact on the total scene. There is some evidence to support this; the Cumbernauld housing put up under the first contracts had back gardens screened from each other, and from the road; those I did manage to see were both pretty and well cultivated

Now I know what landscape architects' current tastes in plant material are, I am more interested in the tastes of the person who lives in the house. The gardener in Seafar 2 who found himself without a front garden and in sheer frustration tore up a paving slab to grow a cotoneaster up his harled wall, is something I find fascinating. Established design taste in Britain has long held (particularly since the time of the Georgian terraces) that the front room and back garden are where we should display our individual taste. But designers today – who in most cases don't and can't know what our current crazes are, increasingly assume responsibility for private and public display. We know that some architects even want to choose window fabrics; for me, the information about the way a house is used is of far more interest than a dubiously organized 'display of good manners'. A city which cannot accept the transient is a dead city

If, as I believe it must be, environmental design is based on human use and human wishes, are we not obliged – even in planting design – to include non-professional landscapers as human beings with human tastes? We talk a lot about easy maintenance, but this must not be the sole criterion on which we base our design ideas. Much as I like the planting of heather and boulders at the Seafar housing, it only tells me that heather grows on the moors nearby, can be cut as turves, laid like grass and never needs cutting

It tells me nothing about the people in the houses, nor does it tell me much about the designer. The consultant landscape architect, G. P. Youngman, has said he is not interested in gimmicks, by which he means Burle Marx, and that the things which really matter, 'the fundamental elements – are not those which people on the whole can appreciate and which therefore they do not value. Shape and form and not merely colour; space and not merely an assortment of objects in space; the local and particular, the twentieth-century version of the genius loci as against the standardized and uniform; but at the same time the total as against the individual, the unified vision as against the partial and fragmentary;

and fundamentally, the spiritual as against the material.'[6] am not sure exactly what this means, unless it is neo-platonism – but see little point in designing things which people are unlikely either to appreciate or value

Youngman is not alone in making a plea for 'timeless qualities' in design. It is a concept peculiarly wedded to the so-called modern movement, and one which we can now see as a falsity. What is so wrong with contemporaneity in an age of the Kleenex aesthetic? 'It is important that an architect through his very design and employment of materials and techniques, makes a real contribution to ensuring that the activity catered for will not have to continue for any reason – economic, structural, etc – beyond its period of social viability.'[7] Something far more easily said than done, even in building, let alone landscape design. But we can start by designing a permissive environment in which we design for plural use, so that the rigidity of our solutions does not preclude alternative uses. Play areas are a good example of what I mean. Children play all the way home from school, inventing their games as they go, and many of the Cumbernauld play areas do have exactly this feeling of casualness; unlike some playgrounds, which

have the air of forlorn monuments to a wrong idea unless children are actually playing in them. But with these it doesn't matter, they are a game in themselves. They don't need the justification of play or sculpture, those concrete biomorphs which do seem to me to be neither playful nor sculpture but products of a mind which accepts abstract art only within the social realists' doctrine of 'the function of art'

Since children do not need or depend on playgrounds as such to play games, I think that if it is necessary for play areas to be designed they should be adaptable to any passing craze.[8] And despite the Opies' claim that children, in their apparently capricious games, are extraordinarily bound by oral codes and traditions often centuries old,[9] I still think they need places to play in, rather than set games to play or things to play with

Coia's primary school is excellently small people sized; big people have to bend from the neck or get reduced in size. But this keen thinking is not witnessed by his playground next door. Brick-in-asphalt railway lines, a castle topped by a metal St Andrews flag and a jungle gym and a maze both in concrete. The play sandpit which forms the centre of Coia's

tough gutted housing[10] is far better. Does sand have to look so permanent? Can't a truckload be dumped somewhere every week and the old carted away? To my mind the best playgrounds are where trees have been retained by stone walls; or underpasses. These are often trowel-finished, and permit children to chalk up their graffiti and conduct internecine slogan fights on the merits of pop singers and taboos. Why not exhibit child art in public?

If I appear to have been critical about Cumbernauld I must make it clear that this is only because I both admire and respect what has already been achieved. And I am fully conscious of the landscape architect's dilemma which is what Youngman seems to be describing. The central difficulty, and it is one unique to the practice of landscape design, is the time scale during which plants and particularly trees take to mature. It is hard enough for a professional landscaper to predict the final appearance of his work and it is not surprising others should find it more difficult. We can plant fairly large trees; but we cannot yet, nor is it likely we ever shall, produce in a short time works of quality which will have the mass appeal of the Marx Brothers, Marilyn Monroe or the Crystal Palace. The art of landscape design is not evanescent, and that does not mean it is either better or worse than those arts which are; only that it is different

The artificial hills in the foreground of Coia's housing are grassed over. In order to protect the grass while it is growing, and maybe afterwards too, the landscaper messes up the town with chestnut pale fencing. And those newly planted trees: by the time they mature the housing will be obsolete. Peter Daniel has said of his housing at Peterlee New Town that he doesn't mind if the houses are scrapped after fifty years; so the trees being planted now will last fifty years longer than the houses. There are 100,000 new trees planted in Cumbernauld, as many as Capability Brown planted on one estate, and I think the British new towns will eventually become the national parks and nature reserves of the future

In Britain, as in other countries, we benefit from the planting done during the past, and we take great pains to preserve those trees and woods and site our structures in relation to them. So should we not now be planting forests where for the present no one is intended to live, so that future generations can site their structures within them? I think we should. I believe we should apply the ability to think of the growth/time scale of an oak tree to the growth/time scale of society. This will call for great anticipation. Or what Buckminster Fuller has called comprehensive anticipatory design science

FOOTNOTES

1 For those who wish to refer to some writers who have, see
Richard Hamilton: The Urbane Image, Living Arts 2. London 1963
Reyner Banham: What is Pop? Motif 10. London 1962
Tomas Maldonado: Notes on Communications. Uppercase 5. London 1961
Lawrence Alloway: Junk Culture. Architectural Design. London, March 1961
All these writers have published extensively on these ideas; so have others; my list is indicative, not exhaustive
2 see Maldonado, Uppercase 5
3 Brian Copland: Advertising and Traffic. New Society, No 46. London, August 1963
4 Of all the eleven acres of land within which J. C. Loudon designed the Derby Arboretum in 1840, six were taken up with tree planting. There were 1,013 different species and varieties of plants. The walk is over one mile in length
5 L. J. Fricker: Organization of Space in Housing Neighbourhoods. Institute of Landscape Architects. London, May 1960
6 Journal of the Institute of Landscape Architects. London, November 1961
7 Cedric Price: Reflections on Team Ten Primer. Architectural Design. London, May 1963
8 At school we acted out in the playground the day's history lesson: Yorkists v Lancastrians, Saracens v Crusaders
9 Iona and Peter Opie: The Lore and Language of Schoolchildren. London 1959
10 Which Theo Crosby considered the best housing in Cumbernauld and probably in Scotland. Cumbernauld New Town. Architects' Year Book 10. London 1962

JOY BOX

JOE TILSON

265   1962/3 Painted wood box
        14 × 9 in (35.5 × 23 cm)

E MAXWELL FRY

266

An enthusiastic French journalist once described Chandigarh as a city built in a desert. It is not, but it depends a good deal on the season in which you first discover the Punjab as to how desert-like it looks. Before I reached the Punjab I met an old lady in Delhi who said to me, 'It is not one climate up there but six', and so it is

I went first up to Chandigarh, or rather up to Simla because Chandigarh hadn't even started, by road from Delhi. It was in the winter, a crisp cool day with a thin blue sky. The road was a line of bluish tarmac with wide dusty verges fit for driving cattle along and from time to time strings of bullock carts drawn by milky cattle offered the first contrast between the immemorial Punjabi life and that with which we were to replace it. There were two dry rivers to pass over and the plain seemed endless before the blue line of the Himalayas came into view. Even at this season, with fields of young wheat and sugar coming on, the sense of dustiness was there and the wheat was the greener for being contrasted with it. But the contrast between the hills and the plain is the dramatic fact about the site of Chandigarh. It is true that the land rises gradually towards the hills. The car stops at a level crossing while the

two-engined mail train puffs and pants up the incline towards Kalkar, the terminal of the broad gauge. But it is still a plain and the surprise is to find within the space of a few miles travelling the line of the Himalayas rising on the skyline: first just a line of blue, and finally the rampart of hills stretching endlessly into the distance on each hand. All this takes place after you have passed through the big military town of Ambala, where the bungalows of the British Army officers stand in gardens wide enough to play polo in, the verandas full of shadow, yellow painted classical facades backed by dusty brick. Ambala is Kipling, a fragment of British India interrupting a plain which by now is closely farmed, field after field of corn, sugar, young wheat and gram, with rutted roads passing between them to villages that rise from the plain like mounds of configured mud topped by feathery trees

The Simla road begins to rise definitely towards the hills for the last few miles and as you pass through the old village of Chandigarh the land is falling on each side into valleys that channel up into the Himalayas, and there is a noise of running water. It is here one branches off through the old moghul town of Mani-Majarh towards the site on which the new Capital now stands. The road that passes across the site is traversing the base of the Himalayas, rising and falling over the spurs and declivities, a wide tree-shaded track of a road with fields on each side and the little mud villages showing up through the crops at easy intervals. We would call these villages hamlets, and their size is conditioned exactly by the agriculture they serve. The rich clayey soil supports an intensive agriculture of wheat, gram and sugar and the size of the village and their spacing are direct responses to a simple set of conditions with no mathematical exactitude. Men and beasts must fan out into the fields each morning and be gathered in at dusk. What men and beasts with primitive tools can do defines the terrain: where water is locates the village

At somewhat similar intervals therefore the tracks between the standing crops gather to where the brown earth rises to the barely distinguishable form that shelters a community of seven or eight hundred souls

Seen from the fields it is little more than an excrescence of moulded mud, topped sometimes by the

Right: Typical decorations done by villagers near Chandigarh in their own housing

267

house of the elder or tax collector, and fringed irregularly with trees among which the giant and holy pipul clearly dominates, marking the site of the pond or tank with its temple nearby

An air view would doubtless reveal a still greater degree of similarity between the hamlets, and what is more interesting, would show, especially in the season of harvest, the exact connection between them and their agriculture, the extent to which they were as much a part of a process of reproduction as the calyx of a flower is a part of the cycle that includes the plant form it decorates, the bee that fertilizes it, and the region that invites them both to flourish

Let us therefore enter the Punjabi hamlet by way of the track that passes the pond, where the water buffaloes stand submerged to their noses. The pipul tree arches immensely over the water; its roots stretch out gnarled fingers: women gather at the well: a temple bell peals faintly: smoke rises

In the twisting alleys of the village goats press against the rounded mud walls or enter with fastidious tread tiny courtyards where beyond, in deepening shade, the small complications of domesticity are received into white structural form. Beauty is everywhere; inherent; no more in the courtyards than in the swelling tree trunk; no less in the sweetly arching ironwork of the well-head than in the mild-eyed milk-white bullocks that wait their turn. All is beauty: timeless

The feeling evoked is one of harmony, as though each part has achieved its proper form in relation to the whole and is different only because nature seldom permits the same circumstances to be repeated. What has remained constant is the common problem, and that it should have remained so while generation after generation built and rebuilt, wore down, smoothed over, white-washed anew after the monsoon, decorated with emblems of the cherished god, with crude representation of the enemy tiger, ensures that each individual solution of the partial problem will approximate towards the whole and bear the common imprint

The land is too near the hills to form part of the great system of irrigation that has converted the Punjab plain from a desert into a great wheat and sugar growing province; the water sources are less regular; the land is more uneven and the feeling of the mountains everywhere about one. In the early days of building these villages were very close to us. Some

of them were yet to be demolished and continued their simple life while our great works came nearer and nearer

For some months Jane Drew and I lived at the old village of Chandigarh on the main road in a rest house surrounded by lawns which the gardeners used to submerge in a thin sheet of water from time to time, and great mango trees shaded it on two sides. Every morning we took the jeep and passed along the shady road through the little town of Mani-Majarh, threading our way through flocks of goats and cattle in a haze of dust in the first heat of the morning, and it was the animals and the bullock carts and the people that we were aware of. But in the evening coming back we used to linger around the tank with its little temple approached by a causeway, because it is in the evening when the great heat of the day is sinking back that colour comes into its own again. In this poetic hour of North India we used to love walking through the bazaar, the narrow stinking little street crowded with stalls where at the cross-roads women gathered round a great stone well that served the whole town. Everywhere was harmony and beauty. There was nothing, except our jeep, that was mechanical; there was nothing that could have changed much over a thousand years

We had no plan in any of these expeditions. It was just that after our day's work we relapsed into the past of the close bazaar, or on the rocky hill where the Hindu temples clustered; but I have the feeling that there was no better way of absorbing the conditions of life and the real effects of sun and climate. We made, with Corbusier, certain codifications of climate – his 'grille climatique' for instance, and these were invaluable as bases for design. But they were not enough. They didn't really indicate the crises through which the year passes; the drama of the monsoon working its way across the Continent to end a nearly intolerable period of mounting heat; the tension of the sunrise in the hot season; or the happiness of the long, calm, cool days of winter

Wherever we went we were in close contact with a virile agricultural community following its calling with the animals and implements of the ancient world, as slow moving as the strings of bullock carts that moved night and day under the shade of the trees along the dusty margins of the roads, the drivers often asleep, or one patriarchal bearded elder erect among a sleeping family

And at the same slow pace a bullock drew the wooden plough through the rich red earth across fields,

269

always in sight of the village to which men and animals would return along the known alleys into their joint compounds, humans and animals barely separated

This is village life, where the organization and the form that enclosed it are commanded by the necessities of the natural circumstances. There is indeed no means of thinking up a community. It is commanded by circumstances or it does not exist

We built some of our housing in village form, and we were right to do so for what it could bring of close association. But these groups of ours were not villages in any proper sense of the word though the people that lived there were villagers by old habit

Many of our staff were Punjabis coming from villages, with the outlook of countrymen and the same rough humour. How far they helped us to design housing of the right sort I would not care to say, but they acted for me as a link between what we saw about us and the families for whom we were to design. Sitting round the ceremonial fire that signals the close of one of the periods of the farming year when it is the custom to tell stories and sing songs, I felt as closely drawn into the community as it was possible for a stranger to be. Looking down the line of seated figures, the firelight throwing into relief their fine profiles, with glossy beards and dark shining eyes, I felt very much a part of them; while there in the clearing before the fire was Madan, our jester, imitating a countryman's first initiation to modern traffic in throaty Punjabi, wafting us in laughter from the old world to the new

CHANDIGARH REALISED

BHANU MATHUR

Punjab, one of the north-west provinces of India, was partitioned in 1947. Its eastern portion was integrated in the Indian Union; the western wing went to Pakistan. The Indian share of Punjab lost its capital to Pakistan. The provincial headquarters of this newly formed State was moved to Simla—a hill station, and the summer capital of India during the British rule. The climate at Simla was not conducive for work throughout the year as it was situated at a height of 7,000 ft. Simla was not easily accessible from the plains, and all essential materials like food and other supplies had to be transported there from various places. These difficulties, and many other considerations, caused the Government to decide to find a permanent capital in the plains. A search for a more apposite site thus started early in 1947

The communal disturbances in Pakistan and in India in August 1947, brought large numbers of non-Muslims to India. Hurried townships were set up for them in Ambala, Amritsar, Jullundur, and at other places in the Punjab. Existing towns swelled in size. As a result, the general opinion at that time was in favour of extending one of these existing towns as the permanent capital of the Punjab

P. L. Verma, then Punjab's Chief Engineer, who was asked by the Punjab Government to recommend a suitable site for the capital, was convinced that the new capital could in no case be an extension of an existing Punjab town, but should be built on virgin soil. He argued that the cost of land acquisition around an existing town would be much more than a completely new site. The recommendation of Verma was accepted by the Government

After a hectic search, a site for the new capital was chosen at the origin of the Ruper road from the Kalka-Ambala highway (lat. 30° 45″ north, long. 76° 45″ east). The capital was christened as 'Chandigarh'. The name is from the goddess Chandi, and the Chandi temple is eight miles from the city

THE SITE

Chandigarh site covers an area of 14 square miles. To the north-east is the backdrop of the Shiwaliks range of hills (part of the Himalayas); the Sukhna Cho range is to the east, and the Patiala Rao to the north-west. On the south and south-west lies a very fertile sloping plain, with elevations varying from 1,175 ft in the north to 1,075 ft in the south or 25 ft per mile. The north-west quandrant of the city is undulating in character, with a somewhat steeper slope of 50 ft per mile

Chandigarh has an annual rainfall of about 30 in. The climate is hot and humid during the summer (which is also the wet season, with rainfalls of great intensity), but the winters are cold and dry. The maximum temperature during the hot weather is above 90° F. and below 75° F. in winter. January and February, however, also have a cyclonic rainfall. Throughout the year, winds from south-easterly direction are usual. During the monsoon, the direction of the wind changes and north-westerlies predominate

Generally the subsoil strata revealed interbedded clay and sand to 300 ft. In places boulders and gravels are sandwiched between these beds. The surface soils is predominantly sandy loam, though patches of sand are not uncommon, the proportion of sand increasing near the Sukhna Cho. The original cover was forest. At present, much of the vegetation is formed by shrubs, mushrooms, acacia trees or munja grass along the choes. Mango groves are a conspicuous part of the landscape

The city derives its water supply from a battery of forty-four tube-wells. The average depression-head works out to be 15 ft. Water supply in these tube-wells is adequate

THE FIRST MASTER PLAN

Albert Mayer (of Mayer and Whittlesey, New York) was in India when the selection of the site was under consideration. He was invited to prepare a master plan. Mathew Nowicki, a brilliant Polish architect who had emigrated to the USA and was a partner in the firm, came to India to work with Albert Mayer on this exciting project

The Mayer master plan was designed for 500,000 people over an area of 28 square miles. Mayer recommended a grid-iron plan, wedged between the Sukhna Cho and the Patiala Rao, with the main roads of the grid-iron pattern laid north-south and east-west to form a number of sectors about 80 acres each in area. The north-south roads were designed as radial roads, while the east-west roads were straight

Mayer suggested the capitol group of building on the

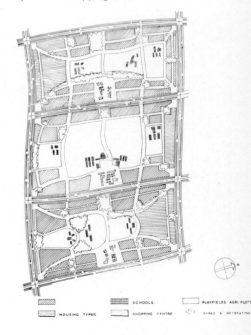

Albert Mayer. Typical sector plan, showing three blocks with their peripheral roads, and central spaces for shopping and schools

low hills on the top of the eastern end of the town, certainly a very commanding location; the city centre's main business areas were in the centre; the industrial areas were on the east, and the educational centre on the west

A typical sector in Mayer's plan was divided into three parts by means of two roads running across the shorter side of the sector. The sector was subdivided into blocks. Each block was provided with space in the centre for subsidiary shopping and for schools. These open spaces were connected with linear parks. The roads around the sector and the two roads cutting through the sector had lanes for slow traffic and fast-moving vehicles. All the traffic generated from the blocks was brought to the intersection of the circumferential road, running round the sector, and the road running through the sector — a typical feature of Mayer's master plan

There is no doubt that Albert Mayer made a fairly sound suggestion for the master plan of Chandigarh. Indeed, Le Corbusier's final plan of Chandigarh coincided with the main lines of his approach. But the sudden death of Matthew Nowicki, in an air crash in Egypt, came as a crippling setback to Albert Mayer. Nowicki during this stay in India had prepared draft plans for residences, schools, shopping centres, railway stations and studied proposals for the capitol buildings. He showed immense respect for the traditional folk art of Punjab, and this had great bearing on his architecture

Finding himself handicapped, Albert Mayer suggested to the Punjab Government that other architects should be engaged to detail out the master plan and design the buildings. Consequently a team of Indian engineers and administrators went round the world in search of architects. Finally, they contacted Le Corbusier in Paris. Corbusier declined to come over to India permanently and take full charge of the project, but suggested as an alternative that Pierre Jeanneret, his cousin and old collaborator, should be approached to take up a permanent assignment at Chandigarh. Corbusier however, agreed to give directions and advice from his Paris studio, and offered to visit Chandigarh twice a year. He further proposed in December 1951 that the Punjab Government should invite E. Maxwell Fry and his wife Jane

B. Drew to take up similar assignments with Pierre Jeanneret. Le Corbusier, Jeanneret and Maxwell Fry came to India, and M. N. Sharma, J. S. Dethe and N. S. Lamba, the Indian architects and town planners who had worked for Albert Mayer, joined them to form a new team. Later, B. P. Mathur, A. R. Prabhawalker, Urmila Choudhury, and Ted Bower also joined the team

LE CORBUSIER'S MASTER PLAN

In India Le Corbusier was shown the recommendations of Albert Mayer. After scrutinizing the layout, Corbusier disagreed with the orientation of the master plan, the location of the capitol on the hill, the size of the sector, and the network of roads recommended for the capital. He further commented that the total road provision was more than adequate for the number of users. Le Corbusier was then asked to prepare a master plan according to his own vision. This was not an easy task; however, Le Corbusier prepared a draft master plan which the Punjab Government considered to be economical, straightforward and more suitable. It was approved

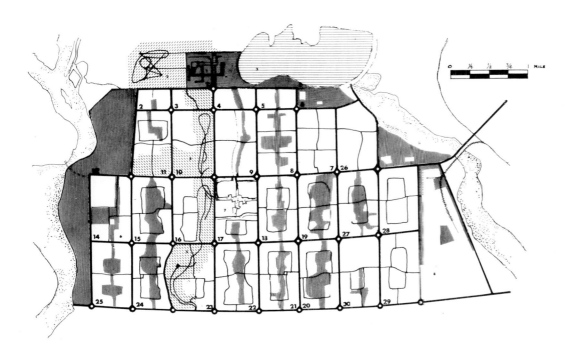

Left: Le Corbusier's master plan. Key:
1 The Capitol   2 Rajindra Park
3 Lake Sukhna Cho   4 Patiali Rao
5 Leisure Valley   6 University Campus
7 City Centre   8 Industrial Area

in January 1951. But it was also mutually agreed that the two sectors of the new master plan would be detailed out on the original principles laid down by Albert Mayer

Le Corbusier's master plan is also a grid-iron pattern. The main roads run north-east, south-west and north-west, south-east, forming sectors half a mile wide and three-quarters of a mile long (240 acres). Above the grid-iron and on high ground he sited the capitol group of buildings of the High Court, Governor's House, the Legislative Assembly building and the Secretariat building. Towards the south-east is the industrial area, separated from the residential sectors by a green belt. In the centre is the main shopping centre or the city centre of the capital and the district headquarters. On the north-west is the University – a city within a city. Thus the city can be further extended by adding more sectors to the south-west of the town

The sectors on the north-east are low-density sectors, about 6,000 to 7,000 people in an area of half a mile by three-quarters of a mile. The central belt of the sectors are medium density sectors and the south-west sectors are high density sectors planned to take 12,000 to 15,000 people. Corbusier recommended an hierarchy of roads for circulation in and to Chandigarh. For example, the V1 road connects the airport with the town. V2 is the main road to reach the important public buildings, ie, the road leading to the capitol. V3 is the road running in the north-east, south-west and north-west, south-east directions, round a sector where a vehicle could run at an increased speed. V4 provides access to the local shopping centres of each sector. These V4 routes are interconnected, and run in the south-east and north-west direction. The V5 roads are the main distribution roads emerging from the V4s in each sector; while the V6 roads which connect the V5s with the doorsteps of each residential unit in a sector. The V7 roads traverse the open spaces of the sectors, and take pedestrian and cycle traffic to the north-east end of the town. Until recently these roads were known in Chandigarh after this system V1 to V7, but proper names have now been given according to their function and location; for example, Madhya Marg or the Central Vista for the road running through the centre of the city

Chandigarh is at present planned in five quarter sectors and seventeen full sectors. Four sectors were kept in reserve unplanned, besides the industrial area and the capitol. However, the reserve sectors have now been planned and released for various purposes. The Punjab Government has built houses, office buildings, schools, etc, on one-seventh of the town while six-sevenths of the town are being developed by private owners. There is great pressure on land; and the Government is now reported to be considering the acquisition of land on the south-west of the city

The principle of sector planning has been laid out by Le Corbusier under the direction of Pierre Jeanneret, E. Maxwell Fry and Jane Drew and the details have been worked out by Indian town planners and architects. As already mentioned, these sectors are based on the Albert Mayer plan. Each sector is entered from the north-west or the south-east side, through the V4–which is generally not a straight road to discourage fast traffic. On the south-west of this road is the subsidiary shopping centre which generally runs along the road. It is from the V4 that the V5 (the main distribution road) emerges and runs through the sector, making a figure of eight. Finally there are the smaller roads, running to each house

As in the Mayer plan, each of these domestic sectors is provided with an open space in the centre, and is planned to take an education building and recreation centres like a club, playing fields, medical health facilities, etc

THE CAPITOL

At the top of the town, between the lake and the Rajindra Park, is Le Corbusier's Capitol, the seat of the Provincial Government, in an area of about 250

272

Below: Le Corbusier's Capitol. Key:

1 Assembly	8 Martyrs Memorial
2 Secretariat	9 Tower of Shadows
3 Museum of Knowledge	10 Pond
4 High Court	11 Cycle Stand
5 'Open Hand'	12 Garden
6 The Basins in front of the Museum	
7 The 'Modulor'	13 Artificial Hills

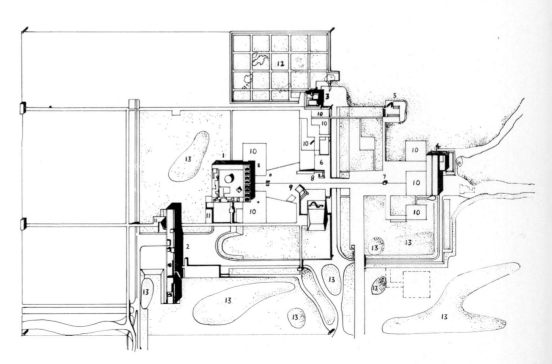

Above: Le Corbusier's Assembly Building
Photo: Rondal Partridge

Right: Workman with donkey transports bricks
during construction of Le Corbusier's Secretariat
Photo: Camera Press

274

Previous page: Le Corbusier's Assembly Building

Below: Court of Le Corbusier's Assembly Building
Photos: Rondal Partridge

acres. This area is detached from the city by a water course culminating in the climax of the town. The Secretariat building, Assembly Chambers, the Raj Bhawan (now the museum of knowledge), and the High Court are set to stand out against the back drop of Shiwalik range and provide a contrast between nature and man-made architecture

In the capitol, the Secretariat and the Assembly are placed on the north-west, the Raj Bhawan on the main axis, i.e., the north-east direction, while the High Court is placed on the south-west side. These buildings are interconnected by footpaths, roads, pools and by a number of monuments

In the capitol, fast moving and slow traffic are canalized at two different levels. The fast moving lanes lanes are 5 metres below the usual ground level, thus creating complete safety for the pedestrian. These

Right: Pierre Jeanneret and B. P. Mathur. Detail of Gandhi Bhawan Panjab University Administration building. Photo: Rondal Partridge

Above: Men and women carry cement, sand and water during construction of Chandigarh's Capitol and University buildings

fast moving roads branch off in the direction of the main building in the capitol, ending in the car parks. The car parks are then connected to the pedestrian ways by means of staircases and ramps

The slow traffic roads which run along the leisure valley, connect with the capitol, uninterrupted by the fast-moving traffic

Between the Secretariat, the Assembly, the Museum of Knowledge and the High Court, the famous diagram of 24 solar hours, the modular scale, the tower of shades, the martyrs' monument and the open hand, form a total composition

Man-made hills between the buildings, roads and monuments with various colours of foliage, have been successfully landscaped. These hills were made out of the excavated earth from the sunken roads for fast-moving traffic

Except for a few essential roads, the hills in the landscape and the Secretariat building, the Assembly building, the High Court with its extension, and a few reflection pools in front of the Assembly and the High Court, have all been constructed. The full conception of Le Corbusier's Chandigarh is still in the making. Nevertheless, when it is completed it will be a source of inspiration for a whole generation of architects

HOUSING

Housing in Chandigarh falls into two categories: housing developed for Government officials, and housing developed by private individuals for their own requirements or for rental purposes

The Government has financed housing for its staff which falls into fourteen graduations. In India, there is a big difference in income between the low-paid and high-paid employees. The low-paid are the peons, clerks, etc; and the highest paid officers are the secretaries to the Government, commissioners and the high court judges. The ministers do not in fact draw the highest salaries, but enjoy many privileges, like free-furnished and Government-maintained residences

The Government housing has been largely designed by Pierre Jeanneret, E. Maxwell Fry, Jane B. Drew and the Indian architects, B. P. Mathur, Urmila Choudhury, Prakash, Jeet Malhotra and M. N. Sharma. One of the main considerations in designing these houses has been cost, which is prescribed and limited. It requires quite a bit of brain-racking to achieve standards within the prescribed financial limits

The climate of Chandigarh has made a noticeable

Above: Pierre Jeanneret and B. P. Mathur. Girls' Hostel, Gandhi Bhawan Panjab University

Right: Pierre Jeanneret and B. P. Mathur. Gandhi Bhawan Panjab University buildings

contribution to the design of houses. Sleeping terraces, various devices to cut the summer sun and glare, a variety of measures to provide good and cross ventilation and welcome the winter sun into each house, had to be provided for. The bricks burnt locally have brought a certain amount of uniformity and scale to the brick structures, although these are occasionally broken up by rubble walls and white-washed architraves

The social and religious pattern and living habits of the people have also contributed to the domestic architecture of Chandigarh. Measures have been taken to ensure privacy, security against theft, protection from flies, mosquitoes and rodents, etc; special arrangements for food preparation, storage and cooking have been made; and in the layout of neighbourhoods, type-clusters of housing in the various sectors have been designed to produce an interrelationship of traditional sub-communities in modern terms

Eighty per cent of the Government housing is for the lower income group. Housing of this type usually has two rooms, a kitchen, bath/w.c., verandah or a courtyard, provided with running water, and connected to a proper sewage disposal. The high income Government houses are mostly three-bedroom houses with living-rooms, dining-room, an office,

kitchen, pantry, store and a garage. The standard of living for the lower income group is something of which the Government can be proud; it is probably for the first time in India that reasonable accommodation has been designed for these people

On the other hand, private houses in Chandigarh are in a somewhat bad way, although plans are properly scrutinized by the estate office before sanction is given. This is largely due to the fact that the general public is not architecturally minded. The result is that very few private architects have been attracted by the city. Various methods to control the architecture of private residences have been tried, but no satisfactory system, except for providing complete designs of terrace housing, has been found. However, Le Corbusier's idea, worked out by Prakash, of providing frame control may prove to be successful, but it is still too early to comment on this system

EDUCATION AND HEALTH

A reasonably large share of development funds has already been spent for the development of educational and health facilities for Chandigarh. Nursery schools for children in the three-five age-group, primary schools, junior secondary schools, high schools, technical schools, colleges, an engineering

college, a Post-Graduate Medical Research Institute, and finally Punjab University, have been built. Similarly health centres, dispensaries, a maternity hospital and a 1,000-bed hospital, properly equipped, have also been constructed at Chandigarh

The location of schools and health facilities centres is according to the population of each sector. In the lower density areas, two to three sectors share a school or a dispensary while in a higher density sector, there may be two nursery schools, a junior secondary school, a health centre or a dispensary. These buildings have been located in the central open spaces of a sector

The outstanding educational buildings are Pierre Jeanneret's nursery school in Sector 16, and his junior secondary schools, Jane Drew's high school and Maxwell Fry's colleges for men and women. The health centre in Sector 22 by Jane Drew is also a successful building. The Post Graduate Medical Institute is one of the largest buildings in concrete, designed by Pierre Jeanneret and Jeet Malhotra

Punjab University, which was uprooted in the partition, administered its affiliated colleges from Solan before 1957, a hill station half way between Simla and Chandigarh. The University suffered immensely in research and scholarship. In 1957, it was decided to move the administrative office of Punjab University to Chandigarh and accommodation was made available to transfer all the teaching departments into a properly designed campus at Chandigarh

A full sector on the north-west end of the town was allotted to the University. The earlier plans for the University campus were drawn by a PWD architect. In 1959, the work was entrusted to Pierre Jeanneret and B. P. Mathur, and Mathur took over as the full-time architect

Punjab University has put up teaching departments both for science and humanities, a six-storey administrative office building, a five-storey air-conditioned library, and hostels for nearly 2,500 students in single rooms. A Gandhi Bhawan, placed in a pool, is the most successful building

The University, which serves a large area of the Punjab, is now planning expansion. More accommodation in the hostel both for male and female students, and housing for teaching staff, is in hand. Another sector, on the south-west of the present University campus, has been acquired for the growing needs of the University

RECREATION

The recreation facilities in Chandigarh include cinemas, theatres, sports clubs, community centres, swimming pools, playgrounds for hockey, cricket and football. There is also a plan to build a sports stadium on the north-west bank of the lake. The leisure valley, which follows the natural contour of a monsoon drain, stretches from the north-east to south-west of the city. In the leisure valley, winding paths for walks and a slow carriageway has been laid out. The sharp contours have been graded, and planted with groves of trees and flower beds in an irregular design. On the eastern side at the top of the town, the Sukhna Cho has been dammed and made into a lake. The work was executed through the irrigation department and completed in ten months. P. L. Verma considers the lake a necessity to reinforce the underground source of water supply, and to stop dust rising over the city from the dry river beds, besides providing a beautiful picnic and sports location

The water of the lake was muddy in the beginning, although Le Corbusier refers to this as Rose Lake. At the junction of the V2 and the dam, an entrance has been designed by Le Corbusier. On the top of the dam, which is 24 metres wide, a road has been

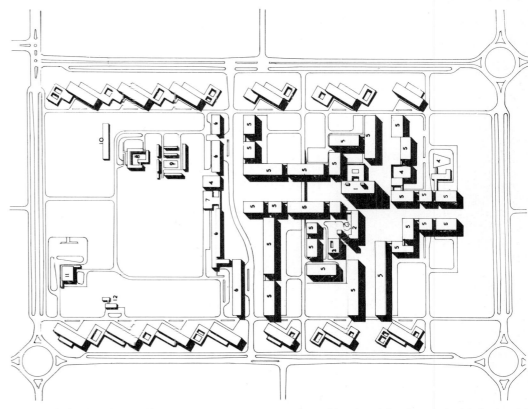

Le Corbusier's Civic Centre. Key:
1 Post Office
2 Town Hall
3 Central Library
4 Cinema
5 4-storey development
6 3-storey development
7 Booths
8 Central Police housing
9 Police housing
10 Treasury and District Courts
11 Regional bus terminal
12 Central Fire Station

constructed for its maintenance. The sides of the road have been beautifully landscaped with grass, hedges, flower beds – and indirect lights which reflect in the water of the lake at night. The road on the dam is a place where pedestrians can walk in peace and in a noiseless atmosphere

On the western bank, it is proposed to have a number of boating clubs. One such club is already functioning there. The building has been designed by Urmila Chunder under the direction of Le Corbusier

Plans for a golf links on the other side of the dam are under way

Rajindra Park, at the top north-west corner of the town, is shaping fast. The park is named after the first President of India, the late Rajindra Prasad, who inaugurated the city. This is probably the only example of Le Corbusier's genius at landscaping. The plan consists of a central road, which ends in a bandstand, and is intersected by a strong form of circular footpaths making a figure of eight. Trees have been planted in groups on the road, providing play with shade and light. Each group of trees in the park has been planned with two or three species of trees, creating different forms and fragrance

277

THE CIVIC CENTRE

The commercial and industrial areas form essential functions of the city, although each sector contains a local market. A civic centre has been planned in the centre of the town at the intersection of the Madhya Marg and Jan path. This sector has two zones, the north-eastern for the civic centre, and the south-west as the district headquarters.

The conception of the civic centre is traditionally around the Piazza, where the city's town hall, business houses, cinemas, etc, are located. A slow carriage-way runs round, and encircles, the Piazza where car parking has been provided. This leaves the Piazza free from fast-moving traffic

The buildings in the civic centre fall under strict architectural control regulations. Exposed concrete with shuttering pattern markings, the grid of the structural columns, the architectural elements, floor levels and heights of building, as well as the use of the

building, have been codified. The centre is being developed outwards from the core, and although the civic centre is still under construction, its full development has been ensured. The commercial strip along the boundary of the sector cannot at present be sold; it will be released only when the other land in the civic centre is sold out

The commercial strips along the central road, dividing the sector for civic and district headquarters, has shops in brick which are in complete contrast to Le Corbusier's civic centre. On the other hand, the general layout of cinemas by Prakash, with option to change the interiors, are designed in concrete box. This was done as cinemas form part of the civic centre

THE INDUSTRIAL AREA

The industrial area occupies the south-east corner close to the railway station and wholesale market.

This area is separated from the residential sector by a green belt consisting of twenty rows of mango trees. The industrial area prohibits the location of heavy industries and chemical factories. The principal industries of the area at present are manufacturing cycle parts, water meters, hosiery and antibiotic medicines. A plan for a further expansion of the industrial area is complete, and it will not be long before land will be released to industrialists

Above left: Pierre Jeanneret and B. P. Mathur. Library building of the Gandhi Bhawan Panjab University

Above right: Pierre Jeanneret and B. P. Mathur. Administration building of the Gandhi Bhawan Panjab University

JANE DREW

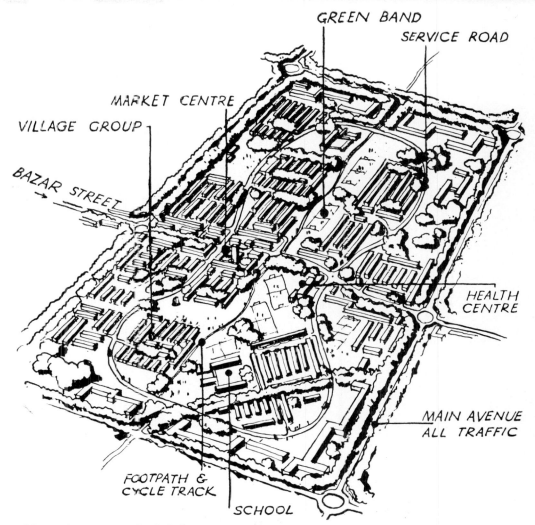

GREEN BAND
SERVICE ROAD
MARKET CENTRE
VILLAGE GROUP
BAZAR STREET
HEALTH CENTRE
MAIN AVENUE ALL TRAFFIC
FOOTPATH & CYCLE TRACK
SCHOOL

This housing was for all grades of Government staff – thirteen of them – the lowest for peons or messengers and the top for judges. We found that the poor sweepers' or cleaners' grade was so low that these untouchables had not even been included in the budget at all. A very detailed budget had been prepared giving us exactly how much we could spend on each grade of house: £244 for the lowest of the thirteen grades, the peons, and the highest category £4,875 for the judges and commissioners – that is the highest excluding the Chief Ministers

Our problem was to design a house to suit the owner within the budget allowance – a considerable problem, since the lowest class, excluding the sweepers who were not budgeted for, were the peons, the office messengers and drivers who, having large families pleaded for two rooms as well as a veranda and kitchen. We were determined to do this and also to provide water-borne sanitation and a tap, and for a long time we tussled with the problem of the separate w.c. and wash place, the w.c. being an innovation in India, and Chandigarh the first town to have a fully water-borne sewage system. In the end we devised housing of about 424 sq ft, consisting of two rooms of about 100 sq ft each. We labelled them living-room and bedroom but our Indian staff was

quick to point out to us that in India every room is also a bedroom. A closed kitchen veranda and a w.c. and wash-room and a closed compound made up the complement for the dwelling unit

These houses were grouped together in 'villages' of 150–200 houses having a central green area and the minimum access paths. We closed the end of the roads to give privacy and security and to carry electric supply cables, thus doing away with extraneous and unsightly street furniture

Above: Drawing of Sector 22, showing figure of eight internal housing road and peripheral fast roads to Sector. For the position of Sector 22 in Chandigarh see Le Corbusier's Master Plan

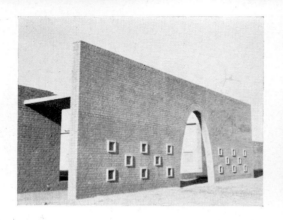

The houses were of local brick (30s. per thousand) and we used prestressed concrete roof beams and brick reinforcing with 4 in of stabilized mud over for the roofs. The houses varied in detail to suit their orientation and we designed special end houses so that the streets became one architectural entity

We found that brick was our cheapest material, then wood, then concrete, then steel and glass, so we had to build these houses chiefly of brick, cutting down the size of our window openings and using wood shutters and louvres rather than glass windows, where possible

This particular grade of society, the peons, was nearly entirely illiterate and yet so strong is the force of the unheralded educator, the cinema and illustrated magazine, that we found them asking us for modern kitchen arrangements, although in the first houses we designed we followed strictly traditional patterns, it having been impressed on us that the normal Indian woman liked to cook squatting

Later we designed yet cheaper houses for the sweeper class even omitting windows where possible, and internal doors and using brick holes for ventilation and curtains for room division

The cheapest housing was thus so dictated by the budget that only minimal variations were possible and we made our chief economies on the layout, the grouping of w.c's and the narrow access roads which were quite sensible in a completely pedestrian society. Indeed, we tried to keep the motor car out of 'the village' just making it possible for a doctor or fireman to enter in case of necessity

It was in the grades above that we met our real

Left above: One of the arches into the peons' village

Left centre: Peons' houses; Type 13-J, Sector 22– architect Jane Drew

Far left: Type 10–house designed by Pierre Jeanneret

Centre above: Front elevation of Type 13 houses, designed by Jane Drew

Centre: House Type 13-J, Sector 22, Clerks' houses

Left: Shops in Sector 22, built by the owners to an agreed design. Designed by Jane Drew

problems. We had many meetings with our future clients who told us all about the intricacies of Hindoo religious observance in the domestic routine, the separation of sexes, castes and occupations, of customs of sleeping and relaxation brought about by the climate. They told us of the need for sleeping on the roof or in the garden at certain times of the year but how there must be a place, a basarti, where the bed could be withdrawn when the rain fell. The bed is a light bamboo and string affair and easy to carry

We, and particularly Maxwell Fry, designed some terrace housing which fulfilled all the various complicated requirements both of the ecology and the climate (just above freezing point in winter to 115° F. before the breaking of the monsoon and with dust storms and hot winds at certain times of the year). This particular house, an early one, was called a type 'G' house and some of our architects were entitled to live in it. We built prototypes and then we had long evening post mortem parties on the roof – which was a wonderful party place with oil wicks alight. It gradually became clear to us that quite a number of the future occupants would rather have a sensible modern house, cool in the warm season and warm in winter with big rooms rather than copy the traditions and taboos of their ancestors and produce a house which was perforce a maze inside to allow separate sweeper access to w.c's, bath, etc. Encouraged, we designed new types that were untraditional and gave our future tenants the choice. In nearly every grade the sensible answer was preferred and only the babu or secretary class remained traditional in taste

We planned our houses within our sectors, using terraces freely, and as time went on we learnt that coolness, obtained as cheaply as possible, was the most important factor. The P.W.D. in the old British hey-day had obtained this by building a verandah right round the house. We, on a critical budget, worked out light angles and faced our houses as far as possible north and south, putting thick walls on the vulnerable side. Unable to build massive walls everywhere we devised sunbreakers to cool our walls and surrounds to our windows, making sure that at certain times of the day the whole house could be closed up. Air conditioning was too expensive to be entertained. We discovered that the lower rooms in a house could have a normal ceiling height, being well insulated by rooms over, but that despite 4 in or more of compacted mud on our roof with tropical asphalt over, upper rooms must be high. Modern

materials, such as expanded polystyrene were not available to us. The result was houses faced with egg-box sunbreakers and ventilated roof walls where ventilation was required for sleepers at night. We found that our early houses did not give our sleepers enough privacy and that overs climb walls. All these innovations began to produce a style we had not sought but a style which we found very popular because it has been much copied in the sectors of Chandigarh and elsewhere where private owners built for themselves. All our houses were for Government officials. Between January 1951 and July 1954 we housed 20,000 people but by then private enterprise began to build too and we had the great problem of how to control it. To do this I had the unenviable job of drawing up bye-laws, drafting Acts for the control of advertisements and the protection of trees, etc

We devised what I believe to be a unique method of control. We had a planning sheet for each sector on which were shown graphically the building lines, permissible heights, area of plot that could be built on, scheduling of trees, controlling boundary walls and showing standard gate designs. In this way we were able to design each sector at a time in three dimensions as a visual conception. On some frontages

on important streets we controlled the heights, profiles and set backs, but we controlled as little as possible since we had no large staff of inspectors to enforce any control and since we wished to leave individual architects as much freedom as was possible so long as major effects were not endangered by this

As far as population distribution and house types were concerned, on the whole we grouped similar grades, v z, 7, 8 and 9 near each other but we placed some of the lowest category near high ones since people should be near their place of work, but we did not otherwise mix the grades much since India, even more than England, is class conscious and people would be unhappy near very differing grades. We have been criticized for this but, in the situation, we still think it was right

Above: Rear elevation facing south–house Type 6, designed by Maxwell Fry

THE RELEVANCE OF
GREEK PLANNING TODAY

THEO CROSBY

The modern dream of a city: vehicles swirling along great highways, burrowing into a towering fabric at many levels. Above this network of mechanical service the pedestrian walks calmly, freely in the sun, through a series of luminous spaces, surrounded by soaring pinnacles, where the vapour trails linger in a sky unstained by smoke or fumes

This vision from the science fiction magazine and an image whose fragmentary reality is constantly about us, owes a good deal to history, Le Corbusier, St Elia (and Piranesi) for the multi-level circulations; to the paintings and realities of the unmotorized cities of the Renaissance, of Rome and Greece, for the pedestrian situation. Prints of Renaissance Florence show churches and palaces standing four square on paved streets containing a few elegantly disposed figures. Today those same buildings have almost vanished under a cascade of vehicles, and the pedestrians are nervously hugging the walls. Venice today is perhaps the only visually surviving city of the Renaissance, a great stone labyrinth where everything is scaled to the walker, where every movement creates a new picture

It is tempting to project such an image into the past, though we know that Rome was so greatly congested

with carts and chariots that wheeled vehicles were forbidden in the city during daylight. Rome was just too big to be organized on a simple pedestrian basis. On the other hand Greek cities, particularly the Hellenistic new towns in Asia Minor were perhaps perfect human environments

Later Greek architecture became consistently more anonymous. Archaic temples were boldly modelled, violently polychromed; by 300 BC the kit of parts, the order, became standardized and individual buildings tended to be submerged into the fabric of the town. The game was not architecture but town-planning

Generally Hellenistic cities followed the Hippo-damian rectilinear system, but there is an infinite constructivist subtlety in the way that the spaces relate to each other, within the grid. The city was conceived as a series of outdoor rooms often with galleries and verandahs, building in spatial sequences to the agora or temple. Each sequence was modulated into the next by a screen of columns, or the insertion of a smaller space. Above all the mode was sufficiently understood for the plan to be implemented, or creatively manipulated, within the system over a period of several centuries

It was a conscious and sophisticated process. Rex Martiennsen showed how the Greeks gradually came to master the most complex spatial problems in planning the temple temenos, and his analytical method can be applied to city plans such as Miletus, Priene and Halicarnassus with much profit

First the city is walled: a clearly identifiable man-made unit in a more or less undisturbed natural setting. The visitor enters through a gate. From this point, at Priene, an avenue leads to the agora around which are the public buildings and from which streets lead directly north to the theatre and south to the gymnasium. The temple precinct is somewhat apart from but readily adjacent to the main circula-tion. The temple dominates a long rectangular space to the west, and is seen, due to the steep slope, rising over the northwest corner of the agora. This was the true centre of Greek life, at first a market, later a civic space where the male citizens spent their days, in discussion. The habit survives in present-day Greece. The men sit in the cafés around the village squares, drinking water, and playing backgammon. In the evening everybody walks around the square, the main social event of the day

Such a space is most useful in a hot climate, and it also compensates for the cramped houses of its poorer citizens. The Greek house was, and is, small and crowded. Each room is a bedroom and there is little space for a man. The house is the woman's preserve and she is not encouraged to go out, except to work in a field, and spends most of the day washing and cooking in the courtyard. The plans of Hellenic and Hellenistic houses vary considerably, but generally consist of an entrance leading to a court-yard around which the various rooms are grouped. The more elaborate examples have complete peri-styles and a complex progression of spaces, a micro-cosm of the city itself

To project such an image of a primitive and coherent life to our own time is a romantic and probably untenable idea, though one very appealing to archi-tects. Most Europeans want something of this kind of urban fabric – the agora, stoa and temple – but no longer wish to act out their lives in this setting. The setting of twentieth-century man is his home, infinitely convenient and comfortable, comfortably in touch with every activity by TV, radio, phone or car, a home that can be a museum, a 'musee imagin-aire' of books, prints, photographs, records of the images, objects and music of all past and present civilizations. The sole reason for leaving this mini-paradise is to buy something, so shopping has become almost our only social activity. Thus shopping centres embedded in suburbia. The agora has thus degener-ated into a mere market place

Yet the need for some kind of centre, or hinge to one's existence, is deeply felt, and something might be encouraged to grow out of a stonily commercial situation. An entirely commercial area without a self-regenerating and regulating cultural component is not a really viable economic proposition. It commands no loyalties, and is constantly menaced by the next ambitious or cut-rate proposal

A truly twentieth-century agora is likely to consist of many diverse elements, apart from shopping of all kinds from barrows to department stores. Increased leisure will be filled, in a mass society, partly by mass entertainment, but also with a multitude of minority and specialist activities. Such a centre, safely segre-gated from traffic tensions, readily identified by an extravagant architecture, would organize the vast bulk of urban building into a meaningful system

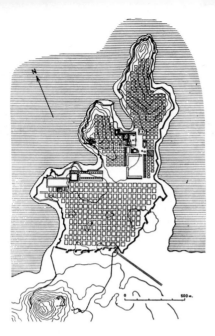

283

Miletus in Asia Minor was rebuilt in the fifth century, the plan being based on the rectangular grid pattern which became the model for most later Greek cities. The site is a peninsula running north-south, with two ports, and the bulk of the town in the lower area at the neck of the peninsula. The civic area is placed to serve the three main residential areas, linked by two markets to the ports. The plan is simple and logical. The geometric order remained viable for many centuries: that is, it was added to, strengthening rather than weakening its original impulse

The plan (lower right) shows the north part of the agora of Miletus in the second century BC, a series of spaces well scaled to the city, the north stoa facing the port. The need for more shops caused new stoas to be built running north-south, making a tighter urban pattern but also a more complex architectural experience. The plan (upper right) shows the same area in the second century AD. Notice the new colonnaded link from the north stoa to the next building on the right, and the way the anteroom so created is linked to the long space between the new stoas, which leads to the bouleterion and the main south agora

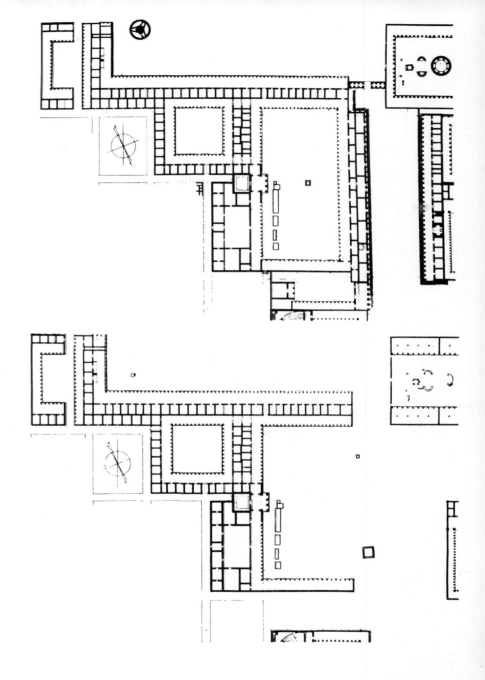

The grid (right, centre) was used as a positive method of organization over the whole site of Miletus. Here the residential area grid is applied to the civic area (plan as at 200 BC); the grid is used as a regulator

Priene, also in Asia Minor, is the classic Hellenistic city plan. The application of a rigid grid to such a romantic site has been criticized because most of the north-south streets are staircases. Seen in three dimensions, however, this produces many virtues. The temple of Athena, which on the plan (extreme right) seems detached from the agora, in fact overhangs the civic area, a most potent juxtaposition, and unlikely to be accidental. The plan is extraordinarily elegant, functional and direct; the various elements – temple, theatre, gymnasium, entrance gates, all form points of attraction linked by the agora

The north stoa of the agora of Priene (below), with the colonnade of the temple precinct high above it

View (below, right) of a reconstruction of Priene from the east. Notice the scale of the public buildings to the residential area, and how their disposition ensures an identifying element in each part of the city

284

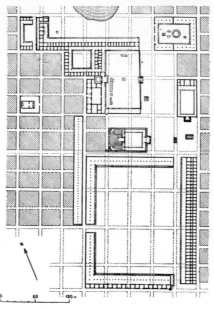

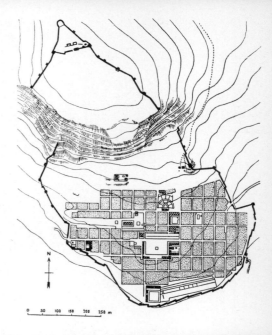

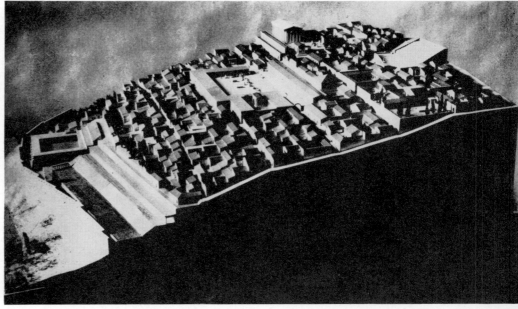

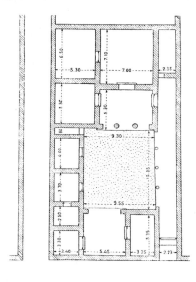

Above: House plans in Priene were microcosms of the city plan, in formed by the same space system. The entrance leads to a covered court which becomes one side of the court, on to which face the porch and the main room. Servants' rooms and the dining loggia are placed on the other side of the court

Top centre and far right: A street 8 ft wide in Lindos on the island of Rhodes. Lindos was a Hellenistic city and still boasts a third-century temple on its splendid acropolis. Although it was completely destroyed, the town as it is now was built from the fourteenth century AD, and is the most perfect environment in Greece. Its housing solution is very similar to ancient Greece, though the space concept is more complex and often haphazard. There are no public buildings on the ancient scale, but many tiny Orthodox churches occur within the townscape, which consists of a maze of narrow streets with doors opening on to courtyards. Each stretch of street forms a 'picture', leading to another 'picture'

Right: Shops occur within the street pattern forming a nucleus of communal life. In the background, a church

Far right: A courtyard in Lindos

Next page: Courtyard floorscape in black and white pebbles; such patterns carry through into the principal rooms

DOXIADIS' CONTRIBUTION TO THE PEDESTRIAN VIEW OF THE CITY

ROLAND WEDGWOOD

From his office and his town apartment Constantinos Doxiadis can gaze across Athens to where the monumental climax to one of man's earliest pedestrian routes breaks the skyline. What has he done to understand, develop and interpret the lesson of the Acropolis for this century? How has the continuous presence of one of the shrines of our civilization reacted on this fifty year-old Thracian?

He was brought to Athens as a refugee in the first world war and his doctor father became Minister for Refugees after the disastrous 1922 Asia Minor campaign. The contrast of this sublime architectural background with his direct experience of hunger, poverty and squalor as a child and as a resistance leader during the last war, probably accounts for the curious combination of realism and idealism in the man today. He gained his doctorate in engineering at the Charlottenburg Technical University for a thesis on 'Planning in Ancient Greece'. He was Minister for Reconstruction after the return of the Free Greek Government in 1945. His determined approach to the enormous problems facing the country secured his tenure under twenty-one successive governments, and his youth gave him the courage to act. 'Architecture', he has written, 'only exists when it is implemented by actual building'. He is one of the few planners of international repute who refuse to do a 'prestige plan' if he knows there is no intention of carrying it out

The problems of existence are simplified and clarified when conditions reach extremes. There is a categorical distinction between life and death. The ancient gods were never crossed with impunity however human they might appear. Time was embedded in the concept of both legends and sanctuaries such as the Acropolis. Doxiadis has fused these legacies with the Christian exhortation 'Render unto God the things which are His and unto Caesar the things which are Caesar's'. In our profane world God is the machine – motor vehicle, aeroplane, rocket, and Caesar the man on his own two feet

Although, like Buckminster Fuller, Doxiadis is concerned to think in total world terms, he is also clear in his conception of the basic element of the broader urban areas, the human sector. This is the largest unit within which architecture remains in direct relation to man without the interference of the machine

'The concept of the Human Sector is born out of the fact that urban settlements of the present no longer have one master but four, ie, man, car, aeroplane and rocket. Under these circumstances we have to recognize the necessity for preserving the first master as the one controlling the whole synthesis of the city. This is not possible over extended areas. Man on foot cannot cover distances much greater than two miles and even such a distance is probably too great

We have therefore to reconcile ourselves to the idea that we must preserve the human scale so far as distances are concerned. These may be half a mile, one mile, or a mile and a half. In very exceptional circumstances they could be greater than that, but they could certainly not exceed two miles. If we assume that urban dwellers could under proper conditions walk for up to thirty minutes in order to go to their jobs, their theatres, their markets, etc, then this distance of a mile and a half appears the maximum distance which can be allowed for a sector under the full control of man. Its ideal shape would seem to be an oblong, from half a mile to a mile in maximum length, so that people need walk no more than a distance of up to half a mile inside it to reach their schools, shopping areas, small parks and cultural and social centres, as well as those other basic requirements of their neighbourhood or community'

These sectors would be surrounded by traffic roads with bridges or underpasses for the safe passage of pedestrians from one sector to another. It is within the sectors that Doxiadis sees the special role of the architect. Important buildings should not be erected along highways where they can attract the attention of drivers

'In the human sector, on the contrary, where people walk, the values of architecture remain the old ones'

Vehicles would be allowed to penetrate these sectors, but only at slow speeds and to a distance a little short of the exclusively pedestrian heart, by means of culs de sac. Incidentally, it is interesting to note the similarity of size of downtown sectors surrounded by urban motorways in proposals for many American cities, eg, Pittsburgh, Philadelphia

The earliest schemes built by Doxiadis were for underdeveloped countries such as Iraq, and an illustration shows on page 291 a typical sector built in Western Baghdad. Here the vehicle population is very low and there are virtually no cars in private ownership. The pattern however is clear. In this case the central pedestrian core contains the mosque, schools, market, baths, health centre, shops, sportsground and administration buildings. The detailed appreciation of local customs and conditions reveals itself beneath the apparently similar plans for areas in different countries. In Iraq for instance, the walk to the well was often the only time a woman was allowed out in public. To introduce piped water at this stage of social development would have been a disastrous imposition on the pattern of life. So Doxiadis retains the distribution system of the past, but provides pipes and taps within the dwellings leading from storage jars or tanks on the roofs. These are filled by the pitchers carried by the women from the water points situated in little gossip and play squares. He also installs drainage, since this does not interfere with any important social custom. Later when a functional need is no longer required as an excuse for the women to venture forth, a piped water supply can easily be added

In later schemes, such as Eastwick Redevelopment Project, Philadelphia, the same basic principles can be seen applied to a very different situation. The illustrations of this project show site plans and some photographs of housing already completed. The sectors are planned to allow implementation of the different scales: the human and the machine. High speed traffic is confined to the speedways surrounding the sector, while 'collector' roads of reduced speed feeding major streets enter each sector. Inside the sector though, a network of walks allows the

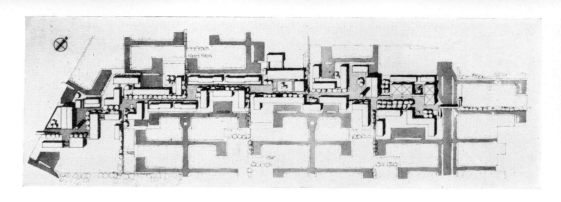

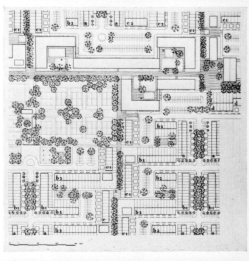

Eastwick Redevelopment Project in Philadelphia,
U.S.A.

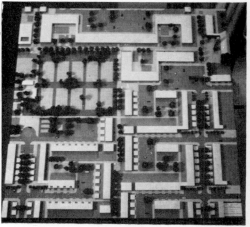

pedestrian to circulate freely within the small cluster of houses into the next cluster, to the parks and open spaces and finally to the main pedestrian greenway or esplanade bisecting each sector. This gives access to the schools, churches, clubs, etc, and is made continuous from sector to sector by bridges over the expressways

To our more northern eyes, used to the infinite range of greys on rain-washed stonework, Doxiadis' incisive rectilinear planning seems over simplified and stereotyped, but it has been evolved as an economical framework in which to rehouse the vast populations of the world in a manner and with facilities befitting the second half of the twentieth century. We must not forget that it is only recently that architects have accepted the task as theirs, of designing the whole environment, including mass housing. For example until this decade the house had never been included in the curriculum of the Ecole des Beaux-Arts in Paris. In Britain, with our strong postwar tradition of public housing, and with the advent of architects into the speculative builder world, it is difficult to recall how revolutionary the preamble to the Fifth Congres of the C.I.A.M. in Paris 1937 sounded at the time

'We feel that it is imperative that in the work of this congress we give top priority to the dominant fact of our time. After a hundred years of conquest, dispute and disorder, modern society has come to the conclusion that the construction of a new home for man is the factor that definitely determines the character of a civilization. By creating a new form of dwelling the second phase of the Machine Age enters a period of universal construction'

Even today the impact of the architect on ordinary dwellings in underdeveloped countries is negligible. For Doxiadis this is the architects' main problem. 'The architect cannot survive as a designer of single buildings, much less of monuments, but only as a co-ordinator of architectural activity; in a word as a Master-Builder'. Doxiadis himself has been worried that, although he tried to develop local styles and give expression to his ideas in a local manner, the resulting solutions to urban problems in Pakistan, Greece, the U S and Iraq were substantially the same

He might have added quotations from Le Corbusier's 'Vers une Architecture'. The same general type of face is the property of every individual – nose, mouth, forehead, etc, and also the same general

proportion between these elements. There are millions of countenances constructed on these essential lines; nevertheless all are different: there is a variation in the quality of the features and in the relationship which unites them. We say that a face is handsome when the precision of the modelling and the disposition of the features reveal proportions which we feel to be harmonious because they arouse deep within us and beyond our senses a resonance, a sort of sour ding-board which begins to vibrate' or again 'It is necessary to press on towards the establishment of "standards" in order to face the problem of "perfection". The Parthenon is a product of selection applied to an established standard. Already for a century the Greek temple had been standardised in all its parts

'When I was confronted with this situation I had to answer an important question. I said to myself "I am often tending towards similar solutions, should I try to be different?" I came to the irresistable conclusion that I had no right to be different where the conditions themselves impelled me to remain the same. We should not be afraid to express ourselves in the same way and repeat something that is good. After all a doctor is not afraid to use a medicine because it has been used before'

Le Corbusier was twenty-three when he reached Athens a few years before Doxiadis was born. The Acropolis has had a profound effect on both these men. Both studied the plan

'The apparent lack of order in the plan could only deceive the unlearned. The balance of the parts is in no way a paltry one. It is determined by the famous landscape which stretches from the Piraeus to Mount Pentelicus. The scheme was designed to be seen from a distance, the axes follow the valley, the false right angles are contrived with the skill of a first-rate stage manager. The Acropolis set on its rock and on its sustaining walls, seen from afar appears as one solid block'

Developing his discussion of Axes' Le Corbusier goes on to write

'In actual fact, a bird's-eye view such as is given by a plan on a drawing board, is not how axes are seen; they are seen from the ground, the beholder standing up and looking in front of him. The eye can reach a considerable distance and, like a clear lens, sees everything even beyond what was intended or wished. The axis of the Acropolis runs from the Piraeus to Pentelicus, from the sea to the mountain. The Propylea are at right angles to the axis, in the distance on the

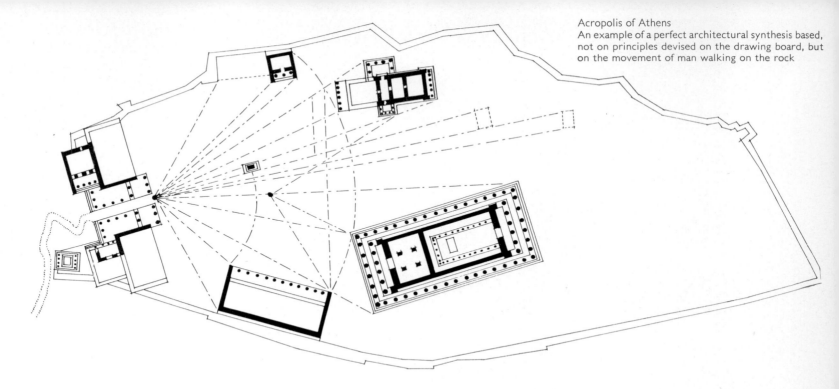

290

horizon the sea. In the horizontal, at right angles to the direction that the architectural arrangement has impressed on you from where you stand, it is the rectangular impression which tells. This is architecture of a high order: the Acropolis extends its effect right to the horizon. The Propylea in the other direction, the colossal statue of Athena on the axis, and Pentelicus in the distance. That is what tells. And because they are outside this forceful axis, the Parthenon to the right and the Erechtheum to the left, you are enabled to get a three-quarter view of them, in their full aspects. Architectural buildings should not all be placed upon axes, for this would be like so many people talking all at once'

The overwhelming message for Le Corbusier was that the 'site' must be obeyed:

'Your building may cube a 100,000 cubic yards, but what lies around it may cube millions of cubic yards, and that is what tells. To sum up, in architectural ensembles, the elements of the site itself come into play by virtue of their cubic volume, their density and the quality of the material of which they are composed. . . . On the Acropolis at Athens the temples are turned towards one another, making an enclosure, as it were, which the eye readily embraces; and the sea which composes with the architraves, etc. This is to compose with the infinite resources of an art full of dangerous riches out of which beauty can only come when they are brought into order'

Doxiadis sought the secret of this order. His thesis 'Raumordnung im Griechischen Staedtebau' takes Corbusier's point on axes and examines various acropolis in terms of the angles subtended at the eye of an observer in certain key positions such as the main ceremonial entrance. He found an order in these angles. The Dorians, believing space to be finite, used a finite division, ie, 10 for their buildings (1/20, $\sqrt{5}$, $\sqrt{2}$, etc) but an infinite division, ie, 12,

for their spaces. These angles turn out to be sub-divisions of 12 of the whole circle, 30° and its simple sub-multiples. The Ionians, believing space to be infinite, used the reverse. Infinite space was terrifying so they, unlike the Dorians, limited it with finite numerology. The Dorians allowed their axes to embrace the horizons, the Ionians fearful of infinity, always closed theirs with a building. Underlying the perhaps mainly academic interest of these theories is a much more vital realization that architecture can only be appreciated by movement around and through it

'I think we must assert that time is the essential dimension if we are to have an architectural synthesis. Time in architecture means movement. If we stop at one point we no longer have architecture but mere scenic design, a theatrical effect. The examples of Ancient Greece and of Luxor in Egypt are sufficient to impress upon us the importance of the axis of movement. . . . In great ages of architecture the

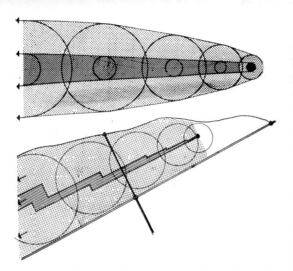

Above: Islamabad. Dynapolis – the Ideal City and Islamabad

Right: Islamabad. The Master Plan of the Metropolitan area

Below: A representative human sector built in Western Baghdad

1 Mosque
2 School
3 Market
4 Public Baths
5 Coffee Houses
6 Administration
7 Red Crescent
8 Cultural Centre
9 Public Health Centre
10 Police Station
11 Shops
12 Public Park
13 Sports Ground
14 Open Air Theatre

notion that architecture implies a time dimension was always thought to be true, so that the result of the synthesis compelled a man to walk through it, to feel and then become part of a piece of architecture, and not remain outside it as a looker on. . . . There is the synthesis in Ancient Greece where we can see that man was compelled to walk through a whole complex of buildings and live within them in order to achieve his end. . . . There are several elements in the Acropolis which prove that the architect deliberately left some part of his building incomplete in order to give visual material expression to his conception of time as the fourth element in the synthesis. . . . This is especially apparent in the walls of the Propylea where the marble blocks have never been completely cut—although the Acropolis and all its buildings remained in full use for many centuries after their construction had been completed'

Doxiadis' philosophy of the linear city is due more to experience, his Greek heritage and his conception of time as a fourth dimension of true architecture, than to any influence of Don Arturo Soria y Mata. As

a city expands it can do so only by adding further human sectors. If some of these are needed for predominantly 'town centre' activities they must be related to the existing sectors with similar functions. Hence quite simply the conception of a linear city in which separate functions can all expand together. For unlike a tree where only the outer layers are alive, and where a new layer is added each year

Far left above and below: Iraq–Dibis Housing Project
A 10 ft wide walkway between the rows of houses

Left above and below: Iraq Housing
Pedestrian squares in communities. Class I (sub-neighbourhood)

Below left and below: Islamabad – the new capital of Pakistan
Pedestrian walkways in a community Class III

292

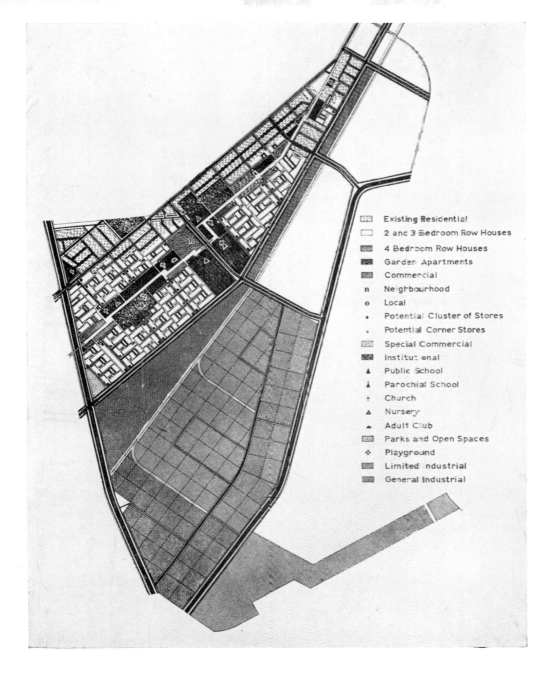

Existing Residential
2 and 3 Bedroom Row Houses
4 Bedroom Row Houses
Garden Apartments
Commercial
n   Neighbourhood
o   Local
•   Potential Cluster of Stores
∘   Potential Corner Stores
Special Commercial
Institutional
▲   Public School
⏧   Parochial School
✝   Church
▲   Nursery
⏥   Adult Club
Parks and Open Spaces
✤   Playground
Limited Industrial
General Industrial

and another layer inside joins the half-dead heart wood, a city must be alive right through

Superficially the message of the Acropolis to these two men might seem almost opposite. The importance of site is not the first impression gained from looking at the apparently similar solutions to urban areas in Baghdad or Washington D.C. prepared by Doxiadis. But in their different ways we can perhaps find a fundamental agreement. To Corbusier the importance of Greece was the realization that the site must be obeyed, that good architecture stimulates one to touch as well as gaze, and is only appreciated by being walked through and traversed inside as well as outside. For Doxiadis the site is not the geographical locality so much as the universal site requirements of the different dimensions of man. The aeroplane which lands in Athens is the same as the one which takes off in Honolulu or Reykjavic and its airport requirements are the same. The same cars drive on the streets of Athens as along the avenues in Washington or the dusty roads of Chandigarh. They have the same lethal potentialities and the same desire for free passage. And the human beings in the ancient capital of western civilization move on two feet at about the same speed as they do in Pekin or Marakesh. Doxiadis, like Corbusier, stresses the inviolability of the 'site'. He also recognizes in the Corbusier sense that the geographical heritage of the inhabitants will greatly determine the nature of architecture within any one human sector. So in a way Doxiadis is reacting to the same message from the Acropolis as Corbusier. Architecture is alive only when walked round and through. Doxiadis is perhaps more preoccupied with achieving the conditions that will enable architecture to live, than with the architectural form itself. But Doxiadis understands that like a tree 'our architecture will not grow overnight. It will take its time and we can only help it grow. We should not think of forms but create space, build and live. Architecture will come'. The remarkable realization in all his thought is that wherever man is legitimately a pedestrian, he is made to feel in scale and dominant

letters; and also that they differ in style from the logotypes of other firms. The house style of a sign involves more than the design of letterforms, it covers the materials and colours used. Sign designers not only use the shop's house style to create an image distinctive from its neighbours, they often place the sign at a different height and in a different size

What restrictions could an architect lay down, to impose some kind of uniformity, but which still respect the need for individual signs to have distinctive characteristics?

LAURENCE CAREY

teristics, which transform them into trademarks. Many large retailers have developed house styles for their signs, based on their logotypes which also appear on their printed matter. A logotype originally meant a whole or part of a word, cast as a single piece of type. It has come to mean the way that a firm presents its name using a particular typeface or drawn letterforms. An obvious example is the word Boots, which in the logotype form refers to a firm of chemists ('The Chemists'); in any other form, it would probably mean footwear. For this reason logotypes differ as much as possible from other standardized ways of assembling the component

RESTRICTIONS IMPOSED THROUGH ARCHITECTURAL DESIGN

The positioning of facilities for fascia boards usually governs the position of the sign; it can also affect the design. For example in the design of shop sites for the Churchill Gardens development scheme in London, unity was achieved by imposing arches which partly obscured the fascia. This was done because the architects (Powell and Moya) knew that they would have no control over the design of signs, and obviously felt that these should be as unobtrusive as possible. In fact where shop fitters have attempted to get round the problem of semi-obscurity, the fault

When an architect designs a row of shops combined with apartments or offices, the shop sites consist of the space left between the ground level and the first floor. The architect has no direct control over the outward appearance of any individual shop when it is eventually designed by shop fitters. Allowed complete freedom, this can change or ruin the architect's original conception of the character of the whole building. In old and unplanned shopping areas new signs, which are obviously not considered in relation to the architecture, are acceptable since they form part of a natural evolutionary process: however, many good new development schemes have been spoilt by fascia signs which are unrelated to one another and which are in themselves badly designed. To avoid this the architect would need to have some control over the positioning and design of fascia signs. In this way the signs would not only relate to one another, but would be integrated with the building

THE PURPOSE OF SHOP SIGNS

Shop signs are slightly more than announcements; they are permanent advertisements. They are differentiated one from another by certain design charac-

of the restriction is just as clear as in the cases where the signs ignore the problem

The architect of a combined block must allow facilities for shop fascias: and these will govern the position of the signs, by alignment along the top and bottom fascia edges. The depth which he chooses for the fascia, will be governed by its height from the road level and the width of the pavement and road: the greater these measurements the larger the size of lettering he will have to allow for

RESTRICTIONS IMPOSED THROUGH PLANNING COMMITTEES AND DEVELOPMENT CORPORATIONS

I Position of Lettering on the Fascia

A common left-hand margin as well as a common margin at the base of the sign may govern the position of the lettering. The result of maintaining a common left-hand margin (the distance between the edge of the fascia and the beginning of the word) is that the lettering always begins at an expected place, continuing for an unexpected characteristic length. A common base line implies one of two things, either that the margin at the base of the logotype remains constant (as in the Basle example where the descenders of one sign align with the base of the capitals in another), or that the base of all the capital letters align with those lower case letters which do not have descenders. This second alternative gives a more satisfactory appearance of alignment, but fails to take into account logotypes, such as the Boots one, which are always set at an angle, and those that have descenders of exaggerated length

2 Materials

If a single set of materials is selected, it is necessary to choose one in which all possible logotypes can be represented without too much adjustment to the design. This requirement limits the selection; for instance if lighting is needed the materials might be limited to some kind of glass box on which the letters of a thin material, would be placed

3 Colour

Restrictions of colour can either be in the form of a single colour combination, or of a limited variety of combinations. The colours of a single combination must be sufficiently neutral not to favour any one

shop which happens to use those particular colours on its normal printed matter. At the same time the colours must have sufficient tone contrast and brilliance, so that the signs are clearly legible and can compete with posters, show cards and other brightly coloured ephemera. One of the two colours applies to the lettering and the other to the fascia background; on some shops the two colours could be reversed, either on some predetermined system or by giving the choice to the shop fitter. This latter would disturb unity, simply because the background colour would dominate by covering a larger area.

The result of giving a limited choice of combinations to a shop fitter can be seen in a recent development scheme. The following colour restrictions were imposed: red or blue lettering on a white ground, or white on a red or blue ground. The number of possibilities is too great, and the colours red and blue too strongly contrasting for the restriction to result in unity. At the same time the selection is so limited that only one or two shops were able to use colours with which they had come to be associated in other forms of publicity. This indicates that a two-colour combination, especially if colour reversal is not allowed, is the most satisfactory form of restriction; this is borne out by the example from Basle

4 Three-dimensional letterforms

The material that is used often makes it necessary for the letterforms to have a third dimension. The thickness may be governed by the materials, particularly where each letter is going to be separately lit. It is also governed by the stroke width of letterforms in all the possible logotypes. Where the materials allow a choice of depth for the third dimension, the amount of depth should allow for the different angles of vision, particularly if the stroke width is very narrow; when it is too great this depth can disturb legibility. The choice of depth may also be governed by characteristic features of the architecture: in the Basle example the surfaces of letterforms have been intentionally placed slightly less than flush with the front surface of the building

5 Height of letterforms

If alignment is established along the base of the lower case letters without descenders and the base of the capitals, it may be desirable to control the apparent height of letters. (Allowing for the use of logotypes and a controlled height it would never be possible to control the apparent size of letterforms. The expanded letters would appear much larger than the condensed letters.) In order to give an impression of similar height of letterform between different signs, it is the height of the lower case letters without ascenders and descenders (that is the 'x-height') that must be controlled, and not the overall height including ascenders and descenders. This second height is roughly the point size of a typeface; but since the proportion of ascender or descender to 'x-height' varies from one typeface to another, the apparent size of a letterform is governed by this 'x-height' (for instance 24 point Times Roman has the same apparent size as 30 point Bembo). If a sign consisted solely of capital letters, these would be measured as though the absent lower case letters conformed to the established 'x-height', because when capitals of one point size appear with lower case letters of a larger point size, the capitals appear to be out of context, even though they are physically higher

6 Stroke width of letterforms

When the height of letterforms is controlled, it is only possible to control their apparent stroke width by adjusting the design of the logotypes. The apparent stroke width of a letter is governed by the width of the vertical strokes: thus where an adjustment has to be made to an existing logotype a proportionate adjustment would need to be made to the horizontal strokes. The width of vertical stroke to be selected must be the mean average of all the known letterforms. This average would probably be a little wider than the width of a normal roman letter. There would have to be a small tolerance on the specified width, otherwise expanded letters would appear lighter than condensed ones. The Basle example shows how

Typeface

Above: Times Roman 24 point

Typeface

Above: Bembo 30 point

well a restriction of stroke width can work: it has the disadvantage that the logotypes which have to make the greatest adjustments are obviously unfairly handicapped

7 Typeface

With all other restrictions, to impose that of a single typeface, would mean that the only form of distinction between signs would be the different shapes made by the words (as it is between words in printed text). Again an unfair advantage would be gained by those shops which happened to use the chosen typeface for their logotype. However, should this restriction be imposed, the typeface should be chosen purely on legibility: and it would, of course, have to be of such a length that the longest name could be accommodated in the given length of fascia

This list of restrictions is ordered according to the degree of stringency they impose on the design. 2 and 4 might involve slight adjustment to an existing logotype; 6 would involve considerable adjustment; 7 would involve its elimination. Because logotypes are basic for creating distinctions, it would seem that they should undergo the minimum adjustment. However, the distinguishing characteristics would be more apparent between one sign and another when every other aspect of their design but their two-dimensional shape conformed; so in fact, the restrictions imposed by the design of the site and the first five remaining restrictions would make the most satisfactory combination

NOTES ON PARTICULAR SITES AND SHOP SIGNS

In the new Nottinghill Gate Development in London (architects Cotton, Ballard and Blow) certain restrictions are imposed by the design itself. The height of the ceiling inside the shops is about 3 ft less than the height of the canopy, which leaves a natural depth for fascia signs. This depth is sufficient to accommodate the size of lettering appropriate, according to the height from ground level and the width of pavement and road. The position of the fascia in the darkest part of the covered way makes it necessary for the signs to be lit artificially

There were no restrictions imposed on graphics through planning committees or development corporations, except that the given fascia area be used. The shop fitters seem to have been free to ignore the base line of this area. The signs demonstrate the unfortunate effect of this lack of control

296

Above: The sign respects the given fascia area. However, it demonstrates an unnecessarily extravagant use of materials and decoration. The cantilevered sign shows that the logotype has more impact flat on a glass box. The removal of the diamond pattern would be an improvement

Left: The given base line for fascias has been ignored. However, the extra depth has not been used except by the tail of the 'f'. No other advantage has been gained by the extra depth. The two words which are intended to be read in sequence bear no relation to one another either in the over-extravagant materials, the design of the letterforms, or the positioning. In any standardization the glass panel shape could be ignored

Lower left: The glass panel does not take full advantage of the fascia area. However, the lettering is clear and legible, and the use of an expanded typeface, by being readable from an acute angle, eliminates the need for a cantilevered sign

LUPUS STREET

Returning to the shops on Lupus Street (which form part of the enormous Churchill Gardens high density housing/commercial development in Pimlico, London) architects Powell and Moya have imposed strong restrictions through design. No physical allowance was made for fascias. The unifying arches act as a hindrance to the visibility of the only area where the signs could possibly go. This area is only visible from about 4 ft away, whereas the pavement is about 11 ft wide

The reason for this was that the architects were unable to gain any form of control through the planning committees and the development corporation; this is why they employed the arches

Right: The given base line has been ignored. The whole sign is very badly designed. Not only the lettering (which in any standardization would have to be accepted as a logotype) but the whole fascia design demonstrates the capacity of a shop sign to defile the architect's conception

Middle right: This illustrates the unfortunate effect of these arches. Even from close to the sign is difficult to read. As it is in deep shadow it should be lit artificially

Far right: This shop is also small enough not to have developed a house style or logotype, and can make allowance for the arches in the design of the lettering. The light shining through from the back of the shop and the strong reflection in the near side view again demonstrate the need for artificial lighting

Middle right: This sign has been set at the same height as the previous ones but as the shop front has been recessed about 4 ft the fascia is more visible from across the road and of course much more visible from the near side. As it is artificially lit it is un-affected by being in deep shadow

Far right: It is not only the ill-chosen colour, pale pink, which impedes the clarity of this sign, it is also the lack of consideration for tone in relation to its position. However, this position means that it is unaffected by the arches

DEVELOPMENT SCHEME IN BASLE

Once again special restrictions are imposed through architecture. Three positions are allowed for shop signs: above the shop entrances, suspended from the ceiling of the covered way at right angles to the shop fronts, and the front of the covered way. The covered way extends over the pavement, so that the entrance signs are in deep shadow, which combined with the supporting columns obscures their visibility from the opposite side of the road. For this reason the fascia signs on the front of the building have been allowed, but in such a way as to restrict their depth. The signs over the shop entrances and the hanging signs are all lit artificially

In addition certain restrictions have been imposed by the planning committee or development corporation. A left-hand margin has been established as well as alignment along the base of the capitals and the descenders, where lower case letters have been used. A single material has been imposed on the fascia signs. The colours have been limited to white lettering on a black ground. The depth of the third dimension is about 2 in. The height of the letterforms has not been restricted, but the narrowness of the fascia imposes a natural limit. Because of the inevitable similarity of letterform heights, a common stroke width has been imposed

298

Above right: This is the only sign which takes advantage of the full length of the fascia. The austerity of the sign, working well within the restrictions, is suited to the expression of efficiency

Middle right: This modified Fractur typeface demonstrates the capacity of the restrictions to allow an individual image, without the unity of the whole scheme being affected

Far right: Apart from the curious treatment of the umlauts, this is a clever logotype design since it takes advantage of the similar shape patterns of the two words. A condensed letter is bound to suffer a loss of apparent size when the fascia is so narrow; the circular Os help to counteract this problem

Middle right: This is a characteristically Swiss treatment of a sans serif typeface. It is well suited to the restrictions of stroke width and third-dimensional thickness

Far right: View through the covered way

Gas station in the United States
Photo: H. R. Domke